SUPREME DISORDER

DISORDER

JUDICIAL NOMINATIONS AND THE POLITICS OF AMERICA'S HIGHEST COURT

ILYA SHAPIRO

REGNERY GATEWAY

Regnery Gateway™ is a trademark of Salem Communications
Holding Corporation
Regnery® is a registered trademark of Salem Communications
Holding Corporation

Cataloging-in-Publication data on file with the Library of Congress

ISBN: 978-1-68451-056-6
eISBN: 978-1-68451-072-6
Library of Congress Control Number: 2020935852

Published in the United States by
Regnery Gateway, an imprint of
Regnery Publishing
A Division of Salem Media Group
300 New Jersey Ave NW
Washington, DC 20001
www.RegneryGateway.com

Manufactured in the United States of America

10 9 8 7 6 5 4 3 2

Books are available in quantity for promotional or premium use.
For information on discounts and terms, please visit our website:
www.Regnery.com.

To Kristin, Jacob, and Charlie

Contents

Introduction   1

Part I—Past
A Short History of Confirmation Battles   9

Chapter 1
The Early Court   11

Chapter 2
Prelude to Civil War   23

Chapter 3
The Civil War and After   31

Chapter 4
The Court Resists the Progressives   47

Chapter 5
Roosevelt's Court   61

Chapter 6
The Post-War Settlement   73

Chapter 7
The New Frontier   83

Part II—Present
The Modern Era   93

Chapter 8
The Burger Court and the Conservative Revolt   95

Chapter 9
The Swinging Seventies   113

Chapter 10
The Calm before the Storm   127

Chapter 11
The Original Sin of Robert Bork   137

CHAPTER 12
Insult after Injury   151

CHAPTER 13
The Souter Disappointment and the Thomas Travesty   159

CHAPTER 14
Ginsburg's Pincer Movement and Breyer's Safe Pick   177

CHAPTER 15
Filibusters and Umpires   189

CHAPTER 16
The Wise Latina and the Nuclear Senate   209

CHAPTER 17
The Garland Blockade, but Gorsuch   223

CHAPTER 18
Kavanaugh and Beyond   241

PART III—FUTURE
DIAGNOSES AND REFORMS   263

CHAPTER 19
What Have We Learned?   265

CHAPTER 20
Term Limits   283

CHAPTER 21
More Radical Reforms   293

CHAPTER 22
A Question of Legitimacy   311

Conclusion   329

Acknowledgments   335

Bibliography   339

Notes   343

Index   381

Introduction

When Justice Charles Evans Whittaker retired in March 1962 after just over five years on the Supreme Court, John F. Kennedy had his first opportunity to shape the high court. The youthful president selected a man of his own generation, Byron White. White had met JFK in England while on a Rhodes Scholarship—after having been runner-up for the Heisman Trophy and spending a year as the highest-paid player in the NFL—and the two became fast friends.

White was a vigorous forty-five and serving as the deputy attorney general under Robert F. Kennedy. Kennedy formally nominated him on April 3, 1962. Eight days later, White had his confirmation hearing, a quick ninety minutes including introductions and supporting testimony from various bar association officials (during which the nominee doodled on his notepad). What questioning there was largely concerned the nominee's storied football career; "Whizzer" White was surely the last person to play a professional sport while attending Yale Law School. The judiciary committee unanimously approved him, and later that day so did the Senate as a whole, on a voice vote.

My, how times have changed.

The battle to confirm Brett Kavanaugh showed that the Supreme Court is now part of the same toxic cloud that envelops all of the nation's public discourse. Ironically, Kavanaugh was nominated in part because he was thought to be a safe pick, with a long public career that had been vetted numerous times. He was firmly part of the legal establishment, specifically its conservative mainstream, and had displayed a political caginess that made some on the right worry that he would be too much like John Roberts rather than Antonin Scalia or Clarence Thomas. As it turned out, of course, 11th-hour sexual assault allegations transformed what was already a contentious process into a partisan Rorschach test. All told, Kavanaugh faced a smear campaign unlike any seen since Robert Bork.

Senate Democrats had warned President Reagan that nominating Bork—a judge on the D.C. Circuit after a storied academic and government career—to the Supreme Court would provoke a fight unlike any he had faced, even after Scalia had been confirmed unanimously the year before. And so, on the very day that Reagan nevertheless announced Bork as his pick, Ted Kennedy went to the Senate floor to denounce "Robert Bork's America" as a place "in which women would be forced into back-alley abortions, blacks would sit at segregated lunch counters, rogue police could break down citizens' doors in midnight raids, schoolchildren could not be taught about evolution, writers and artists could be censored at the whim of the government, and the doors of the federal courts would be shut on the fingers of millions of citizens."

It went downhill from there, as the brusk Bork refused to adopt the now well-worn strategy of talking a lot without saying anything. A few years later, Ruth Bader Ginsburg would refine that tactic into a "pincer movement," refusing to comment on specific fact patterns because they might come before the Court, and then also refusing to discuss general constitutional principles because "a judge could deal in specifics only."

Confirmation processes weren't always like this. The Senate didn't even hold public hearings on Supreme Court nominations until 1916, a tumultuous year that witnessed the first Jewish nominee and the resignation of a justice to run against a sitting president. It wouldn't be until 1938 that a nominee testified at his own hearing. In 1962, the part of Byron White's hearing where the nominee himself testified lasted less than fifteen minutes.

But while the confirmation process may not have always been the spectacle it is today, nominations to the highest court were often contentious political struggles. For the republic's first century, confirmation battles, including withdrawn and postponed nominations, or those upon which the Senate failed to act—Merrick Garland was by no means unprecedented—were a fairly regular occurrence.

George Washington himself had a chief justice nominee rejected by the Senate: John Rutledge, who had lost Federalist support for his opposition to the Jay Treaty. James Madison, the "Father of the Constitution," also had a nominee rejected. And John Quincy Adams, who himself had declined a nomination from Madison, had a nominee "postponed indefinitely" during the lame duck period after Andrew Jackson had stopped his bid for reelection.

Jackson then had a nominee thwarted, but a change in Senate composition allowed Roger Taney to become chief justice a year later—and eventually author *Dred Scott*. John Tyler, who assumed the presidency in 1841 after the one-month presidency of William Henry Harrison, never lived down his nickname of "His Accidency." Congressional Whigs disputed his legitimacy and their policy disagreements extended to judicial nominations: the Senate rejected or declined to act on four Tyler nominees (three of them twice) before finally confirming one.

Indeed, most 19th-century presidents had trouble filling seats on the high court. Millard Fillmore was prevented from filling a vacancy that arose during his tenure, as was James Buchanan. Congressional elimination of Supreme Court seats stopped Andrew Johnson from replacing the two justices who died during his presidency. It took Ulysses Grant seven tries to fill three seats. Grover Cleveland ran into senatorial traditions regarding seats reserved for certain states—which he overcame only by nominating a sitting senator.

In the 20th century, Presidents Harding, Hoover, Eisenhower, Johnson, Nixon, and Reagan all had failed nominations—although Harding and Ike got their picks confirmed after resubmitting their names. FDR never had anyone rejected—although his court-packing plan was rejected both in Congress and at the polls. And LBJ's proposed elevation of Justice Abe Fortas led to the only successful filibuster of a Supreme Court nominee, a bipartisan one over ethical concerns, which wasn't even a true filibuster because Fortas never had a majority of pledged votes. Douglas Ginsburg withdrew before President Reagan could send his name to the Senate for having smoked marijuana with his law students.

Then of course there's Merrick Garland, the first nomination the Senate allowed to expire since 1881—but then the last time a Senate controlled by the party opposite to the president confirmed a nominee to a vacancy arising in a presidential election year was 1888. As we now know, Senate Majority Leader Mitch McConnell's gamble worked: not only did it not hurt vulnerable senators running for reelection, but the vacancy held Republicans together and provided the margin for Donald Trump in key states. Trump rewarded his electoral coalition with the nomination of Neil Gorsuch, who was confirmed only after the Senate decided, on a party-line vote, to exercise the "nuclear option" and remove filibusters.

Opportunities for obstruction have continued—pushed down to blue slips, cloture votes, and other arcane parliamentary procedures—even as control of the Senate remains by far the most important aspect of the whole endeavor. The elimination of the filibuster for Supreme Court nominees was the natural culmination of a tit-for-tat escalation by both parties.

More significantly, by filibustering Gorsuch, Democrats destroyed their leverage over more consequential vacancies. Moderate Republican senators wouldn't have gone for a "nuclear option" to seat Kavanaugh in place of Anthony Kennedy, but they didn't face that dilemma. And they won't face it if President Trump gets the chance to replace Justices Ruth Bader Ginsburg or Stephen Breyer, which would be an even bigger shift.

Given the battles we saw over Gorsuch and Kavanaugh, too many people now think of the justices in partisan terms. That's too bad, but not a surprise when contrasting methods of constitutional and statutory interpretation now largely track identification with parties that are more ideologically sorted than ever.

Why all the focus on one office, however high? If Secretary of State John Kerry had died or resigned in the last year of the Obama presidency, it certainly would've been a big deal, but there's no doubt that the slot would've been filled if someone with appropriate credentials were nominated. Even a vacancy in the *vice presidency* wouldn't have lasted unduly long.

But of course executive appointments expire at the end of the presidential term, while judicial appointments usually outlast any president. A president has few constitutional powers more important than appointing judges. Justice Scalia served nearly thirty years on the high court, giving President Reagan's legal agenda a bridge to the 21st century. A big ruling on nonprofit-donor disclosures was made in April 2016 by a district judge appointed by *Lyndon Johnson*.

Pundits always argue that judicial nominations should be among voters' primary considerations when choosing a president. Well, the Supreme Court's future truly did hang in the balance in 2016. The election was so consequential in part because people knew that its winner would have the first chance in more than twenty-five years to shift the Court's ideological balance. Indeed, the Court now stands starkly split 5–4 on many issues: campaign finance, the Second Amendment, religious liberty, and regulatory power, to name a few. If Hillary Clinton had been able to appoint a progressive jurist—even a "moderate" one— these policy areas would be headed in a substantially different direction.

And that goes just as much if not more for the lower courts, which decide fifty thousand cases annually even as the Supreme Court hears fewer and fewer. Every four-year term, the president appoints about a fifth of the judiciary. On Inauguration Day in January 2017, there were already 105 vacancies—and that rose to more than 150 before a tweak in Senate debate sped up confirmations. To put it another way, when Obama took office, one of the thirteen appellate circuit courts had a majority of judges appointed by Democratic presidents; after his fifty-five appointments, nine did. Trump has partly reversed that, "flipping" three circuits and getting a record thirty circuit judges confirmed in his first two years—about the same number as Bush and Obama *combined* at that point in their presidencies. And more than fifty overall, better than anyone in one term except Jimmy Carter, for whom Congress created many new judgeships to fill, as a sort of consolation for not having any Supreme Court vacancies on his watch.

Even if politics has always been part of the process, and even if more justices were rejected in our country's first century than in its second, we still feel something is now different. Confirmation hearings are the only time that judges go toe-to-toe with politicians—and that's definitely a different gauntlet than even President Tyler's nominees ran. So is it all about TV and Twitter, the 24-hour news cycle, and the viral video? Is it that legal issues have become more ideologically divisive? No, the nomination and confirmation process—an interplay among president, Senate, and outside stakeholders—hasn't somehow changed beyond the Framers' recognition, and political rhetoric was as nasty in 1820 as it is in 2020. Even the "novel" use of filibusters is anything but. All these parts of the current system that we don't like are symptoms of a larger phenomenon: as government has grown, so have the laws that courts interpret, and their reach over ever more of our lives.

Senatorial brinksmanship is symptomatic of a larger problem that began long before Kavanaugh, Garland, Thomas, or even Bork: the courts' self-corruption, aiding and abetting the expansion of federal power, then shifting that power away from the people's legislative representatives and toward executive branch administrative agencies. And the Supreme Court is also called upon to decide, often by a one-vote margin, massive social controversies, ranging from abortion and affirmative action to gun rights and same-sex marriage. The judiciary affects public policy more than it ever did—and those decisions increasingly turn on the party of the president who nominated the judge or justice.

So as the courts play more of a role in the political process, of course the judicial nomination and confirmation processes are going to be more fraught with partisan considerations. This wasn't as much of a problem when partisanship meant rewarding your cronies. But it's a modern phenomenon for our parties to be both ideologically sorted and polarized, and thus for judges nominated by presidents from different parties to have markedly different constitutional visions.

Is there anything we can do to fix this dynamic, to turn down the political heat on Supreme Court vacancies? Reform proposals abound: term limits, changing the size of the Court, setting new rules for the confirmation process, and more.

But before we get to all that, let's see how we got to where we are. This book proceeds in three parts. The first part you can think of as "the past," roughly George Washington through Lyndon Johnson and the rejection of Justice Abe Fortas's nomination to be chief justice. The second part is "the present," the modern age of judicial politics, covering developments on the court from Richard Nixon to now. That includes the "big four" controversies over Robert Bork, Clarence Thomas, the Antonin Scalia vacancy, and Brett Kavanaugh, but also the escalating battles over the lower courts. The third part is "the future," diagnosing problems and offering solutions.

It turns out that politicization of judicial nominations isn't a new phenomenon—the Founders themselves lived it—but do we have to settle for politics as usual?

Part I—Past

A Short History of Confirmation Battles

CHAPTER 1

The Early Court

W hen they set out to design the Supreme Court, the Framers debated various ways to appoint the members of the judicial branch. We know from James Madison's notes of the Constitutional Convention that, by July 1787, the delegates seemed to have settled on having the Senate appoint federal judges. It looked like the judiciary, or at least the high court, was one more part of the young republic that would have state interests paramount, as filtered through the upper house of Congress.

As the delegates moved on to other aspects of their deliberations, discussion of the judiciary focused on the scope of its powers and the sorts of cases federal judges would consider. It was understood, without being written into the Constitution, that the justices would "ride circuit," traveling to designated parts of the country to preside over cases when the high court wasn't sitting. The Judiciary Act of 1789, which established that the Supreme Court would have six members and created the lower federal courts, designated one local U.S. district court judge and two Supreme Court justices to preside over cases— which required such arduous travel that Congress soon reduced the number of justices required to hold circuit court from two to one.

Still, the mechanism for choosing justices confounded the delegates until the Convention's final days in September, when a draft emerged that balanced the views of those like Benjamin Franklin and John Rutledge, who called for a legislative role to prevent monarchical tendencies in the executive, and those like James Wilson, Alexander Hamilton, and Gouverneur Morris, who favored strongly independent executive prerogatives.[1] The final text reflected a Madisonian compromise that the president "shall nominate, and, by and with the advice and consent of the Senate, shall appoint…Judges of the Supreme Court." This last-minute change seems to have been lost in the debate over the legislative and executive branches; at least two delegates continued to write and speak about the Senate's naming federal judges.[2]

But what did this "advice and consent" mean? In *Federalist* No. 76, Hamilton wrote that the provision requires "cooperation" between the president and Senate, a body some delegates generally viewed as an informal advisory council to the president, somewhat akin to the modern cabinet. Hamilton explained that senatorial advice and consent "would be an excellent check upon a spirit of favoritism in the President.… It would be an efficacious source of stability."

Historians and political scientists have continued to debate the meaning of the Advice and Consent Clause, but all we know for sure is its simple text: it's the president's duty to *nominate* judicial candidates and the Senate's to decide whether to *consent* to such nominations (after giving whatever advice senators wish to give)—and if not, to reject, table, or otherwise take no action according to Senate rules. To date, presidents have officially submitted 163 Supreme Court nominations to the Senate, which has confirmed 126 of them (seven of whom declined to serve); the others were rejected (twelve), withdrawn (twelve), postponed (three), or had no action taken (ten).[3]

For obvious reasons, George Washington had the most opportunities to make Supreme Court appointments. All told, the first president made fourteen nominations, twelve of which were confirmed, one rejected, and one withdrawn and resubmitted to satisfy the constitutional rule that a sitting member of Congress can't be appointed to an office created during his tenure. Notably, two of the confirmed picks declined to serve.

Washington had seven criteria in choosing his justices, to which he adhered rigorously: (1) support for the new Constitution; (2) service in the Revolution; (3) participation in state or national political life; (4) prior judicial experience; (5) either a "favorable reputation with his fellows" or personal ties with Washington himself; (6) geographic diversity; and (7) "love of our country."[4] The most important one was undoubtedly the first, as Washington sensed that, much as he himself was creating the mold for all future chief executives, the early Supreme Court would flesh out the young republic's constitutional *mores*, including the establishment of a distinct national government with a strong judiciary. In commissioning letters to his nominees to the original six-member Court in September–October 1789, he wrote, "The Judicial System is the chief Pillar upon which our national Government must rest."[5]

Although not a lawyer himself, Washington had meaningful experience with and respect for the law. He had served seventeen years as a state legislator and seven as a justice of the peace and county court judge, and had administered at least nine estates. Accordingly, all but one of his appointees had served in some judicial capacity, the one exception being the brilliant legal theorist and constitutional framer James Wilson. And seven of those whom the president tapped for the high bench had participated in the Constitutional Convention.

Washington was also sensitive to various state controversies in ratifying the Constitution, so his first justices were from Maryland, Massachusetts, New York, Pennsylvania, South Carolina, and Virginia, respectively. And when the Maryland nominee declined his commission, his replacement was from yet another state, North Carolina. The members of the "original six" had varied backgrounds but a clear commitment to the Constitution and the Federalist cause of building a nation out of disparate states. While Washington made some political calculations when deciding who should serve, he had more trouble convincing potential nominees to accept the nomination than in securing congressional approval.

Despite Washington's high hopes, the early Supreme Court suffered from a lack of both prestige and work, not to mention the unglamorous circuit-riding, which led to significant turnover, as well as difficulties in filling seats. Justice John Rutledge left the Court after two years, before hearing any cases, to become chief justice of South Carolina. Washington unsuccessfully offered the seat to two other South Carolinians, including Rutledge's brother Edward, the youngest signatory of the Declaration of Independence. Chief Justice John Jay, who spent part of his tenure serving as minister to Great Britain—he negotiated what became known as the Jay Treaty, resolving issues left over from the Treaty of Paris that ended the Revolutionary War—resigned from the Court in 1795 to become governor of New York.

After Jay resigned, Washington received a letter from John Rutledge asking to be reappointed. Washington immediately offered Rutledge the position, which became a recess appointment because the Senate was not in session. But before formally taking the judicial oath, Rutledge gave a controversial and intemperate speech against the Jay Treaty that set off the nation's first confirmation controversy. Not that opposition to the treaty, premised on the idea that Jay had conceded too much to secure the final withdrawal of British troops, was an unpopular position. At a public meeting in New York, people literally threw stones at Hamilton for defending it, while residents of Rutledge's own Charleston burned Jay in effigy and dragged the Union Jack through the streets before burning it in front of the British consulate. Still, Rutledge's language was extreme; the *South Carolina State-Gazette* quoted the chief justice-designate as saying he'd rather the president die than sign the treaty.[6]

Reports of Rutledge's remarks cost the new chief justice the support of administration officials and the Federalist-friendly press. Rutledge presided over the Court for nearly four months, until the Senate rejected him 10–14. (Ironically, at the Constitutional Convention, Rutledge had led the charge against Wilson's suggestion that the president be allowed to name justices without Senate assent.)[7] Vice President John Adams wrote to his wife Abigail that it "gave me pain for an old friend, though I could not but think he deserved it. Chief Justices must not go to illegal Meetings and become popular orators in favor of Sedition, nor inflame the popular discontents which are ill founded, nor propagate Disunion, Division, Contention and delusion among the people."[8]

Rutledge left the Court as the only justice among fifteen recess appointees who wasn't eventually confirmed. Despondent at this outcome, and so soon after his wife's death, Rutledge attempted suicide by jumping into Charleston Harbor. He was rescued by two slaves.

As the fight over the chief justiceship proceeded—it would go to Oliver Ellsworth, who had defended the Supreme Court's power of judicial review at the Constitutional Convention—Washington had one more seat to fill. Having chosen Rutledge over Samuel Chase, the chief justice of Maryland, the president now named Chase, though not without reservation. Chase had served in the

Continental Congress and signed the Declaration of Independence, but voted against the Constitution at Maryland's ratifying convention and advocated against it in a series of Antifederalist essays under the name "Caution." He was also voted out of legislative office when it was discovered that he had tried to corner the flour market using information gained through his service in Congress. A few years later, foreshadowing what was to come when he joined the high court, the Maryland legislature considered removing him from state judicial office.

After Maryland nonetheless ratified the Constitution, Chase saw the light and, with the zeal of a convert, gave impassioned speeches denouncing the Democratic-Republican Party. During the 1796 election, while a sitting justice, he predicted that with a Thomas Jefferson victory, "our republican institution will sink into a mobocracy."[9] When Adams won, Chase advocated the enactment of the Alien and Sedition Acts, which posed obvious threats to the freedom of speech. For these and many other instances of ill-tempered behavior, the House of Representatives approved eight articles of impeachment in March 1805.

Although Republicans had a 25–9 majority over the Federalists in the Senate, Chase was acquitted outright on six counts and only convicted 18–16 on two others (short of the two-thirds necessary for removal). He remains the only justice ever to be impeached, but many senators felt that removal was too harsh a penalty. Senator John Quincy Adams expressed concern that, in the absence of contrary precedent, impeachment could destabilize the judiciary if reasons could be developed for emptying the entire Supreme Court.[10] Chief Justice William Rehnquist would write that some senators declined to convict Chase despite their hostility to him—partisan and personal—because they doubted that the mere quality of his judging was grounds for removal.[11]

All judicial impeachments since Chase have been based on legal or ethical misconduct, not performance. For their part, federal judges since that time have generally been more cautious to avoid the appearance of partisanship.

Although he did have one nominee rejected, the stately Washington was able to use his judicial nominations to strengthen the new republic and bolster political support for the Constitution. Geographic considerations, as well as a commitment to a unified federal government, were thus of paramount importance in selecting judges who could convince the various states to bind themselves in the American project.

The End of the Beginning

Washington's successors, regardless of their party, shared his goal of using the judiciary to advance the federal cause. Geography would thus remain a central concern in the selection process, both to continue forging national unity and for more immediate political interests.

Some of our most storied justices were chosen out of a concern for maintaining balanced state representation. The fact that there had been no Virginian on the Court since 1796 weighed on President John Adams, leading him to offer his first nomination to John Marshall, already a distinguished lawyer and diplomat but whose judicial service was limited to a minor state tribunal. Marshall initially declined for financial reasons, but accepted two years later when the chief justiceship came open.

Picking Marshall was the masterstroke of the Adams presidency. Ironically, Adams had first wanted John Jay to return to his previous post, and the Senate confirmed that nomination, which commission was signed by Marshall, then serving as secretary of state. But Jay declined, out of a distaste for circuit-riding and because the Court still lacked "energy, weight, and dignity."[12] Adams was then importuned to appoint any number of politically connected choices, but demurred because, having by this point lost the election of 1800 to the "radical" Thomas Jefferson, he needed to be assured that his own man would be in place. So he went with Marshall, who although Jefferson's second cousin, was the incoming president's avowed political enemy. The nomination is a defining moment in U.S. history, even if the Senate at the time would have preferred sitting Justice William Paterson—whom Adams passed over because he was of the Hamiltonian faction—and stalled consideration of the nomination in hopes of reconsideration. When Adams, now a lame duck with nothing to lose, held firm, the Senate yielded to Marshall's overwhelming qualifications and confirmed him by acclamation.

While it may be hard to believe that a legal titan as universally esteemed as John Marshall could have been the subject of a nomination dispute, political factions are always keen to express their self-interest. Marshall, who served longer than any other chief, is remembered for finally establishing the Court as the institution that many Founders had wanted it to be. It's no exaggeration to say that Marshall's labors realized the Federalist dream of a united and powerful country, operationalizing the Washington-Adams ideology perhaps more than any other justice with respect to the president who made the appointment.

In the early days, political battles over the judiciary had less to do with individual nominees and more with ironing out the Supreme Court's function. Shortly before John Adams's single term expired, the Federalist Congress passed the Judiciary Act of 1801, the purposes of which were, first, to relieve the circuit-riding burden on Supreme Court justices and, second, to preempt Thomas Jefferson's influence on the judiciary. Accordingly, it reduced the number of Supreme Court seats from six to five, effective with the next vacancy, doubled the number of circuits from three to six, and added several judges to each circuit. It also reorganized the district courts and created various other judgeships. Adams filled all the vacancies in the nineteen days before the end of his term, so the legislation became known as the Midnight Judges Act. It was the appointment of one of these "midnight judges" that led to *Marbury v. Madison*, which at base was a dispute over whether President Jefferson's secretary of state, James Madison, had to deliver judicial commissions that had been signed by President Adams and sealed by Secretary of State Marshall.

Upon assuming office in March 1801, Jefferson set out to repeal the Midnight Judges Act, which the narrow Democratic-Republican majority in Congress managed to do in January 1802—before any vacancy came on the Supreme Court, whose size thus remained unchanged. Congress then passed the Judiciary Act of 1802, which repealed the doubling of the circuits but without adding judges, because Jefferson was wary that the judiciary would start impinging on the executive.

The new law also eliminated the Supreme Court's summer session, which meant that the court wouldn't meet again until ten months after the 1802 act was passed. Critics charged that this delay was engineered solely to prevent the Supreme Court from finding the repeal of the 1801 act unconstitutional. For his part, Chief Justice Marshall doubted the constitutionality of the repeal but recognized that he could not sway a majority of justices.

Once the dust had settled from the partisan politics, Jefferson ended up with three Supreme Court appointments, the third after Congress added a seventh justice in 1807 to cover the new western Seventh Circuit (Kentucky, Ohio, and Tennessee). The new president made it known that he had two big criteria, which by this point already shouldn't be a surprise: loyalty to the Democratic-Republican party and geographical balance. Although Jefferson met with little resistance from the Senate, he still failed to wrest the Court away from Marshall. Even William Johnson, the rare early justice who didn't come to sing from Marshall's hymnal, was a nationalist patriot who read the Constitution to strengthen federal power.

James Madison had another opportunity to move the Court away from a Federalist majority, the party itself having collapsed. But he had to try four different nominees before filling his first vacancy, for what was considered the New England seat. Two men, including John Quincy Adams, declined the appointment after the Senate confirmed them, while another, Alexander Wolcott, was voted down for being an unqualified party hack who would bring shame to the office. The fourth time would be the charm. Madison went with the precocious nephew of a longtime friend. Joseph Story had graduated Harvard at nineteen and was the only Democratic-Republican lawyer in Essex County (Salem), Massachusetts, a published poet, and newly elected speaker of the state house of representatives. During a brief stint in Congress, he led the effort to repeal the Embargo Act of 1807, by which Jefferson had stopped maritime commerce. Indeed, Story's Federalist flirtations enraged the former president, who called Story a "pseudo-Republican," a "political chameleon," and an "independent political schemer."[13]

On November 15, 1811, at the age of thirty-two years, fifty-eight days, Story became the youngest person nominated to serve on the U.S. Supreme Court, a record unlikely ever to be broken. A Senate weary of the political battle over this seat confirmed Story by voice vote three days later.

Justice Story remains one of the most significant figures in early American constitutional history, shaping the Court together with John Marshall, with whom he developed a shared jurisprudence. He wrote many of the landmark decisions of the early republic, based on the idea that the Union could be made stronger through judicial oversight and by crafting a more uniform national jurisprudence founded on property rights and free interstate commerce.[14] Unlike his poetry, his legal writings, foremost his *Commentaries on the Constitution of the United States*, first published in 1833, remain indispensable. Indeed, Justice Story was one of the most successful American authors of the first half of the 19th century.

While the early presidencies had their fair share of political battles over judicial nominees, disagreements were more personal than ideological and most justices fell in line with the "Great Chief" Marshall. Particularly as the founding period gave way to the "era of good feelings" dominated by the Democratic-Republican Party, presidents took care to manage political ambitions—James Monroe didn't trust potential nominee Martin Van Buren, then a senator—and otherwise not rock the boat.

This soon began to change. John Quincy Adams, having been put into office in 1825 by the House of Representatives after nobody received an Electoral College majority, lost to Andrew Jackson in his bid for reelection. Adams nevertheless made a lame duck nomination of prominent Kentucky lawyer John Crittenden. Crittenden, aligned with Henry Clay—who had become secretary of state in the "corrupt bargain" that gave Adams the presidency—was squarely in the National Republican (later Whig) faction that had split from the Jackson-aligned wing. Irate senators from the rechristened Democratic Party refused even to consider the nomination, which was "postponed" by a 23–17 vote in February 1829. This wasn't much of a surprise; Clay had written Crittenden that if his nomination were rejected, "the decision will be entirely on party ground; and ought, therefore, to occasion you no mortification."[15] But it was the end of the "era of good feelings," judicially as much as politically.

CHAPTER 2

Prelude to Civil War

By the time Andrew Jackson came to power, the Supreme Court was enshrined in the federal government. Loyalty to the Constitution and eagerness to advance the Federalist project were no longer existential concerns for leaders of the fledgling republic. As a result, judicial nominations became less about institution-building and more a matter of political wrangling.

In his two presidential terms, the pugnacious Andrew Jackson could have been expected to have significant battles over Supreme Court nominees. But only two of six vacancies proved difficult. Only two presidents put more justices on the Court than Jackson: George Washington, who of course got to fill all the original seats, and Franklin Roosevelt, who would have three-plus terms to work with. In so doing, he moved the Court, like the country, in a more democratic, populist, and state-oriented direction. To get there, Jackson ensured that hardball politics played a major part in judicial selection.

Jackson wouldn't have trouble ushering a nominee through the Senate until well into his second term. That allowed him time to consolidate his grip on the Democratic Party, so his later picks reflected a greater commitment to party principles, rather than just being politically useful. James Moore Wayne of Georgia was a rare Unionist southerner, thus mollifying Whig concerns while maintaining partisan loyalties. To replace Gabriel Duvall, Jackson picked his close friend Roger Taney, like Duvall from Maryland. Taney had been attorney general and then treasury secretary on a recess appointment after his predecessor refused to authorize the withdrawal of federal funds from the national bank.

This was Jackson's biggest nomination fight. After the Senate rejected Taney's treasury nomination in June 1834—the first-ever rejected cabinet nominee—the president had pledged to his Senate opponents that they had not heard the last of his loyal sidekick. When the Court nomination came half a year later, Chief Justice Marshall, no friend of Jackson, viewed Taney so highly that he sent a favorable note to a Virginia senator.[1] Nonetheless, the still-furious Senate not only voted to postpone Taney's nomination, but passed a bill to eliminate the seat altogether. The House did not approve the measure, however, and Jackson would've vetoed it anyway. Still, this pointed to the "sticky" relations between president and Senate.[2] When Jackson got word of the postponement, he said he "would receive no more messages from the damned scoundrels."[3]

Jackson refused to make another nomination until the Senate confirmed Taney, but fate intervened to shift the dynamic. On July 6, 1835, after thirty-four and a half years on the bench, Marshall died. With two vacancies to fill, the president bided his time. There was some agitation to elevate the brilliant Justice Joseph Story, but Jackson wasn't about to pick someone who out-Marshalled Marshall in his strong view of the judiciary and national government. On December 28, 1835, Jackson announced that he was nominating Taney for the chief justiceship and Philip Barbour—former House speaker and judge on both state and federal benches—for the Duvall vacancy.

The battle over Taney was intense, with the Senate giants—Henry Clay, John Calhoun, and Daniel Webster—all lined up against Taney and Jackson. One New York newspaper called Taney "unworthy of public confidence, a supple, cringing tool of power,"[4] while another attacked him as a "political hack."[5] But when the vote came, it wasn't nearly as close as the bitter debate had suggested. On March 15, 1836, Taney was confirmed 29–15.

Chief Justice Taney was the first Catholic to serve on the Supreme Court—though he had an interesting arrangement with his Episcopalian wife whereby their sons would be raised as Catholics and their daughters as Episcopalians.[6] He endeavored to enhance the role of the states in national political and legal life, but largely guided the court along lines of compromise and (attempted) conciliation. Far from taking down Marshall's accumulated judicial power and institutional gravitas, the Taney Court secured it, and largely without complaint from those who had disagreed with the Marshall Court.[7]

While Taney is regarded a skilled jurist, shrewd tactician, and strong leader, his record is marred by his majority opinion in *Dred Scott v. Sandford* (1857). *Dred Scott* held that people of African descent were ineligible for citizenship; that Congress can't ban slavery in federal territories (and thus the Missouri Compromise was unconstitutional); and that the federal government can't free slaves brought into the territories. This was an attempt to forestall civil war, but instead foreclosed any non-violent means of resolving the slavery question.

Dred Scott was abetted by another expansion of the Supreme Court, very late in the Jackson presidency. As a result of population movements westward, Congress on March 3, 1837 passed the Eighth and Ninth Circuits Act. It was still customary for each circuit to have an assigned justice, so this legislation expanded the high court by two seats. John Catron, who had served with Jackson in the War of

1812 and gone on to be chief justice of Tennessee—a unique combination of pro-Jacksonian and pro-judiciary—was the president's choice for the former. Catron's inauguration-eve nomination stretched into the first few days of the Van Buren administration; the new president readily allowed the nomination to continue through a relatively easy confirmation. William Smith, who as a South Carolina senator had cast one of the two votes *against* Jackson's nomination of Justice Henry Baldwin, had since moved to Alabama and became the outgoing president's nominee to the second new seat. Although Van Buren likewise continued his nomination and the Senate confirmed him, Smith declined, citing the low salary.[8]

Jackson preferred men loyal to him above all else, and that affected the nomination process. After all, he was hardly the most popular president among powerful senators and doubled-down on Taney to mock them. Still, Jackson had more fights with the justices than had previous presidents. After the Court upheld federal jurisdiction over Indian territory to protect the Cherokee Indians from various oppressions, Jackson is widely quoted as having said, "Well, John Marshall has made his decision, now let him enforce it." And yet Marshall declined to enforce it by sending federal marshals.

Jackson stopped just short of defying judicial rulings, instead resting on a defense of each branch's authority under the separation of powers. His message on vetoing the re-charter of the Bank of the United States in 1832 confirms this view: "The authority of the Supreme Court must not ... be permitted to control the Congress or the Executive when acting in their legislative capacities but to have only such influence as the force of their reasoning may deserve."[9]

For all Jackson's tough talk, his judicial criteria didn't differ much from his predecessors, though he didn't make them explicit other than to make clear that political (not necessarily ideological) loyalty would take primacy. Ironically, the president's nominees, once on the bench, didn't necessarily go along with his views on popular sovereignty. While shifting towards the states on federalism, they maintained Marshall's creed of judicial strength and independence.

Jackson's immediate successors returned to business-as-usual politicking, but their experiences likewise show that the success or failure of a nominee was often due more to the political currency a president had with the Senate than to ideology.

John Tyler, whose serendipitous accession to the presidency earned him the nickname "Your Accidency," failed with eight of nine nominations thanks to his complete lack of political standing among leaders of both parties. Tyler had broken with the Democrats to join the Whig ticket in 1840, so he lacked a personal political base when William Henry Harrison died after thirty-one days in office. Most of Tyler's cabinet resigned over policy differences, and he would be expelled from the Whig Party and become the first president to have a veto overridden. Despite picking only high-caliber nominees from what we would now call the legal elite, nearly all were shot down, in part because Tyler refused to work with senators to find compromise picks.

In the 1850s, slavery reared its head in judicial battles as in all of political life. When Justice Levi Woodbury died in September 1851, President Millard Fillmore noticed abolitionists' criticisms of the Court's pro-Southern stance. (The Court had been majority-Southern since 1791—counting slave-state Maryland—and this wouldn't change until Lincoln's presidency.) Accordingly, he wanted a strong lawyer who had an understanding of contemporary politics. He also wanted a Whig, someone relatively young, and a New Englander.[10]

Fillmore found such a man in Benjamin Robbins Curtis of Massachusetts. But Curtis continued to opine on major issues while being considered, including the Fugitive Slave Act of 1850, which he opposed as policy but thought was constitutional. He was confirmed after abolitionists delayed the process two months. Curtis became one of two dissenters in *Dred Scott*, after which he resigned out of disgust at the court's acting out of political expediency rather than legal principle (and because the pay was lower than what he commanded in private practice).[11]

Fillmore had even more trouble with a second seat, which opened up in July 1852 in the face of a presidential election that didn't look good either for him or his party. By the time the Senate reconvened in January 1853, not only had Democrat Franklin Pierce won the election, but Fillmore hadn't even been the Whig candidate. Still desperate to fill the vacancy, Fillmore put up a senator, George Badger of North Carolina, a conservative Whig not identifiable as either pro- or anti-slavery. Although rejecting one of its own was breaking an unwritten rule, the Democratic Senate majority was not about to deprive its own party's incoming president of this plum assignment. The Senate voted 25–26 to "permanently postpone" the nomination.

Franklin Pierce was a tragic figure both personally and professionally, losing all three sons in childhood and failing miserably at stopping the country from careening toward civil war. Pierce's efforts to please both North and South placated neither, and his party leadership suffered to such an extent that he became the only president serving a full term not to be renominated. His sole Supreme Court appointment proved to be one of the few bright spots. A strong advocate of "states' rights," John Archibald Campbell of Alabama nonetheless believed in the Union and improving slaves' lives. He was so universally supported that all the sitting justices wrote to Pierce to support Campbell. The Senate approved him by acclamation and he went on to serve with distinction until what he felt was a duty-bound resignation in 1861, despite his opposition to secession, war, and slavery. Before resigning, Campbell tried fruitlessly to mediate between three Confederate commissioners and the Lincoln administration, which refused to see them.

By the time James Buchanan, long eager for the presidency and having himself declined Supreme Court nomination several times, finally attained it in the 1856 election, war was nigh. It was an inauspicious time, and two things would've been necessary to keep the country together: (1) a Solomonic decision in *Dred Scott* to uphold the Missouri Compromise and thus presumably allow slavery to wither away, and (2) a strong president able to act decisively to bring together people of conflicting passions. Alas, neither occurred, and Buchanan's inaptness for the moment was reflected too in his controversial Supreme Court nominations.

In his inaugural address, Buchanan called slavery a "judicial question, which legitimately belongs to the Supreme Court of the United States, before whom it is now pending, and will, it is understood, be speedily and finally settled."[12] When *Dred Scott* was decided several days later—with Buchanan's foreknowledge of the result through a leak by Justice Catron—the 80-year-old Chief Justice Taney may have thought he was indeed "solving" the slavery issue and keeping the country together. Instead, he made civil war inevitable.

When Buchanan had an opportunity to nominate justices and set a new tone for the Court, the already embattled president dithered over geographic and other secondary considerations. One need only consider his pick of Nathan Clifford, a Maine Democrat who had been President James K. Polk's attorney general, to see his massive failure to seize the moment. With *Dred Scott* already inserting the Court into national debate, the Clifford nomination further divided the nation. Clifford's views on slavery "could be best described as being somewhere between pro-slavery and fuzzy."[13] Senate abolitionists engaged in an acrimonious five-week debate. The closing of Democratic party ranks and the absence of several key northern opponents led to Clifford's confirmation by a 26–23 vote on January 12, 1858.

When Justice Peter Daniel died on May 30, 1860, the Court was left with four northerners and four southerners. Buchanan, who decided not to seek re-election, moved slowly, considering "moderate" southerners before naming a fellow Pennsylvanian, Jeremiah Black, in February 1861. Black was a solid Democrat, a Union man but not an abolitionist—a gambit that might have worked earlier, but was too little, too late. Many southern senators who would've supported Black had already withdrawn as the first step to secession; Republicans weren't going to do the outgoing president any favors. The Senate rejected Black by one vote, 25–26, eleven days before Abraham Lincoln's inauguration.

Between the Jackson and Lincoln presidencies, the Senate confirmed only eight of the twenty-one Supreme Court nominations it received, often invoking procedural blocks or not acting rather than rejecting outright. Presidents lacked Senate support or bristled at having to kowtow to the other end of Pennsylvania Avenue. Both sides of the slavery question often preferred gridlock to the possibility of losing in the courts. After Buchanan, relations between presidents and the Senate on judicial nominations would improve— Lincoln didn't have to deal with recalcitrant southerners, of course, which greatly reduced the Democratic opposition—though not without some important battles.

CHAPTER 3

The Civil War and After

Within two months of his March 4, 1861, inaugural address, Lincoln had three vacancies to fill. Focusing on the war and smarting at the Court's oversized influence after *Dred Scott*, Lincoln delayed in filling the seats. As he said in his inaugural address, "If the policy of the government upon vital questions ... is to be irrevocably fixed by decisions of the Supreme Court ... the people will have ceased to be their own rulers."[1] The illnesses of Chief Justice Taney and Justice John Catron further eroded the Court's functions, which suited Lincoln just fine.

For all the controversy that embroiled the nomination process in the lead up to the Civil War, the fact that the slavery question moved from the bench to the battlefield allowed for political tensions to ease around the judiciary. As with the need of Washington and Adams to stand up a strong Court that would entrench the new Constitution, Lincoln wanted justices who would be helpful in the war effort. He received no resistance from a Senate that understood the gravity of the moment and was aided by the fact that his biggest detractors had left the Union.

Notably, for a "frontier" seat, Lincoln picked native Kentuckian Samuel Miller, who had moved to Iowa over the slavery issue. Justice Miller strongly favored Lincoln's wartime positions, including the suspension of habeas corpus, blockade of southern ports, and trial by military commissions. After the war, however, his narrow reading of the Fourteenth Amendment—most notably in the *Slaughterhouse Cases* (1873), in which three other Lincoln appointees dissented—limited the effectiveness of federal protections for individual rights. And with the wartime contraction of the southern circuits, Lincoln was free to fill a southern seat with a judge from his own home state of Illinois: David Davis, who had been Lincoln's campaign manager. Davis was loyal to Lincoln's prosecution of the war, but would write the unanimous opinion in *Ex parte Milligan* (1866), holding unconstitutional the trial of civilians by military tribunals where civilian courts are available. And when the president and his congressional allies engineered the Tenth Circuit Act to provide a tenth justice for California and Oregon, Lincoln picked the chief justice of California Stephen J. Field—a Democrat who was a committed Unionist. This represented the first real instance of a president's crossing major-party lines to fill a high court vacancy. Although a Buchanan Democrat, Field did not impede Lincoln's war efforts and ended up serving nearly thirty-five years, second-longest to date, and becoming one of the pioneers of a robust interpretation of the Fourteenth Amendment's protections for individual liberty.[2] His views on substantive due process ushered in what would become known as the *Lochner* era, with strong protections for freedom of contract and private property.

On October 12, 1864, less than a month before the presidential election, Chief Justice Taney died at age 87. Lincoln waited until a month *after* the election to fill this key vacancy. The obvious candidate was Salmon P. Chase, Lincoln's former treasury secretary who had saved the Union financially during the war. The president never trusted this superbly talented but ever-scheming man, however, so he spent weeks looking for alternatives before conceding that Chase was uniquely suited to bringing together his party's disparate factions. Lincoln's evaluation of Chase, good and bad, was essentially borne out. Chase had sought the presidency in 1856 and 1860, and from the bench would seek the nomination of *both* parties in 1868. But the chief justice voted strongly pro-Union and later to enforce Reconstruction. He would've displeased Lincoln, however, in joining with Justice Field in ruling against making paper money ("greenbacks") a legal tender—over the dissents of Lincoln's three other appointees, who would get their revenge the next year when the Court overruled that decision, after President Grant had gotten a couple of his own justices confirmed.[3] Chase's greatest contribution may have been in presiding over Andrew Johnson's impeachment trial. Supreme Court historian Henry J. Abraham opined that his "no-nonsense" performance "may well have saved the institution of the presidency itself."[4]

Thus began the very brief period of ten justices, lasting less than six months, until John Catron died on May 30, 1865, his seat remaining vacant until it was abolished. On the whole, Lincoln's Court nominations were above average; by taking his time and listening to senators' concerns, he had no difficulty getting them confirmed. That wasn't true of his two successors.

With slavery decisively settled by the Civil War, Supreme Court nominations would once again be determined by more mundane political concerns, including Republican distrust of Andrew Johnson—a Union Democrat who never became a Republican. Although Johnson's sole nominee, the prominent Republican Henry Stanbery, was legally skilled and well-respected, "it is doubtful that the Senate would have approved God himself had he been nominated by

Andrew Johnson."[5] Not only did the Senate refuse to act on the nomination but, together with the House, eliminated the seat, stipulating that the next two vacancies would also not be filled once the grandfathered incumbents were gone. This legislation, which Johnson signed into law, also ensured a Lincoln-appointed majority for the foreseeable future.

Even with Johnson's ambitions thwarted, however, the Supreme Court did not match congressional Republicans' zeal for Reconstruction. Despite the Lincoln-appointed majority, the Court repeatedly avoided deciding major constitutional issues attending Reconstruction legislation, removing itself from the struggle between Congress and the executive branch over the enforcement of the post-war order. Johnson's successor Ulysses S. Grant—"a failure in everything except marriage and war," the Ken Burns miniseries put it—thus returned to making decisions based on geography and party loyalty, without regard to ideology, other than support for greenbacks. Grant ultimately needed eight nominations to seat four justices; one reason he had so many chances was that the Judiciary Act of 1869 returned the Supreme Court to nine justices, no longer reflecting the number of circuits and remaining fixed ever since. Grant ran into particular trouble with his first and last nominations. Attorney General Ebenezer Hoar was rejected for refusing to play ball with the Senate on civil-service patronage and lower-court picks, while Grant offered the chief justiceship after Chase's death in 1873 to seven people—two of whom would be formally nominated and rejected—before finally achieving a winning result.

After this tumultuous period of party reorganization and attempted conciliation after the war, the next decades would bring decidedly less controversy regarding Supreme Court appointments— which still remained political plums that presidents negotiated with the Senate.

The Gilded Age

As the political landscape became more fractured, the selection of nominees became more contentious even if the final votes were rarely close, with a couple of exceptions. When Rutherford Birchard Hayes won the 1876 election through the Compromise of 1877, which essentially ended Reconstruction by leaving the South to govern itself, the nomination process became more controversial overnight. Hayes was tasked with removing federal soldiers from the South, which would be a tragedy for southern blacks, ushering in Jim Crow and facilitating legal, political, and social second-class status. In this atmosphere, Hayes would have three Supreme Court nominations, and he worked hard, with these picks as in the rest of his administration, to reunite the country by choosing moderate Republicans who would be reasonably acceptable to the southern states. To do so, he discarded the historic links between seats and regions or circuits, nominating justices based on political and ideological considerations, without regard to geography. The change in criteria didn't prevent Hayes and his immediate successors from getting their nominees approved, but it did cause some hiccups, including with regard to the cronyism and party machines that would become dominant at the end of the 19th century.

When Justice David resigned on Inauguration Day, having been elected to the Senate, Hayes had his first vacancy, which he did not rush to fill. In mid-October he proposed forty-four-year-old John Marshall Harlan, who had grown up in a Kentucky slaveholding family but ended up reluctantly supporting the Union. Although Harlan played a major role in campaigning for Hayes in the border states, he was viewed as both independent and bipartisan, having been a Democrat (and Clay Whig) before the Civil War and supporting George McClellan over Lincoln in the 1864 election. He still ran into some opposition, including from a hard-core Republican faction that resented not having been consulted, others who disliked the geographic deviation, and others, led by New York Senator Roscoe Conkling, who opposed Harlan on patronage grounds.[6]

Despite the terms of Hayes's electoral win and radical Republicans' worries, the "paternalistic egalitarian"[7] Harlan would not only become a defender of Reconstruction, civil rights, and federal power, but was a trailblazer in applying the Bill of Rights against the states through the Fourteenth Amendment. He became known as "The Great Dissenter," most notably for his solo dissents in the *Civil Rights Cases* (1883) and *Plessy v. Ferguson* (1896). Justice David Brewer once observed that Harlan "goes to bed every night with one hand on the Constitution, the other on the Bible, and so sleeps the sweet sleep of justice and righteousness."[8]

The Senate nearly rejected Hayes's third nominee, the savvy political chameleon Stanley Matthews, but not for either ideological or patronage reasons. Matthews instead drew opposition for his close ties to railroad and financial interests. An angry Senate Judiciary Committee refused to report the nomination to the floor, in what was perhaps the first time interest groups entered the confirmation process, this time led by the National Grange and similar agrarian populists.[9] The Senate had taken no action by the time Hayes left office, but to some surprise, President Garfield renominated Matthews right after taking the oath of office on March 4, 1881. The *New York Times* called it "a sad and inexcusable error" that doubled down on one of Hayes's "most injudicious and objectionable acts."[10] Although it's not clear why Garfield stuck with Matthews, the reluctant president—delegates at the 1880 convention picked him as a compromise on the 38th ballot—did want to heal the rifts in a badly divided Republican Party.

Weighing against the nominee were not only his business ties but nepotism charges, because the president's brother-in-law had married Matthews's sister. Financier Jay Gould, a Matthews client, likely provided the marginal influence to shift the necessary votes into a 24–23 confirmation, the narrowest approval of all time. Matthews served for less than eight years and confounded those who predicted that he'd be a tool of business interests, often voting to uphold economic regulations.

Garfield would die on September 18, 1881, lingering four months after being shot in July by a disgruntled office-seeker—emblematic of the battle over patronage appointments to offices low and high—leading to the immediate swearing-in of Chester Alan Arthur. Arthur, although a product of New York machine politics, tried to buck the cronyist trend and imposed merit-based judicial selection. This caused a rift with his old patron Conkling, which Arthur ultimately healed by tapping the party boss for the high court. Although the Senate quickly confirmed him, Conkling decided not to take the seat—the last person to decline after being confirmed—but Arthur had paid his political debts, which allowed him to return to his meritocratic ways.

Although Grover Cleveland was the only Democrat to win the White House between James Buchanan and Woodrow Wilson, he was so free market-oriented that Wilson jokingly regarded himself as the first Democratic president since 1860.[11] He would look for Supreme Court nominees who were Democrats for sure, but who shared his property-rights bent rather than being populists or "reformers."

Cleveland's first nominee was the impossibly named Lucius Quintus Cincinnatus Lamar, the first southerner nominated since before the Civil War, and indeed the first person with a background in both the Union and Confederate governments. An opponent of Reconstruction, Lamar labored to conciliate the North and South. After six weeks of fierce debate, the Senate approved him 32–28 on

January 16, 1888 (with sixteen senators not voting), aided by two Western senators who didn't want to establish a bar against former Confederates. Only six affirmative votes were from northern states, for both ideological and partisan reasons.[12]

Two months after Lamar's confirmation—March of a presidential election year—Chief Justice Morrison Waite suddenly died. After several false starts, Cleveland turned to his old friend Melville Fuller, a minor Illinois political figure whose business ties the president figured would make him acceptable to the Senate, which had a Republican majority. A Philadelphia newspaper called him "the most obscure man ever nominated as Chief Justice," but he shared the president's generally conservative ideas: sound money, free trade, federalism, and less economic regulation.[13] Fuller's opponents pointed out that he hadn't served in the army even though he was in his twenties during the Civil War, but Robert Todd Lincoln, son of the former president, came to his defense, so nine Republicans joined the Democrats in support. Chief Justice Fuller would be the last Supreme Court nominee approved by a Senate controlled by the opposing party to a vacancy arising in a presidential election year. (Sorry, Merrick Garland.)

Benjamin Harrison beat Cleveland in the electoral college in 1888 and would have four opportunities to name justices, a rare bounty for a one-term president. He made no secret of his selection criteria: party loyalty, political and economic conservatism, significant legal/judicial experience, and being at least from the same circuit or area as the departing justice—a brief return of the geographic criterion.[14] Harrison's nominees easily sailed through the Senate, and went on to vote in ways that surely pleased the president who appointed them.

When Grover Cleveland returned to the presidency, he encountered confirmation problems again based on patronage squabbles.

The Senate rejected his first two nominees for a seat that had been held by a New Yorker, because they were New Yorkers who had run afoul of powerful Democratic Senator David B. Hill. While the president had navigated the demands of party and geography, he had run aground on the shoals of senatorial courtesy. Frustrated with Empire State shenanigans, Cleveland looked South, and to the Senate itself, nominating Majority Leader Edward Douglass White of Louisiana. White's colleagues confirmed him unanimously the same day they received his nomination.

Cleveland would later return a "southern seat" to New York, appointing Rufus Peckham, the brother of failed nominee Wheeler Peckham, after swallowing his pride and consulting with Senator Hill.[15] Hill acquiesced because, unlike his brother, Rufus hadn't been involved in the patronage fights within the Democratic Party. Rufus Peckham was a shrewd jurist with a political philosophy very much in line with President Cleveland's: anti-populist, anti-regulation, socially conservative. He famously wrote the 5–4 majority opinion in *Lochner v. New York* (1905), finding that the maximum-hours provisions of New York's bakeshop infringed the freedom of contract and were unrelated to health and safety; in truth, they were protectionist measures sought by established, larger, unionized bakeries against upstart immigrant shops.[16]

Curiously, nominees of both Republican and Democratic presidents could be found on either side of the case, which might not be surprising given that Grover Cleveland had a deregulatory mien even as Theodore Roosevelt was a trust-busting economic reformer.

In modern times, *Lochner* and the jurisprudential era named after it is opposed by progressives for disallowing greater government involvement in economic matters and by conservatives for allowing courts to police rights that aren't specifically listed in the Constitution. But *Lochner* has enjoyed a rehabilitation in the last decade, as originalists of a more classical-liberal stripe rediscover the virtues of an "engaged" judiciary that protects individual liberty against encroachments from left, right, and populist attacks.

Into the 20th Century

While different presidents may have had their own priorities when nominating justices, Teddy Roosevelt revolutionized the way justices are picked. Ever one to break the presidential mold, TR went about his judicial nominations in a way that would last. He wanted progressives who would be for labor interests and federal regulation, and against corporate concentrations of wealth and power, but asserted that moral character was paramount.

In one of what we would now call "State of the Union" messages to Congress, Roosevelt wrote—these wouldn't be oral until Woodrow Wilson—that a judge's "view on progressive social philosophies are entirely second to his possession of high and fine character."[17] He was also the first president to *explicitly* reject geography as a factor. Indeed, two of his three nominees would hail from Massachusetts.

As it happens, Roosevelt's first vacancy came from the September 1902 death of a justice from Massachusetts anyway, Horace Gray, whose failing health had led President William McKinley to prepare for a nomination. The new president didn't feel bound by his slain predecessor's preferences, and actively reviewed many candidates before focusing on already-distinguished jurist Oliver Wendell Holmes Jr.

Holmes had served on the Massachusetts Supreme Court for twenty years, the last three as chief justice, as well as being on the Harvard faculty and a noted author, editor, and general man of letters. His *The Common Law*, a collection of lectures and essays, has been continuously in print since 1881, and remains controversial for rejecting formalism and leading ultimately to the "legal realism" school that looked behind the words on the page to legal actors' political and sociological motivations.

Holmes's sensibility would dovetail nicely with Woodrow Wilson's progressive theory of the Constitution, whereby the Framers' "Newtonian" system of separation of powers and checks and balances—"ambition counteracting ambition," in Madison's terms—was replaced with a "Darwinian" public law that evolves with society.[18]

Appropriately, then, the Progressive-Republican Roosevelt was most concerned with registered-Republican Holmes's "real" politics, perhaps even more than his stated criterion of "high and fine character."[19] He corresponded with Holmes's fellow Bostonian Henry Cabot Lodge precisely to ascertain whether, and ultimately be satisfied that, the man's philosophy was sufficiently anti-trust, pro-labor, and liberal on race. The president nominated Holmes on December 2, 1902; the Senate unanimously confirmed the intellectual Brahmin two days later.

Holmes became one of the most influential justices of all time, revolutionizing progressive jurisprudence through a legal-positivist and "living Constitution" view that was a stark contrast to the natural law theory that held sway before. Holmes famously dissented in *Lochner v. New York* (1905), explaining that "the Fourteenth Amendment does not enact Mr. Herbert Spencer's *Social Statics*"—meaning that courts should defer to legislatures rather than protecting economic and contractual rights based on what Holmes perceived to be the then-prevailing laissez-faire theories. [20] He later infamously upheld Virginia's forced-sterilization program for the "feeble-minded" in *Buck v. Bell* (1927), writing that "three generations of imbeciles are enough."[21] Holmes's deference to the legislative process—"If my fellow citizens want to go to Hell I will help them. It's my job."—made him the progenitor of the "judicial restraint" school that, ironically, conservatives adopted in the second half of the 20th century. [22]

Somewhat surprisingly, Roosevelt considered Holmes "a bitter disappointment ... not because of any one decision but because of his general attitude"—though this conclusion came most from Holmes's "anti-antitrust" vote in *Northern Securities v. United States* (1904).[23] And yet Holmes generally put into practice TR's social philosophies. William Howard Taft, meanwhile, who would go on to be Holmes's chief justice toward the end of his career, complained that "his opinions are short, and not very helpful."[24]

If Holmes disappointed Roosevelt for quixotic reasons, the Rough Rider's next appointee must have been a more systematic source of frustration. In the summer of 1902, the president approached William Howard Taft, who was then serving as governor of the Philippines. Despite his ambition to be chief justice, Taft declined twice, and suggested his former Sixth Circuit colleague and fellow Ohioan, William Rufus Day, a loyal Republican, who was duly nominated and confirmed. Although TR had satisfied himself with Day's "real" (progressive) politics, and the new justice supported the government position in *Northern Securities* and other antitrust cases, Day would go on to vote against federal regulations and various executive actions.

Roosevelt's third and final chance came when Justice Henry Brown announced that he would retire at the end of the 1905–06 term. TR first looked to Senator Philander Knox, who had been Roosevelt's first attorney general. Knox declined, viewing the Court as a political dead end; he would go on to unsuccessfully contest the 1908 Republican presidential nomination before becoming Taft's secretary of state. The president then again turned to Taft, who was back from colonial service and serving as secretary of war, but he too declined, despite his desire to be on the Court some day. Roosevelt ended up going with his loyal attorney general William Henry Moody. Near and dear to the president's heart, Moody had launched legal assaults on the beef, sugar, and oil trusts. His nomination was mildly controversial in that it represented a second Massachusetts pick in four years, but Moody was still confirmed by voice vote.

Although he didn't share Roosevelt's politics, William Howard Taft took the same approach to filling court vacancies as his predecessor, focusing on potential candidates' "real" politics. If Jimmy Carter was the unluckiest president by not having a single Supreme Court seat to fill while serving a full term, Taft was the luckiest. Serving only four years, he made six high court appointments, including a chief justice, more than any other president in one term except Washington. Taft, who to date is the only person to serve as both president and justice, chose his candidates carefully. He didn't care about nominal political affiliations—appointing several southern Democrats—but rejected such progressive legal luminaries as Learned Hand, Louis Brandeis, and Benjamin Cardozo, whom he regarded as "destroyers of the Constitution."[25]

Taft would get five appointments in the 12-month period running from December 1909 to December 1910, the only such span in our history since Washington's original six. (FDR came close with six in an 18-month period.) This was also a string of easy confirmations, most notably Charles Evans Hughes, the youngish (48) governor of New York whom Taft saw as a potential political rival. An April 1910 vacancy was a chance to get Hughes out of the way, so Taft even dangled a future chief justiceship to get him to accept. Taft wouldn't follow through on that incentive but, after leaving the bench to reenter the political world, Hughes would ironically succeed Taft as chief justice.

In his six years as associate justice, Hughes was a well-rounded defender of constitutional liberty—what we might now call a classical liberal—protecting individual rights across both their economic and civil dimensions. At the same time, he rejected many congressional attempts to expand federal power, while recognizing that the federal government could void state regulations that interfered with interstate commerce.[26] Taft was surely pleased with all of this.

Taft's other appointments similarly checked the president's ideological boxes. Willis Van Devanter, an Eighth Circuit judge who was originally a TR-style progressive, had grown more conservative with his time in the West. Choosing him appeased a certain part of the GOP and indeed Van Devanter became the senior member of the "Four Horsemen" who stood against many New Deal policies. Van Devanter suffered from extreme writer's block, writing fewer opinions than any justice appointed between 1853 and 1943.[27] Still, Taft, as chief justice, regarded him to be the best justice on his Court in his approach to the law.[28]

With Taft's emphasis on ideological purity came a renewed fight to get his final nominee confirmed. By the time the president made that pick, Mahlon Pitney, the great-grandfather of Superman actor Christopher Reeve, he faced a veritable confirmation battle over the nominee's "real politics."[29] Progressives and labor advocates questioned Pitney's judicial philosophy and mounted a campaign against him, but were unable to stop his confirmation. After receiving his nomination in February 1912, the Senate confirmed Pitney by a vote of 50–26—the first recorded vote in eighteen years, breaking a string of eleven straight voice-vote confirmations and showing that judicial confirmations couldn't be taken for granted.

Justice Pitney was a strong supporter of the Fourteenth Amendment's protections for economic liberty, opposing state laws that infringed on the freedom of contract to protect unions.[30] Pitney served just over a decade on the Court and was one of only two Taft appointees who would serve alongside the former president when he joined the bench. Chief Justice Taft would call Pitney a "weak member" of his court, to whom he would "not assign cases."[31] On the other hand, libertarian legal scholar Richard Epstein considers Pitney to be his favorite justice because "he was the most consistent classical liberal,"[32] also saying that Pitney "has done the most to protect the core constitutional values."[33]

In sum, despite Roosevelt and Taft's explicit focus on "real" politics—one progressive, the other conservative—both consulted with senators before making nominations and had little problem with any of their high court nominees even as their relationships with the Senate overall had their ups and downs. Indeed, in a long period where most judicial nominees got through the Senate, the failures could be explained by a lack of consultation with—or caring about—senatorial preferences, regardless of party alignment.

CHAPTER 4

The Court Resists the Progressives

Woodrow Wilson, former professor, Princeton president, and governor of New Jersey, reoriented American governance by introducing the administrative state that FDR would build on. A student of German political science, Wilson was impatient with the Founders' Constitution because, unlike parliamentary systems, it failed to provide anyone with the power to "decide at once and with conclusive authority what should be done."[1] And of course it also stymied many of the progressive reforms he envisioned, which just needed the empowerment of technocrats who knew "what should be done" without the interference of enumerated and thus limited powers, or checks and balances.

It's surprising, then, that his three Supreme Court appointments were a mixed bag, with one of the so-called Four Horsemen hellbent on opposing government regulation (sharing only Wilson's racism), one progressive who didn't stay very long, and one social-reform giant, Louis Brandeis, whose nomination presaged modern confirmation battles. Had an aged Court not allowed the one-term Taft a half-dozen appointments, the two-term Wilson could've had a much greater impact, which perhaps would've forestalled the massive legal battles FDR had in the early New Deal against an old guard resistant to the progressive rewriting of the Constitution.

Wilson's appointment criteria built on TR and Taft, looking to candidates' "real" politics rather than formal party affiliation— Brandeis himself was a registered Republican—requiring a commitment to progressive public policy and trust-busting. The major way in which his nominee profiles differed from that of essentially all his predecessors was that judicial background didn't matter; his three nominees had a combined two years of such experience.

The president quickly nominated his attorney general, James Clark McReynolds, a Tennessean who was a renowned trust-buster. Having served as an assistant attorney general under both Roosevelt and Taft, McReynolds eventually left the GOP over what he felt were undue compromises with corporate interests. Continuing his trust-busting, McReynolds maintained Wilson's faith in his progressivism, although his sharp edges were beginning to show such that the president resolved to "kick him upstairs."[2] Strongly backed by the overwhelming Democratic Senate, McReynolds was easily confirmed on August 29, 1914.

McReynolds was prejudiced against Jews, blacks, women, and many others, including smokers and drinkers. He didn't speak to Brandeis, the first Jewish justice, for three years after his appointment, left the conference room when Brandeis spoke, and in 1939 refused to sign his customary retirement letter.[3] McReynolds also refused to sit next to Brandeis for the Court's annual picture, which led Chief Justice Taft to cancel their 1924 photo session. Brandeis in turn considered McReynolds to be "lazy" and moved by the "irrational impulses of a savage."[4]

Justice McReynolds turned out to enforce constitutional limits on federal power and defend economic liberty, voting fairly consistently against everything Wilson wanted. Even before Warren

Harding's appointments completed the conservative Four Horsemen, McReynolds led the charge against all manner of progressive and then New Deal reforms. Still, even those who agreed with him on law found him disagreeable; Justices Pierce Butler and Willis Van Devanter, two other Horsemen, transferred from the Chevy Chase country club to get away.[5]

Woodrow Wilson's next and most consequential appointment produced a firestorm rivaled only by the Robert Bork, Clarence Thomas, and Brett Kavanaugh nominations. Indeed, the process for confirming Louis Dembitz Brandeis lasted longer than any of those, or any others, starting with his nomination on January 28, 1916, and ending with an anticlimactic confirmation on June 1 by a 47–22 largely party-line vote. Twenty-seven senators didn't vote, twenty-four of them "paired" (an equal number of yeas and nays absent with notice), so the "unofficial" tally could be considered 59–34, with all but one Democrat in favor and all but five Republicans opposed. Brandeis, originally from Kentucky, had entered Harvard Law School at nineteen and would become one of the most prominent lawyers in Boston, turning to social causes around the turn of the century after having amassed a fortune in private practice. Co-author with his law partner of the groundbreaking "The Right to Privacy"—perhaps the most influential law review article of all time—he also made frequent appearances at the Supreme Court, having developed what became known as the "Brandeis brief," which presents scientific and other extra-legal information about a case's practical impact.[6] Brandeis was a revolutionary in many ways, and it was Wilson's intent to shake up the Court with his nomination.

This was very much a personal selection by the president. Brandeis had advised Wilson during the 1912 campaign, shaping the Democratic platform on social and economic matters, and then became his friend and collaborator. Knowing the controversy that selecting Brandeis would cause, Wilson kept his own counsel—unlike his practice with most high-profile appointments—consulting only one senator, progressive Republican Robert LaFollette of Wisconsin.

The nomination caused the sensation Wilson had expected. Former president William Howard Taft, whom Brandeis had embarrassed over an Interior Department scandal, called Brandeis a "muckraker," "emotionalist," "socialist," and "hypocrite," as well as "a man of infinite cunning" and "of much power for evil."[7] Further opposition came from former attorney general George W. Wickersham, former NAACP president Moorfield Storey, Harvard President A. Lawrence Lowell, and former presidents of the American Bar Association such as ex-Senator and Secretary of State Elihu Root, who called Brandeis "unfit" to serve on the Supreme Court.[8]

While anti-Semitism surely played a role in the heated opposition, those kinds of impolitic objections may have been muted had it not been for the nominee's "radical" politics. "In all the anti-corporation agitation of the past, one name stands out," wrote the *Wall Street Journal*, "where others were radical, he was rabid."[9] The *New York Times*, meanwhile, argued that as a noted "reformer," Brandeis would lack the "dispassionate temperament that is required of a judge."[10] Justice William O. Douglas, many years later, wrote that the nomination of Brandeis "frightened the Establishment" because he was "a militant crusader for social justice."[11] Supporting Brandeis, on the other hand, were Felix Frankfurter and eight of eleven members of the Harvard Law School faculty, columnist Walter Lippman, Frances Perkins (who would become FDR's labor secretary), union leader Samuel Gompers, former Harvard President Charles Eliot, the *New Republic*, and the *New York World*.[12]

The controversy was such that the Senate Judiciary Committee, for the first time ever, held public hearings on the nomination. Although Brandeis himself was not called to testify—that was seen as unseemly—the process was a far cry from previous experience. For decades, there had been simple up-or-down votes on the Senate floor, often within days of nomination, or decisions to postpone or take no action on controversial picks. This time, things would be different.

When the committee asked the White House to provide the endorsement letters that traditionally accompanied a Supreme Court nomination, Attorney General Thomas Gregory found that there were none, because of Wilson's secretive process in arriving at the decision. Accordingly, Wilson wrote a letter to Chairman Charles Culberson, attesting in poetic terms to the esteem in which he held the nominee's character and abilities.[13]

Although five of the Democratic members of the judiciary committee originally opposed Brandeis—both due to is politics and the standoffish manner in which Wilson picked him—they were eventually swayed, in part by an informal visit Brandeis had with two of them at a journalist's apartment.[14] The full committee reported the nomination favorably on May 24, 1916, leading to the final Senate confirmation a week later.

Brandeis would become the most reliable vote on the Court's progressive wing, first joining with Oliver Wendell Holmes—a very different man but a kindred spirit—and later with Benjamin Cardozo and Harlan Stone. Brandeis later advised FDR behind the scenes, as was not uncommon in those days, and served long enough to see the New Deal Court's codification of progressive legal theories, before retiring at the age of 83 in February 1939.

Nine days after Brandeis was confirmed, Justice Charles Evans Hughes resigned to run for the presidency, thus allowing his presidential opponent to pick his judicial successor. Unlike the notoriety, in very different ways, of Wilson's two previous appointments, this final one was both uncontroversial and insignificant.

The president picked a progressive fellow traveler with a strong antirust background, federal district judge John Hessin Clarke, whose tenure would be decidedly Wilsonian jurisprudentially but unhappy personally. Clarke became disillusioned with the Court's ideological direction, typically joining with Holmes and Brandeis in dissent, and was turned off by McReynolds's animosity. He resigned after just six years to pursue the causes of peace and international relations, especially the United States' joining the League of Nations.

A focus on "real politics" would continue to dominate the nomination process well after Wilson, even if nominees weren't always taken to task for their political convictions. Confirmations still relied on the politics-as-usual approach of consulting senators, or at least making them feel like they were being heard. When presidents leveraged personal connections to grease the process, there was rarely a hiccup; when they failed to do so, they could expect significant resistance.

Warren G. Harding continued the trend, often with the assistance of his first nominee and White House predecessor William Howard Taft, to whom he had promised the chief justiceship when that opened up. Taft was confirmed the same day he was nominated, June 30, 1921, without hearings and after a brief debate that revealed opposition only from three progressive Republicans and a southern Democrat. While philosophically conservative, Taft was neither a precursor to the Four Horsemen, nor a classical liberal with expansive views of constitutional rights. Taft was a master administrator, technical leader, and consensus-builder, discouraging dissents and taking an expansive view of the chief justice's role. He would also have more influence on nominations than any sitting justice, and typically got his way, at least in blocking candidates who might be an "off horse" like Benjamin Cardozo (eventually appointed after

Taft's death) or anyone else who might be "offside" with that "dangerous twosome," Holmes and Brandeis.[15] When vacancies occurred, Taft sought the advice of many people before bringing suggestions to the president, essentially serving as a one-man advisory committee.

Counting the appointments he made as president, those of Harding and Calvin Coolidge, and even his own successor under Herbert Hoover, Taft had direct influence on a dozen Supreme Court picks, significantly more than any other justice. Despite worsening health, Taft refused to resign, in an attempt "to prevent the Bolsheviki from getting control" should the too-progressive Hoover name his replacement.[16] He eventually retired in February 1930, having been assured that Charles Evans Hughes would be his successor rather than Harlan F. Stone.[17]

The day after a disenchanted Justice Clarke left the Court, Harding named and the Senate approved George Sutherland, who would become the intellectual leader of the Four Horseman, joined by Van Devanter, McReynolds, and the next nominee, Pierce Butler. For Sutherland, even more than the others, the Constitution spoke to the libertarian credo of using the government in service of our natural rights, and the Fourteenth Amendment meant keeping technocratic regulatory schemes away from the economic liberties of both working man and tycoon.

At this point, Taft had convinced Harding that that the Court was perceived as "too Republican," so they needed a Democrat who was congenial yet conservative.[18] After John W. Davis, Wilson's solicitor general—who would become the 1924 Democratic nominee for president—declined for financial reasons, they turned to Butler. Butler did his politicking behind the scenes, but became notorious when, as a University of Minnesota regent, he forced out several faculty members for "unpatriotic behavior," "pro-Socialist attitudes," and "incompetence and insubordination"—and became known for being impatient with "kooks," "Bolsheviks," and "Germany-lovers."[19] Taft didn't care much for all that, but still led Butler's campaign, plotting strategy around the Senate hearings, supported by the Minnesota bar association and business interests. Harding found Butler's politics and life story attractive—his Irish parents had fled the potato famine—and liked that he'd be appointing someone from a minority (Catholic) religion. For that reason, he was opposed by the Ku Klux Klan, then at the apogee of its influence.

Justice Butler would validate the hopes of the conservatives and fears of the progressives, opposing labor and business regulations as violating economic liberty and freedom of contract under the Fourteenth Amendment, and federal welfare programs as going beyond the government's enumerated powers. They thus represented the last bulwark of the *Lochner* era against unfettered state economic regulation and a virtually limitless national government.

Harding accepted Taft's recommendation for the next vacancy as well, after the chief justice dissuaded the president from appointing one of the most prominent judges in the country, Learned Hand of the Second Circuit, for being too progressive. A southerner made sense because of the president's support in the region, but it was also time to appoint a Republican, particularly because the other southerner on the Court, McReynolds, was still technically a Democrat. Tennessee federal judge Edward Sanford had lengthy judicial experience, which Sutherland and Butler had lacked, and as a plus was supported by some labor leaders. He was easily confirmed.

Justice Sanford typically joined the Four Horsemen, but even more paired with Taft to show flexibility on some aspects of government regulation, particularly antitrust.

A Return to Normalcy?

Calvin Coolidge was even more a businessman's businessman than Harding, and his calm demeanor fit with the times' demand for "normalcy" after the personal and political controversies surrounding Wilson and Harding. But in his five-and-a-half-year presidency, Coolidge only got to make one Supreme Court appointment, and it was one that would help cement the New Deal and put in place a national legal order very much different than what Silent Cal would've preferred. When octogenarian Justice Joseph McKenna retired in January 1925, nudged by Taft and other brethren, who had determined the previous year that they wouldn't let the essentially senile McKenna's vote be outcome-determinative in any case, Coolidge knew whom he wanted: his attorney general, Harlan Fiske Stone.[20]

The Vermonter Coolidge had known the New Hampshirite Stone since their Amherst college days, so the president discarded any notions of geographical balance or "real politics" to pick a personal friend and ally, one who had been quite helpful in the 1924 campaign. Before cleaning up the Justice Department in the wake of the Teapot Dome scandal, Stone had been dean of Columbia Law School, where he had encouraged the development of a "legal realism" that rejected formal legal rules in favor of human experience and practical legal results—which foreshadowed his approach on the bench.[21]

Despite Stone's own protestations that the seat should go to New York Court of Appeals Judge Benjamin Cardozo, "the outstanding jurist of our times," Coolidge announced Stone's nomination. Stone faced opposition because he continued to pursue a corruption investigation against a powerful sitting senator, so the Senate moved to recommit the nomination to the judiciary committee. At that point,

Stone himself requested to testify before the committee, which would be the first time that a nominee personally appeared—although questions were limited to the one investigation. Stone came through the rather hostile questioning with flying colors. The Senate easily confirmed him, with nary a concern for his iconoclastic legal theories.

On the Taft Court, Justice Stone, allaying fears that he was too closely tied with New York financial interests, joined with Justices Holmes and Brandeis in calling for judicial restraint and deference to the (progressive) legislative will. On the Hughes Court—more on the new chief justice momentarily—Stone, Brandeis, and Cardozo would form a progressive bloc called the Three Musketeers that opposed the Four Horsemen in upholding an expansive view of federal power that undergirded the New Deal. Stone's majority opinions in *United States v. Carolene Products Co.* (1938, ending the *Lochner* era by describing economic regulations as "presumptively constitutional") and *United States v. Darby Lumber Co.* (1941, upholding the Fair Labor Standards Act under a broad reading of the Commerce Clause) created new, more deferential standards of judicial scrutiny of federal laws. In short, Stone's jurisprudence was about as surprising and disappointing to Coolidge as McReynolds's was to Wilson.

Herbert Hoover's made three significant Supreme Court appointments based on pure merit—they were very different ideologically—as well as suffering one surprising rejection of an otherwise capable nominee. When the president picked Charles Evans Hughes to replace Chief Justice Taft on February 3, 1930, he expected another relatively smooth confirmation for the former justice. But Hughes's process wouldn't be quite as comfortable this time around, in part because he now had more of a partisan mien, but also for the very different concerns of progressive Republicans and conservative southern Democrats. The former were suspicious of Hughes's ties to Wall Street; Nebraska Senator George Norris remarked that

Hughes had appeared before the Supreme Court fifty-four times to defend "corporations of untold wealth."[22] The latter were wary of Hughes's citified attitudes that could be seen to favor the national government over the states on both economic and social regulation. Still, this was more a political skirmish that the all-out brawls we'd later see; opposition voices were neither numerous nor unified. Hughes secured the support of both Democratic senators from New York (his home state) and was confirmed 52–26, with eighteen senators abstaining.

Chief Justice Hughes would shift with the times to maintain his leadership role and emerge as a key vote between the conservative Four Horsemen and progressive Three Musketeers, a voting dynamic akin to what we've seen on the modern Supreme Court with various "swing" justices holding the balance of power. Although the Hughes Court struck down several New Deal programs in the early and mid-1930s, after FDR was reelected in 1936, Hughes noticed the shifting winds and started going the other way—convincing the other "swing" justice, Owen Roberts, to go with him. But not because of pressure from FDR's court-packing plan, against which Hughes worked both behind the scenes and in an influential letter to the judiciary committee, which was also signed by Justice Brandeis.[23]

The political challenges to nominees would only increase after the appointment of Chief Justice Hughes. When Hoover nominated the well-regarded Fourth Circuit Judge John Parker of North Carolina to replace Justice Sanford, he found himself in a political dogfight because of Parker's rulings upholding so-called "yellow-dog contracts" prohibiting employees from organizing, as well as racist comments Parker had made ten years earlier when campaigning for governor, after being accused by his Democratic opponents of being too progressive.[24] Both the American Federation of Labor and the NAACP thus opposed him.

Hoover was unwilling to logroll or otherwise pressure progressive Republicans, so six weeks later the Senate voted Parker down 39–41 (again with bipartisan coalitions on both sides), with sixteen paired senators not voting.[25] Parker was the first nominee rejected by roll-call vote in nearly four decades—presaging the modern role of interest groups and digging up dirt on nominees—and the last senatorial rejection for nearly another four decades.

Hoover then turned to Owen Roberts, a successful Philadelphia attorney who had earlier investigated the Teapot Dome scandal. The Senate confirmed him by voice vote eleven days later, literally one minute after the judiciary committee had unanimously sent him to the floor.[26] Even though Roberts was supported by both the conservative/business and progressive wings of both parties, he fully satisfied neither. Indeed, his record is better characterized as inconsistent rather than the more simplistic view that he was initially conservative and flipped in 1937, whether from the pressure of FDR's court-packing plan or otherwise. For example, while Roberts, like Chief Justice Hughes, generally voted with the Four Horsemen pre-1937, there were important exceptions. And Roberts's famous "switch in time that saved nine" in *West Coast Hotel v. Parrish* (1937), where he voted to uphold a minimum-wage law after having earlier voted against such provisions, isn't the inflection it's made out to be, let alone evidence of pressure by FDR. For one thing, Roberts had indicated before the 1936 election that he was open to reevaluating his view if the issue were squarely presented.[27] For another, the influence of the suave Hughes seems more instrumental than any shift in Roberts's thinking. Indeed, post-1941, after the last Horseman (McReynolds) retired, Roberts reverted to his old ways.

On January 15, 1932—another election year—Oliver Wendell Holmes, almost 91, accepted an entreaty from Chief Justice Hughes and retired. Hoover let it be known that he was generally looking for a "non-controversial western Republican," but Judiciary Chairman George Norris, a progressive Republican, made it clear that his committee was looking for someone in Holmes's mold.[28] Everyone whom we would now call a legal elite mobilized for Benjamin Cardozo, now chief judge of the New York Court of Appeals and the most respected jurist not on the Court. Hoover was not unaware of Cardozo, a Sephardic Jew whose ancestors had come from Portugal and Spain, who had also published *The Nature of the Judicial Process*, which remains in print. But Cardozo had three major strikes against him: Two other New Yorkers were already on the Court (Hughes and Stone, though Stone offered to resign[29]); his nomination would mean a second Jew on the Court (controversial to more than Justice McReynolds); and he was a northern Democrat who wasn't as conservative as Hoover (who wasn't all that conservative). Nevertheless, after consulting with Norris and other senators, Hoover announced Cardozo's nomination on February 15. The Senate duly confirmed him by voice vote nine days later.

While Hoover appeared pleased at this process, particularly after the Parker fiasco, it couldn't have either surprised or heartened him that Cardozo immediately joined the Court's progressive wing, aligning with Brandeis and Stone as the third Musketeer, filling Holmes's seat if not necessarily his shoes. Cardozo, 62 when appointed, died a little over six years later, having written more than one hundred elegant opinions—most notably a trio of 1937 cases upholding unemployment compensation and Social Security, and establishing the "selective incorporation" theory of applying some but not all constitutional protections against the states.[30] He had perhaps the most impact of any justice serving so short a time, and heralded a constitutional revolution.

CHAPTER 5

Roosevelt's Court

After significant churn in the Court's personnel in the decade leading up to FDR's election in 1932, the new president was stymied by the "Nine Old Men" who kept rejecting his ambitions. Yes, he had Justices Brandeis, Stone, and Cardozo on his side—favoring the New Deal, holding an expansive view of federal power, and practicing judicial restraint that deferred to the political branches—but three out of nine is only good for batting averages. Frustrated at not being able to get any new blood onto the Court in his first term, the landslide-reelected Roosevelt sent to Congress on February 5, 1937, a plan for a massive "reorganization" of the judiciary that would allow the president to appoint an additional federal judge for each one who didn't retire within six months after turning 70.

Court-Packing

The Judicial Procedures Reform Bill capped the number of total additional judges at fifty and the size of the Supreme Court at fifteen. Conveniently, six members of the Court, including all four Horsemen and the swing Chief Justice Hughes, were over seventy. In a

March 9 "fireside chat," Roosevelt assailed the Supreme Court majority for "reading into the Constitution words and implications which are not there, and which were never intended to be there" and argued that Congress "must take action to save the Constitution from the Court, and the Court from itself."[1] But the president overplayed his hand, sending a disingenuous message to Congress about "insufficient personnel" that was countered by Hughes himself, in an influential and statistics-laden letter to powerful Senator Burton Wheeler (D-Montana) that was co-signed by Brandeis.

The plan was met with fierce opposition, splitting the Democratic super-majority in Congress and drawing a public rebuke from FDR's own Vice President John Nance Garner. Curiously, three future justices supported the plan: Senator Sherman Minton was enthusiastic, scrapping his own bill that would've required a 7–2 vote to hold a law unconstitutional, as were Senator Hugo Black and Wiley Rutledge, dean of Iowa Law School, who was an important academic supporter. Meanwhile, Oswald Garrison Villard, publisher of the left-wing *The Nation*, testified that the bill "opens the way for dictatorship."[2] The judiciary committee negatively reported the bill; a month later the full Senate recommitted it to the committee 20–70—where it was stripped of its court-packing elements, becoming a technical reform that Roosevelt signed in August.

Of course, two important developments took place between the plan's announcement and Senate action. First, the Court started upholding legislation of the sort it had previously invalidated, with Chief Justice Hughes and Justice Owen Roberts shifting their allegiance to the Three Musketeers in *West Coast Hotel* (minimum wage), then *NLRB v. Jones & Laughlin Steel* (labor regulation), and finally *Steward Machine* (unemployment insurance) and *Helvering* (Social Security). The duo to their graves denied that their shift was politically motivated—FDR's court-packing scheme would almost certainly have failed regardless—but even so, the pragmatic Hughes surely moved out of a recognition of the handwriting on the wall.

But second, and perhaps even more importantly, Justice Willis Van Devanter, the oldest and longest-serving of the Four Horsemen, announced that he would retire on June 1, 1937. Finally, four-and-and-half years into his consequential presidency, FDR would have a Supreme Court vacancy. As it turns out, this was the first of nine, a number surpassed only by George Washington's table-setting. And they came quickly: by mid-1941, just four years after court-packing failed, only two justices remained whom FDR hadn't appointed—and one of those, Harlan Stone, Roosevelt had elevated to chief justice. In a very real sense, then, FDR packed the Court the old-fashioned way, by maintaining control of the White House and Senate and waiting for natural attrition—although Republicans capitalized on his political impatience to pick up eight Senate seats in the 1938 election, plus eighty-one in the House.

Roosevelt's criteria in selecting his plethora of nominees were simple: loyalty to the New Deal's regulatory intervention, relative liberalism on civil rights, and, later, support for executive power in wartime. Except for one or two picks, geography played a minor role, not anything determinative. Indeed, much like the New Deal is said to have been a third founding, FDR sought jurists favorable to that institutional realignment as much as George Washington did for the initial constitutional construction and Abraham Lincoln for the forging of a new Union.

For the Van Devanter seat, the leading candidate was Joseph T. Robinson, the Senate majority leader, who had supported all of the president's legislative initiatives, including as an indefatigable advocate for the judicial-reorganization bill. An Arkansas Democrat, Robinson was perhaps more conservative than FDR wanted, so the president, while eager to name his first justice, delayed his announcement—in part because the Senate made it awkward for him, having passed a unanimous resolution urging Robinson's appointment. As fate would have it, six days before the final court-packing vote, Robinson had a fatal heart attack, to which he succumbed while clutching the *Congressional Record*.[3]

Roosevelt then instructed Attorney General Homer Cummings to survey potential nominees and ensure that his pick would be "a thumping, evangelical New Dealer."[4] The four finalists were Solicitor General Stanley Reed, Senators Black and Minton, and Assistant Attorney General Robert Jackson, all of whom eventually joined the Court. FDR settled on Black because, beyond the humble origins, voracious educational appetite—attaining both medical and law degrees after dropping out of high school, understated record as local judge and lawyer, and utter devotion to the New Deal, the Alabaman had advocated for the less fortunate.[5]

Roosevelt nominated Hugo Lafayette Black on August 12, 1937. Although senators nominated for judicial or executive office normally received great deference, the Senate departed from its tradition for the first time since before the Civil War and referred it to the judiciary committee. The nominee proved more controversial than expected, with the intellectual and soft-spoken Black attacked as unqualified, intemperate, and radical. While Black had championed civil rights in the Senate, he had been a member of the KKK in the 1920s, when the organization virtually controlled local politics in the Deep South. Walter Francis White, the improbably surnamed executive secretary of the NAACP, helped assuage critics—who would regardless be mollified by his record on the bench, starting with *Chambers v. Florida* (1940), where Black wrote an opinion overturning the convictions of four black men whose confessions were coerced.

The judiciary committee approved Black 13–4 on August 16 and, after six hours of debate the next day, the Senate voted 63–16 to confirm, with ten Republicans and six Democrats voting against. After the vote but before Black's formal investiture, when he and wife were on a European vacation, rumors broke that apparently the justice-designate had been given a "grand passport" to lifetime membership in the KKK.[6] Black was besieged by reporters abroad and stepped before radio microphones to make an 11-minute statement upon his return, disavowing the Klan and denying any relationship with the group after his resignation in 1925.[7] Three days later, he sat on the bench. That same day, three attorneys filed a motion in the Supreme Court challenging his eligibility under the Emoluments Clause, Article I, Section 6, because justices' compensation had been increased while Black was a senator. The Court dismissed this petition in a brief unsigned opinion, for lack of standing.[8] Recent scholarship suggests there may have been something to the claim after all.[9]

Thus began Justice Black's thirty-four-year tenure on the Court. For his last twenty-five, he would be the senior justice, an unprecedented period. He was known for judicial restraint, a strongly textualist reading of the Constitution, and the wholesale incorporation of the Bill of Rights against the states. An absolutist on free speech, he had a narrow view of what constituted speech, thus dissenting in famous cases on student-armband protests (*Tinker v. Des Moines*, 1969), flag-burning (*Street v. New York*, 1969), and a "Fuck the Draft" jacket (*Cohen v. California*, 1971). A great protector of civil liberties, Black nevertheless wrote the majority opinion in *Korematsu v. United States* (1944), upholding Japanese-American internment during WWII. And as a result of his opposition to substantive due process because of its earlier use to invalidate economic regulations, Black believed that there was no constitutional right to privacy, voting against it in *Griswold v. Connecticut* (1965), the case invalidating a state ban on the use of contraceptives. Black was an iconoclast, a formalist progressive who carried a pocket Constitution with him wherever he went.

FDR's second appointment came less than half a year after his first. To nobody's surprise, he picked his solicitor general, Stanley Forman Reed, who had argued ardently for New Deal legislation before the Supreme Court. Reed had entered public service at President Hoover's behest and stayed into the Roosevelt administration. Although some expected another confirmation fight given Black's troubles, the Senate approved Reed by voice vote ten days after his nomination. Justice Reed spent nineteen fairly quiet years on the bench, a true moderate who was economically progressive—supporting the New Deal and other federal regulations, as well as desegregation—but conservative on speech, national security, and criminal-justice issues. Toward the end of his tenure, he found himself dissenting more and more and decided to retire because the Court's jurisprudential center had moved too far left for him to be effective.

Frankfurter and Douglas

Roosevelt's next opportunity to name a justice came with the untimely death of Benjamin Cardozo in July 1938. The president asked his friend Felix Frankfurter, a storied Harvard law professor, co-founder of the ACLU, and kingmaker for young lawyers looking to go into public service, to find candidates from west of the Mississippi to balance the Eastern bench.[10] Frankfurter, who hailed not just from New York and Boston, but had immigrated from Vienna when he was twelve, failed in that task, because he wanted the seat himself and was pushed by a groundswell of support. FDR's advisers, including new Solicitor General Robert Jackson and Justice Stone, urged him to place "excellence over geography."[11]

Frankfurter became just the second nominee to testify personally before the judiciary committee, withstanding a blistering attack from Senator Pat McCarran (D-Nev.), who tried to tie Frankfurter to communism due to his ties to several people on the ACLU advisory board and other intellectuals. Frankfurter was nevertheless confirmed by voice vote. McCarran need not have worried; whatever anyone thinks of Frankfurter's jurisprudence, the man's devotion to his adopted country and its institutions was clear.

Justice Frankfurter served on the Court for twenty-three years, building a reputation for judicial restraint above all else—which aligned him with New Deal progressives initially, conservatives later on. He was fully comfortable in deferring to the elected branches on regulations that burdened either economic or civil and political liberties, regardless of what his own policy preferences might have been. Like Justice Holmes before him, Justice Frankfurter would essentially allow majorities to legislate and enforce the law so long as what they did didn't "shock the conscience."[12] In short, Frankfurter was an institutionalist who believed in a minimal role for the courts, which could all too easily exhaust their political capital.

Four weeks after Roosevelt nominated Frankfurter, Louis Brandeis retired, giving the president his fourth Supreme Court vacancy in two years. Still wanting a Westerner, FDR began to eye his youthful (40) chairman of the new Securities and Exchange Commission, William Orville Douglas. But Douglas, who was raised in Washington state after having been born in Minnesota, had spent half his life in New York, New Haven, and D.C., so Roosevelt viewed him as "two-thirds Easterner" and he had promised a "true Westerner."[13] Similar to the dynamic with the previous nomination, with legal elites wanting someone who shared their ideological vision, pressure began to build to appoint Douglas. Brandeis also strongly urged his fellow progressive and New Dealer, who believed that the law had to grow with the times.

After two weeks of perfunctory processing in the Senate—the nominee waited outside the hearing room but was told there were no questions for him—William O. Douglas was confirmed 62-4, with the four dissenting senators bizarrely accusing him of being a "reactionary tool of Wall Street."[14] Justice Douglas, the youngest appointee since Joseph Story in 1811, would go on to serve thirty-six years and 211 days, a record unlikely to be broken any time soon.

While "judicial activism" has become an empty term meaning simply that the commentator doesn't like the ruling in a particular case, Douglas truly was an activist on the bench, writing pithy, result-oriented opinions that relied on philosophy, contemporary politics, and literary insights more than legal text, history, or precedent. An early environmentalist, Douglas asserted in *Sierra Club v. Morton* (1972) that inanimate objects like rivers and trees should have standing to sue. Similarly, in cases pitting claims of civil rights and liberties against government power, Douglas sided with the former even if the Constitution failed to provide the precise protection he sought. It was Douglas, after all, who in *Griswold v. Connecticut* (1965) devised the infamous "penumbras, formed by emanations" articulation of rights protected in the interstices of Bill of Rights provisions, which would play a central role in the legal debate over abortion and become a standard trope of criticisms of the Warren Court.[15]

When Justice Pierce Butler died on November 16, 1939, FDR knew he wanted to appoint his attorney general, Frank Murphy, who had previously been governor of Michigan. A loyal New Dealer and before that a savvy advocate for the poor and ethnic minorities, Murphy was a lackadaisical administrator of the Justice Department. FDR told Murphy that he would get the nod the very morning of Butler's death, but Murphy, who had a history of depression and eventually a drug problem, demurred because he felt "utterly inadequate."[16] The nomination still came, and the Senate confirmed him by voice vote less than two weeks later.

Justice Murphy suffered a fatal heart attack nine years later, not having reached the age of sixty, and established a record of utter loyalty not just to the New Deal but to civil liberties. He alone among the progressive bloc of Black, Douglas, and Wiley Rutledge (FDR's last appointee; see below) dissented from *Korematsu*, writing an impassioned attack on the internment program as one that "goes over the very brink of constitutional power and falls into the abyss of racism."[17] Frankfurter disparagingly nicknamed Murphy "the Saint," criticizing his decisions as being rooted more in passion than reason, sacrificing logic to help the little guy, "tempering justice with Murphy."[18]

The last of the Four Horsemen, James McReynolds, announced his retirement in early 1941, soon after FDR's unprecedented second reelection, lamenting that he had tried to protect the country but "any country that elects Roosevelt three times deserves no protection."[19] FDR was expected to finally name Robert Jackson, who had become attorney general after Murphy was "kicked upstairs." But Jackson had been in office barely a year, so Roosevelt decided to keep him there a bit. Influential senators pushed one of their colleagues, Senator James Byrnes of South Carolina, who had been the president's stalwart political ally on New Deal programs, even supporting the court-packing scheme. On June 12, 1941, the same day Byrnes was formally nominated, his colleagues confirmed him.

Byrnes, the last justice who never attended law school, was more conservative than FDR's other appointees, but by that point it didn't matter because the New Deal was judicially secure. He didn't last very long on the Court anyway; a man of action who felt uncomfortable on the bench, he stepped down just over a year later to become what Roosevelt called "assistant president for economic affairs." He would live another thirty years, becoming secretary of state and governor of South Carolina and, with his endorsements of Dwight Eisenhower, Richard Nixon, and Barry Goldwater—as well as blessing his own state's Strom Thurmond's party switch in 1964—signaling the South's shifting partisanship, though he himself remained a Democrat.

Stone and Jackson

Ten days before the Byrnes confirmation, Chief Justice Charles Evans Hughes let it be known that he would be retiring. With five of his nominees now on the high bench and a sixth about to join them, FDR felt no urgency to act, particularly because his choice was quite obviously between Justice Harlan Stone and Attorney General Robert Jackson. The president's heart was with New Deal loyalist Jackson, who had made it clear that he was interested in the position, but Roosevelt hesitated because he was aware of the institutional and popular support for Stone. "On personal grounds I'd prefer Bob [Jackson]," Justice Frankfurter opined, but "from the national interest I am bound to say that there is no reason for preferring Bob to Stone— quite the contrary," because Stone was a Republican, and as war loomed, it would truly make FDR a unifying president to name him.[20]

Frankfurter was so confident that it would be Stone, that he so informed his fellow justices. FDR came to the same conclusion, and also nominated Jackson to the vacancy that Stone's elevation was creating. Stone's nomination was made public June 12, the same day Byrnes was confirmed, and he was confirmed by acclamation two weeks later.

Stone was almost 69 when he succeeded Hughes, the oldest chief justice-appointee to date and the only justice to have occupied all nine seniority positions on the Supreme Court. "Not a first-rate administrator like Taft, not a skillful and disciplinary Court-master like Hughes, not a ruthless craftsman like Marshall, not so persuasive as Taney, not so innovative cum activist as Warren, not so elegant a writer as Jackson,"[21] Stone was much more effective as part of a "team of nine"—to use Justice Brett Kavanaugh's formulation—than as its leader.

Jackson's confirmation took a bit longer than Byrnes and Stone's because of the idiosyncratic opposition of Senator Millard Tydings (D-Md.), over Jackson's decision not to prosecute a columnist who had allegedly libeled the legislator.[22] The judiciary committee still approved the nominee unanimously, and the full Senate approved him by voice vote. Jackson was the last justice not to have graduated from law school and the only person to have been solicitor general and attorney general before joining the Court.

Justice Jackson's jurisprudence is now best known for three opinions, a majority, a concurrence, and a dissent. In *West Virginia v. Barnette* (1943), he wrote a magisterial paean to the freedom of conscience in overturning a public-school flag-salute mandate. In *Korematsu* (1944), he dissented in a warning about excessive deference to executive power over individual liberty. And in *Youngstown Steel & Tube Co. v. Sawyer* (1952), his concurring opinion disallowing President Truman's seizure of steel mills for the Korean War effort remains to this day the standard against which executive authority is measured in the face of congressional acquiescence, disapproval, and silence, respectively. Indeed, the *Steel Seizure Case* is one of the few instances where the law was shaped by Jackson personally, rather than as part of a group of FDR appointees. Jackson's effectiveness was no doubt hampered by his feud with Hugo Black, which started in their first year on the Court together when Jackson bristled at Black's penchant for importing his personal preferences, policy and otherwise, into his jurisprudence.[23] Their often public disagreements even hurt Jackson's chances of being promoted to chief justice, which FDR had informally promised him but which vacancy didn't arise until after FDR died.

Unlike all eight of Roosevelt's previous vacancies, when Justice Byrnes unexpectedly resigned in October 1942, there was no obvious successor waiting in the wings. Perhaps FDR would finally find his "true" Westerner? Roosevelt went with Judge Wiley Rutledge, who had been considered for earlier vacancies and had lost out in part because FDR didn't know him. A long-time academic who had taught in five states, FDR had appointed him to the D.C. Circuit in 1939. After a brief chat in the White House, the president decided to elevate Rutledge, making him Roosevelt's only nominee with federal judicial experience.

The Senate confirmed Rutledge without a roll call or committee hearings less than a month after his nomination. Rutledge fit into the Court's liberal wing alongside Justices Black, Douglas, and Murphy, as opposed to Justice Frankfurter's judicial restraint, which, as the New Deal era faded into the past, made for more conservative results.

It's hard to gauge whether any individual justice among FDR's nine led to major changes in jurisprudence because, coming as they did in rapid succession, they diluted each other's personal impact. In retrospect, Roosevelt's appointees shared little other than faith in and legal support for the New Deal; often bitter enemies personally and professionally, they would split on all sorts of issues that went beyond economic regulation and federal power.

CHAPTER 6

The Post-War Settlement

I t's quite possible that FDR's first choice of running mate in 1944 was Justice William O. Douglas rather than Harry S. Truman, but that Democratic National Committee Chairman Robert Hannigan put his thumb on the scales when the convention choice came down to the two.[1] As President Truman's popularity sunk ahead of the 1948 election, Douglas's name again circulated in political circles, including a "Draft Douglas" campaign before the justice withdrew his name from consideration. After Truman easily won the nomination, he approached the justice about being his vice president, but Douglas turned him down. Douglas's associate Tommy Corcoran was later heard to ask, "Why be a number two man to a number two man?"[2]

Whatever Truman's presidential merits, rising as they've been in the popular conception lately, his nominations valued loyalty (political and personal) over ideology, merit, geography, or any other considerations. His four Supreme Court appointments were all old buddies who knew each other well and spent relatively short and insignificant tenures on the Court. Truman lost their votes on occasion—most notably two defections in the 1952 *Steel Seizure Case*—but they generally sided with his views in favor of federal regulatory power and national security.

Truman's most expansive effort to shape the Court came when Chief Justice Stone died April 22, 1946. It was an awkward moment for the Court to be getting a new chief, in light of the increasing tensions between Justices Black and Jackson and a growing fracture between the liberal bloc, led by Black, and the increasingly conservative judicial-restraint school, led by Justice Frankfurter. Truman was aware of Jackson's claims to the center seat, but, for the sake of maintaining harmony, turned to Treasury Secretary Fred Vinson. Vinson, in addition to being the president's friend, had already had a distinguished career, having served on the D.C. Circuit and presided over several New Deal agencies before Truman moved him into the cabinet. The Senate received Vinson's nomination on June 6 and confirmed him two weeks later.

Vinson served for just seven years, an unhappy period when he was unable to heal the Court's personal and professional rifts. Although the Jackson-Black feud became less public, the percentage of 5-4 opinions was about as high as any comparable period before or since.[3] Vinson's final Court appearance was to read the decision not to review the death sentence of Julius and Ethel Rosenberg; after Justice Douglas granted a stay of execution, Vinson called the justices back to Washington to deny their petition for review. Vinson was the last chief justice to have been appointed by a Democrat and to have presided over a Court whose members were all appointed by presidents from the same party (FDR and Truman).

Truman's other three picks, Harold Burton before Vinson and Tom C. Clark and Sherman "Shay" Minton after him, were political allies whom the president sought to reward. Because the nominations weren't ideologically motivated, Senate Republicans accused Truman of cronyism. The *New York Times*, for example, called Clark "a personal and political friend [of Truman's] with no judicial experience and few demonstrated qualifications."[4] He also faced objections from civil libertarians for his work implementing the administration's anti-communist agenda—although he had the support of other groups associated with the political left. Minton, meanwhile, remains the last justice to have served in Congress, and he kept up with politics, getting into hot water in 1956 when, as a sitting justice, he endorsed Adlai Stevenson and disparaged Dwight Eisenhower.[5] Both were confirmed fairly easily—despite refusals to testify before the judiciary committee—though the fact that they got harsh treatment from Republicans showed that the stakes of nominations were rising. Ironically, Minton disappointed Democrats because his partisanship didn't transfer to the bench. He would join the more conservative Frankfurter wing because, from his New Deal experience, he believed that judges shouldn't overturn the will of the people, and so stuck to judicial restraint above any practical outcomes.

The Unexpected Warren Court

Eisenhower had a very different approach to Supreme Court nominations than Truman, which gave him a greater impact—not always in a direction he liked, ironically. Ike spelled out his considerations in his memoir: (1) character and ability that would earn the "respect, pride, and confidence of the populace"; (2) ideological moderation, common sense, and the "absence of extreme views"; (3) after Earl Warren, who would be the president's biggest disappointment, prior judicial service that would "provide an inkling of philosophy"; (4) geographic and religious balance; (5) an upper age limit of sixty-two, unless "other qualifications were unusually impressive"; and (6) successfully passing a thorough FBI background check *and* approval of the American Bar Association.[6] He would have five chances to apply these criteria.

President Eisenhower's first vacancy came eight months into office, when Chief Justice Vinson died in September 1953. "This is the first indication I have ever had that there is a God," cracked Felix Frankfurter, who detested Vinson's leadership and intellectual inadequacies.[7] Contrary to common belief that Ike had promised this seat to California governor Earl Warren as a reward for his machinations at the 1952 Republican Convention, there was never a guarantee, even if Eisenhower felt a political debt. When the president spoke to Warren before Vinson's death, he was satisfied "that his views seemed to reflect high ideals and a great deal of common sense," so "told the Governor that I was considering the possibility of appointing him to the Supreme Court."[8]

Ike considered other possible nominees before returning to Warren. The president asked Attorney General Herbert Brownell to go to California and learn more about the governor's record, including as a district attorney and the state's attorney general, where he had gained a reputation as a corruption fighter. Ike was hoping to confirm that he would be getting an experienced tactician who could appeal to liberal Republicans as well as law-and-order conservatives, noting privately that Warren "represents the kind of political, economic, and social thinking that I believe we need on the Supreme Court."[9] The president's closest advisers agreed that the leadership qualities of the three-term governor would serve him well in reining in a badly fractured Court, and they were pleased that he had opposed court-packing and supported the Court's anti-steel-seizure ruling. The politically savvy Brownell put it more than once that Warren was a bona fide "middle-of-the-road," "moderate" Republican.[10] Moreover, California's GOP leadership, which included Vice President Nixon, were itching to remove this independent-minded, larger-than-life figure from state politics.[11]

After Brownell re-interviewed Warren in the lounge of McClellan Air Force Base near Sacramento, Ike gave the go-ahead, giving

Warren a recess appointment on October 5, 1953, because Congress wouldn't be in session until January. Confirmation was supposed to be perfunctory, but when Warren's name officially reached the Senate in January, he faced opposition from Judiciary Committee Chairman William Langer of North Dakota, who was going against all Supreme Court nominees until someone from his home state was picked. Several Southern Democrats opportunistically joined the attack based on what they (correctly) perceived as Warren's very liberal views, but only succeeded in delaying the final vote until March 1, 1954, when Warren was waved through.

Just two months after his confirmation, Warren arranged for the Court's decision in *Brown v. Board of Education* (1954) to be unanimous, after which the Court continued to issue rulings against segregation, Jim Crow, and state resistance to federal civil rights oversight. The Warren Court also radically changed constitutional criminal procedure, redistricting, privacy rights, and other areas. *Gideon v. Wainwright* (1963) established a criminal defendant's right to an attorney. *Miranda v. Arizona* (1966) required the police to give the now-famous warning to criminal suspects before what they said could be used against them. *Katz v. United States* (1967) extended the Fourth Amendment's protections against unreasonable search and seizure beyond homes and property to the "reasonable expectation of privacy." *Griswold v. Connecticut* (1965) voided a state law that restricted access to contraceptives, establishing a constitutional right to privacy of another kind—in a way that would prove controversial when applied to abortion eight years later—while *Loving v. Virginia* (1967) set aside state laws against interracial marriage.

Not all of these developments would've been unwelcomed by President Eisenhower, but they certainly would've been unexpected, not gradual enough, and not accomplished by the right branch of government. As one Warren biographer, who had been his law clerk, wrote, "neither Brownell nor Eisenhower sensed Warren's instinctive Progressivism. Warren was appointed as something he was not: an Eisenhower Republican."[12] Warren moved cautiously at first, but eventually instituted an active progressivism that led to bumper stickers and billboards urging his impeachment. More impressive than his legal acumen was his skill at coalition-building. When Warren was appointed, all the other justices had been tapped by either FDR or Truman, but they disagreed about the role that courts should play. Warren's belief that the judiciary must seek to do *justice* placed him with the Black and Douglas liberals without stepping on the others' toes.[13] And yet he let William Brennan, who would join the Court three years later, become the liberal-activist Court's intellectual leader; Brennan complemented Warren's political skills with the legal skills Warren lacked.[14] At base, Warren, who served for fifteen years and led what *New York Times* columnist Anthony Lewis called "a revolution of judges,"[15] believed that vindicating the Constitution's moral principles as he saw them was more important than doctrinal clarity or textual faithfulness.

Eisenhower's next nomination came later the same year, when Justice Jackson suffered a fatal heart attack. Recently appointed Second Circuit Judge John Marshall Harlan II, named after his grandfather, the justice, was a lifelong Republican with a low political profile: just what Ike wanted. Harlan ran into opposition from Southern Democrats, who considered the nominee to be "ultra-liberal," intent on rewriting the Constitution by "judicial fiat."[16] It was an odd accusation to throw at Harlan, of all of Ike's nominees, but it reflected the political atmosphere post-*Brown*. Harlan had to testify before the Senate Judiciary Committee, as every nominee has since, but confirmation still came, by a 71–11 vote.

Sherman Minton resigned in October 1956, three weeks before the presidential election. The president moved quickly to install a fifty-year-old New Jersey supreme court justice, William J. Brennan Jr., on a recess appointment. Brennan came recommended by Arthur Vanderbilt, chief justice of his court and one-time Supreme Court contender, along with the ABA, New Jersey Bar Association, and Cardinal Francis Spellman. For Brennan was a Catholic and a Democrat from the Metropolitan Northeast, all of which appealed to Eisenhower's sense of bipartisanship ahead of the election. As with Harlan, Brennan's confirmation was delayed once the Senate returned in January, mostly by Senator Joe McCarthy, whom the nominee had criticized in the past. The secularist National Liberal League also opposed him, out of fear that he would base his rulings on Church doctrine rather than the Constitution.[17] Past the height of his influence, McCarthy in the end managed only an audible "no" on the confirming voice vote.

Brennan became a reliable member of the Court's liberal wing, first alongside Chief Justice Warren and later with Thurgood Marshall. He had many opinions that are considered landmarks, including on civil rights, women's rights, freedom of the press, and reapportionment. He also helped Harry Blackmun write the majority opinion in *Roe v. Wade* (1973), which put his religious beliefs in conflict with what he saw as the Constitution's right to privacy. In what may be the most obvious case of legislating from the bench, in *United Steelworkers of America v. Weber* (1979), Brennan cobbled together a 5–4 majority to allow racial quotas in employment, despite express statutory language *and* congressional intent to the contrary, citing the "spirit" rather than the "letter" of Title VII of the Civil Rights Act of 1964.[18] Indeed, his influence on modern affirmative action jurisprudence, the disingenuous muddle that it is, can't be understated.

Not as doctrinaire as Justices Black or Douglas, for Brennan the most important rule on the Court was "the rule of five"—the votes needed to form a majority. Called the "playmaker," Brennan was good at devising majority coalitions, though in his later years he was more often in dissent. When Brennan retired in 1990, he was the sixth-longest-serving justice and second only to the longest-serving one, William O. Douglas, in number of opinions written.[19] Justice Antonin Scalia would call him "probably the most influential justice of the [20th] century."[20]

Eisenhower's remaining two nominees would have less of an imprint than his first three. Charles Evans Whittaker, a high school dropout who had gone to law school in the evenings while working as an office boy for the prominent Kansas City law firm, had a meteoric rise during the Eisenhower administration but proved utterly unsuited to the job. Although he was a moderate conservative, and thus the swing vote on a divided Court (which no doubt pleased Eisenhower), Whittaker had difficulty composing sentences and was uncomfortable with the docket and his colleagues, especially Justice Douglas. When he first joined the Court, Whittaker said he was "scared to death,"[21] and "used to come out of our conference literally in tears."[22] In 1962, he suffered a nervous breakdown—because "he changed his mind so often," cracked Douglas—and resigned from the Court after five unhappy and unproductive years.[23] He then returned to the comforts of the private sector, where he became a critic of the Warren Court and Civil Rights Movement.

Eisenhower's fifth and final nomination came when Justice Burton, diagnosed with Parkinson's Disease in the 1957–58 term, retired at the start of the following term. When the time came, Ike was ready with a recess appointment of Potter Stewart, a young (43) Ohioan he had appointed to the Sixth Circuit. Stewart's nomination process is more noteworthy than his time as a justice, as it reflects the mounting tensions over the Court's role in civic life.

When Stewart's name was submitted to the Senate in January 1959, the nominee faced stern opposition from Southern Democrats for his views on civil rights. Before the judiciary committee, Stewart told Senator John McClellan of Arkansas that "I would not like for you to vote for me on the assumption that I am dedicated to the cause of overturning [*Brown*], as I am not."[24] The committee still voted him out 12–3. The dissenters, led by Chairman James Eastland of Mississippi, filed a minority report objecting to the recommendation, writing, "We are further opposed to Justice Stewart, because it is evident from the hearings that Justice Stewart thinks the Supreme Court has the power to legislate and to amend the Constitution of the United States."[25] Stewart's opponents were able to delay the final vote for four months, before he was finally confirmed 70–17 on May 5. All but five senators from the old Confederacy voted no.[26]

Justice Stewart, ever the Eisenhower moderate, started his high court career on the more conservative side of the Warren Court—particularly on criminal procedure and redistricting—and ended it nearly twenty-three years later as a centrist swing vote on the Burger Court. His most famous line is that the Constitution protects all but "hard-core pornography," which is hard to define, but "I know it when I see it."[27]

Eisenhower is famously quoted as saying that he had made only two mistakes during his presidency, "and they are both sitting on the Supreme Court" (Warren and Brennan), but it's not clear that he ever expressed the sentiment in precisely those terms.[28] Ike's disappointment with Warren is well-documented, such as when he called the appointment "the biggest damnfool mistake I ever made."[29] Brennan must have been similarly disconcerting; *New York Times* columnist Arthur Krock recorded in a memorandum after a ninety-minute conversation on April 6, 1960, that "the President has been disappointed in the far Leftist trend of Chief Justice Warren, and has been equally astounded at the conformity to this of Justice Brennan."[30] But Brennan's ideological slant shouldn't have been surprising; the fact that he was a Northeastern Democrat was one of the reasons

Eisenhower's team liked him, and the jurist hardly hid his liberal tendencies on the state bench. So it may well have been that, just as Eisenhower considered Warren a kindred moderate because of the support he had given him in the fight for the Republican nomination in 1952, he thought that the political advantages he purportedly gained from picking Brennan in 1956 would extend onto the Court. Maybe Ike should've been focusing instead on his nominees' "real" politics, in the style of TR and Taft.

Chapter 7

The New Frontier

T he 1960 presidential election had plenty of innovation and intrigue, including the first televised debate and a nail-biting conclusion marred by fraud. Senate Democrats, fearing further recess appointments to the Supreme Court—three of five of Eisenhower's nominees had started that way, with Brennan's recess appointment coming a month before the 1956 election—passed a resolution "expressing the sense of the Senate that the president should not make recess appointments to the Supreme Court, except to prevent or end a breakdown in the administration of the Court's business."[1] The resolution was non-binding, but we haven't had any justices recess-appointed since Potter Stewart in 1958.

JFK

President John F. Kennedy, in his tragically short time in office, had the opportunity to pick two justices. His criteria were standard: professional qualification and intellectual capacity, personal integrity, judicial temperament, and "real" politics sympathetic to his administration.[2] There were plenty of outstanding people satisfying those requirements, so the president and his brother, Attorney General Robert F. Kennedy, could also get themselves personally comfortable with a nominee, checking that they were on the same wavelength, in the parlance of the new era.

Kennedy's first vacancy came with Charles Whittaker's merciful retirement after a tenure filled with decisional paralysis. The final shortlist included two members of the administration, Deputy Attorney General Byron White and Labor Secretary Arthur Goldberg; one federal judge, William Hastie of the Third Circuit; a leading law professor, Paul Freund of Harvard; and two highly regarded state supreme court justices. The Kennedys didn't really know the state jurists, while Hastie, the first black federal circuit judge, was thought too controversial and, at least in the view of Justices Warren and Douglas, too conservative.[3] The brothers knew Freund, but he had his detractors among the progressive legal elite for being too much like Justice Frankfurter, a judicially restrained conservative. In any case, the choice came down to White and Goldberg.

Byron White, all of 44, was the perfect pick for a youthful president obsessed with "vigah." A popular All-American at the University of Colorado, where he was also student body president, "Whizzer" White was runner-up for the Heisman Trophy in 1937. He also won a Rhodes Scholarship, which he deferred so he could play in the NFL for the Pittsburgh Pirates (now Steelers), where as a rookie he was both the highest-paid player and leading rusher. While in England, he met JFK, whose father was ambassador to the Court of St. James. On his return, he enrolled at Yale Law School, where he earned the highest grades in his class, but turned down a spot on the *Yale Law Journal* to play for the Detroit Lions, again leading the league in rushing.[4] He continued his pro-football career while at Yale—using his earnings to pay his tuition—surely a feat that will never be repeated.[5] During World War II, White was a naval intelligence officer and wrote up the report on the sinking of JFK's PT-109, after which he graduated first in his Yale class and clerked for Chief Justice Vinson—becoming the first clerk to become a justice.

Seeing him serve with distinction as deputy attorney general, Kennedy tapped White for the Supreme Court on April 3, 1962. Eight days later, White had his confirmation hearing, a quick ninety minutes during which the nominee himself was questioned for less than fifteen minutes, mostly about his football career; otherwise he smoked and doodled on a notepad. The judiciary committee unanimously approved him and, later that day, so did the full Senate.

Justice White proved to be independent-minded and, other than in cases of racial and later gender discrimination, more conservative than President Kennedy likely expected. White normally supported the government in criminal-justice cases and was critical of reading broad liberty and privacy rights via substantive due process. He dissented in *Roe v. Wade*, which he called "an exercise in raw judicial power," and only concurred in *Griswold v. Connecticut*, declining to join the "penumbras and emanations" majority. As the Warren Court became the Burger Court, White became a key swing vote, alongside Justice Potter Stewart, and relished his role as a pragmatic centrist.

On August 28, 1962, Felix Frankfurter, no longer able to serve after a stroke, resigned in a heartfelt letter to President Kennedy. The next afternoon, JFK announced that he had chosen Goldberg for the seat. Goldberg had previously served as the chief negotiator and legal adviser in the AFL-CIO merger in 1955 and also as general counsel of the United Steelworkers of America. If there was any reluctance on the president's part, it was that he hated to lose such a skilled cabinet member and personal adviser. Sailing through the Senate Judiciary Committee, Goldberg was confirmed by voice vote, with only South Carolina Senator Strom Thurmond registering oral opposition.[6]

Although Goldberg's personal history as the son of Russian-Jewish immigrants paralleled Frankfurter's, his jurisprudence diverged from his predecessor and, at least in result, more closely matched the previous occupants of that seat, Justices Oliver Wendell Holmes and Benjamin Cardozo. Goldberg quickly slotted into the left side, joining in the decisions on civil rights and criminal justice that defined the Warren Court. His *Griswold* concurrence, finding "additional fundamental rights" in the Ninth Amendment, has gained far more respect as a basis for privacy rights than the majority's penumbras and emanations.[7]

Justice Goldberg clearly enjoyed his work, so it was surprising that in July 1965 he accepted Lyndon Johnson's offer to succeed the deceased Adlai Stevenson as U.N. ambassador. Goldberg made this move out of a belief that he could thus negotiate the end of the Vietnam War. "I had an exaggerated opinion of my capacities," he later explained, "I thought I could persuade Johnson that we were fighting the wrong war in the wrong place."[8] He also thought he'd return to the Court, which opportunity never materialized, although LBJ considered recess-appointing him after Fortas's proposed elevation to chief justice was withdrawn in the face of Senate opposition.[9] Among Goldberg's clerks during his brief tenure were future Justice Stephen Breyer (who now sits in the same seat) and celebrity law professor Alan Dershowitz.

LBJ

It's certainly possible that, had Kennedy lived, Byron White wouldn't have gone quite as far to the right, but it's almost certain that Goldberg would've stayed on the Court. Of course, that's not the world we live in, so Johnson got to fill the Goldberg seat—and would have three other attempts to appoint justices. He only succeeded once, but made history nonetheless by nominating the first black justice. Indeed, other than Thurgood Marshall, whose nomination was noble, politically strategic, and a capstone on an already historic legal career, Johnson's picks, while capable attorneys, were cronies whose defects the president simply ignored.

The first nomination went to close personal friend and longtime adviser Abe Fortas, who had represented then-Congressman Johnson in a legal dispute over his 1948 Senate primary that reached the Supreme Court on an emergency motion. Fortas had earlier been a law professor at Yale (on William Douglas's recommendation), went with Douglas to the Securities and Exchange Commission, and became general counsel of the Public Works Administration. He later co-founded a law firm that's now Arnold & Porter, one of the world's largest, from which perch he defended those ensnared in Joe McCarthy's investigations, as well as other pro bono clients like Clarence Gideon, whose Supreme Court case *Gideon v. Wainwright* (1963) established the right to government-provided counsel in criminal cases. Even though the president had orchestrated Goldberg's move to the U.N. to open up the seat for him, Fortas had to be cajoled in typical LBJ style. Indeed, Fortas never actually said yes; during a meeting at the White House in late July, the president simply told him that he was going to the East Wing to "announce your appointment," and Fortas could either stay or come along.[10]

Justice Fortas would continue advising Johnson, including on military and diplomatic matters, and rendering legal advice on racial controversies. He had a private line to the White House installed in his office; Fortas's biographer counted 254 contacts between the justice and the president from October 1966 to December 1968.[11] His colleagues thought that this was perhaps too much, but generally got along well with him, except Hugo Black, a onetime close friend with whom Fortas had a falling out over Black's textualist approach—whereas Fortas liberally construed the law and was more result-oriented.

Justice Tom Clark's retirement at the end of the 1966–67 Supreme Court term—to allow his son Ramsey to become attorney general free of conflicts—would be the second and final vacancy President Johnson filled. The choice was easy: his solicitor general Thurgood Marshall, who had previously been a Second Circuit judge and executive director of the NAACP Legal Defense and Educational Fund. Johnson was said to have appointed Ramsey Clark precisely to force his father out and thus make Marshall the first African-American justice.[12]

With the Legal Defense Fund, Marshall executed a targeted litigation strategy of ever-expanding challenges to Jim Crow, arguing many civil rights cases before the Supreme Court, most of them successfully. As solicitor general, Marshall won fourteen of nineteen cases he argued for the government before the Supreme Court. Marshall knew what was to come, having faced significant opposition from Southern Democrats and an 11-month delay before being confirmed to the Second Circuit in 1962. LBJ said that he had to "armor [Marshall] with the kind of battleplates that no opposition could penetrate."[13]

Southern senators recognized the inevitability of a black appointment, so focused their attacks on Marshall's liberal ideology and allegedly deficient knowledge. Three senators led the questioning— John McClellan (D-Ark.), Sam Ervin (D-N.C.), Strom Thurmond (R-S.C.)—attacking Marshall for being sympathetic to criminal defendants, enamored of a "living Constitution," judicially unrestrained, and unsympathetic to federalism.[14] The judiciary committee approved him 11–5. The floor vote was then delayed until the end of August, with Senator Ervin summing up the argument against: "This is no time to add another judicial activist to the Supreme Court."[15] In other words, the appeals against Marshall weren't overtly racist, but most of the cases on which ideological attacks were based involved racial questions. On August 30, Marshall was confirmed 69–11, with all no votes coming from Southern senators except Robert Byrd (D-W.V.), and all but one of those being Democrats—the lone exception being Strom Thurmond, who had switched parties three years earlier. Four other southern Democrats paired against Marshall, opposite one border-state and three northern Democrats.

Justice Marshall took his oath on October 2, 1967, and quickly began siding with the progressive bloc: Warren, Douglas, Brennan, Fortas, and sometimes Black. As the Court grew more conservative under Chief Justice Warren Burger, he became an even more predictable ally of the activists, especially Brennan. Justice Marshall once described his legal philosophy as: "You do what you think is right and let the law catch up."[16] Marshall was particularly interested in civil rights cases, but to such an extent that he neglected other areas of statutory and constitutional interpretation, and frequently delegated opinion-writing to clerks.[17] As an admirer put it, Marshall was a "social engineer and a partisan for individual and social justice. Upon becoming an 'objective' judge, [he] resolved the challenging problem of intellectual integrity by transferring his lawyer's partiality from persons to principles of law."[18]

After Chief Justice Warren wrote to LBJ on June 13, 1968, that he would retire "effective at your pleasure," the president, with Warren's agreement, announced the retirement two weeks later while nominating Fortas to succeed him in the middle chair.[19] Although the choice wasn't surprising, this was now an election year and Republicans smelled blood in the water from the self-imposed lame duck Johnson. Fortas was confirmable, but historian Henry J. Abraham concludes that LBJ made three key errors: (1) misjudging Republican support, particularly when the party's nominee, Richard Nixon, was looking to wound the Democratic administration; (2) antagonizing influential Democratic Senator Richard Russell of

Georgia by allowing the controversial attorney general, Ramsey Clark, to delay a federal judgeship for a Russell favorite; and (3) simultaneously nominating his childhood friend Homer Thornberry for the putative Fortas vacancy.[20] The president also failed, uncharacteristically, to consult other key senators.

Then there was the sentiment expressed by Senator Robert Griffin (R-Mich.), who argued that since LBJ had already declined to seek reelection, the choice of chief justice should be left to the next president: "I would hope and expect that [the president] would not seek to deny the people and the next President of their appropriate voice in such a crucial decision."[21] Another sixteen senators joined in a petition to that effect.[22] Warren didn't help things by holding a press conference to announce that he would stay on the Court if Fortas weren't confirmed.[23]

Justice Fortas didn't do himself any favors before the judiciary committee, denying having given legal advice to LBJ or that he had participated in any policy decisions. In the words of his biographer, Laura Kalman, "He simply lied."[24] When he told the committee that he didn't recall making personnel recommendations to the president, LBJ ordered the White House staff to destroy all notes from Fortas.[25] Then Fortas began defending the Warren Court, which didn't make him any friends among conservatives, Southern Democrat or otherwise. To that end, Senator Thurmond had gotten hold of several of the pornographic films that were the subject of the Court's ongoing obscenity cases and began showing them while the hearings were out of session. The "Fortas Film Festival," as it was called, had its intended effect.[26]

Shortly after Fortas finished four days of tense testimony, it came out that he had accepted a large honorarium to give a series of lectures at American University, funded by private sources connected to Fortas's former clients and partners. While the payment was legal, its size—more than forty percent of a justice's salary at the time, and seven times what any other AU seminar instructor had ever gotten—raised ethics concerns. Fortas declined an invitation to explain himself further to the committee, which still approved him, 11–6. The *New York Times* had a neutral headline with an ominous subhead, "Fortas Approved by Senate Panel: Possible Obstacles Arise Over Fund for Seminar."[27]

Fortas ran into a buzz saw on the Senate floor, bipartisan opposition that he could not overcome. Both Senator Russell, the powerful chairman of the armed services committee, and Minority Leader Everett Dirksen (R-Ill.) opposed cloture and, after a strenuous White House effort, the motion to end debate achieved a 45–43 majority on October 1, 1968, a moral victory of sorts, but far short of the sixty-seven senators needed to move to a final vote on the nomination. Fortas thus became the first and only Supreme Court nominee blocked by filibuster—although it's unlikely that he had even a majority of the full body in his corner. LBJ withdrew the nomination, making Thornberry's moot, and Earl Warren remained on the Court.

In short, a combination of cronyism, timing, political climate, ethical issues, hostility to the Warren Court, and the sense of impropriety over Fortas's role as presidential consigliere, coalesced into an insurmountable obstacle to confirmation *even though the Democrats had a 64–36 Senate majority.* And if that weren't enough, Fortas would be off the Court altogether less than a year later after *Life* magazine revealed that the justice had accepted a $20,000 retainer from the family foundation of a former client who was under investigation—and would soon be indicted, and then imprisoned—for securities fraud.[28] This was the first payment of what was to be an annual stipend for unspecified legal advice, which may have included an attempt to secure a presidential pardon. On the advice of Chief

Justice Warren, and days after an impeachment resolution had been filed, Fortas resigned a week after the article was published.

A month later, Earl Warren's retirement took effect. The Warren Court was done, but not before raising the temperature on legal battles that added a cultural dimension to the desegregation struggles of the 1950s. As the Vietnam War escalated, battles over civil liberties and the sexual revolution thrust the judiciary into people's lives more than ever.

At the same time, the collapse of the Fortas elevation led to the establishment of two significant norms: (1) a justice shouldn't retire during a presidential election year; and (2) a justice shouldn't serve as a presidential advisor.[29] The former had happened seven times before 1968 (not counting deaths), but as late as 1956, nobody thought anything was wrong with Justice Minton's retiring and President Eisenhower's appointing his successor.[30] The latter was also not unusual; such prominent justices as Louis Brandeis, William Howard Taft, and Felix Frankfurter were White House regulars. Some of these actions may have been seen as inappropriate had they been more widely known at the time, but now they're unthinkable, beyond the pale. In so many ways, 1968, an inflection point in American political and cultural history, also represents a turn into the modern age of judicial confirmations.

Part II—Present

The Modern Era

CHAPTER 8

The Burger Court and the Conservative Revolt

R ichard Nixon's election was in part a reaction to the excesses of the Warren Court. Although the rejection of Justice Fortas's elevation wasn't wholly apolitical—Nixon himself cajoled the opposition of key Republican senators—cronyism and ethical concerns tied into the perception that Earl Warren was presiding over a Court untethered from the Constitution and the social mores that people felt were slipping away. A weakened LBJ was simply unable to convince the Democrats' sizeable Senate majority to confirm his pick, leaving the choice to his successor in what proved to be a realigning election.

Campaigning on the restoration of law and order amid riots and social upheaval, Nixon very much ran against Warren and a Supreme Court that had been implementing liberal policies on civil rights, criminal justice, the separation of church and state, and other hot-button issues. The former vice president promised on the campaign trail to appoint judges and justices who would be less active on social policy. Instead, he wanted "strict constructionists" who saw their job as "interpreting law and not making law," who would be "properly conservative" to protect against "criminal forces" and "see themselves as caretakers of the Constitution and servants of the people, not superlegislators with a free hand to impose their social and political viewpoints upon the American People."[1]

So perhaps it's politically appropriate that Nixon got to replace Warren, since that was part of his electoral mandate. Although the new president hinted that southern nominees might be best, the judicial correlate to his political Southern Strategy didn't play too well, with geography a factor only in Nixon's two failed nominees. Nor did religion play a role, with no discussion of Catholics versus Protestants or maintaining a "Jewish seat"—though Nixon once asked about William Rehnquist: "Is he Jewish? He looks it."[2] As for judicial experience, two of his appointees, Warren Burger and Harry Blackmun, were on lower federal courts, while two others, Lewis Powell and Rehnquist, had never been judges. Like most presidents, Nixon cared about party affiliation, though Powell was a Democrat whose "real" politics turned out to be mixed, and Blackmun, a lifelong Republican, became one of the most liberal justices and authored *Roe v. Wade*.

President Nixon had the unique opportunity to name four justices in his first term, and was able to swing the Court's balance of power away from an activist orientation toward judicial restraint. But that series of appointments, encompassing a three-year political battle with the Senate, didn't come close to auguring a reversal of the previous decade.

Warren Burger

That decade ended judicially in June 1969 when, keeping to a deal he made with President Nixon, Chief Justice Earl Warren would retire at the end of the Supreme Court term. After an unprecedented expansion of federal judicial power, Nixon was looking for a change in appointing the nation's 15th chief justice, and he didn't wait until the end of the term to decide. On May 21, 1969, he announced that Judge Warren Burger, whom President Eisenhower had appointed to the D.C. Circuit and who had caught Nixon's eye with his public criticisms of the Warren Court, was his choice. Nixon, himself a lawyer, was vested in the selection process because he knew the judiciary's significance; it was "the most personal choice of [my] Presidency to date."[3] The president told a news conference that he had ruled out personal friends, and made a point to say that he hadn't met with Burger and hadn't "cleared" the pick with any political leaders.[4] Instead, it was a political calculation, but not in the partisan or ideological sense. He was looking for a strong law-and-order jurist who also had a more modest view of the judicial role: Burger had established a solid if understated record of restrained rulings, of the sort that Nixon expected would reverse the previous fifteen years' jurisprudence.

The choice was uncontroversial and even welcome. Despite the lack of Senate consultation, Burger drew approval from a wide swath of senators in a process that was the antithesis of Fortas's a year earlier. He testified before the judiciary committee for less than two hours on June 1—with no other witnesses—and was approved unanimously that afternoon. Some liberal senators attempted a delay, but the full Democrat-controlled Senate still confirmed Burger 74–3 after three hours of debate.

Conservatives expected the Burger-led Court to be a different animal than the Warren Court. By the early 1970s, however, it became apparent that the new chief justice was either unwilling or unable to reverse his predecessor's precedents and might even extend some of them. The Burger Court's first major opinion was an unsigned unanimous order to desegregate public schools, updating the failed "all deliberate speed" formulation of *Brown v. Board of Education II* (1955).[5] Two years later, the Court issued another unanimous ruling, this time explicitly authored by Burger, approving forced busing to combat de facto school segregation.[6]

Chief Justice Burger personally continued the Warren Court's doctrine on the separation of church and state when he wrote the majority opinion in *Lemon v. Kurtzman* (1971), where the Court invalidated a state law that allowed school superintendents to reimburse Catholic schools for the salaries of teachers. Thus he originated the "*Lemon* test" for determining when a law violated the Establishment Clause, but whose prongs are so indeterminate that courts have struggled to apply them. Twenty years later, Justice Antonin Scalia likened the test to "some ghoul in a late-night horror movie that repeatedly sits up in its grave and shuffles abroad, after being repeatedly killed and buried…frightening the little children and school attorneys."[7]

President Nixon also wouldn't have been happy about *New York Times v. United States* (1971), otherwise known as the *Pentagon Papers Case*, where the 6–3 Court allowed newspapers to publish then-classified documents regarding the origins of the Vietnam War, which the administration wanted to keep secret for national security purposes. Burger dissented but was only able to get two colleagues to join him. Then came the Court's unanimous ruling in *United States v. U.S. District Court for the Eastern District of Michigan* (1972), which rejected the administration's desire for warrantless wiretapping of domestic criminal suspects.

Chief Justice Burger was also instrumental in the Court's unanimous decision in *United States v. Nixon* (1974), requiring the president to release secret Oval Office recordings, leading to his resignation two weeks later. Burger was originally going to vote in Nixon's favor, but tactically changed his vote to assign the opinion to himself and thus restrain its rhetoric.[8] Ironically, Nixon had asked Burger in the spring of 1970 to be prepared to run for president in 1972 if the political repercussions of the Cambodia incursion were too much to endure. A few years later, Burger was on Nixon's short list of replacements for Vice President Spiro Agnew, before Gerald Ford was appointed after Agnew's resignation in October 1973.

Burger failed to assemble durable majorities to steer a clear course among disparate legal approaches and was overshadowed by the legal pens of Justice William Brennan on the left and Justice William Rehnquist on the right. And his haughty leadership style rubbed colleagues the wrong way.[9] In part to placate the American Bar Association, many of whose members had become alienated by the Warren Court—how the ABA's politics have changed!—he instituted an annual State of the Judiciary Address, which quickly became a major event on the legal landscape. This address has since taken written form, with the chief justice issuing a relatively short memo on December 31, which I find to be a fun addition to my New Year's Eve festivities.

Clement Haynsworth and Harrold Carswell

President Nixon's next appointment would not go as smoothly. Justice Fortas resigned in May 1969, just as Nixon was gearing up to replace Chief Justice Warren. Fortas had broken no law but showed bad judgment that detracted from the Court's reputation and distracted from its work, and indeed that built on the revelations that came out during his own failed elevation a year earlier. In part to solidify his Southern Strategy, President Nixon took the advice of Attorney General John Mitchell and nominated Fourth Circuit Judge Clement Haynsworth of South Carolina. Haynsworth was a Harvard-educated conservative Democrat—"real politics" trumping party identification again—and met the approval of senior senators who had made things difficult for previous nominees.

The nominee was well-regarded and expected to be confirmed, but was opposed by northern Democrats, Rockefeller Republicans, unions, and the NAACP. He was alleged to have made rulings favoring segregation and being reflexively anti-labor. Haynsworth asserted that civil rights groups were "condemning opinions written when none of us was writing as we are now." When asked if he'd changed, he responded, "Haven't we all?"[10]

To the president's dismay and embarrassment, however, it wasn't Haynsworth's jurisprudence that ultimately sank him, but financial improprieties and conflicts of interest that came out during his judiciary committee hearing. It appeared that the nominee had ruled in cases benefiting companies in which he held stock, and had sold stock when his court decided a case but before the decision was public.[11] There was no claim of fraud or other legal infraction, but the Senate could hardly apply a different standard than it did with Fortas. The ABA, which had unanimously found Haynsworth well-qualified, reevaluated him and split 9–3. Although the judiciary committee approved him 10–7, the full Senate rejected him 45–55—with seventeen Republicans voting no, including Minority Leader Hugh Scott (Pa.) and Whip Robert Griffin (Mich.)—the first voting down of a nominee since John Parker's defeat nearly forty years earlier. Justice Lewis Powell, after his retirement, felt that the defeat "reflected badly on the Senate."[12] A frustrated Nixon blamed "anti-Southern, anti-conservative, and anti-strict constructionist" prejudice, pledging to pick another "worthy and distinguished protagonist" of Southern, conservative, and strict-constructionist persuasion.

And so he did, though this was someone less-regarded than the smart but ethically challenged Haynsworth: G. Harrold Carswell, a very new Nixon appointee to the Fifth Circuit, whom President Eisenhower had placed on the federal district court in Tallahassee.[13] This was essentially the president's revenge, vindicating the judgment of those senators who had counseled confirming Haynsworth, lest the next nominee be even worse. But a Senate resigned to confirming Carswell quickly soured on the new nominee.

First came the revelation that, as a twenty-eight-year-old campaigning for the Georgia legislature in the late 1940s, Carswell had said that "I yield to no man as a fellow candidate or as a fellow citizen in the firm, vigorous belief in the principles of White Supremacy, and I shall always be so governed."[14] Later in that speech, he intoned that "the so-called civil rights program [would] better be called the civil wrongs program."[15] The nominee, citing his youth and inexperience, disavowed those statements. But then it came out that, while serving as U.S. attorney in Florida, he had assisted in transferring a municipal golf course to a private club, to evade Supreme Court desegregation rulings. And as a judge, already in the 1960s, he had handed down decisions that slowed integration efforts.[16] The Leadership Conference on Civil Rights concluded that Carswell "has been more hostile to civil rights than any other federal judge in Florida."[17]

Still, the administration's full-court press may have mollified a Senate otherwise disposed to avoid the appearance of repeatedly obstructing a popular president—except that Carswell's record didn't hold up to scrutiny even aside from the civil-rights controversy. If Haynsworth was considered an above-average jurist, Carswell was far below. As an objective matter, he was reversed nearly 60 percent of the time, more than all but seven of the 400-plus district judges.[18] Chief Justice Burger, after initially supporting the nomination, referred to Carswell as "a zero," while Yale Law School Dean Louis Pollak attributed to the nominee "more slender credentials than [those of] any Supreme Court nominee put forth in this century."[19]

One of the first to take the Senate floor in opposition was Republican Edward Brooke of Massachusetts, the first black senator since Reconstruction. It went downhill from there, as several senators who had supported Haynsworth came out against Carswell. Future Senate

Majority Leader Mitch McConnell, then a Senate aide, wrote in the *Kentucky Law Journal* that Carswell "had been reversed more than twice as often as the average federal judge.... had no publications, his opinions were rarely cited... [had] no expertise in any area of law.... [and was] unable to secure the support of his fellow judges on the Fifth Circuit."[20] Minority Leader Hugh Scott, who had come out for Carswell to make up for any offense he caused by voting against Haynsworth, moved to opposing him. Still, the judiciary committee, after voting not to reopen its hearing to have Carswell address the new allegations, approved the nomination 13–4.

Senator Roman Hruska (R-Neb.), the nomination floor manager, tried to make Carswell's insufficiencies into a strength in his memorable explanation that "there are a lot of mediocre judges and people and lawyers [who] are entitled to a little representation, aren't they?"[21] Making a similar observation, Senator Russell Long (D-La.) asked, "Would it not appear that it might be well to take a B student or a C student who was able to think straight, compared to one of those A students who are capable of the kind of thinking that winds up getting us a 100-percent increase in crime in this country?"[22] Even the ABA unanimously approved Carswell.

It wasn't enough; the Senate rejected the nomination 45–51 on April 8, 1970. Thirteen Republicans voted no, fewer than against Haynsworth. Nixon thus became the first and only White House occupant to suffer consecutive Senate rejections of Court nominees— not forced withdrawals, fatal non-actions, filibusters, or any other technical knockout, but full-blown no votes. The president fulminated that "I cannot successfully nominate to the Supreme Court any federal appellate judge from the South who believes as I do in the strict construction of the Constitution."[23] This wasn't entirely accurate, as there were distinguished jurists in the South who broadly shared Nixon's philosophy of law and whom the Senate would've easily confirmed. It was the White House selection process that was shown to be lacking.

Harry Blackmun

President Nixon, having announced that the Senate would never confirm a southern strict-constructionist, now went with a northerner. Harry Blackmun of Minnesota had served on the Eighth Circuit for eleven years, having been appointed by Eisenhower while serving as in-house counsel to the Mayo Clinic. A lifelong Republican and old friend of Chief Justice Burger, Blackmun was highly regarded by fellow judges.

When the nomination came in April 1970, the *New York Times* declared that "Judge Blackmun appears strikingly like Mr. Burger in judicial philosophy," adding that the two "seem most alike in their reluctance to follow the Warren Court's lead in expanding the rights of criminal defendants."[24] Five days later, however, a follow-up piece was presciently titled "Blackmun May Prove a Surprise for Nixon."[25] Nixon was not as directly involved in the selection as he had been previously, but Blackmun was recommended by Attorney General Mitchell and supported by Minnesota's two Democratic senators, Eugene McCarthy and future Vice President Walter Mondale, as well as former Vice President Hubert Humphrey. The judiciary committee approved him unanimously, as did the full Senate, the first unanimous roll call on a high court appointment. Finally Fortas's seat was filled.

Justice Blackmun was initially all that Nixon expected, voting with Chief Justice Burger in 87.5 percent of the closely divided cases during his first five terms (1970–75), and with Justice Brennan, the Court's leading liberal, in only 13 percent.[26] For example, Blackmun joined Burger and the other two Nixon appointees in dissent in *Furman v. Georgia* (1972), which imposed a moratorium on capital punishment until states reformed their laws, before voting to end that moratorium in *Gregg v. Georgia* (1976). From the First Amendment to criminal justice and other areas of public law, Blackmun went along with Burger's law-and-order project, pushing back on the Warren Court's approach to cultural issues.

All that began to change in the next five years, at which point Blackmun joined Brennan more than half the time in divided cases. Shortly after Blackmun dissented in *Rizzo v. Goode* (1976, limiting federal power over state agency actions), activist lawyer William Kunstler "welcom[ed] him to the company of the 'liberals and the enlightened.'"[27] During the last five years that Blackmun and Burger served together, Blackmun joined Brennan in more than 70 percent of close cases, and Burger in less than a third.[28]

The blockbuster opinion for which Blackmun is best known, and which signaled his shift away from his erstwhile commitment to judicial restraint, was *Roe v. Wade*.[29] The product of more than a year of painstaking labor spanning two arguments and a change in Court personnel, *Roe* came down on January 22, 1973, a day now marked by the March for Life in Washington. The Court ruled that the right to privacy, found in the Ninth and Fourteenth Amendments, protected the right to terminate a pregnancy, and that a fetus wasn't a "person" for purposes of constitutional protections, but that the right wasn't absolute. Not wanting to take a position on when life begins, Blackmun devised a trimester framework: (1) a state couldn't restrict abortion in the first trimester (other than minimal medical safeguards like requiring a licensed physician to perform it); (2) higher risks to the mother's health gave the state a compelling interest in the second trimester, such that it could regulate the procedure "to the extent that the regulation reasonably relates to the preservation and protection of maternal health";[30] but (3) once the fetus becomes viable, which then was the beginning of the third trimester, the state gained a compelling interest in protecting prenatal life, so could prohibit abortions except to save the mother's life or health.

It was a 7–2 ruling, with only Justices Byron White and William Rehnquist dissenting. Chief Justice Burger wrote separately to suggest that "the Court today rejects any claim that the Constitution requires abortions on demand."[31]

Suffice it to say, *Roe v. Wade* was controversial when it was announced and remains so to this day, inciting passions that are personal, not just ideological. In a famous *Yale Law Journal* article published in the months after the decision, John Hart Ely, one of the leading legal scholars of the 20th century, who personally supported abortion rights, strongly criticized *Roe* as a decision that was disconnected from American constitutional law, writing that *Roe* is "a very bad decision. Not because it will perceptibly weaken the Court—it won't; and not because it conflicts with either my idea of progress or what the evidence suggests is society's—it doesn't. It is bad because it is bad constitutional law, or rather because it is *not* constitutional law and gives almost no sense of an obligation to try to be."[32]

Harvard law professor Laurence Tribe, then in the early years of his academic career, said the same: "One of the most curious things about *Roe* is that, behind its own verbal smokescreen, the substantive judgment on which it rests is nowhere to be found."[33] Justice John Paul Stevens, while agreeing with the decision, has suggested that it should have focused more on the issue of privacy, without constructing trimester systems or musing on when life begins.[34] Justice Ruth Bader Ginsburg, before joining the Court, criticized the decision for short-circuiting the growing political movement for more liberal abortion legislation[35]—and later faulted the Court for being "physician-centered" rather than "woman-centered."[36] Similar sentiments have been expressed by a host of lefty scholars and pundits, let alone conservative critics. *Roe*, more than any other case or issue, is central to the modern war over the Court and the judiciary writ large.

It also marked Justice Blackmun's "evolution" from Nixon conservative to joining Justices Brennan and Marshall on the Court's left wing. On race, gender, and religion, his agreement with the two liberal lions for the last two decades on the bench was pretty much complete. On affirmative action, he justified remedial and compensatory racial preferences. On capital punishment, a year before his retirement, he wrote: "From this day forward, I no longer shall tinker with the machinery of death."—after which point he would dissent each time the Court declined to review or overturn a death sentence. [37] And on abortion, he lamented with acute self-awareness in *Planned Parenthood v. Casey* (1992) that "I am 83 years old. I cannot remain on this Court forever, and when I do step down, the confirmation process for my successor well may focus on the issue before us today."[38]

By Blackmun's retirement in 1994, the estrangement from his boyhood chum Warren Burger was complete. Having been Burger's best man, Blackmun didn't even attend his wife's funeral that year. "By the end of their long lives," Blackmun biographer Linda Greenhouse wrote, "the two men had become strangers."[39]

Lewis Powell

In September 1971, Hugo Black and John Marshall Harlan II, both gravely ill, retired within a week of each other. Black would be dead a week later; Harlan in two months. Both were highly influential and long-serving justices, so it was a tremendous opportunity for Nixon. The president was at least ready with a list of some one hundred names assembled by Deputy Attorney General Richard Kleindienst and Assistant Attorney General Rehnquist, and indeed 36 names were leaked to the press.[40] Although some accounts accuse Nixon of anti-Semitism for not prioritizing the mythical "Jewish seat" that had been vacant since Fortas's retirement, several people on the list caught Nixon's eye precisely because they were Jewish—or so the president thought.

Nixon decided to send six names for ABA appraisal, which list became public and included generally undistinguished lawyers and jurists. The leading contenders were California state court of appeals judge Mildred Lillie (the first woman to be considered) and an Arkansas municipal-bond lawyer named Herschel Friday, who was recommended by Justice Blackmun. The Nixon tapes reveal certain misogynistic attitudes—"I don't think a woman should be in any government job, whatever, mainly because they are erratic."—but the president was quite serious about Lillie.[41] The president's list—"The Six," as they were known—was widely panned, with thirty-four members of the Harvard Law School faculty signing a protest petition.[42] The ABA committee, led by Lawrence Walsh (later Iran-Contra independent counsel), urged the president to "add some people with stature," rating Lillie "unqualified" and Friday "not opposed." When these ratings became public, Nixon withdrew The Six and made it known that he would no longer submit nominees to the ABA for pre-screening.[43] The ABA in turn announced that it would still make evaluations post-nomination, a dance that has continued under every Republican president since.

On October 21, 1971, President Nixon, having failed to teach the Senate and ABA a lesson—"a bunch of sanctimonious assholes"—went on national TV to announce his "formal" nominees.[44] It's possible that he wasn't really serious about The Six, but the new selectees were much more weighty personages: Lewis F. Powell Jr. of Virginia, a past ABA president and respected corporate lawyer with views on criminal justice that jibed with the president's; and Rehnquist, the youthful (forty-seven) and brilliant head of the Justice Department's Office of Legal Counsel. The two were submitted to the Senate together the next day, Powell for Black's seat and Rehnquist for Harlan's. Their hearings were also held together, two weeks later.

Three days before the nominations, after Powell had twice declined Attorney General Mitchell's entreaties—he was concerned about abandoning his comforts for a "hermitlike" existence, but also questioned his own qualifications given his corporate law background—President Nixon had called Powell at his Richmond home and repeated the offer, which Powell accepted after consulting his law partners. In addition to the ABA, Powell had held leadership positions in the American College of Trial Lawyers, Virginia Board of Education, Virginia State Library Board, and other civic and charitable organizations. He had led the opposition to, and ultimately defeated, the state's "massive resistance" to integration and, as chairman of the Richmond Public School Board, presided over the desegregation of that city's schools.

The ABA called Powell "the best person available" and the Virginia NAACP endorsed him. The Senate Judiciary Committee unanimously recommended confirmation, which advice the full body took 89–1. The sole no vote came from populist Senator Fred Harris (D-Okla.), who considered Powell to be "an elitist [who] has never shown any deep feelings for little people."[45] On the other hand, Senator Henry "Scoop" Jackson (D-Wa.) wondered "why it has taken so long to propose a man of Mr. Powell's stature."[46]

Cautious and conservative in a genteel, mild-mannered way, Justice Powell was part of the Court's growing group of centrists, alongside Justices White and Stewart, and to be joined by Justice Sandra Day O'Connor. Although Powell had, as a private citizen, supported the Nixon administration's wiretapping of groups it deemed subversive, as a justice, he wrote for a unanimous Court that the practice violated the Fourth Amendment.[47] On the Establishment Clause cases that were the Court's bread and butter in the late 1970s and early 1980s, Powell was a swing vote, approving some practices and displays, disapproving others. He sided with Chief Justice Burger and Justice Rehnquist in limiting the scope of federal power under the Commerce Clause, but joined the majority in *Roe v. Wade* and a decade later wrote for the Court in a group of cases that reaffirmed *Roe*.

But the case for which Justice Powell is most famous is *Regents of the University of California v. Bakke* (1978). There was no overall majority opinion in this challenge to the University of California at Davis medical school's use of racial quotas in admissions, but Powell was the hinge between pluralities that struck down the quota but allowed the use of race as a factor for purposes of achieving educational diversity. Powell urged "strict scrutiny" to be applied to affirmative action programs, but allowed that some programs might pass muster. The ruling was both Solomonic and sophomoric, forcing our debate in this fraught area to focus on an amorphous "diversity"—not the merits of righting wrongs or making up for structural disadvantages—that avoided quotas but achieved racial balancing through a nebulous "holistic" review of the kind that Harvard had originally developed to restrict Jews.

Setting Justice Powell's principled but unpredictable jurisprudence aside, he was a jurist widely admired for his civility and thoughtfulness, whose retirement in 1987 after fifteen years of faithful service was hailed as the end of an era. More accurately, he represented a sort of throwback nonideological nominee, free of controversy of any kind, and was thus unique among the LBJ-Nixon series of confirmation battles. After Powell came the deluge, as Robert Bork was President Reagan's choice to replace him.

William H. Rehnquist

Rehnquist, meanwhile, had no idea that he was under consideration even as he put together Nixon's list of contenders, but had strong ties to the president's inner circle. But Rehnquist hadn't made a good first impression—"who is this guy dressed like a clown?" the president remarked about the future chief justice's early-'70s fashion—or perhaps little impression at all, judging by a hilarious Oval Office exchange between the president and top aide John Ehrlichman where they can't remember his name, positing "Renchburg" before settling on "Renchquist."[48] When asked whether he was in the running for one of the Court vacancies, Rehnquist replied in the negative, "because I'm not from the South, I'm not a woman, and I'm not mediocre."[49] But he overcame those disadvantages by being, more than the other Nixon nominees, a conservative constitutionalist.

Rehnquist had significant political involvements in his home state of Arizona, but his legal credentials were nonpareil, having graduated at the top of his class at Stanford Law and clerked for Justice Jackson before landing a top Justice Department job. The debate over his nomination, which didn't go as smoothly as Powell's, thus focused on his would-be judicial philosophy rather than legal acumen. Rehnquist was demonstrably more conservative than Powell and had deeper intellectual architecture for those commitments than probably anyone in the Nixon administration. But those sorts of views, including on such law-and-order issues as "no-knock" police raids, compelled self-incrimination, wiretapping, and demonstrators' rights, made him more controversial than a qualified nominee without ethical lapses had been in some time. "Those sons of bitches," Nixon intoned about Senate opponents. "They made a point of excellence. Now they are going to oppose him on the grounds they disagree with his views."[50]

The ACLU for the first time in its then fifty-two-year history formally opposed a nominee for public office, calling Rehnquist "a dedicated opponent of individual civil liberties."[51] There was another speed bump when it came out that Rehnquist had authored a memo while clerking for Justice Jackson arguing that *Plessy v. Ferguson* shouldn't be overturned. The nominee explained that the memo fleshed out Jackson's own thoughts. The judiciary committee approved him 12–4. Evan Bayh (D-Ind.), who had been active in the fights against Haynsworth and Carswell, led a filibuster that failed to achieve the necessary two-thirds by eleven votes. With Christmas looming and then a presidential election year, the opponents agreed to hold a vote four days after Powell. Rehnquist was confirmed 68–26, which at that point was one of the highest number of nays for a successful nominee; still, the yeas included a majority of Democrats and all but three Republicans. Rehnquist and Powell were then sworn in together, but Powell received and accepted his commission first, so he was technically of higher seniority.

Rehnquist would serve for fourteen and a half years as an associate justice, becoming a leader of the Court's conservative wing, most frequently joined by Chief Justice Burger and then Justice O'Connor, but also by Justice Powell on redistricting and busing, Justice White on criminal justice, and Justice Stevens on affirmative action. The best example of Rehnquist's work as an associate justice was his fiery, airtight dissent in *United Steelworkers v. Weber* (1979), where, joined by Burger, he showed how the majority's holding that minority set-asides in a training program complied with Title VII of the Civil Rights Act—which said its provisions can't be interpreted "to require any employer...to grant preferential treatment to any individual or group because of the race...of such individual or group"[52]—was legally unjustifiable. "Thus, by a *tour de force* reminiscent not of jurists such as Hale, Holmes, and Hughes, but of escape artists such as Houdini, the Court eludes clear statutory language, 'uncontra-dicted' legislative history, and uniform precedent in concluding that employees are, after all, permitted to consider race in making employ-ment decisions."[53]

Justice Rehnquist held the fort until Justice Scalia (and later Thomas) arrived, not just with votes but with new constitutional theories to replace the imprecise "strict construction." It's no wonder that Rehnquist was the most frequent sole dissenter on the Burger Court, earning him the nickname "the Lone Ranger."[54] More impor-tantly, he had sown the seeds for the federalism revolution to come.

With the confirmation of Powell and Rehnquist, the country seemed relieved at having dodged another Haynsworth/Carswell bul-let, which almost certainly would have resulted had President Nixon insisted on picking someone from his original shortlist. Set against the backdrop of an escalating Vietnam War and growing countercul-ture, the nomination battles that President Nixon faced built on those that LBJ endured. Even as no controversies attended the next few nominations, the Senate had given notice that it would not simply roll over for presidential prerogative—particularly when it was con-trolled by the opposing party. Not that it necessarily had in the past, but something had changed in 1968 that made "real" politics the whole ballgame.

The Swinging Seventies

Richard Nixon's resignation on August 9, 1974, was precipitated by a Supreme Court order two weeks earlier to turn over tape recordings and other subpoenaed materials. *Nixon v. United States* was a unanimous ruling joined by all of Nixon's appointees except Justice Rehnquist, who was recused for having been assistant attorney general during the relevant time.

Gerald R. Ford brought a sense of decency and quiet confidence to the White House that had been sorely lacking. He also provided a picture-perfect nomination model when Justice William O. Douglas resigned in November 1975, albeit one that may no longer be replicable.

Douglas had served for thirty-six and a half years, longer than anyone else then or since. He had suffered a debilitating stroke the previous winter and was essentially incapacitated, such that his colleagues agreed to hold over until the following term any cases where Douglas might be the deciding vote. Retired justice Abe Fortas, a close friend, finally convinced him to move on, which is somewhat ironic given that Douglas had written to Fortas five years earlier to say that he felt out of step with the Court's jurisprudential direction and was pondering retirement.

What had no doubt prompted Douglas's melancholic mood in mid-1970 was an attempt to impeach him. Douglas maintained a busy speaking and publishing schedule to supplement his income—the demands on which only grew from three divorce settlements; he married a fourth wife, forty-five years his junior, in 1966. Grumblings about "Wild Bill's" lifestyle and choice of where to publish—including in the risqué magazine of a convicted pornographer (conviction affirmed by the Supreme Court, over Douglas's dissent) who also lost a libel suit brought by Barry Goldwater (review denied by the Court, over Douglas's dissent)—came to a head when compounded by ethical concerns over certain dealings of the Parvin Foundation. Douglas had been the foundation president since 1961, accepting a salary from casino financier Albert Parvin until May 1969, when Fortas resigned "to save Douglas," thinking that the inquiries would stop.

Urged on by President Nixon, then-House Minority Leader Gerald Ford, disgusted by Douglas's behavior and aware that Fortas had resigned over a similar scandal, started an impeachment investigation.[1] Although supported by forty-nine Republicans and fifty-two Democrats, that process went nowhere and was quickly closed, without a formal vote.[2]

John Paul Stevens

It was thus ironic that Ford himself would have the opportunity to fill the seat of his erstwhile nemesis Douglas. The new president wanted to avoid his predecessors' controversies, so when he asked Attorney General Edward Levi to put together a list of potentials, he emphasized objective professional merit and (literally) unimpeachable ethical standards. Ford insisted that his pick "be of such known and obvious professional quality, experience, and integrity that valid opposition will not be possible."[3] Although the president assuredly wanted someone he could agree with, ideology, and especially partisanship, was as secondary a consideration as it could've been. Indeed, while presidents generally appoint members or affiliates of their own party to well over 90 percent of their judicial vacancies—Presidents Reagan and Clinton were over 98 percent, though Bush I, Hoover, and Taft were under 90—only 81 percent of Ford's nominees were Republicans.[4] And there was one more consideration: "Don't exclude women from the list," Ford instructed.[5]

While Levi gathered and vetted names, Ford took advice from senators, congressmen, and other stakeholders, particularly the Republicans and conservative Democrats who would need to be on board for a successful confirmation. Several senators convened a hearing on the Constitution's Advice and Consent Clause, at which Senator Edward Kennedy (D-Mass.) said, "Our hope is that the President will seek out the best and ablest person to fill the Douglas vacancy."[6]

The administration ended up submitting more than twenty names to the ABA for pre-nomination review. An initial list of eleven included two members of Congress; Solicitor General Robert Bork (whom Ford thought too controversial ahead of the 1976 election year); and five federal circuit judges, including Arlin Adams (a prominent Jewish Republican and runner-up for the Rehnquist seat) and John Paul Stevens. The ABA labeled the list "a good one, which was responsibly drawn," implying a contrast to Nixon's lists.[7] A supplemental list included at least three women. Betty Ford pressured her husband to pick a woman, while Senate Republican leader Hugh Scott pushed his colleague Robert Griffin (R-Mich.)—whom Ford ultimately passed over out of fear of hearkening to LBJ's cronyism.

The decision came down to Adams and Stevens, with the nod going to the latter, in part based on the familiarity and high recommendation of Attorney General Levi, who served with him on staff at the House Judiciary Committee and on the faculty of the University of Chicago Law School, where Stevens taught antitrust. When Ford announced his nomination, he called him simply "the best qualified."[8]

While there was mild disappointment from women's groups and some conservatives, the nomination was well-received in the Senate. The judiciary committee unanimously approved Stevens, as did the Senate two days later, on December 17, 1975. The confirmation process lasted less than three weeks and, remarkably for the first nomination since *Roe v. Wade*, only touched on abortion in testimony by Margaret Drachsler of the National Organization for Women, with no follow-up from senators and no questioning of the nominee on the subject.[9]

Ford had been looking for a moderate like himself, someone to aid Chief Justice Burger's effort "to limit federal jurisdiction and let state courts make more judgments themselves."[10] It looked like he'd succeeded. After all, Stevens was a centrist conservative on the Seventh Circuit, perhaps the last of the Rockefeller Republicans. But he gradually moved left and became the co-leader, with Justice Ruth Bader Ginsburg, of the Supreme Court's liberal bloc.

Although Ford would later say that the Stevens appointment was the proudest point of his presidency,[11] the justice's shift must've at least surprised the former president, and certainly would've disappointed him in certain areas. Most notably on federalism, where Ford, a Yale Law School graduate, had expressed disapproval of expansive federal power, Stevens consistently sided with assertions of congressional authority to regulate "interstate commerce." He dissented in *United States v. Lopez* (1995, Gun-Free School Zones Act) and *United States v. Morrison* (2000, Violence Against Women Act), cases that for the first time in decades found that Congress had exceeded its constitutional power under the Commerce Clause. Five years later, he authored *Gonzales v. Raich* (2005), which allows the federal government to ban marijuana, even from people who grow the plant for their own medical use consistent with state law.

These sorts of rulings, when combined with his opinions on property takings, flag-burning, the Second Amendment, and campaign finance, show that Justice Stevens didn't really believe in either structural or rights-based protections for individual freedom, at least with the exception of presidential power and criminal procedure. His jurisprudence was difficult to characterize as a matter of conventional methods and modes, but the results were what we'd now call progressive. In other words, he was a lawyer's lawyer—as well as a classy gent who had lived an amazing American life that included witnessing Babe Ruth's "called shot" and a valorous WWII stint in the Navy—but no great friend of liberty. Stevens, who died in July 2019 at age 99, was the longest-lived justice—a bow-tied throwback to a legal culture to which we should all aspire but are unlikely to see again unless the Supreme Court does, as President Ford hoped, stop federal overreach by courts, Congress, and presidents alike.

Carter's Lower-Court Legacy

Ford's successor Jimmy Carter didn't get to appoint any Supreme Court justices—the first such presidency since Andrew Johnson and the fourth overall—but was the only one elected to a full four-year term. Carter's consolation prize was that he got to appoint more lower-court judges than any other president over a four-year period. That's because the Omnibus Judgeship Act of 1978, which created

152 new judgeships—more than a fifth of the then-total—enabled President Carter to appoint a total of 262 Article III judges. Carter appointed about 40 percent of the federal judiciary in his single term. Every two-term president since has surpassed Carter in total number of judges, because of further judicial expansion, but only Clinton appointed a (slightly) higher percentage.

One of Carter's lasting judicial legacies is the Ninth Circuit, which received ten of the new 1978 judgeships. Carter was able to fill those seats, largely with very liberal nominees. While some of those judges, upon death or retirement, have been replaced by moderates, most judges still aim to retire when a president of the same party as the one who appointed them is in power. Accordingly, most of those "Carter judges" are now "Clinton judges" and "Obama judges." That's why the Ninth Circuit, to this day, skews left: not because of geography—presidents of both parties appoint federal judges in all states—but history.[12]

Two of Jimmy Carter's court of appeals appointees, Ruth Bader Ginsburg and Stephen Breyer, ended up on the Supreme Court, elevated by President Clinton. Notably, Breyer was nominated on November 13, 1980—*after* Carter lost the White House to Ronald Reagan—and confirmed by the lame-duck Senate. Breyer had been a key staffer for Judiciary Committee Chairman Ted Kennedy, who muscled him through the committee. The Breyer example puts paid to the so-called "Thurmond Rule" that confirmations stop at a certain point during presidential election years, named after Senator Strom Thurmond's efforts to block Abe Fortas's elevation in 1968. Indeed, Thurmond himself, as judiciary committee chairman, held hearings and confirmed nominees in 1984, while a 2008 Congressional Research Service report couldn't find any "consistently observed date or point in time after which the Senate ceased processing district and circuit nominations during the presidential election years from 1980 to 2004."[13] Similarly, a 2012 Brookings Institution study showed that confirmations slow but don't stop in the final year of a presidential term.[14] In short, the Thurmond Rule is neither a rule nor even a norm—but that's separate from the debate over filling Supreme Court vacancies arising in election years, particularly when the Senate is run by the opposing party.

Equally significant to the *number* of judges Carter appointed was his commitment to "representativeness," meaning an affirmative action program that trumped other considerations. Attorney General Griffin Bell testified that "Mr. Carter was prepared to appoint to the Federal Bench a black, Hispanic, or woman lawyer who was found to be *less qualified* than a white male as long as the appointee was found qualified."[15] To that end, he created a circuit judge commission and instructed each nominating panel to "make special efforts to seek out and identify well qualified women and members of minority groups as potential nominees."[16] As the president admitted: "If I didn't have to get Senate confirmation of appointees, I could tell you flatly that twelve percent of my judicial appointments would be black and three percent would be Spanish-speaking, and forty percent would be women, and so forth."[17] But regardless of Senate process, Carter succeeded in his project, particularly in light of the small pools of women and minority lawyers to choose from. On Inauguration Day 1977, eight women had been appointed to Article III courts since the founding of the Republic;[18] Carter appointed forty. Thirty-eight blacks, Hispanics, or Asians had been appointed previously; Carter chose fifty-five.[19] The next Democratic president, Bill Clinton, would broaden that commitment, while Barack Obama would go even further. Both Clinton and Obama would be criticized, however, for appointments that weren't as jurisprudentially strong or progressive enough, which is of course the trade-off for a focus on demographics.

Sandra Day O'Connor

Ronald Reagan made the Supreme Court a campaign issue more than any candidate before him, promising "to appoint only those opposed to abortion and the judicial activism of the Warren and Burger Courts."[20] He also pledged to put a woman on the Court: "One of the first Supreme Court vacancies in my administration"—not necessarily the first—"will be filled by the most qualified woman I can find, one who meets the high standards I will demand for all my appointments."[21] That pledge, borne at least in part of political calculation, would be in some tension with Reagan's opposition to quotas, and indeed with Attorney General William French Smith's April 1981 "Memorandum on Judicial Selection Procedures," which focused on "the principle that federal judges should be chosen on the basis of merit and quality" alone.[22]

This was to be a return to traditional criteria and away from either demographic correctness or social engineering. Beyond general Republican identification, the search process looked for relatively young candidates (under 50 for the lower courts), with judicial or teaching experience (for the circuits), who were in general philosophical agreement with the new president's governmental philosophy.[23] And President Reagan would use it effectively to seat about half the federal judiciary, 383 appointments. This is a percentage that no president is likely ever to reach again and a number that won't be reached unless there's a significant expansion in the number of judgeships (there were 749 when Reagan left office, and 860 now). That includes four Supreme Court appointments, two of which would be completely uncontroversial, one of which ran into some opposition, and one that's the main reason you're reading this book.

The first high court opportunity came five months after Reagan's inauguration, when Justice Potter Stewart retired at the end of the

Court's term in June 1981. The administration had known of Stewart's intent to leave since March, so had three months to search for a nominee without media speculation or political pressure.[24] Attorney General Smith and Counselor to the President Ed Meese (later attorney general himself) led the search. In late June, Smith gave Reagan a list of about twenty-five names, about half of whom were women—largely state and federal judges, including a young black liberal Carter appointee, Second Circuit Judge Amalya Kearse.[25] Those were quickly winnowed to five candidates, Arizona Court of Appeals Judge Sandra Day O'Connor and four men: Dallin Oaks of the Utah Supreme Court, Ninth Circuit Judge J. Clifford Wallace, former solicitor general Robert Bork—all of whom had been considered by President Ford—and Ninth Circuit Judge Anthony Kennedy. According to Deputy Chief of Staff Michael Deaver, when Reagan was initially given the background of the short-listers, he pointed to O'Connor and said, "That's the one I want."[26]

O'Connor had grown up on a ranch in southeastern Arizona, near the New Mexico border, and went to Stanford for both college and law school, where she met and briefly dated classmate William Rehnquist. A 2018 biography of O'Connor revealed that, after Rehnquist graduated Stanford Law School a semester early and went to Washington to clerk on the Supreme Court, he wrote a letter to his ex-girlfriend proposing marriage.[27] She turned him down, having started to date her eventual husband. O'Connor had a hard time finding a job because of her gender, but eventually settled back in Arizona to start a family and become active in politics. After stints in the Arizona attorney general's office and state senate—where she rose to majority leader, the first woman in any state to do so—she was elected to the Maricopa County (Phoenix) superior court and elevated to the state court of appeals. She got rave reviews in each job as a sharp legal thinker and meticulous judge.

Although President Reagan wanted to fulfill his campaign pledge, he insisted that he wouldn't appoint a woman "simply to do so." Still, a man with O'Connor's background was unlikely to have been considered. While the ABA gave her a "qualified" rating and praised her temperament, the committee was concerned that her experience "has not been as extensive or challenging as that of some other persons who might be available for appointment."[28] But the president also wasn't choosing the "highest-ranking" female lawyer, making clear that political and ideological criteria were as important as in his other judicial selections. He didn't want to repeat President Eisenhower's experience of looking for a Catholic and ending up with Justice Brennan—or, for that matter, Reagan's own selection of Donald R. Wright to be chief justice of the California Supreme Court, who had burned him on the death penalty. His administration's painstaking vetting revealed that O'Connor was definitely in the Republican mainstream, but that wasn't saying very much because she hadn't had the time to develop a jurisprudence on the hottest legal controversies. And this was before Ed Meese and Antonin Scalia began popularizing "originalism"—the idea initially that constitutional interpretation should be based on what the Founders intended and, later, that the text meant what it meant when written—with only general notions of "strict construction," "judicial restraint," and "deference" to guide conservative judge-makers.

When President Reagan interviewed O'Connor in the Oval Office, the only candidate he met with, she quickly charmed the president and, strongly supported by home state senators Barry Goldwater and Dennis DeConcini (a moderate Democrat), she got the nomination. It was a shrewd political move, but not an ideological one; O'Connor was a Republican, but one devoted to precedent and pragmatism rather than overarching theories of constitutional interpretation.

Women's rights groups and prominent liberal politicians, including Senator Ted Kennedy, quickly came out in favor. Representative Morris Udall (D-Ariz.) commented that O'Connor was "about as moderate a Republican you'll ever find being appointed by Reagan."[29] Echoing that sentiment, Michigan Law School's Yale Kamisar said of Reagan: "Give the devil his due; it was a pretty good appointment."[30]

Conversely, this meant that conservative organizations were wary. Abortion in particular became a flashpoint, as pro-life and religious groups suspected, correctly, that she would be reluctant to overturn *Roe*.[31] Jerry Falwell, head of the evangelical Moral Majority, said that "good Christians" ought to be concerned. Goldwater responded in his characteristically frank style: "Every good Christian ought to kick Falwell right in the ass."[32] President Reagan wrote in his diary, "Already the flak is starting and from my own supporters. Right to Life people say she is pro abortion. She declares abortion is personally repugnant to her. I think she'll make a good justice."[33] Certain Senate Republicans conveyed their dismay directly to the president, with Don Nickles (Okla.) saying that he and "other pro-family Republican senators would not support" the pick.[34] None of them ended up mounting an opposition campaign in the Senate, however, and all voted for confirmation, but they represented the emergent influence of the religious right and the centrality of any nominee's views, real or perceived, on cultural issues.

O'Connor had the first televised confirmation hearing, lasting three days and focusing largely on abortion. Presaging the now-standard line of committee questions and nominee responses, O'Connor refused to say how she would rule on that or any other issue. More broadly, O'Connor hewed to her reputation as a minimalist: "I do not believe it is the function of the judiciary to step in and change the laws because the times have changed. I do well understand the difference between legislating and judging."[35]

Senators Howard Metzenbaum (D-Ohio) and Pat Leahy (D-Vt.) lambasted O'Connor's critics for engaging in single-issue politics. "An agreement to vote a certain way can never be the price to be paid for confirmation by the United States Senate," Leahy said, adding that requiring such a commitment would "destroy the independence and integrity of the Federal court system."[36] The judiciary committee approved the nomination 17–0–1, with Senator Jeremiah Denton— the first Alabama Republican since Reconstruction and the first Catholic elected there state-wide—voting "present" because O'Connor refused to criticize *Roe*. Six days later, the full Senate confirmed her 99–0 (including Denton).

Justice O'Connor began as a conservative voice, similar to Rehnquist. Her voting record aligned with her law school classmate 87 percent of the time her first three years on the Court and, in nine of her first sixteen years, she voted with Rehnquist more than with any other justice.[37] Through a combination of drifting a bit left and more conservative newcomers—especially Clarence Thomas, whom she didn't join in a single dissent in the 1992–93 term—O'Connor occupied the center in the last decade or so of her tenure, if still shading a bit to the right. From 1994 to 2004, she joined the conservative bloc of Rehnquist, Scalia, Kennedy, and Thomas eighty-two times, while joining the liberal bloc of John Paul Stevens, David Souter, Ruth Bader Ginsburg, and Stephen Breyer only twenty-eight times.[38] Indeed, during the eleven and a half years from 1993 to 2005 when the Court's composition didn't change, she was in the majority in 77 percent of 5–4 decisions, ahead even of Kennedy.[39] O'Connor's role as the "swing vote" meant that her idiosyncrasies—case-by-case decision making and a politician's eye for compromises—had an outsized impact on Supreme Court jurisprudence. As with Justice Kennedy, this dynamic is most evident in cases concerning "cultural issues," where Reagan's nominees split: O'Connor and Kennedy joined the liberals, while Rehnquist and Scalia stuck with the conservatives.

Her most famous majority opinion is undoubtedly *Planned Parenthood v. Casey* (1992), co-authored with Justices Kennedy and David Souter (who would replace Justice Brennan). *Casey* reaffirmed *Roe v. Wade*'s constitutional right to abortion but replaced its trimester rubric with an "undue burden" standard for evaluating restrictions on the right to abort a nonviable fetus. *Casey* validated the fears of those who opposed her nomination.

Justice O'Connor's most lasting legacy, in addition to being the first female justice and preserving *Roe*, was as the linchpin in the 2003 University of Michigan affirmative action cases. Justice O'Connor was uneasy with racial preferences, but felt that they were justified, at least for now, to achieve the goal of educational diversity that Justice Powell had approved in the *Bakke* case twenty-five years earlier. "We expect that 25 years from now," she concluded, "the use of racial preferences will no longer be necessary to further the interest approved today."[40]

Sandra Day O'Connor was the last addition to the Burger Court, and the only one added from 1975 until Chief Justice Burger's retirement in 1986. Those who were expecting the Burger Court to reverse the Warren Court in significant part were sorely disappointed. Particularly on racial questions and free expression, the Court continued in a more liberal direction, while not touching the criminal-justice rulings that so angered the "silent majority" who swept Nixon into power. And that's not to mention the extension of the right to privacy/abortion and church/state relations. The failure to reverse the Warren Court wasn't so much a "growing" in office, other than perhaps by Blackmun, but in the ability of Douglas, Brennan, and Marshall to get fourth and fifth votes, not only to keep but to expand on Warren-era doctrine, especially regarding race and substantive due process/privacy. Of all of Nixon's appointees, only Rehnquist dissented in all of those.

The replacement of Douglas by Stevens and Stewart by O'Connor didn't change that dynamic in the least, as Burger represented an interregnum, a transition from the liberal excess of the Warren Court to the conservative retrenchment of the Rehnquist Court.

CHAPTER 10

The Calm before the Storm

T hree weeks shy of the end of the 1985–86 Supreme Court term and within months of his 79th birthday, Warren Burger, having served longer than any other 20th-century chief justice, submitted his resignation, saying he wanted to focus on leading the 1987 bicentennial of the U.S. Constitution. There had been no public hints of his retirement, which caught even his colleagues by surprise, but President Reagan was ready for it, immediately announcing his intent to elevate Justice William Rehnquist and to appoint D.C. Circuit Judge Antonin Scalia in his place. Reagan was keen on finding "strict constructionist" stalwarts. With these two intellectual, articulate, highly credentialed nominees, he accomplished his goal.

Rehnquist Elevation

The Rehnquist nomination was welcomed by his colleagues, including those who were on the other side ideologically, but the confirmation process ended up being more contentious than expected— what Senator Orrin Hatch (R-Utah) called a "Rehnquisition."[1] At his hearing, the man who had already spent more than fourteen years on the Court made clear that his approach to the law would not be changing. Senator Ted Kennedy (D-Mass.) had a problem with that, arguing that Rehnquist's record showed him to be "too extreme on race, too extreme on separation of church and state, too extreme to be Chief Justice."[2] Senator Howard Metzenbaum (D-Ohio) agreed, claiming that Rehnquist's ideological views were "so extreme that they are outside the mainstream of American thought."[3] Foreshadowing his attack on Robert Bork a year later, Kennedy said Rehnquist had "a virtually unblemished record of opposition to individual rights in cases involving minorities, women, children and the poor," and explaining that senators aren't supposed to be a "rubber stamp" after checking for basic qualifications.[4]

Part of Kennedy's claim that Rehnquist was bad for civil rights was his ownership of properties that had (unenforceable) racially restrictive covenants and his alleged intimidation of black and Latino voters as a party official in Arizona in the early 1960s, which Rehnquist denied.[5] Many criticisms from his first confirmation process, at which Kennedy and Metzenbaum claimed he was "less than candid," returned, notably questions over a memo he wrote as a law clerk urging Justice Jackson to uphold *Plessy v. Ferguson*.[6] Rehnquist repeated that the memo had not expressed his own views, but Justice Jackson's. Ultimately, the more liberal senators were unable to win over their colleagues, and the judiciary committee approved the nomination 13–5. It took another month and a half of debate and a fairly close vote on the motion to end debate, just 10 nay votes short of sustaining a filibuster, before the Senate confirmed Rehnquist to be the sixteenth chief justice on September 26, 1986. The final vote was 65–33—49 Republicans and 16 Democrats for, 31 Democrats and 2 Republicans against—which was then the most votes against a successful Supreme Court nomination.

Rehnquist's predecessor had alienated colleagues with an over-bearing manner, inability to manage conference sessions, and abuse of his seniority. Rehnquist, in contrast, was easygoing, and humorous, but also a stickler for timely and orderly conferences, as well as scrupulously fair in assigning opinions. The new chief justice also successfully lobbied Congress in 1988 to give the Court control of its own docket, cutting back on mandatory appeals, and started a decline in certiorari grants that continued throughout his tenure.

Rehnquist stayed true to his word that his jurisprudence wouldn't change—although with some surprises, like his 7–2 majority opinion in *Dickerson v. United States* (2000) that reaffirmed *Miranda v. Arizona* (1966) despite his own personal misgivings, largely because "Miranda warnings" had become ingrained in our culture.

Chief Justice Rehnquist also became known for his Court's short-lived federalism revolution—an incomplete insurrection, really—writing the majority opinions in *United States v. Lopez* (1995) and *United States v. Morrison* (2000), both of which held that Congress exceeded its constitutional power to regulate interstate commerce. "We start with first principles," he wrote in *Lopez*. "The Constitution creates a Federal Government of enumerated powers."[7] In both of these 5–4 Commerce Clause cases, *all four* of President Reagan's appointees were in the majority, indicating a more successful selection process than George H.W. Bush would have, with his nominees splitting in both cases (Clarence Thomas in the majority, David Souter dissenting). But the fact that every one of the Reagan justices were essential to *Lopez* and *Morrison* also shows that even one errant nomination can have a significant impact on the Supreme Court's trajectory, as Presidents Eisenhower and Nixon learned in spades.

Although conservatives were disappointed that the Rehnquist Court couldn't reverse more of the left's earlier judicial successes, this is more a function of personnel than the chief justice's shortcomings.

And Rehnquist accomplished far more than his immediate predecessor. As one academic wrote months before Rehnquist's death in 2005, "It is telling to see how many of Rehnquist's views, considered outside the mainstream at the time by professors and commentators, the court has now adopted."[8]

Antonin Scalia

While the timing of Chief Justice Burger's retirement came as a surprise and the selection of Rehnquist to take his center seat a bit of a fight, the nomination of the gregarious yet scholarly fifty-year-old Antonin Scalia for the resulting associate justiceship was neither. A year earlier, the New Republic had written that a Scalia pick "makes political sense," further quoting an unnamed White House official who called him "a political symbol. Nino would be the first Italian-Catholic on the Court. He's got nine kids. He's warm and friendly. Everybody likes him. He's a brilliant conservative. What more could you want?"[9] The only question about Scalia was whether he would be picked for this vacancy or the next one, ultimately edging out perennial candidate Robert Bork by being a decade younger and more easily confirmable—despite also being what Time magazine characterized as "a more energetic true believer."[10]

Scalia easily met Attorney General Meese's three criteria for nomination: intellectual and lawyerly capability, integrity, and "a commitment to the interpretation of the law rather than making it from the bench."[11] White House Counsel Peter Wallison urged the president to go with Bork first, because that wouldn't change the balance of the Court, leaving the more personable Scalia for the next, more consequential vacancy. Reagan wouldn't go for that strategy. In announcing the nomination, he said that Scalia's "great personal energy, the force of his intellect and the depth of understanding of our constitutional jurisprudence uniquely qualify him for elevation to our highest court."[12]

The nominee's background and resume were irresistible: the only child of an immigrant father and second-generation mother, valedictorian at Georgetown and *magna cum laude* graduate of Harvard Law School, Scalia had a series of academic and government positions—including as assistant attorney general for the Office of Legal Counsel soon after Rehnquist—before President Reagan appointed him to the D.C. Circuit in 1982.

Given what we know now about the larger-than-life lightning rod Justice Scalia became—love or hate his jurisprudence, he's "the most influential justice of the last quarter-century," Judge Richard Posner wrote nearly a decade ago, understating the man's impact—it's hard to imagine the acclamation his nomination received.[13] And it's hard to believe in this woke, intersectional time that being the first Italian-American nominee was a big deal. Every press account noted it and politicians of Italian descent from both parties lauded what Senator Pete Domenici (R-N.M.) called a "magnificent tribute" and Congressman Marco Baggi (D-N.Y.) said was "special pride...for consideration based on merit."[14] The Senate confirmed him 98–0 after "about seven minutes of discussion."[15] Scalia undoubtedly benefited from the Senate's being distracted by the Rehnquist elevation, but his adept handling of controversial questions during his hearing— expansive responses while puffing on a pipe—also inured to his benefit, even if he later called it "an absurd spectacle."[16]

Scalia's legacy is so much more than just being a conservative stalwart. For one thing, before he joined the Court, legal arguments over constitutional and statutory interpretation often failed to consider the actual constitutional and statutory text. While Scalia wasn't wholly responsible for the advent of originalism and revival of textualism, he was their highest-profile and most powerful expositor.

Legal experts still disagree about constitutional meaning, often vehemently. But we're all originalists now, playing on Scalia's field— or at least paying lip service to it, as then-Solicitor General Elena Kagan did at her confirmation hearing. Look no further than the competing opinions in *D.C. v. Heller* (2008), where Justice Scalia for the majority and Justice Stevens for the dissent argued over the historical understanding of the individual right to keep and bear arms.

Plus Scalia went about his craft with unprecedented verve. As law school casebooks began acquiring a more serious intellectual rigor, they also began filling up with his writings—at first dissents, but then a healthy dose of majority opinions and concurrences. Indeed, those dissents often ended up carrying the day, as with *Morrison v. Olson* (1988), a case that came to be so discredited that both parties in Congress decided not to renew the independent counsel law a decade later. We shouldn't underestimate the impact of Scalia's personality, eloquence, and leadership on the strength of his influence. Another justice with an identical outlook but a different personality may not have been able to gain as much traction for the conservative legal movement as a whole, both in the courts and in the court of public opinion.

Scalia knew that he was writing for more than the lawyers before him and that the Court's reputation depended on the clarity and logic behind its rulings. Agree with him or not, there was a method to his acerbic pen. It was not mere "legalistic argle-bargle" or "interpretive jiggery-pokery," to quote two witticisms from his dissent in the same-sex marriage case, *Obergefell v. Hodges* (2015).

Moreover, to say that Scalia was "conservative" is to misunderstand what that means in the judicial context. His personal views were very much what we'd call "socially conservative," but it's hard to argue that he made his legal decisions that way. Take *Texas v. Johnson*, for example, the 1989 case where Scalia voted to uphold the right to burn the American flag. "If you're going to be a good and faithful judge," he explained in a 2005 speech, "you have to resign yourself to the fact that you're not always going to like the conclusions you reach. If you like them all the time, you're probably doing something wrong."[17]

Perhaps the best example of Scalia's going against his preferences would be in the area of criminal procedure. Scalia's conservative contemporaries, including Rehnquist, Bork, and others coming of professional age in the Nixon era, were "law and order" types concerned about criminals getting off on technicalities. But there was no greater supporter of those constitutional "technicalities" than Scalia—whether the Fourth Amendment right to be free from unreasonable searches, the Sixth Amendment right to confront witnesses testifying against you, or the right to be sentenced based only on facts found by a jury.

When Justice Scalia died unexpectedly in February 2016, after nearly thirty years of service, he set off a political showdown the effects of which are still with us. After all, it's one thing to replace a conservative with a conservative. Both Rehnquist's succession of Burger and Scalia's replacement of Rehnquist were, more or less, replacing like for like. But it's quite another thing to change the Court's balance, particularly when it's on a 5–4 razor's edge over so many issues.

That's what would've happened with the Scalia seat if Hillary Clinton had won the 2016 election, which is why the vacancy loomed so large during the campaign, and effectively provided the margin of Donald Trump's victory. It's also what did happen with both Clarence Thomas's replacing Thurgood Marshall and Brett Kavanaugh's replacing Anthony Kennedy, which is a large part of why those confirmation processes were so apocalyptic.

Of course, before Thomas and Kavanaugh came Bork, an all-consuming battle for the vacancy that arose the year after the

Rehnquist-Scalia twofer. It's interesting to think about what would've happened had Bork gone first, with Scalia coming along the following year. These two intellectuals with outsized personalities were by Reagan's second term the clear picks for the next two vacancies. Had their order been flipped, both would've likely gotten through.

There are three main factors that changed from 1986 to 1987. First, Scalia was paired with the more controversial Rehnquist, who drew fire away from the nominee for associate justice. Second, Republicans had a Senate majority in 1986, but lost it in that November's elections. Third, and perhaps most important, the first vacancy was to replace a conservative, Rehnquist, while the second was to replace the swing vote, Justice Lewis Powell.

To put a finer point on it, had President Reagan, who sought committed conservatives, revealed Bork as his nominee alongside his elevation of Rehnquist, Bork may well have gotten through. And had Scalia in this scenario been the nominee the following year, he likely would still have been confirmed, probably with a couple dozen no votes given that all the focus would be on him and the Democratic Senate majority would be out to wound the president.

Of course, that swap didn't occur. But it's important to note that the Bork conflagration didn't come out of nowhere. The Reagan administration, under the leadership of Ed Meese, had been making a concerted effort to appoint not simply loyal Republicans, but those who espoused what Meese would characterize in a 1985 speech as "a jurisprudence of original intention," seeking to "resurrect the original meaning of constitutional provisions."[18] Meese refused to accept the idea that the judiciary should conform to the bar and the academy, searching instead for the types of "counterculture" judges President Reagan had secured an enormous mandate to appoint. Understandably, the left-leaning legal establishment didn't take kindly to that shift, so when the Democrats took over the Senate in 1987, they began executing a playbook against *lower court* judges—a trial run of what was to come with the next Supreme Court vacancy. Their innovation was to attack nominees on ideological rather than merely partisan grounds.

Most notable was the effort to take down Bernard Siegan, a libertarian legal theorist nominated to the Ninth Circuit. Siegan ran into opposition from liberals and judicial-restraint conservatives because of his view that courts should return to their pre-New Deal enforcement of economic liberties.[19] He faced one of the longest judiciary committee delays in history to that point; after being nominated in February 1987, he had one hearing that November and another the following February, but his inquisitors weren't satisfied. "No 'iffy' nominees are going to get through now," Senator Leahy said.[20] Siegan withdrew in September 1988, by which point Bork's battle was raging.

As we've seen, there have been political battles over judicial nominations between parties and within party factions since George Washington's time. But in the past, the nation wasn't watching and following along—not quite in real time as in our age of twenty-four-hour cable stations, digital livestreams, and social media, but close enough. It's not often that the direction of the Supreme Court can turn on one seat, and at a time when the White House and Senate are controlled by different parties. But the war over that seat, and the "absurd spectacle" of those confirmation hearings, is what faced Robert Bork when he finally got his moment in the arena.

The Original Sin of Robert Bork

When Justice Lewis Powell unexpectedly announced his retirement in June 1987, it set the stage for what people already recognized was a pivotal moment in the fight for the Supreme Court. The Robert Bork nomination represents the moment when the scales fell from conservative eyes over what they perceived were unfair tactics in defeating a nominee who would finally, *finally*, start reversing the activism of the Warren and Burger Courts. And not because the nominee was perceived as unqualified, unethical, too much of a crony, or assorted parochial concerns that had sunk nominees in the past. This was purely about ideology.

This battle royale came about in part because whoever was nominated would be replacing a "determined moderate" whose resignation "gave President Reagan a historic opportunity to shape the future of the Court."[1] Justice Powell was the key vote on issues ranging from abortion and affirmative action to criminal justice and religion. Senate Democrats, who had a 55–45 majority, asked liberal leaders to form a "solid phalanx" to oppose any "ideological extremist" nominee.[2] More specifically, they warned Reagan there would be a fight if Bork were to be the nominee—even though in November 1986,

Judiciary Committee Chairman Joe Biden had said that he would support Bork if "after our investigations, he looks a lot like Scalia... and if the [special-interest] groups tear me apart, that's the medicine I'll have to take."[3]

Bork was the obvious choice, head and shoulders in intellectual reputation and resume above other contenders. Then serving on the D.C. Circuit, to which he was unanimously confirmed in 1982, Bork had been solicitor general in the Nixon and Ford administrations, the number three man at the Justice Department and the government's lawyer before the Supreme Court. Considered a potential justice for at least fifteen years, Bork had once been promised a seat by President Nixon, but then Nixon resigned before he could fulfill that pledge.[4]

Upon learning of Powell's resignation, Reagan asked for a list of potential nominees, which was prepared by his chief of staff, former senator Howard Baker, along with Attorney General Edwin Meese and White House Counsel A.B. Culvahouse. Baker took the list to key senators, revealing several possibilities but asking for discretion to avoid leaks. Biden, who was on the presidential campaign trail and had now heard from those activist groups, flew back to Washington to meet with Reagan and give advice. "If you nominate [Bork]," a chastened Biden said, "you'll have trouble on your hands."[5]

The Opening Salvo

President Reagan announced Bork's nomination on July 1, describing him as "well prepared, evenhanded and openminded" and highlighting his exceptional academic and professional qualifications.[6] The strategy was to portray Bork as neither a conservative nor a liberal, someone who would use his towering intellect to follow the law wherever it led. On pure legal merit, he was widely considered the most qualified nominee since Felix Frankfurter.

Within forty minutes of Reagan's announcement, Senator Ted Kennedy took to the Senate floor with a strong condemnation:

> Robert Bork's America is a land in which women would be forced into back-alley abortions, blacks would sit at segregated lunch counters, rogue police could break down citizens' doors in midnight raids, and schoolchildren could not be taught about evolution, writers and artists could be censored at the whim of the Government, and the doors of the Federal courts would be shut on the fingers of millions of citizens.[7]

It was a declaration of war, catching the administration on its back foot. Republicans had hoped to woo Southern Democrats who were uneasy about the Court's direction on abortion and religion, but the allegations of racial insensitivity put these senators in an awkward position because of their need for black votes. Coupled with the decline of President Reagan's political fortunes toward the end of his second term and the pent-up frustration that Republican presidents had appointed the last eight justices, liberal groups were spoiling for a fight.

Bork was the anti-O'Connor, someone with clearly defined views and a track record of writings on just about every legal controversy, in a style that pulled no punches about the progressive project. Building on the work of his professor Alexander Bickel, who later became his Yale faculty colleague—who urged judges to reconcile their often counter-majoritarian role with legitimate governance by exercising "passive virtues" and deciding as little as possible so as not to disrupt the political process—Bork developed a theory to resolve that "Madisonian dilemma" of the judiciary's making law without popular approval. "We are increasingly governed not by law or elected representatives," he wrote, "but by an unelected, unrepresentative, unaccountable committee of lawyers applying no will but their own."[8]

The problem is that Bork got the Madisonian vision wrong. "How can a judiciary dedicated to restraint be, in Madison's terms, 'the bulwark of our liberties'?" asked Roger Pilon, who served in the Reagan administration and was my predecessor as director of the Cato Institute's Center for Constitutional Studies. "When courts extend a presumption of constitutionality to statutes and executive actions, they simply buy into the majoritarianism that grew out of the Progressive Era. On the contrary, the Founders took every step to protect our liberties, even from the majority—indeed, especially from the majority."[9]

Indeed, Bork's commitment to judicial restraint—which became a conservative hallmark, even though it originated with Oliver Wendell Holmes and the progressives—left him open to caricature as being unfeeling in the face of injustice. His dedication to the Founders' "original intent" subjected him to attack for being overly rigid and outside the mainstream. And, it should be said, Bork's appearance and demeanor—an irascible manner to go along with an irascible beard, which in this day and age would likely have its own Twitter feed—made him easier to demonize. One writer later commented that Bork's problem wasn't his conservatism, but that he "looked like a warrior in that cause."[10]

The most famous attack ad was run by the heavily financed People for the American Way, which labeled Bork an extremist. The ad was narrated by Gregory Peck, who portrayed Atticus Finch in the 1962 film version of *To Kill a Mockingbird*. Bork's penchant for academic provocation didn't help. Take, for example, a talk at the University of Michigan questioning the excesses of the freedoms of speech and of the press, or one at Catholic University arguing that the Supreme Court had created rights nowhere found in the

Constitution. He criticized the "one man, one vote" *Reynolds v. Sims* (1964) decision, as well as other now-sacred Warren Court rulings where he felt the Court had gone beyond its constitutional authority in remedying wrongs. Father Robert Drinan, the Jesuit pro-choice former congressman turned Georgetown law professor, wrote in the *National Catholic Reporter* that "Bork's anti-civil rights positions are almost unbelievable. He wrote in 1971 that the Supreme Court was wrong in 1948 when it ruled that the 14th amendment forbade state-court enforcement of racially restrictive covenants."[11] Bork became only the second Supreme Court nominee, after Rehnquist, to be opposed by the ACLU, while NAACP executive director Benjamin Hooks said his organization would "fight [the nomination] all the way—until hell freezes over, and then we'll skate across on the ice."[12]

The Reagan administration's 11th-hour attempts to rehabilitate Bork couldn't overcome the poor planning in selling the nominee as both an intellectual giant and logical heir to Justice Powell's middle-of-the road legacy. Bork was unlike Powell both jurisprudentially and temperamentally, but the White House didn't pivot when the predictable attacks came. Bork's opponents controlled what we now call "the narrative." By the time the judiciary committee hearings began in early September, the perception that Bork was supremely intelligent but also had an agenda was baked in. The ABA's unusual rating of the nominee, released on the eve of those hearings, reflected that Dr. Jekyll/Mr. Hyde persona: ten committee members rated Bork "well qualified," while four found him "not qualified," and one was "not opposed," a rating reserved for minimally qualified nominees whom the evaluator considers not to be among the best candidates available.[13] In other words, two-thirds of what was then still a widely respected professional organization gave Bork their highest rating, while the rest gave him their lowest. The White House touted the ABA "endorsement," but it was really a sign of the trouble to come.

The Longest Hearing

Starting September 15, there would be an amazing twelve days of hearings, five of which involved questioning of Bork himself, including a rare Saturday session. This was more than for any other nominee before or since, except Louis Brandeis in 1916—which was perhaps a mirror image of the Bork nomination, with Brandeis perceived as a towering intellect but an extreme social crusader. Senator Paul Simon (D-Ill.), a member of the judiciary committee, later wrote that, despite all the controversy in the preceding two months, and even though he personally opposed the nomination, if a vote had been taken when the hearings began, Bork would have been approved 9–5 or 8–6.[14] In other words, Bork was his own worst enemy.

A panel of august introducers began the hearing. President Ford, who had picked John Paul Stevens over Bork, called the nominee "uniquely qualified" and commended his conduct during Watergate.[15] Senate Minority Leader Bob Dole then praised Bork's judicial restraint, likening his jurisprudence to that of Oliver Wendell Holmes—which shows that "restraint" is neither progressive nor conservative, but majoritarian. Finally, Senator John Danforth (R-Mo.), who studied under Bork at Yale Law School (and as state attorney general hired Clarence Thomas), formally presented the nominee to the committee. He saw how Bork, living in D.C., didn't have a home-state senator as would otherwise be traditional.

As the senators then turned to their opening statements, Ted Kennedy continued his calumny, saying that "Robert Bork has shown that he is hostile to the rule of law and the role of the courts in protecting individual liberty.... In Robert Bork's America, there is no room at the inn for blacks and no place in the Constitution for women, and in our America there should be no seat on the Supreme Court for Robert Bork."[16] Senator Pat Leahy (D-Vt.) called

the nominee "an intellectual of the first order...with a more comprehensive and clearly expressed judicial philosophy than any
nominee to the Supreme Court in recent history," but expressed
concern about Bork's criticism of decisions on free speech, privacy,
and equal protection.[17] Joe Biden presented a vague theory of a
living Constitution and how protected rights expand with the times,
to contrast Bork's view of constitutional meaning and bias against
those rights not listed in the Bill of Rights. Republicans generally
sided with Bork, with the exception of Arlen Specter (Penn.), who
held his cards close to the vest and became a pivotal player in the
Senate debate.

The Republican strategy was to allow Bork to explain himself, at
last to rebut the charges against him. On race, Charles Grassley
(R-Iowa) asked Bork to explain his views on the now decade-old
Bakke case that ushered in modern affirmative action. Bork acknowledged that he disagreed with affirmative action as a policy beyond a
transition period, but made no broader comment on the law. That
led Specter to question how his conception of "original intent"
squared with the equal protection clause and *Brown v. Board*. Bork
claimed that the Fourteenth Amendment's drafters had relied on an
assumption that racial separation would produce equality, but that
this assumption had now been disproven, constitutionally requiring
integration. He further stated his belief that all equal protection cases
should be judged based on whether the government has a "reasonable
basis" for its challenged action. This represented somewhat of an
evolution from earlier views, in which Bork suggested that the Constitution's equal protection guarantee applied narrowly to blatant
racial abuses. Bork also demurred from his published views that
rights couldn't evolve, conceding to Grassley that the definition of
"cruel and unusual punishment" under the Eighth Amendment could
change with changed circumstances.

These walk-backs didn't help Bork, in part because all of his responses were couched in turgid language—"He's too professorial," Senator Howell Heflin (D-Ala.) complained to a Justice Department staffer—but also because they made him seem disingenuous.[18] Senator Kennedy mused that "a switch at a convenient time should not be sufficient to make Mr. Bork one of the nine."[19] Kennedy and others tried to paint Bork as bad on sex discrimination, citing aB (unanimous) D.C. Circuit opinion that allowed a chemical company to require female employees to either become sterilized or quit their jobs, because they would be exposed to substances likely to cause birth defects.[20] Howard Metzenbaum (D-Ohio) accused Bork of supporting forced sterilization and read a message from one of the plaintiffs after Bork misspoke and said that some of the women "didn't want to get pregnant." Yale's Paul Gewirtz later testified that "Judge Bork stood against all of those [civil rights] legal developments when it counted, and no latter day recantation or acceptance of prior precedent can really erase that."[21]

Another flashpoint was the right to privacy, which Bork had written was "invented" in *Griswold v. Connecticut*, the contraceptive case. Under questioning before the committee, Bork maintained that this nebulous right was a "radical innovation" and that, while he may have been able to achieve the same result—protecting married couples' right to use contraceptives—Justice Douglas's "penumbras" and "emanations" were not to be found in the Constitution. Questioned by Senator Heflin about how his analysis applied to abortion, Bork surprisingly said that he could imagine considering a straightforward right to abortion, if that were argued in a case, but that he was highly skeptical of a general right to privacy under the Fourteenth Amendment leading to that conclusion. Similarly, he told Senator Kennedy that "a generalized, undefined right of privacy is not in the Bill of Rights."[22]

Bork's views on privacy were part and parcel of his criticism of a "general right of freedom," which, he testified on the first day, Alexander Bickel had convinced him didn't exist.[23] He was highly critical of the expansive view of the Ninth Amendment that judges and academics were taking on, likening to an indecipherable ink blot the constitutional provision specifying that "[t]he enumeration of certain rights shall not be construed to deny or disparage others retained by the people." This view was essentially shared by Justice Scalia and other judicial-restraint conservatives, who recognized that the Constitution protected unenumerated rights but claimed not to have the tools for discerning or enforcing those rights. It was, and remains, a blind spot, as Randy Barnett's work on the original meaning of the Ninth Amendment has shown.[24]

Bork presented his positions, controversial as they were on the substance, in a gruff and standoffish manner, lecturing rather than having a conversation. White House staff tried to get Bork to change, but he couldn't hide his disdain for the process. At the beginning of the hearing, Senator Specter had expressed concern about the Rehnquist and Scalia hearings not getting to some of the issues, but there were few evasions here. This was all against how a nominee would've been coached by White House and Justice Department staff, but *this* nominee didn't want coaching, blowing off so-called "murder board" training sessions. "Bork tended to want to score debate points, rather than appeal to the Committee for votes."[25]

Bork had claimed in a 1971 law review article that the Free Speech Clause of the First Amendment was meant to be limited to political speech that affected political discourse.[26] During his testimony, Bork stated that his views had changed and that he considered this part of the article to be overly narrow; while he was not sure that the Court's doctrine here was completely right as a matter of original intent, he accepted it as precedent and acknowledged that the First

Amendment was broader than he had written. He stood by the part of his article in which he outlined a general theory under which justices need to base their opinions on specific rights listed in constitutional text. Specter asked Bork if he believed the Court could strike down a state or local law restricting obscenity. Bork replied that he didn't believe this type of expression was constitutionally protected, but if a state's definition of pornography was at variance with the Supreme Court's then the law could be struck down.

On the still-controversial subject of *stare decisis*—the idea that some erroneous precedent should be maintained in the interest of legal stability—Bork explained that some cases which were wrongly decided had accrued so many expectations and reliance interest that they should not be overturned. Bork explained that he would consider overturning established precedent if a case were not only wrong but "dynamic," in the sense of being able to spawn future bad law.

Many senators came to Bork's defense, saying that the attacks he faced weren't about his qualifications, which were unimpeachable, but pure politics. Orrin Hatch (R-Utah) stated that the nominee "will be counted by history as belonging alongside a few select justices, like Oliver Wendell Holmes, Louis Brandeis, Felix Frankfurter, Potter Stewart…and Lewis Powell, as well."[27] Hatch assailed his colleagues for trying to exert control over presidential prerogative rather than weeding out unfit nominees. He quoted southern progressive journalist Hodding Carter as saying that "we [liberals] are depending in large part on the least democratic institution…to defend what it is we no longer are able to win out there in the electorate."[28] Hatch also referred to a number of cases in which Bork sided with women and minorities. Indeed, a 1988 study showed that, as solicitor general filing *amicus curiae* (friend of the court) briefs, Bork took liberal positions as often as Thurgood Marshall did during the Johnson administration and more often than Wade McCree did during the

Carter administration, in part because Bork filed in favor of the plaintiffs in civil rights cases 75 percent of the time.[29] At one point, Senator Alan Simpson (R-Wyo.) gave Bork the opportunity to respond to the charge that he was arrogant, to which he replied: "I never have thought of a way to respond to that."[30]

Judge Bork also had a string of star witnesses supporting his nomination. Chief Justice Warren Burger called him "well qualified."[31] Stanford law professor Thomas Campbell, later a congressman, analyzed several of Bork's judicial decisions to show that the AFL-CIO's allegation of anti-union bias was unfounded.[32] Jimmy Carter's former White House counsel Lloyd Cutler described the nominee as "a highly qualified, conservative jurist, who is closer to the moderate center than to the extreme right,"[33] while Carter's attorney general, Griffin Bell, said, "I would vote to confirm Judge Bork, and I do so on the view that he is sensitive and he has never taken any right away from anyone."[34] All this after President Carter himself had sent in a letter opposing Bork's "obnoxious" views on civil rights that would have a "deleterious effect on future decisions involving personal freedom, justice for the deprived, and basic human rights."[35]

All in all, the hearings consumed more than six thousand tightly laid out pages, published in five bureaucratic-green volumes by the Government Printing Office. The judiciary committee voted 5–9 against the nomination—party-line except Specter voted no—sending it to the full Senate with a recommendation that it be rejected. The committee hearings had reinforced the anti-Bork campaign of the preceding two months, a far cry from the initial media analysis that "Bork is likely to be confirmed."[36] Public opinion had shifted, too. Before the hearings, a Gallup poll showed 31 percent for Bork, 25 percent opposed, while after the hearings it was 32 percent for, 52 percent opposed, with nearly all of the undecideds breaking against.[37]

Many now expected Bork to withdraw, but he issued a statement that even though he was under "no illusions," he would stay the course because "a crucial principle is at stake. That principle is the way we select the men and women who guard the liberties of all the American people. That should not be done through public campaigns of distortion. If I withdraw now, that campaign would be seen as a success, and it would be mounted against future nominees."[38] Of course, Bork's valiant effort to stand for principle would in no way defuse future confirmation battles or preempt public campaigns of any kind.

The battle would rage for an entire month, with senators loading up the *Congressional Record* with editorials and other materials. Biden inserted into the record the names of 1,925 law professors who were against Bork, representing about 40 percent of law school faculty members nationwide. Senator Daniel Evans (R-Wash.) noted that "I have had . . . over 15,000 letters which probably, if you measure them for and against, give me little solace for they are split almost precisely evenly."[39] Senators Biden and Thurmond, the judiciary committee leaders from each party, led the formal debate on the Senate floor, which focused on what the Constitution says about privacy and civil rights. Most senators had decided how to vote, but party leaders knew the vote would be close so maintained their oratory for the sake of any gettable votes. President Reagan himself made national appeals in five of his weekly radio broadcasts and a national TV address.

Robert Bork's nomination was defeated 42–58 on October 23, 1987. It was close to a party-line vote, with two Democrats voting in favor and six Republicans opposed. It was the biggest rejection margin ever and only the fourth Supreme Court nomination to be rejected in the 20th century, spawning a new verb, to be "borked."

While lots of people had lots of disagreements with Robert Bork, it's undeniable that the man had an outsized impact on law and legal policy that included fomenting the pushback against the progressive excesses of the Warren Court. Best known for his failed Supreme Court bid, his enduring legacy lies elsewhere. His work on antitrust law, in line with the nascent law-and-economics movement, transformed the field into one focused on consumer welfare rather than government management of industry and continues to influence legal doctrine and jurisprudence. His pioneering development of originalism as the one coherent method of constitutional interpretation led to a revival of the once-quaint idea that constitutional text, structure, and history matter more than the subjective policy views of particular judges.

Bork was inexcusably wrong in emphasizing judicial restraint over getting the law right—John Roberts's votes in the Obamacare cases were fruits of that poisonous tree—and in reading unenumerated rights out of the Constitution. He also misunderstood the "Madisonian dilemma" of judges making unpopular rulings, positing that majorities are entitled to rule in wide swaths of life, with limited exceptions for individual freedom; that's exactly backwards. And he, like Justice Scalia, too easily made peace with the New Deal's abandonment of the doctrine of enumerated powers, which resulted in the government's getting the benefit of the doubt almost as much as from liberal jurists. In the end, we should remember him as an intellectual powerhouse who fought the progressives' hijacking of the law until better reinforcements came. And his experience unfortunately produced a chilling effect on ambitious would-be judges and their academic writings or public pronouncements, especially when testifying before the Senate.

CHAPTER 12

Insult after Injury

W hen it became clear that Robert Bork's nomination was in trouble, President Reagan told one audience: "If I have to appoint another one, I'll try to find one that they'll object to just as much as they did for this one."[1] Well, less than a week after the Senate rejected Bork, the president announced the nomination of Bork's D.C. Circuit colleague, Douglas Ginsburg. Judge Ginsburg, just 41 years old, the youngest nominee in half a century, was among several judges Reagan had considered. Senator Warren Rudman's (R-N.H.) suggestion of a judge from his state, David Souter, was rejected as being unknown and unremarkable.[2]

The White House strategy was to find someone as conservative as Bork, but "less visible and controversial."[3] Several Democratic senators had advised that Ginsburg might be the hardest to confirm, given his youth and conservative reputation—"Judge Bork without the paper trail," Senator Ted Kennedy called him, after having praised him as "open-minded" and compassionate the year before—but he was the favorite of Attorney General Meese.[4] He had also been confirmed twice in recent years and was moderate in style and temperament.

Ginsburg was (and is) more of a libertarian than a social conservative, so while it's likely that progressive groups would've attacked him for being "extreme" on deregulation, there wouldn't have been the same purchase over the more politically salient issues of privacy and civil rights. Indeed, Ginsburg's jurisprudence turned out to be more in the judicial "engagement" school, skeptical of government power of all sorts, than Bork's judicial restraint.

But there'd be no chance to test Reagan's hypothesis, because it came out that Ginsburg had smoked marijuana as a law student and, more importantly, as a law professor. Although he'd passed several background checks, the FBI in those days didn't ask their whether you'd "used" drugs, just whether you'd ever abused them, to which Ginsburg could truthfully answer no. He withdrew his name a mere nine days after he was picked and before the White House formally submitted his name to the Senate.

Anthony Kennedy

Four days after Ginsburg withdrew, President Reagan nominated Judge Anthony Kennedy, who had been appointed to the Ninth Circuit by President Ford after having been in private practice in Sacramento. While engaged in local affairs in his hometown, Kennedy advised then-governor Reagan on a state tax-limitation proposal, leading Reagan to recommend him to Ford. Based on his moderately conservative judicial record, civic service, and affability, Kennedy was much more in the Powell model than either Bork or Ginsburg. There was nothing controversial or provocative in his background; he had literally been an altar boy and led a life of quiet excellence and community involvement. Combined with his talent at "schmoozing Senators," he seemed a shoo-in for confirmation.[5] Senator Biden described the nominee as more "open minded" and less of an ideologue than Bork.[6]

Kennedy's lack of overarching theories placed him in the "mainstream" of legal thought in the eyes of Democrats, contrary to how they viewed the previous nominees for this seat. Senator Howell Heflin (D-Ala.) would comment that Kennedy's "conservatism, while pronounced, is not so severe as to prevent him from listening."[7] In his judiciary committee questionnaire, Kennedy had written that "life tenure is in part a constitutional mandate to the federal judiciary to proceed with caution, to avoid reaching issues not necessary to the resolution of the suit at hand, and to defer to the political process." And that the "expanded role of the courts tends to erode the boundaries of judicial power and also threatens to permit the individual biases of the judge to operate."[8] This sort of homage to judicial restraint could have been written by Bork, but here it went over a lot better—showing both that the messenger matters and that successful nominees are savvy enough to know how to strike the right tone.

During his relatively uneventful confirmation hearings, Kennedy said of privacy rights that "I would like to draw the line and not talk about the *Griswold* case so far as its reasoning or its result."[9] He also discussed "a zone of liberty, a zone of protection, a line that's drawn where the individual can tell the Government, 'Beyond this line you may not go.'"[10] The Senate confirmed him 97–0 on February 3, 1988. Paul Simon (D-Ill.) and Al Gore (D-Tenn.) were out campaigning for the president and Joe Biden, whose own campaign had ended under a cloud during the Bork hearings, was home with a pinched nerve.

Initial reports called Justice Kennedy "as conservative as any justice nominated by President Ronald Reagan"[11] and "a predictable conservative."[12] He quickly joined Justice O'Connor in the middle, however, particularly on divisive social issues like abortion, affirmative action, and gay rights. They would be met there temporarily by David Souter, as he transitioned from moderate right to definite left (see next chapter). The trio would come together in a rare co-authored plurality opinion in *Planned Parenthood v. Casey* (1992), reaffirming *Roe v. Wade* but replacing its trimester/viability rubric with an "undue burden" standard for evaluating abortion regulations. Kennedy played the key role in applying this test in later cases, finding a right to end a pregnancy but recognizing that, as one author of a book on his jurisprudence put it, "[T]his is a liberty that is bounded by important state interests...that permit the state to require the woman to exercise her liberty in an informed and responsible manner."[13] Kennedy's bounded-liberty rubric was even more on display in *Stenberg v. Carhart* (2000) and *Gonzales v. Carhart* (2007). In *Stenberg*, a 5–4 majority overturned Nebraska's ban on partial-birth abortion because it wasn't limited to late-term abortions and had no exception for maternal health. Kennedy dissented. In *Gonzales*, Kennedy wrote the opinion for a different five-justice majority, upholding a federal partial-birth abortion ban that likewise lacked a maternal-health exception.

After taking heat from conservatives for *Casey*, Kennedy now took heat from liberals for seeming to contradict *Casey* and for not recognizing that he would have to overrule *Stenberg* to achieve his desired result, rather than creating a contradiction. In *Whole Women's Health v. Hellerstedt* (2016), Kennedy voted to invalidate an abortion law for the first time since *Casey*, in a case where Texas required clinics to meet the safety standards of surgical centers and have physicians with nearby hospital-admitting privileges. Thus, we're left with an outcome whereby abortion rights are now both stronger and narrower than before Kennedy got his hands on them—and an "undue burden" was whatever gave him a headache.

Justice Kennedy accepted racial diversity as a legitimate goal but, until the quixotic *Fisher v. UT-Austin II* (2016), had never voted to uphold a policy trying to achieve that goal. In the 2003 University of Michigan cases, Kennedy labeled the concept of critical mass a "delusion used by the Law School to mask its attempt to make race an automatic factor in most instances and to achieve numerical goals indistinguishable from quotas."[14]

As important as Kennedy's role in the abortion and affirmative action fights were, he's now most identified with 2015's landmark ruling on gay marriage. *Obergefell v. Hodges* was the fourth sexual-orientation case in which Kennedy not only voted against a restriction, but wrote the majority opinion. In *Lawrence v. Texas* (2003), Kennedy led the majority striking down a Texas anti-sodomy law, a result he found so obvious that he wrote the opinion in one weekend. Georgetown law professor Randy Barnett—the intellectual godfather of the challenge to Obamacare's individual mandate—called it Kennedy's "libertarian revolution" because the opinion was grounded in "personal liberty" rather than "privacy."[15]

Alas, Kennedy's *Obergefell* opinion was a doctrinal mess. What should've been a case about justifications for certain marriage-licensing schemes and the equality of gays and lesbians in the eyes of the law instead became a purple disquisition on how the Constitution protects "a liberty that includes certain specific rights that allow persons, within a lawful realm, to define and express their identity."[16] The rule of *Obergefell* seems to be that you take a scoop of due process and a cup of equal protection, wrap them in dignity, and away you go. That's poetic, but it's not law. For one thing, the due process clause should've had nothing to do with the case because the right to "due process of law" means that the government can't take away your life, liberty, or property for no good reason. It's the equal protection clause that says the government can't treat people differently without reason. While the clauses can overlap, they often don't, because the discrimination might concern something that's not life, liberty, or property.

Such is the case here: there's no natural right to the state recognition of marriage. Marriage—the civil institution, not the religious rite—is a kind of government benefit. To put it in the context of injustices perpetrated against gay people, marriage is not like the right to have sex with a consenting partner. *Obergefell* thus differed from *Lawrence*, but also from *Loving v. Virginia* (1967), which overturned a law that banned interracial cohabitation.

Perhaps Kennedy's synthesis can best be called "equal liberty": a rejection of the idea that people seeking protection for their intimate conduct must seek it politically. Regardless, these rulings led some to call Kennedy the "first gay justice." It's an odd appellation for the genteel country-club Republican, but it'll stick until someone who's openly gay joins the Court.

Justice Kennedy was a leader of a very pro-speech Court. While no absolutist like Justice Hugo Black, he more than anyone else had no tolerance for content-based restrictions. According to First Amendment scholar Eugene Volokh, in the latter half of the Rehnquist Court, Kennedy took the pro-speech position three-quarters of the time, by far the most.[17] In case after free-speech case, Kennedy showed the importance of tolerance in the free market of ideas.

An underappreciated part of Justice Kennedy's legacy is his relatively solid record on the Constitution's structural protections for liberty. Separating powers vertically, not just horizontally, is a key part of the Founding project, as is the principle of dual sovereignty—the idea that the state and federal governments shouldn't interfere in each other's respective spheres.

The clearest exposition of Kennedy's federalism came in *United States v. Bond* (2011), where the government prosecuted a woman who used a household chemical against a romantic rival for violating the federal law that implements the international Chemical Weapons Convention. "Federalism is more than an exercise in setting the boundary between different institutions of government for their own integrity," he wrote for a unanimous court; it "protects the liberty of the individual from arbitrary power."[18]

Using the judicial power to stop government abuse was the theme of Justice Kennedy's magnum opus in this area, the joint dissent he co-authored with Scalia, Thomas, and Alito in *NFIB v. Sebelius* (2012), otherwise known as the first Obamacare case, which concludes:

> The values that should have determined our course today are caution, minimalism, and the understanding that the Federal Government is one of limited powers. But the Court's ruling undermines those values at every turn. In the name of restraint, it overreaches. In the name of constitutional avoidance, it creates new constitutional questions. In the name of cooperative federalism, it undermines state sovereignty.[19]

I was in the courtroom when the ruling was announced from the bench, including Kennedy's dramatic summary of that dissent. The starkness of his language and passion in his voice could have made you mistake him for Scalia. It was his finest hour—and really makes you wonder how the same jurist could have signed onto *Gonzales v. Raich* (2005), which ratified the federal government's power to regulate plants you grow in your backyard for your own use.

Although Justice Kennedy hated being called a "swing" justice—"The cases swing, I don't," he protested during an appearance at Harvard Law School in October 2015—anyone with even a passing interest in the Supreme Court knows that for more than a decade he provided the deciding vote in nearly all the controversial cases that rile the nation.[20] The statistics bear this out: in every term but three from Alito's replacement of O'Connor in January 2006 until Kennedy's retirement in June 2018, Kennedy was the winningest justice, typically in the majority over 90 percent of the time. In 2006–07, the first full post-O'Connor term, Kennedy was in the majority in all twenty-four of the 5–4 cases and dissented but twice out of seventy-two cases overall. And in the seven terms from Justice Elena Kagan's arrival until Justice Gorsuch, Kennedy was on the winning side of 85 percent of 5–4 splits, while his colleagues were clustered between 48 and 57 percent. As SCOTUSblog founder and frequent Supreme Court advocate Tom Goldstein put it, "it's Justice Kennedy's world, and you just live in it."[21]

The problem with Kennedy in the contemporary account of our politics isn't that he sometimes agreed with progressives and sometimes with conservatives. It's that, even if he had a coherent view of the Constitution, his jurisprudence was often inscrutable. Decisions that come from such special access to legal truth undermine the rule of law, which values predictability and transparency. Regardless of how convincing anyone's explanation of his methods may be, if the perception is that he decided cases like a magic eight-ball, whether based on a unique legal theory or personal predilections, that doesn't instill faith in the system.[22]

But even apart from what Justice Kennedy did on the Court, the way he got on the Court affected how all future nominees would be treated. When he was confirmed, Senator Howard Metzenbaum (D-Ohio), who had been one of Bork's leading opponents, called it "a triumph of process as well as justice," adding that Kennedy "would not have been my nominee" but his views were "well within the constitutional mainstream." Senator Arlen Specter (R-Penn.), meanwhile, said that the confirmation process was "a growing experience for the Senate and for the country." Senator Leahy called it "a turning point in Senate history." Indeed, the Bork-to-Kennedy confirmation established for modern times that, in Specter's words, "judicial philosophy is relevant and important."[23] While some Republicans criticized the Democrats for imposing what Senator Alan Simpson (R-Wyo.) called a "political litmus test," this was hardly something new. But the fights to come were spectacles of a kind we didn't have when you had to read about Senate debates several days after they took place.

CHAPTER 13

The Souter Disappointment and the Thomas Travesty

G eorge H. W. Bush, who was elected to "Ronald Reagan's third term," had a sterling record of public service and was about as well-prepared to be president as anyone can be. He admitted that he lacked "the vision thing," but recognized that he needed support from the large swaths of the country upset with the Supreme Court's direction on things like abortion and school prayer. While labeled the "Religious Right," the appellation doesn't accurately describe those God-fearing voters who aren't necessarily regular churchgoers—working-class folks who are motivated by cultural issues more than economic ones. "Reagan Democrats" was the old moniker for them, and we'd probably call them Obama-Trump voters now, though they tend to sit out elections where neither major-party candidate speaks to them.

If the first President Bush "spoke conservatism as a second language," he knew that an easy way to get conservatives to trust him would be to continue his predecessor's strong record on judicial nominations. While Justice O'Connor turned out to be more moderate than hoped, and Justice Kennedy was a third-choice compromise after the Bork saga, everyone recognized that President Reagan and his team had a clear direction on judges.

Bush would try to replicate that. He batted .500, with one cipher who proved quite liberal and one bitter battle that seated a man who is, to this day, the Court's most conservative member.

David Souter

With the advanced age of several justices, much thought had gone into possible replacements, so when Justice William Brennan retired on July 20, 1990, Bush was ready. His chief advisers, Attorney General Dick Thornburgh, Chief of Staff John Sununu, and Counsel C. Boyden Gray, had whittled a list of fifty they had inherited on Inauguration Day down to eighteen.[1]

The list of eighteen was reduced to eight, and then to four: two judges whom Bush himself had recently appointed, Clarence Thomas of the D.C. Circuit and David H. Souter of the First Circuit, and two Reagan appointees, Edith Jones of the Fifth Circuit (and Bush's adopted state of Texas) and Laurence Silberman of the D.C. Circuit. Bush went with Souter out of a desire to pick someone with no paper trail and thus avoid controversy ahead of the 1990 midterm elections. Jones was more ideologically defined, but she was young (41, having been previously confirmed just before her 36th birthday) and so would presumably have another chance. Given these two jurists' records, however, with Jones becoming a conservative stalwart, this choice turned out to be one of American political history's great mistakes.

Souter, a double-Harvard Rhodes Scholar who had been a career prosecutor and then his state's attorney general before beginning his judicial career, certainly fit the bill of being a "stealth" candidate. He had written few opinions on federal issues and just one insignificant law review article. Justice Thurgood Marshall said he had "never heard of him."[2] Souter was also quiet, diffident even. While his intellect and legal acumen were evident, there was no record of his having taken a position on anything remotely controversial. If Bush wanted someone who was the polar opposite of Robert Bork, he got him. Bush made the announcement on July 25, 1990, adding that he had no "litmus test" and didn't know the nominee's views on anything. "You might just think that the whole nomination had something to do with abortion. It's something much broader than that. I have too much respect for the Supreme Court for that."[3]

Of course, Souter was as much a cipher to Democrats as he was to Republicans. The left was especially wary that their loyal lion, Brennan, would be replaced by *whomever* Bush thought was good enough to placate his right wing. The NAACP organized a letter-writing campaign, while the National Organization of Women staged a protest as Souter's hearings began. NOW president Molly Yard testified that Souter would "end freedom for women in this country."[4] Despite the unease of outside interest groups, he was warmly received by a Senate Judiciary Committee that was still composed of eight Democrats and six Republicans. After an opening statement that focused on the effect judicial rulings had on actual human beings, Souter was mum on just about every subject that had gotten Bork into trouble. Under sustained questioning from Senator Ted Kennedy, he acknowledged a right to privacy and gave a touching tribute to Justice Brennan, but drew the line at the insistent queries aimed at teasing out his views on *Roe v. Wade.* One of the more heated exchanges on that score involved Republicans asking about the decision of a hospital (on whose board Souter sat) to begin performing abortions. With polite answers that gave little indication of a judicial philosophy over five days of testimony, he frustrated conservatives and thus defused the liberal opposition.

The committee voted to approve him 13–1, with Kennedy alone in the negative. A few others expressed reservations but went along out of recognition that they were unlikely to get a more moderate nominee. The full Senate confirmed Souter 90–9 on October 2, with eight liberal Democrats who weren't on the committee adding their dissent.

On the Court, Justice Souter was initially a moderate, shading a bit to the right alongside Justice O'Connor. Indeed, the duo voted together in all but two cases during Souter's first term. That meant that Souter provided the fifth vote in several cases that would've gone the other way if Brennan was still on the bench. But there were other cases where Souter, with O'Connor, took the Court left. And, of course, the following term, Justice Kennedy would join them in co-authoring *Planned Parenthood v. Casey* (1992). The trio wrote, in a section that sounds very much like what we know about Souter's hidebound approach to precedent, that *Roe* shouldn't be overturned because it would be "a surrender to political pressure.... So to over-rule under fire in the absence of the most compelling reason to re-examine a watershed decision would subvert the Court's legitimacy beyond any serious question."[5]

Casey signaled a leftward shift for Souter. Never again would he agree with Justice Scalia more than Justices Blackmun and Stevens, or later Justices Ginsburg and Breyer.

While Souter ended up about as liberal as Brennan, he lacked the coalition-building talent that made his predecessor such an effective justice. Accordingly, his main impact was to amplify the power of the swing justices; had Souter been a traditional conservative, Justices O'Connor and Kennedy would only have been able to flip the Court if they *both* joined the liberals. Most prominently, Souter and Kennedy joined Justice Stevens's 5–4 opinion in *Kelo v. City of New London* (2005), which okayed the forcible transfer of property from one private owner to another under the guise of "public use." That prompted a vehement dissent by Justice O'Connor, as well as an attempt to have Souter's farm seized and turned into the "Lost Liberty Hotel," featuring a "Just Desserts Cafe."[6]

In short, in all but the first two of his nineteen terms on the Court, Justice Souter could be a reliable part of a four-justice liberal bloc in ideologically salient cases. But he wasn't a leader; he didn't write the majority opinion in any big case, for example, and was rarely the lead dissent in the major ones that the liberals lost.

Never quite happy on the Court, the lifetime bachelor thought often about retiring. But he stuck it out until 2009, letting the White House know of his intent to retire a few months after President Obama was inaugurated. Allowing a Democratic president to fill his seat was perhaps the final insult to those who had urged President Bush to appoint a better-known quantity, and an object lesson. For example, when President George W. Bush considered nominating his attorney general, Alberto Gonzales, who was perceived to have liberal views on certain issues, conservative Senate staffers popularized the slogan, "Gonzales is Spanish for Souter."[7]

Clarence Thomas

When Thurgood Marshall, in failing health and despite having vowed to "die in office," announced his intent to retire on June 27, 1991, the administration had its short list ready to go. But Bush was fighting Congress over new civil rights legislation, labeled the "quota bill," and also faced pressure to maintain the "African-American" seat. How was he supposed to argue against aggressive affirmative action while also picking someone based on race? Even if he had been grooming Clarence Thomas for elevation, this was awkward. Bush considered appointing a woman or Hispanic judge, adding several people to his list. Ultimately Bush stuck with Thomas, who was then 43 and had been a federal judge less than sixteen months.

Announcing the nomination on July 1, the president said he had found "the best person at the right time."[8]

From Thomas's perspective, it may be that he was the right person at the wrong time, walking into a firestorm. At the celebration of Souter's swearing in, Sununu promised to fill the next Supreme Court vacancy with a "true conservative" and predicted a "knock-down, drag-out, bloody-knuckles, grass-roots fight."[9] And that would be the case not simply because the iconic Marshall was being replaced by a black conservative, but because the next justice would be joining five GOP-appointed justices to form what many liberals feared would be an unassailable super-majority against *Roe v. Wade* and much besides. *Any* nominee Bush put up would face stern opposition in a Senate where the Democrats had grown their majority 56–44.

Unlike Souter, Thomas had a paper trail and a record of government service that put him in controversial positions. As assistant secretary of education for civil rights and then chairman of the Equal Employment Opportunity Commission, he had given speeches and written articles sympathetic to natural law—the moral rules preexisting any political order—criticizing racial preferences, supporting property rights, and other themes that established conservative bona fides. "I am confident it can be shown," he wrote in a Cato Institute-edited volume called *Assessing the Reagan Years*, "that blacks at any level, especially white-collar employees, have simply not benefitted from affirmative action policies."[10] These writings would provide fodder for his confirmation hearings and grist for progressive opposition groups. The ABA voted 12–2 to rate Thomas "qualified," with two committee members voting "unqualified" and one abstaining, a record low for a Supreme Court nominee. One academic commentator described the Thomas nomination as "a bold political move calculated to make it more difficult for many of the same civil rights organizations and southern blacks, who opposed Judge Bork's nomination, to oppose

Justice Thomas."[11] Nevertheless, the NAACP and National Urban League came out against him. And in perhaps the most famous early use of the verb "to bork," at a National Organization for Women conference in July 1991, Florynce Kennedy said of the nomination, "We're going to bork him. We're going to kill him politically.... This little creep, where did he come from?"[12]

Clarence Thomas came from the small, slave-descended community of Pin Point, Georgia, located on the Moon River near Savannah and mired in deep poverty in the Jim Crow South. His father left when the future justice was an infant, and several years later his beleaguered mother sent him and his brother to live with their grandfather and his wife. Thomas originally entered the seminary, but was troubled by the church's poor stance on racial prejudice, which had culminated in a student's elation at Martin Luther King's assassination. He left and matriculated at the College of the Holy Cross, where he founded the Black Student Union and organized a walk-out over disparate treatment in disciplinary actions.

Thomas felt uncomfortable at Yale Law School because employers assumed he had gotten in due to affirmative action. Unable to find work in corporate law in Atlanta or other cities, he went to work for fellow Yale alum and future patron, Missouri Attorney General John Danforth, who later as a senator would play a key role in the support of Thomas's Supreme Court nomination. During an eight-year tenure as EEOC chairman, Thomas moved the agency away from its group-based focus toward an individual-rights approach to civil rights, rejecting quotas and timetables. Based on the reputation he garnered there, President Bush picked him to replace Robert Bork on the D.C. Circuit.

Judge Thomas's Supreme Court hearings began September 10 and initially lasted ten days, with the nominee appearing in five of them. "In this time of change, fundamental constitutional rights which have been protected by the Supreme Court for decades are being called into question," ominously began Chairman Biden.[13] Well aware of the different outcomes between Bork's loquacious approach and Souter's taciturn politesse, Thomas aimed to follow the now-standard playbook of avoiding squarely answering controversial questions as much as possible. He even said that he'd never really thought about or discussed *Roe v. Wade*, which was decided while he was in law school.[14] But he was largely prevented from doing the same thing on other issues because of his extensive writings, as when Biden waved a copy of legal scholar Richard Epstein's book, *Takings: Private Property and the Power of Eminent Domain,* and asked Thomas whether he agreed with the arguments contained therein. Biden also asked him about Stephen Macedo, another political theorist who had written about constitutional protections for individual rights, about whom Thomas had spoken favorably. The Cato Institute would paraphrase this line of questioning as, "Are you now or have you ever been a libertarian?"[15]

Ranking member Strom Thurmond (R-S.C.), who had already spent forty-seven years in the Senate and participated in hearings for a fifth of all Supreme Court justices, opened his side's questioning. He argued, counter-historically, "To reject a nominee based solely on ideology is inappropriate."[16] Orrin Hatch (R-Utah) said pointedly, "I don't think President Bush could have made a better decision."[17] As was to be expected, the Republicans generally threw Thomas softballs; Arlen Specter (Penn.) was an exception to that, as he had been in the Bork hearings.

Democrats, meanwhile, tried to pin the nominee down. Senator Kennedy asked about how Thomas had said that our entitlement programs were "a short road" from socialism because "a right has come to mean... the legal claim to receive and demand something," and an article where he complained about "[o]ur current explosion of rights" (because that trivializes actual rights).[18] The nominee backed away from many of these statements. Senator Howell Heflin (D-Ala.) called the disparity between Thomas's previous writings and his testimony a "confirmation conversion."[19] Later, Heflin lamented Thomas's criticism of Justice Oliver Wendell Holmes, which was a sophisticated critique of nihilism as uniting left and right against natural law.[20] Finally, even as polls showed three-quarters of African Americans supporting Thomas, the leaders of national black organizations testified against him. But the president of the Liberty County, Georgia, NAACP asked, "Who is to tell blacks that we are compelled to join in a lock-step mentality toward the best approaches to improve the life of blacks and other minorities?...Clarence Thomas has demonstrated that he is an independent thinker, maybe too independent for some self-appointed spokesmen against his confirmation."[21]

Although the opposition to Thomas wasn't quite as vociferous as four years earlier with Bork, the only major civil rights group that didn't line up against him was the Southern Christian Leadership Conference. Along with his opposition to racial preferences and group rights, his attachment to natural law, as well as his religious faith, made many of the Democrats uneasy. Even though Senators Biden, Kennedy, and Pat Leahy (D-Vt.) were also Catholic, they wanted to see some acknowledgment of the right to abortion. Thomas held firm, despite twenty-eight separate attempts by Senator Metzenbaum to get the nominee to express an opinion.[22]

On September 27, 1991, the Senate Judiciary Committee split 7–7, with one Democrat, Dennis DeConcini of Arizona, voting for Thomas. This was a surprise, because several other Democrats had hinted that they might vote for him. The committee then voted 13–1 to send the nomination to the Senate floor without any recommendation—the lone no vote belonging to Senator Simon, who always voted no on such motions. Accordingly, Senate Majority Leader George Mitchell

(D-Maine) set the final vote for October 8, with the conventional wisdom being that there would be a safe margin for confirmation. Fifty-three senators had already announced support, including thirteen Democrats.[23] Justice Souter, who had just celebrated his first anniversary of running the same gauntlet, sent a note of congratulations. Chief Justice Rehnquist's assistant called to offer help in setting up chambers. But Thomas was wary, writing in his 2007 memoir that he "didn't trust my enemies" and "wouldn't rest easy until the votes were tallied."[24]

"High-Tech Lynching"

Two days before the scheduled vote, NPR's Nina Totenberg aired information from a leaked statement submitted to the judiciary committee by University of Oklahoma law professor Anita Hill. The statement accused Thomas of having made unwanted advances when she worked for him at the Department of Education and then the EEOC.[25] Biden had asked for an investigation and the FBI completed its work before the committee vote, but Biden did not postpone that vote when the report came in.[26] Thomas wrote that he "never feared the results of the FBI's investigations, not merely because I was innocent but also because I trusted the agents to behave professionally. What I feared was that if Anita's charges became public, the media would jump to its usual conclusion that I was the villain—and that was what happened."[27] Hill initially wanted her name to be kept confidential, but after the allegations leaked to the national media, she held a press conference and announced that she was willing to testify. Facing pressure from women's groups, Biden reopened the hearings, only the third time this had been done with a Supreme Court nominee and the first since Harlan Stone's nomination in 1925. Party leadership worked out a deal to set a hard deadline of one week for the reexamination.

Hill testified wearily, recounting that Thomas had asked her out a few months after they began working together. She recited the indignities she claimed her new boss visited upon her after she declined his entreaties, including references to bestiality, group sex, and his own sexual prowess. Hill said that Thomas had mentioned a porn star named Long Dong Silver—which happened to match an item in an EEOC case file—and related the following incident: "Thomas was drinking a Coke in his office, he got up from the table at which we were working, went over to his desk to get the Coke, looked at the can and asked, 'Who has put pubic hair on my Coke?'"[28] The lurid detail captivated media coverage during a time of debate over sexual harassment. *Time* labeled Hill a modern-day Rosa Parks or Harriet Tubman.

Republicans chipped away at Hill's credibility, pointing to how she had followed Thomas from the Department of Education to the EEOC. They also introduced phone logs showing she talked to him even after that. After Hill equivocated on her reasons for doing so, offering several variations, Senator Specter accused Hill of "flat-out perjury" and suggested her testimony was the "product of fantasy."[29] Senator Hatch suggested that she got the idea for one of her charges from *The Exorcist*. In the book, which the movie was based on, a character references "an alien pubic hair floating around in my gin."[30] Democrats were sometimes awkward in trying to defend Hill's motives. Senator Heflin asked, "Are you a scorned woman.... Are you a zealoting civil rights believer.... Do you have a martyr complex?"

Thomas testified unequivocally that the accusations were false. In his testimony's most famous passage, Judge Thomas called the process a "high-tech lynching":

This is a circus. It's a national disgrace. And from my standpoint, as a black American, it is a high-tech lynching

for uppity blacks who in any way deign to think for themselves, to do for themselves, to have different ideas, and it
is a message that unless you kowtow to an old order, this
is what will happen to you. You will be lynched, destroyed,
caricatured by a committee of the U.S. Senate rather than
hung from a tree.[31]

On the relationship between his political opponents and the media,
Thomas further commented: "This is a case in which this sleaze, this
dirt, was searched for by staffers of members of this committee. It was
then leaked to the media. And this committee and this body validated
it and displayed it in prime time over our entire nation."[32]

Thomas was questioned for ninety minutes about sex, pornography, and other uncomfortable subjects. Before he left the witness
chair, Thomas told the committee, "There has never been one minute
of joy in having been nominated to the Supreme Court."[33]

The committee heard from several other witnesses. Thomas's special assistant at the EEOC, J.C. Alvarez, said that Thomas "demanded
professionalism and performance" and that Hill's allegations were
self-serving: "Women who have really been harassed would
agree...you don't follow them to the next job—especially, if you are
a black female, Yale Law School graduate. Let's face it, out in the corporate sector, companies are fighting for women with those kinds of
credentials."[34] Another special assistant, Phyllis Berry-Myers, testified
that Thomas "was respectful, demand[ed] of excellence in our work,
cordial, professional, interested in our lives and our career ambitions."
Berry-Myers said her "impression" was that Hill desired a personal
relationship with Thomas.[35] Diane Holt, Thomas's secretary for six
years and a friend of Hill's, said, "At no time did Professor Hill intimate, not even in the most subtle of ways, that Judge Thomas was
asking her out or subjecting her to the crude, abusive conversations

that have been described."[36] Nancy Altman, who worked with Hill and Thomas at the Department of Education, concluded, "It is not credible that Clarence Thomas could have engaged in the kinds of behavior that Anita Hill alleges, without any of the women who he worked closest with—dozens of us, we could spend days having women come up, his secretaries, his chief of staff, his other assistants, his colleagues—without any of us having sensed, seen or heard something."

Two former EEOC staffers, Angela Wright and Rose Jourdain, made statements to Senate staff in support of Hill, but did not testify. Wright said that Thomas made repeated comments about her appearance and pressured her for dates.[37] She said that after she turned him down, he began to express discontent with her work and eventually fired her. Thomas explained that he fired Wright for poor performance and for using a homophobic epithet.[38] Jourdain said Wright had told her about Thomas's behavior at the time, and that she, Wright, had become "increasingly uneasy" from her boss's commentary about her body.[39] Another former Thomas assistant, Sukari Hardnett, didn't claim any harassment, but told judiciary committee staff that "if you were young, black, female, reasonably attractive and worked directly for Clarence Thomas, you knew full well you were being inspected and auditioned as a female."[40] Wright was the only person other than Hill who publicly claimed that Thomas had made sexual advances, but ultimately declined to testify, for reasons that remain in dispute. Republicans wanted to avoid the prospect of a second woman describing inappropriate behavior by Thomas, to be sure, but Democrats were even more concerned about Wright's credibility.

While salacious and provocative, the second hearing failed to prove the truth of Hill's claims. Partisans on both sides saw what they wanted to see. Despite a media skewed against the nominee, the public as a whole believed Thomas by about a 2:1 ratio and a majority favored confirmation, including more than 70 percent of blacks.[41]

Women believed Thomas over Hill by a 54–26 percentage. Even the *Washington Post* concluded that Anita Hill did not meet a low burden of proof.[42] Still, in April 2019, as he geared up for his final presidential run and seeing a political vulnerability in the #MeToo era, Joe Biden called Anita Hill to express "his regret for what she endured."[43] No apology to Justice Thomas has been forthcoming.

In any event, enough senators gave Thomas the benefit of the doubt, with a final vote of 52–48, the smallest margin for a successful 20th-century Supreme Court nominee. Eleven Democrats voted to confirm Thomas and two Republicans voted against him: Jim Jeffords of Vermont, who would leave the party a decade later, and, ironically, Bob Packwood of Oregon, who resigned a few years later after allegations of sexual misconduct. Three of the thirteen Democrats who had pledged to vote for Thomas ended up voting against: Joe Lieberman of Connecticut and both Nevada senators, Richard H. Bryan and Harry Reid.[44]

Thomas refused to watch the final vote, and instead went home and took a bath. When his wife, Virginia, told him he was confirmed, all he said was, "Whoop-dee-damn-doo," before sliding into the water. He wrote in his memoir, "Mere confirmation, even to the Supreme Court, seemed pitifully small compensation for what had been done to me."[45] A magnanimous Thomas met with reporters outside his home later that day and said, "No matter how difficult or painful, this is a time for healing in our country. We have to put these things behind us. We have to go forward."[46] Justice Thomas was sworn in by Chief Justice Rehnquist a week later.

Thomas has repeatedly said that the confirmation battle embittered him, leaving a weariness behind his booming laugh. Yet he has taken all the slings and arrows—some remarkably nasty, like the political cartoons depicting him as a lawn jockey or Uncle Tom, or as Justice Scalia's puppet—in stride, maintaining his judicial lodestar of originalist and textualist interpretation. To attribute any jurisprudential effect to enmity, or to ignore the continuity between his thinking pre- and post-confirmation, is to misunderstand the man's approach to the judicial role. As two *Washington Post* reporters themselves noted in a 2007 biography, Thomas "strives for intellectual consistency," which sometimes "puts helping someone in need or righting an obvious wrong beyond his reach."[47] His view of the judge's role is evident in his dissents in *Hudson v. McMillian* (1992) and *Lawrence v. Texas* (2003). In *Hudson*, Thomas argued that while "abusive behavior by prison guards is deplorable conduct," and may even be constitutionally remediable, it does not constitute "cruel and unusual punishment" such that the Eight Amendment becomes "a National Code of Prison Regulation."[48] In *Lawrence*, Thomas called a sodomy law "uncommonly silly," but ultimately found himself, as a federal judge, lacking the power to do anything about it.[49]

Replacing Thurgood Marshall with Clarence Thomas meant, on most issues, replacing the Court's most liberal member with its most conservative, marking perhaps the greatest shift in jurisprudence in the Court's history. But simply calling Thomas "conservative" misunderstands his judicial project and lumps him in with Rehnquist, Bork, and especially Scalia, without differentiating his jurisprudence. One of his early biographers characterized his approach as "classical original liberalism" rather than "Borkian conservative originalism."[50] That gets it about right, because Thomas isn't about "judicial restraint" or "law and order," but rather reading history and being faithful to constitutional original meaning or statutory text as he can best determine it, with everything else secondary.

Although Justice Thomas hasn't had the opportunity to write many majority opinions in landmark cases—those assignments typically go to the "swing" vote, chief justice, or most senior associate justice if the chief is in dissent—he has made his scholarly opinions clear. He has repeatedly planted the flag for a more limited understanding of the federal power to regulate interstate commerce, as in his dissent in *Gonzales v. Raich* (2005): "Diane Monson and Angel Raich use marijuana that has never been bought or sold, that has never crossed state lines, and that has had no demonstrable effect on the national market for marijuana.... This makes a mockery of Madison's assurance to the people of New York that the 'powers delegated' to the Federal Government are 'few and defined,' while those of the States are 'numerous and indefinite.'"[51]

The justices write about the same number of majority opinions each year, but Thomas quickly established a pattern of writing many more concurrences and dissents. Part of this is his desire always to present his precise view of the law, whereas others may be satisfied to go along with the majority or lead dissenting opinion. That's why Thomas has long led the Court in solo dissents.[52] Another part of it is the work ethic that his grandfather instilled in him, typically making him the hardest-working justice as measured by pages, not just number, of opinions. Many years he has more than doubled the justice with the fewest pages.

And Justice Thomas's impact has been felt beyond the U.S. Reports, where Supreme Court opinions are printed. More than a dozen of his former clerks have gone on to become judges, with ten nominated to federal judgeships under President Trump thus far. These include such highly reputed judges as Greg Katsas and Neomi Rao of the D.C. Circuit, Jim Ho of the Fifth Circuit, David Stras of the Eighth Circuit, and Allison Jones Rushing, who was confirmed to the Fourth Circuit in her mid-30s.

In the end, there was little in common between President George H. W. Bush's two Supreme Court nominees, other than the fact that they had spent their early careers in the offices of state attorneys general who later became senators and were instrumental in their protégés' confirmation process. Bush would experience more push-back in his attempts to shape the judiciary, nominating eleven people to ten federal circuit judgeships that the Democratic-controlled Senate refused to process, including John G. Roberts Jr., who would be confirmed to the D.C. Circuit under George W. Bush. And none of these unprocessed nominations were made after July 1, 1992, the middle of the presidential election year that some people consider to be a confirmation moratorium under the apocryphal Thurmond Rule.

The Thomas fight represented the second shoe dropping after Robert Bork. But alas, there would be more shoes. "It is safe to assume that no other successful nominee to the Supreme Court will ever have to endure the firestorm Justice Clarence Thomas experienced," historian Henry J. Abraham still wrote in the last (2008) edition of his magisterial tome on the history of high court appointments.[53] He would be proven wrong a decade later, however, when the Anita Hill playbook was dusted off for use against someone whose background was very different from Clarence Thomas's. But first we had a period of relatively smooth Supreme Court nominations that belied turbulence in the battle for the judicial branch.

CHAPTER 14

Ginsburg's Pincer Movement and Breyer's Safe Pick

On June 25, 1992, Senator Biden went to the Senate floor to urge President Bush not to nominate anyone to the Supreme Court if a vacancy opened up before that fall's election. "Should a justice resign this summer and the president move to name a successor," he counseled, "a process that is already in doubt in the minds of many will become distrusted by all. Senate consideration of a nominee under these circumstances is not fair to the president, to the nominee, or to the Senate itself."[1]

Biden noted that, among the previous seven nominations, two were not confirmed and two were approved over major opposition. Under the circumstances, if Bush were to nominate someone anyway, the judiciary committee "should seriously consider not scheduling confirmation hearings on the nomination until after the political campaign season is over."[2] There was no election-year vacancy, so any showdown was averted. But that speech would resurface twenty-four years later, when President Obama made a Supreme Court nomination in the final year of his second term, which led to plenty of debate over the "Biden Rule."

The next vacancy came the following year, when Byron White, the last member of the Warren Court, announced barely a month after Bill Clinton's inauguration that he would be retiring at the end of the term. This would be the first chance for a Democratic president in twenty-five years. The new president told aides to look at his written testimony against the Bork nomination, which emphasized pragmatism and an "agenda of unity" over legal doctrine.[3] He stressed that his goal would be "unquestioned intellect, judicial temperament, broad experience," as well as aiming to appoint more women and minorities to instill public confidence in the judiciary.[4] While those sorts of neutral criteria are all well and good, in his presidential campaign Clinton let slip some ideological factors. He criticized Presidents Reagan and Bush for "selecting judges who shared their restrictive views of constitutional rights," and instead promised to "bring the federal courts back toward their traditional role as guardians of constitutional rights."[5] Candidate Clinton made public his litmus test that "I would look for someone who believed in the constitutional right to privacy... [people] who were pro-choice."[6]

Ruth Bader Ginsburg

Clinton's first choice was New York Governor Mario Cuomo, who fulfilled his requirement of having a "big heart," but also the savvy to lead the Court. Cuomo declined, choosing to stay in politics. After flirting with the idea of appointing a legal scholar like Laurence Tribe or a political philosopher like Michael Sandel—or even the first lady, Hillary Clinton!—the president looked to Senate Majority Leader George Mitchell (D-Maine), who had briefly been a district judge before being appointed to the Senate, but who also declined in favor of his political career.[7] After considering several of his cabinet secretaries, Clinton turned to more conventional candidates—federal judges.

Clinton was set to nominate Eighth Circuit Judge Richard S. Arnold, a longtime friend and supporter from Arkansas, but shied away because of health concerns and to avoid cronyism accusations. Several judges withdrew their names, and time was flying by as Clinton pursued his deliberate process.

The president seemed to settle on First Circuit Judge Stephen Breyer, a staff favorite. But Breyer had been hit by a car while biking a few days earlier, causing him to be in pain and short of breath at his brief interview. The two didn't click, with Clinton labeling Breyer "heartless." It also later came out that Breyer had a mini-"Zoë Baird problem," referring to Clinton's failed attorney general nominee, who had hired illegal aliens and not paid their Social Security taxes. Breyer had hired an elderly woman to clean his house but neglected to pay Social Security, because he thought he didn't have to because she was already a recipient of the program.[8]

On June 15, 1993, after interviewing D.C. Circuit Judge Ruth Bader Ginsburg and briefly reconsidering Cuomo—whose son Andrew, then an administration official, now governor of New York, called the president to ask him to do so—Clinton announced that Ginsburg was his nominee. She thus became the second female nominee and the first successful Jewish nominee since Abe Fortas in 1965. She would also be the last justice to date to be clearly more liberal than the justice being replaced.

Ginsburg had already served thirteen years on the D.C. Circuit and had a compelling personal story. Having lost her mother to cancer the day before her high school graduation, she excelled at Cornell and was one of nine women in her Harvard Law School class. Married to a fellow student and with a young daughter, she ended up transferring to Columbia when her husband took a job in New York, and finished tied for first in her class. Like Justice O'Connor, however, Ginsburg had a hard time finding employment due to her gender.

Justice Frankfurter denied her a clerkship, and she ended up clerking for a district judge only after famed Columbia law professor, Gerald Gunther, threatened never to send another student his way. She learned Swedish to co-author a book on Sweden's civil procedure, before getting her first academic position at Rutgers. In 1972, she moved to Columbia. That same year she co-founded the ACLU's Women's Rights Project, under whose auspices she argued six cases before the Supreme Court. She picked her battles carefully, building on successive victories and sometimes having male plaintiffs to show that gender discrimination hurt both men and women.[9]

In announcing the nomination, President Clinton highlighted three reasons why he picked her: first, her distinguished judicial career. Second, her litigation project, which made her "to the women's movement what Thurgood Marshall was to the rights of African Americans,"[10] a comparison that originated with former solicitor general and Harvard Law School Dean Erwin Griswold, and which Justice Scalia would repeat in *Time* magazine's 2015 tribute to the one hundred "most influential people."[11] Third, her ability to build consensus as a "moderate liberal."

That sense of moderation and strategy got her in hot water because just a few months earlier, in a lecture at NYU Law School, she questioned the rationale and timing of *Roe v. Wade*, blaming the Court's overbroad decision for the continued political controversy over abortion.[12] It seems amazing that anyone had doubts about Ginsburg's pro-choice commitments, but Kate Michelman, then president of the National Abortion Rights Action League, asked senators to determine "whether Judge Ginsburg will protect a woman's fundamental right to privacy, including the right to choose, under a strict scrutiny standard."[13] At her hearing, Ginsburg would say that restricting abortion "controls women and denies them full autonomy and full equality with men."[14]

In light of Ginsburg's qualifications and bipartisan support, she sailed through three days of testimony. Her methodical performance managed both to reassure liberals that her relatively restrained judicial record on the oft-technical D.C. Circuit didn't mean that she no longer shared their social-justice goals, and to satisfy conservatives that she was no wide-eyed activist. And she did so by talking a lot without saying much, except on those subjects, like abortion and gender discrimination, on which she had written. Indeed, she refined that tactic into a "pincer movement," refusing to comment on specific fact patterns because they might come before the Court and then also refusing to discuss general principles because "a judge could deal in specifics only."[15]

The judiciary committee, which now included two women, unanimously approved the nomination. A few days later, on August 3, 1993, the full Senate concurred 96–3. That overwhelming approval now seems like it's from another time, particularly for someone with a record, at least earlier in her career, of pushing the legal envelope. The main difference from the Bork and Thomas imbroglios is that, with Ginsburg, Democrats controlled both the White House and the Senate, though even that unified power wouldn't guarantee easy nominations forever.

On the high bench, Justice Ginsburg quickly joined the left of the Court, particularly on gender, race, and religion, as well as questions of federal power. In nearly all high-profile cases with ideological salience, she's either been on the short end of 5–4 dissents or joined opinions assigned to the deciding justice, typically Sandra Day O'Connor or Anthony Kennedy. That means that she's had few landmark majority opinions, the most prominent being *United States v. Virginia* (1996), where she authored the 7–1 ruling—Scalia in dissent, Thomas recused because he had a son attending the Virginia Military Institute, whose men-only admissions policy the Court held violated the Fourteenth Amendment's Equal Protection Clause.

When Ginsburg became the sole woman on the Court after Justice O'Connor's retirement, she "found her voice," with stemwinding dissents in the 2007 cases *Ledbetter v. Goodyear Tire & Rubber Company*, strictly enforcing the statute of limitations on claims of gender pay discrimination—which Congress would reverse in the first legislation signed by President Obama—and *Gonzales v. Carhart*, upholding the federal ban on partial-birth abortions.[16]

Since Justice Stevens's retirement in 2010, Justice Ginsburg has been the senior member of the Court's liberals, getting to assign the lead dissenting opinion in the 5–4 decisions that split on "conventional" ideological lines. She has used that power not only to pen key dissents, but to have her bloc speak with one voice, without separate opinions, unlike the unpredictability of the supposedly dominant conservatives.[17] Also in this last decade, Justices Breyer and Kagan have shaded to the middle on occasional pragmatic compromises. But Justice Ginsburg, together with Justice Sotomayor (Stevens's replacement), has stuck to her guns, in cases ranging from *NFIB v. Sebelius* (2012), the Obamacare constitutional challenge where Breyer and Kagan joined the conservatives to invalidate coerced Medicaid expansion, to *Masterpiece Cakeshop v. Colorado Civil Rights Commission* (2018), which found the state civil rights agency guilty of anti-religious bias in applying antidiscrimination law to a baker who wouldn't create a wedding cake for a same-sex marriage, to *Trump v. Hawaii* (2018), the travel ban case where Ginsburg and Sotomayor were the only justices who found anti-Muslim animus.

Justice Ginsburg has thus become a hero of the progressive left, gaining the unlikely moniker Notorious R.B.G. and becoming a staple of Saturday Night Live skits. Her growing collection of jabots ("neck doilies"), including a particularly striking one she uses when dissenting from the bench, has contributed to her iconic status. Her increasing visibility in that role has gotten her in hot water at least once, when in July 2016 she criticized presumptive Republican presidential nominee Donald Trump, saying that she didn't want to think about the possibility of a Trump presidency and might consider moving to New Zealand.[18]

How long can the 87-year-old justice keep it up? Having been treated for cancer four times and hospitalized for various other ailments over the years, her health is of morbid concern in these polarized times. Her trainer even wrote a book that became a local bestseller. Although progressive lawyers and activists criticized her for not retiring under President Obama, when Democrats had the Senate majority before the 2014 election, she has maintained that nobody as good as she is could be confirmed.[19]

Stephen Breyer

When Harry Blackmun announced his retirement in April 1994, President Clinton would have his second opportunity to shape the Court. Clinton continued his elusive search for political experience, making it known that his top choice was George Mitchell, who was retiring from the Senate. Mitchell demurred, wanting to shepherd the president's health care legislation. He then considered Interior Secretary Bruce Babbitt again, but concerns about his regulation of western lands that had been raised in the process to fill the previous seat remained. Although Judiciary Committee Chairman Biden assured the president that he had the votes to confirm Babbitt, Clinton feared that a contentious hearing would hurt the Democrats in both 1994 and 1996. The president saw district judge José Cabranes as "personally distant," so he decided to elevate him to the Second Circuit instead. But Clinton was mindful of the Hispanic vote in politically important states like California, Florida, and Texas, and sent his staff on a fruitless search for any other appropriate Hispanic nominee.[20]

Meanwhile, Breyer's supporters had been trying to rehabilitate him. Ted Kennedy met with Clinton and insisted that he had misjudged his former counsel. A few days later, worn down in trying to find either a politician or "diversity" pick, and eager not to have to spend more time on the vacancy, the president announced that he would nominate Stephen Breyer. Breyer got the nod despite being nowhere near the top of the short list for either the White or Blackmun vacancy. As one senior official put it, "He was the one with the fewest problems."[21] In retrospect, three factors sealed the deal in Clinton's mind: (1) Breyer's broad professional record, having worked in the Justice Department and Senate, as well as being a Harvard professor until President Carter tapped him for the bench; (2) his reputation as an amiable consensus-builder; and (3) bipartisan backing despite being a Bay Area/Bay State liberal—in part because his expertise was in the technical field of administrative law rather than constitutional law or other areas with more ideological resonance.

Senator Kennedy shepherded his former staffer's nomination through the judiciary committee, but there really wasn't much to shepherd. Having already gotten the support not only of Democratic leadership, but also of key Republicans Orrin Hatch and Strom Thurmond, Breyer's July hearings were anticlimactic. Quiet by modern standards, the questioning was more heated than what his future colleague Justice Ginsburg faced. Republicans queried the nominee's embrace of expected liberal beliefs, particularly on church-state issues, but the harshest attack came from a liberal Democrat. Ohio's Howard Metzenbaum criticized the jurist's allegedly pro-business philosophy on antitrust cases, as well as his investments in Lloyd's of London, which insures companies against pollution liability. Ralph Nader testified that Breyer was "extraordinarily one-sided" in favor of big business, while others called him "an unfeeling and elitist advo-cate for America's corporations."[22] Indeed, Breyer's non-recusal in a series of "Superfund" (hazardous waste cleanup) cases in the 1980s troubled many senators and played a key role in the eventual votes against him on the Senate floor.[23]

Despite continuing debate over his investments and other busi-ness-ethics issues, Breyer was confirmed ten days later on an 87–9 vote, with nine Republicans voting nay and two senators from each party not voting. As with Ginsburg, it's worth asking why there wasn't more opposition to such a liberal nominee. Especially since abortion was now a litmus-test issue—explicitly so given Clinton's campaign promise—and in view of Justice Thomas's treatment two years earlier. It could be that the ethical issues didn't galvanize public opinion, plus Clinton's judgment that the nominee's unique constellation of profes-sional background and interests would forestall controversy was cor-rect. Moreover, Republicans must have realized they were unlikely to get anyone "better." There was no Tony Kennedy waiting in the wings, after all.

Indeed, while Justice Breyer instantly became a member of the Stevens-Souter-Ginsburg liberal bloc, with the first two later replaced by Sotomayor and Kagan, his technocratic approach sometimes finds him as the sixth or seventh vote in the direction of compromise. In *Bush v. Gore* (2000), he and Justice Souter joined the 7–2 ruling that there was an equal protection violation in allowing different ballot-counting standards in different counties, but stuck with the liberals in dissenting from the 5–4 decision to stop a recount that couldn't have been completed before the statutory deadline. In *NFIB v. Sebe-lius* (2012), he and Justice Kagan joined the 7–2 majority in disal-lowing Obamacare's requirement that states expand Medicaid rolls if they wanted to receive *any* Medicaid funds. And in *Trump v. Hawaii* (2018), his dissent, joined by Kagan, would've remanded the travel ban for consideration of whether its waivers and exemptions operated in such a way as to show religious neutrality, instead of invalidating the policy then and there.

Justice Breyer has a pragmatic interpretive method that looks beyond text, structure, and history to the purpose of a given statutory or constitutional provision and the consequence of any given ruling on it. Apparently that's synonymous with extreme judicial restraint, at least with respect to the federal government, given that Breyer votes to uphold acts of Congress and administrative regulations more than any of his colleagues.[24] The francophile justice, whose wife is descended from British aristocracy, is also known for invoking foreign law to help explain American law, famously debating Justice Scalia on that point in 2005.[25]

A Judiciary That Looks Like America

Determined to make the judiciary "look like America," President Clinton nominated more women and racial minorities, particularly African Americans, than any of his predecessors. Nearly two thirds of those ascending to the federal bench were such "nontraditional" picks. But his selection process comprised typical Clintonian hesitancy and overthinking. This, when added to the GOP takeover of the Senate after the 1994 election, led to delays in filling seats. In all, he appointed 378 Article III judges, second only to Ronald Reagan's 383.

At the same time, Clinton had an unprecedented number of unsuccessful court of appeals nominations—twenty-four people for twenty judgeships—a sign of a gradual increase in partisan tensions and the pushing down of confirmation battles below the Supreme Court level. Interestingly, in all eight years of the Clinton presidency, only one nomination was formally rejected. Instead, and in particular once Republicans took the Senate in the 1994 elections, the judiciary committee just wouldn't process nominees with significant opposition, leading to a few withdrawals and many more returns of nominations to the White House at the end of each Congress.[26] Three unprocessed nominations were made after July 1, 2000, the traditional start of the Thurmond Rule (for those who celebrate).

Some of the more notable Clinton-era confirmation battles, carrying over into his successor's tenure, were over the Fourth Circuit, which covers Maryland, the Virginias, and the Carolinas. This court had the largest black population of any circuit, but a long streak of conservative judges, so Clinton decided to make it the cornerstone of his diversification efforts. Powerful North Carolina Senator Jesse Helms refused to return blue slips—the form where a home-state senator indicates an opinion about a judicial nominee—while Chief Judge J. Harvie Wilkinson testified before Congress that his court's workload didn't justify filling the vacancies. Part of this opposition was no doubt retaliation for the Democratic stonewalling of two George H. W. Bush nominees, and this gamesmanship continues to this day.

Beyond that one court, the opposition to Clinton's attempt to transform the judiciary took on new urgency once Republicans regained the Senate. In addition to insisting on positive blue slips from at least one home-state senator, there were delays in scheduling hearings and floor debates. Senator Leahy called it a "pocket filibuster," which is a non sequitur but conveys the frustration of the moment.[27] And the number of roll-call votes—as opposed to uncounted voice votes—increased with every Congress. Democrats would repeatedly mention the slow-down of Clinton's circuit nominees during the controversy over George W. Bush's judges.

But there were only three cloture votes (a motion to stop debate and proceed to a final vote) during the entire eight years on nominees who all ended up confirmed. For all the hand-wringing about

Republican obstruction, when President Clinton departed the White House, he left about thirty fewer judicial vacancies than George H. W. Bush had four years earlier. Clinton appointed a record number of district judges, as well as more circuit judges than anyone before or since other than Ronald Reagan.[28] So we can look back on what then seemed to be a tense period as a halcyon era of good feelings compared to what came next.

CHAPTER 15

Filibusters and Umpires

With Democrats already upset about the slowdown in lower-court confirmations over the last two years of the Clinton presidency, *Bush v. Gore* put them—and the progressive legal establishment—on war footing. And the battlefield was about as even as it could be. Although George W. Bush narrowly won the 2000 election, Democrats picked up five Senate seats, deadlocking the upper chamber 50–50, with Vice President Dick Cheney as the tiebreaker.

The new president didn't rush ahead with any judicial nominations. Instead, he focused on his cabinet and other executive appointments, and tried to negotiate a new détente with the opposition party. It wouldn't be easy. Less than a month into the Bush presidency, storied Yale law professor Bruce Ackerman published an article urging the Senate not to confirm any new justices. "Forty senators should simply make it plain that they will block all Supreme Court nominations until the next presidential election," Ackerman wrote, putting a finer point on it.[1]

Circuit Court Filibusters

As President Bush was set to announce his first wave of judicial nominees, Senate Democrats held a retreat in rural Pennsylvania to strategize. Two more giants from legal academia, Laurence Tribe and Cass Sunstein, suggested they play hard ball. Minority Leader Tom Daschle told his caucus to avoid endorsing *any* Bush nominee. At a time when "blue slip" policy—the ability of a home-state senator to hold up a nomination—was up in the air, Judiciary Committee Ranking Member Pat Leahy sent a letter to the White House, signed by all committee Democrats, insisting on a greater role in judicial selection.

Against that backdrop, and with no Supreme Court vacancies for four years, President Bush announced his first eleven circuit court nominees on May 9, 2001. "Every judge I appoint will be a person who clearly understands the role of a judge is to interpret the law, not to legislate from the bench," he said, noting that he "sought and received advice from senators of both parties" and was submitting these nominations "in good faith."[2] It was a group the *New York Times* said was "notable for its inclusion of women and minorities,"[3] and included John G. Roberts Jr. and Terrence Boyle (both of whom had been nominated by the first President Bush), Miguel Estrada (the first Hispanic nominated to the D.C. Circuit), Barrington Parker (who had been appointed to his district judgeship by President Clinton), and Roger Gregory (already serving on a Clinton recess appointment). Although Leahy initially made positive noises about the slate, Senator Chuck Schumer (D-N.Y.) accused Bush of "trying to create the most ideological bench in the history of the nation." Moreover, Schumer said, "Until the blue slip issue is resolved, our intention is not to move forward with any judges."[4]

Fifteen days later, while those nominees, and others who were named the following week, began their confirmation dance, Vermont

Senator Jim Jeffords threw a monkey wrench by becoming an independent and caucusing with the Democrats. It was the only time in history that a party switch led to a change in Senate control, and it effected a seismic shift in the judicial contretemps. The only nominees from the May 9 list who were confirmed in 2001 were the two Clinton-associated peace offerings, Parker and Gregory, as well as Edith Brown Clement. Only three other appellate nominees were confirmed that year. District nominees proved easier to confirm, though delays still pushed most of their confirmation to the last few months of the year. This despite Leahy's having said during the 2000 election that "although we are different parties, I have agreed with Gov. George Bush, who has said that in the Senate a nominee ought to get a vote, up or down, within 60 days."[5]

The following year saw the process loosen, perhaps out of a post-9/11 deference to a wartime president. Eleven circuit judges were confirmed, including two from the original May 9 list. Sixty-one district judges were also confirmed, which was the fourth-highest in one year.

Republicans regained the Senate in the 2002 elections—one of the rare times in modern history that the incumbent president's party gained seats at the midterms—achieving a bare 51–49 majority. No longer able to block nominees in committee, Democrats began to filibuster, denying the sixty votes needed for "cloture," to end debate and proceed to a vote. On February 12, 2003, Miguel Estrada became the first lower-court nominee ever to fail a cloture vote, despite having enough declared votes to be confirmed. That September, after seven more failed cloture votes and twenty-eight months in limbo, Estrada withdrew. President Bush called Estrada's treatment "disgraceful," noting his excellent qualifications, compelling personal story as an immigrant from Honduras, and bipartisan support.[6] It later came out, from internal judiciary committee minority staff memos that had been saved on a hard drive accessible by majority staff, that the main reason

Democrats made him the focus of their opposition was to deny Bush the opportunity of naming the first Hispanic Supreme Court justice.

Nine other circuit nominees would also be filibustered, generally those considered to be the most ideological and intellectual, two of whom also later withdrew their nominations.

In November 2003, Senate Republicans staged a 30-hour overnight talk-athon, a sort of anti-filibuster filibuster, to protest the treatment of the blocked judicial nominees. They also began to threaten to change Senate rules to eliminate the filibuster for judges by requiring only fifty-one votes for cloture, a procedure that Senator Trent Lott (R-Miss.) coined as the "nuclear option."[7] With only a two-vote majority, however, they were in a weak position to implement the maneuver. One academic commentator wrote of the worsening atmosphere going back to the Clinton years and beyond: "The recent withdrawal of George W. Bush's nomination of Miguel Estrada to the D.C. Circuit, bemoaned by Senate Republicans as the first-ever successful filibuster of an appeals court nomination, underlines a growing sense that the federal judicial appointments process has degenerated, in the words of one senator, into a vicious cycle of 'payback on top of payback on top of payback.'"[8]

On October 7, 2004, a month before the presidential election, Senate Democrats issued a statement arguing that they weren't obstructing nominees.[9] Although district court nominees were being confirmed at a higher rate than under Presidents Reagan and Clinton, President Bush had less success with circuit nominees (67 percent) than either Reagan (85 percent) or Clinton (71 percent) in their first terms.

Bush's 2004 reelection also saw the president's party gain in the Senate, giving Republicans a 55–45 edge. Filibusters continued, however, with Majority Leader Bill Frist (Tenn.) edging closer to the nuclear option, even as Judiciary Committee Chairman Arlen Specter (Penn.) criticized the tactic and suggested that his party might not have the votes for it. On May 23, 2005, seven Republicans and seven Democrats, the most moderate members of their respective caucuses, worked out a deal, good for that 2005–06 Congress only, to end the filibusters of three of the seven remaining affected nominees. The Democrats in this "Gang of 14" agreed not to filibuster the future except in "extraordinary circumstances," while the Republicans agreed not to use the nuclear option. Frist criticized the deal as falling short of giving each nominee an up-or-down vote, while Minority Leader Harry Reid (Nev.)—who would use the nuclear option himself eight years later—hailed it as "good news for every American."[10] As a direct result of the deal, the two filibustered nominees not mentioned in it were confirmed, as was the man nominated to replace Estrada after his withdrawal. There would be no further filibusters under President Bush—not even for White House insider Brett Kavanaugh, who was confirmed to the D.C. Circuit with fewer than sixty votes in May 2006—except for an aborted attempt to stop a Supreme Court nominee (see below).

John G. Roberts Jr.

After President Bush's reelection, the composition of the Court had been unchanged for more than a decade, the second-longest such period in American history. Chief Justice Rehnquist was widely expected to retire, due both to age (80) and his battle with thyroid cancer, although there were also rumors of Justice Sandra Day O'Connor's possible retirement. While younger than Rehnquist, she had served on the Court almost twenty-five years, and wanted to spend time with her husband, who was suffering from Alzheimer's. Before deciding to retire, O'Connor consulted Rehnquist on his plans, to avoid having two vacancies at the same time. Being assured that her longtime friend had no intention of leaving the Court that year, right after the conclusion of the 2004–05 term, O'Connor sent a letter to the White House announcing her retirement "effective upon the nomination and confirmation of my successor."[11]

This was a prime opportunity for President Bush to put his mark on the Court, replacing a centrist with someone more conservative. Having waited five and a half years for the occasion, the administration was prepared. There were about a dozen serious candidates, including nine circuit judges and an intriguing outside-the-box trio: Senator John Cornyn (R-Tex.); Attorney General Alberto Gonzales (who had also served Bush as White House counsel)—both of whom had also served on the Texas Supreme Court—and PepsiCo General Counsel Larry D. Thompson (who had been deputy AG in Bush's first term). Republican elites reacted positively to most of these names, but conservatives opposed Gonzales for what they feared were liberal proclivities. Democrats, meanwhile, threatened to filibuster any "extreme" nominee.[12]

On July 12, Bush met for breakfast at the White House with the Senate's party and judiciary committee leaders—Frist, Reid, Specter, and Leahy. The Democrats suggested the names of three "moderate" Hispanic judges whom they could accept: Ricardo Hinojosa, a Reagan-appointed district court judge in Texas; recently Bush-appointed Fifth Circuit Judge Edward Prado; and Clinton-appointed Second Circuit Judge Sonia Sotomayor, who had been named to the district court by the first President Bush in a deal with New York senators. These three were quickly dismissed as being offered in bad faith because they were too liberal.[13] That same day, First Lady Laura Bush indicated on the *Today* show, in an interview while she was traveling in South Africa, a preference for her husband to nominate a woman. A surprised President Bush said he would be open to hearing her advice when she returned from her trip.[14]

The president moved quickly, interviewing D.C. Circuit Judge John Roberts, Third Circuit Judge Samuel Alito, Fourth Circuit

Judges Michael Luttig and J. Harvie Wilkinson, and Fifth Circuit Judge Edith Brown Clement. Roberts had been underwhelming in an earlier interview with Cheney, Gonzales, White House Counsel Harriet Miers, and others, playing his cards close to the vest and not admitting an overarching legal philosophy.[15] In the days that followed, speculation was rampant that Judge Clement had the edge; replacing a woman with a woman while moving the Court in a more conservative direction offered the president a twofer—but ultimately Bush went with his gut instinct of what a justice was like.

In a primetime ceremony broadcast live across the nation on July 19, 2005, President Bush announced that his nominee was John Roberts, who had been a highly regarded Supreme Court litigator before becoming a judge. Roberts, who was born in Buffalo and moved to Indiana as a child, had graduated with honors from Harvard College and Law School, going on to clerk for esteemed Second Circuit Judge Henry Friendly and then-Justice Rehnquist. Besides his sterling professional credentials, he had established his conservative—or at least Republican—bona fides. Roberts worked for Reagan's attorney general, William French Smith, in the White House counsel's office, and as principal deputy solicitor general. He was confirmed to the D.C. Circuit by voice vote in 2003, although three Democrats voted against him in committee.

Recognizing that Roberts was a boy scout with no professional or personal flaws, Democrats and liberal interest groups knew that they would have to attack him for being conservative. There was speculation about Roberts's membership in the Federalist Society, the conservative/libertarian legal network. "So what? What are we talking about here: the Communist Party? The Ku Klux Klan?" retorted the Cato Institute's Roger Pilon.[16] It was an early indication of the role the then-35,000-member—now double that—organization of law students, lawyers, professors, and judges plays in the nation's legal life, countering the left-leaning legal academy and ABA. Indeed, when President Bush announced that the ABA would not be given nominees' names to pre-screen, critics worried that the mantle had effectively passed to the Federalist Society.

For their part, conservatives became concerned when it came out that, while in private practice, Roberts had advised gay rights advocates on the *Romer v. Evans* litigation, which culminated in a 1996 Supreme Court decision invalidating a Colorado constitutional provision extending antidiscrimination law to sexual orientation.[17] Representatives of the Congress of Racial Equality, the National Center for Neighborhood Enterprise, Project 21, the Center for New Black Leadership, and some members of the U.S. Commission on Civil Rights held a press conference to emphasize that liberal advocacy groups didn't speak for all minority communities.[18]

But then fate played its hand: on September 3, less than a week before hearings were due to begin, Chief Justice Rehnquist succumbed to his illness. Former clerk John Roberts would serve as a pallbearer for his casket as it was placed onto the Lincoln catafalque to lie in state in the Supreme Court's great hall.

Rehnquist's death ended the longest period of unchanged Supreme Court personnel since the bench was fixed at nine seats in 1869: exactly eleven years and one month since Justice Breyer received his commission. Having waited five and a half years for a Supreme Court vacancy to fill, Bush now had two in two months.

The president didn't hesitate. Although the pool of serious contenders for this vacancy was considered to be somewhat different than that for O'Connor's—less pressure to pick a woman, the possibility of elevating Justice Scalia—within thirty-six hours Bush announced that he was withdrawing John Roberts's nomination to be associate justice and tapping him for the center seat. It was a strategic choice. He avoided the sort of fight that would've attended a Scalia elevation or the nomination of someone with a longer record of conservative juris-prudence, like Jones or Luttig. And it was at a time when Bush was politically weakened by criticism of his Iraq policy and the govern-ment's response to Hurricane Katrina. It also prevented the Court's starting its new term, set to begin in less than a month, without a confirmed chief justice. Given that preparations for Roberts's hearing were already well under way, it was pushed back by only a week.

Roberts put on a clinic, emphasizing his dedication to precedent and restraint, and to a limited role for the judiciary. Judicial "mod-esty" became his watchword, likening the role of a judge to that of a baseball umpire, to "call balls and strikes and not to pitch or bat," or write the rules of the game.[19] And this wasn't some "confirmation conversion": memos from his time in the Reagan White House showed that he was critical of the Court intervention in too many cases.[20] Like Justice Ginsburg, Roberts would demur from respond-ing on specific issues, while also not getting too deep into abstract theory. It was a strategy that a young Roberts had suggested to San-dra Day O'Connor ahead of her 1981 hearings. Roberts endorsed a right to privacy but wouldn't say how it applied to specific issues, noting simply that *Planned Parenthood v. Casey*, which reaffirmed *Roe v. Wade*, "is a precedent of the court that is entitled to respect under the principles of *stare decisis*."[21] He likewise allowed that reli-gious faith would play no role in his rulings, that he would look to the law, not the Bible. Although Democrats were "pledging to subject Judge Roberts to more intensive scrutiny than they had so far," he likely had an easier time replacing the conservative Rehnquist than he would have had he been replacing the moderate O'Connor, regard-less of the significance of the chief justiceship.[22]

The judiciary committee approved the nomination 13–5, with three Democrats, including Ranking Member Leahy, joining all the Republicans in the affirmative. A week later, September 29,

2005—the Thursday before the first Monday in October that's the traditional start of the new Supreme Court term—John Roberts was confirmed as the nation's seventeenth chief justice. The vote was 78–22, with all 55 Republicans and half of the 44 Democrats (plus Independent Jim Jeffords, who caucused with the Democrats) in favor. Among the no votes were Minority Leader Reid, Joe Biden, John Kerry, Hillary Clinton, Barack Obama, and Chuck Schumer.

Roberts thus became the youngest chief justice (50) since his hero John Marshall. At first he seemed understandably daunted by his new responsibilities, but it didn't take long for a man who had planned for this moment seemingly all his life to settle in. And it didn't take long for him to make his mark. To the extent that Roberts's project is to have the Court speak more often "with one voice," his first term saw a marked increase in unanimous decisions: 45 percent, up from 21 percent the previous year and a five-year average of just over 25 percent.[23]

The Roberts Court hasn't hit that level of agreement every term, and some terms a high rate of unanimity has been complemented by a relatively high rate of 5–4 decisions. But the statistics do bear out the fact that, if you go below the highest-profile culture-war cases, this Court is more united now than it has been since the days of FDR. Of course, those "big" cases matter, both for public confidence in the Court and for the development of the law. The 2013–14 term, for example, saw a record two-thirds of the cases decided unanimously in the judgment. Many of those, however, had strident concurring opinions that were dissents in all but name, essentially accusing the Roberts-led majority of splitting the baby in a way the law doesn't allow.[24]

Even beyond the behind-the-scenes leadership to assign opinions strategically and orchestrate narrow decisions when possible, Chief Justice Roberts personally practices what he preaches, writing fewer opinions than all of his colleagues. When he's in dissent, someone else is typically writing that opinion—and to this day he has *never* issued a solo dissent.[25] As one might expect, he has generally been in the majority more than any justice not named Anthony Kennedy. With Kennedy's replacement by Brett Kavanaugh, Roberts should lay undisputed claim to being the biggest winner, although the rookie justice pipped the chief in his first term.[26]

But that doesn't mean Roberts was, or has become post-Kennedy, either a "swing" vote, going back and forth depending on the political winds or what he had for breakfast, or a moderate. It's readily apparent that the chief justice has a conservative judicial philosophy—see his record on abortion, gay rights, and pretty much everything except Obamacare—but it's a conservatism of restraint and minimalism, rather than originalism or any other interpretive theory. "If it is not necessary to decide more to a case, then in my view it is necessary not to decide more to a case," Roberts explained in a speech towards the end of his first term. "Division should not be artificially suppressed, but the rule of law benefits from a broader agreement."[27]

Where he has supported "big" changes in the law, those have been preceded by small moves in that direction. *Citizens United v. FEC* (2010), which threw out the restriction on using corporate and union funds for independent political speech, with Roberts as the deciding vote, was preceded by several campaign-finance cases rejecting justifications for various other parts of the 2002 Bipartisan Campaign Reform Act. *Shelby County v. Holder* (2013), which invalidated the "coverage formula" for determining which jurisdictions had to "preclear" their electoral rules with the Justice Department under Section 5 of the Voting Rights Act was preceded by *Northwest Austin Municipal Utility District No. 1 v. Holder* (2010), in which Roberts raised concerns about Section 5's continued constitutional viability.

In other cases, he took the lead in achieving a conservative result, as in *Parents Involved in Community Schools v. Seattle School District No. 1* (2007), where the 5–4 Court invalidated two school districts' use of race to assign students to different schools. "The way to stop discrimination on the basis of race is to stop discriminating on the basis of race," Roberts concluded his opinion, in a part not joined by Justice Kennedy.[28]

Of course, Roberts is most famous (or infamous) for his role in upholding the Affordable Care Act, first against constitutional attack in *NFIB v. Sebelius* (2012), and then statutory attack in *King v. Burwell* (2015). In both cases, the chief justice attempted to show judicial restraint or even "modesty" by merely tweaking Congress's work rather than striking it down.

Unfortunately, he failed on his own terms. As the four *NFIB* dissenters wrote, "The Court regards its strained statutory interpretation as judicial modesty. It is not. It amounts instead to a vast judicial overreaching. It creates a debilitated, inoperable version of healthcare regulation that Congress did not enact and the public does not expect."[29] The chief's judicial passivism, combined with the activism of the four liberal justices who saw no judicially enforceable limits on federal power, created a Frankenstein's monster. It's certainly gratifying to those of us who were involved in that fight that a majority of justices rejected the government's assertion of power to compel commerce in order to regulate it. But justifying a mandate with accompanying penalty for noncompliance under the taxing power doesn't rehabilitate the statute's constitutional abuses. It merely creates a "unicorn tax," a creature of no known constitutional provenance that will never be seen again. And by letting Obamacare survive in such a dubious manner, Roberts undermined the trust people have that courts are impartial arbiters rather than political actors.[30]

The sad thing about this episode is that the chief didn't have to do what he did to "save the Court." For one thing, Obamacare was at that point highly unpopular—particularly its individual mandate, which even a majority of Democrats thought was unconstitutional.[31] For another, Roberts only damaged his own reputation by making this move after warnings from pundits and politicians that striking down the law would be "conservative judicial activism." Had the Court sent Obamacare back to the drawing board, it would have been just the sort of thing for which the Court needs all that accrued respect and gravitas. Instead, we had a strategic decision dressed up in legal robes, judicially enacting a new law and feeding public cynicism.

With Justice Kennedy's retirement, Roberts is the first chief justice to be the median vote in half a century. What we have now is truly the Roberts Court: in the 2019–20 term, the chief justice was in the majority in 97 percent of cases, including all but one of the 5–4 splits. And while it's possible that Roberts might be voting differently had he become an associate justice instead of the chief, he was never a Scalia or Thomas (or Gorsuch) type to begin with. Conservative, yes; originalist, no.

Anyone can judge the success of Chief Justice Roberts's project to depoliticize the judiciary; tacking left and right while issuing narrow decisions, even if marginally improving public perception, does nothing to address an underlying dynamic that's driven by irreconcilable legal philosophies.

Harriet Miers

Four days after John Roberts was sworn in, President Bush announced his pick for the other vacancy. The new nominee was Harriet Miers, the White House counsel who, in a Dick Cheney-like situation, was heading up the nomination committee. That search had added several female judges to those previously considered, but the prize ultimately went to Miers herself. A Bush loyalist from Dallas, she had previously been deputy chief of staff and staff secretary, which controls information flow to the president, a post in which she was succeeded by Kavanaugh. At a time of escalating tensions, when Democrats threatened to filibuster anyone they deemed too conservative for O'Connor's swing seat, Harry Reid had recommended Miers and said that "the Supreme Court would benefit from the addition of a justice who has real experience as a practicing lawyer."[32] Senators Specter and Leahy, meanwhile, had urged the president to consider candidates outside the federal judiciary.[33]

The sixty-year-old nominee certainly had a successful career, but it was largely as a corporate litigator and local leader—the first woman president of the Dallas Bar Association and Texas Bar, as well as a term on the Dallas City Council—rather than Supreme Court advocate or judge. She also had a different academic pedigree than we had come to expect, having attended both college and law school at Southern Methodist University rather than an Ivy League or "top 14" law school. This background led to attacks over qualifications, which, when combined with her close ties to Bush, who had been a personal client and who had appointed her to the Texas Lottery Commission before taking her to the White House, drew charges of cronyism. The White House pointed out that forty of 109 justices hadn't had any judicial experience when they were appointed, including such 20th-century luminaries as Louis Brandeis, Robert Jackson, Earl Warren, Lewis Powell, and Bill Rehnquist. In addition, ten of the thirty-four justices appointed since 1933 had been members of the administration, again including Jackson and Rehnquist.

Although Miers was, like Bush, an evangelical Christian, and had taken on the ABA over its decision to take a pro-choice stance without a membership vote, conservatives were concerned that she had no real record. Pundits who expressed serious reservations included Pat Buchanan, Ann Coulter, Charles Krauthammer, Rush Limbaugh, and Ramesh Ponnuru. "For this we need a *conservative* president?" asked George Will.[34] Former Bush speechwriter David Frum called it an "unforced error,"[35] while former Reagan speechwriter Peggy

Noonan labeled it a "misstep" that didn't make sense as either policy or politics.[36] Robert Bork wrote a *Wall Street Journal* op-ed to decry a "stealth candidate" with no record on originalism and castigate President Bush for being "like his father ... indifferent if not actively hostile, to conservative values."[37] In the face of this opposition, President Bush's response was essentially, "Trust me."

As Miers went about the typical rounds nominees make before their hearings—meetings with senators, "murder boards" of live questions, other preparations for the harsh spotlight—she did not do herself any favors. When Senator Leahy asked who her favorite justice was, she said, inexplicably "Warren,"[38] presumably meaning the moderate conservative Burger rather than Earl Warren, hero of the left, but still not an answer anyone had ever given. She apparently told Senator Schumer that she'd have to "bone up" on constitutional law.[39] In mid-October, the judiciary committee asked Miers to redo her nominee questionnaire after members complained that her answers were "inadequate," "insufficient," and "insulting."[40] Ultimately, Miers's abysmal performance at prep sessions led Chief of Staff Andy Card to urge Miers to withdraw.[41] Republicans had wanted the appointment squared away by Thanksgiving, so the hearings were less than three weeks away. She just wouldn't make it. On the morning of October 27, 2005, she walked into the Oval Office and handed President Bush a letter, which he accepted with regret. She became the first Supreme Court nominee withdrawn since LBJ's Fortas/Thornberry fiasco—not counting Douglas Ginsburg, whose name wasn't formally submitted to the Senate—and the last one before that was in the Grant administration.

Samuel Alito

Bush moved quickly to replace Miers, returning to the list that she herself had prepared. The president's task was to placate his conservative base and leading influence-makers, while also not opening up a hornet's nest among Democrats. He considered four judges who had been previously considered, solid conservatives who would be easily accepted by those who had been up in arms about Miers. It took him just two days to go with the man who had been Miers's first choice, Samuel Alito. Bush announced his nomination on October 31, 2005, saying that Alito "understands judges are to interpret the laws, not to impose their preferences or priorities on the people."[42]

Alito was the anti-Miers. A New Jersey native whose father had immigrated from Italy, he graduated *summa cum laude* from Princeton, where he had jokingly written in his yearbook that he "intends to go to law school and eventually to warm a seat on the Supreme Court."[43] Alito graduated from Yale Law School a year behind Clarence Thomas and became an assistant U.S. attorney under Maryanne Trump Berry, who would later be his judicial colleague. He then spent four years as an assistant to Solicitor General Rex Lee, where he lost only two Supreme Court cases. After two years as a deputy assistant attorney general in the Justice Department's elite Office of Legal Counsel, and just ten years out of law school, Alito became the U.S. attorney for New Jersey. In 1990 he was unanimously confirmed to the Third Circuit.

Judge Alito's fifteen and a half years on the bench gave him more judicial experience than any high court nominee in the previous seventy years. There was no doubt about his competence and no charges of cronyism for this serious, sober jurist. At the same time, his conservative record, as both a judge and prosecutor, made him a target for liberal organizations. The ACLU came out against him, only the third time it had done so, citing concerns over civil liberties at a time when the Bush administration was embroiled in a debate over warrantless surveillance and enemy combatants.[44] NARAL Pro-Choice America sounded the *Roe v. Wade* alarm. The Democrats' next presidential nominee, freshman senator Barack Obama, said that Bush had "wasted an opportunity to appoint a consensus nominee,"[45] while their last nominee, John Kerry, asked, "Has the right wing now forced a weakened President to nominate a divisive justice in the mold of Antonin Scalia?"[46] Some in the press had taken to calling the nominee "Scalito," based on nothing but the fact that they were both Italian-American conservative jurists.

Hearings were set for the second week of January. The White House had wanted a confirmation by Christmas, but Alito's long judicial paper trail made that impossible. This processing delay allowed activist groups like Alliance for Justice and People for the American Way to mount well-funded opposition campaigns, though Senate Democrats realized that, with Republicans still in control, their only hope of stopping Alito would be to filibuster him. It would be a tough assignment, particularly given the Gang of 14 standard requiring "extraordinary circumstances" and the ABA's again giving Alito a unanimous "well qualified" rating.

The hearing began on January 9, with three days of questioning starting the following day. Unlike Bork, Alito was a cooperative respondent, soft-spoken and engaging, yet following what Brett Kavanaugh would later call the "nominee precedent" of not answering on specifics. At one point, Specter referred to *Roe v. Wade* as a "super-duper precedent." Alito explained that the difference between the freedom of speech and right to abortion is that the former appears explicitly in the Constitution, while for the latter, the key word is a more general "liberty."[47]

Alito was questioned on his alleged membership in a college alumni group that had been formed to oppose coeducation and affirmative action in the wake of Princeton's ROTC building being burned down by anti-war activists. He had no recollection and his name didn't appear on any membership lists. When Republicans expressed disapproval of how the nominee was being treated—"Are you a bigot?" Lindsey Graham (R-S.C.) asked, mocking the Democrats' attack—Alito's wife Martha Ann burst into tears and left the hear-ing.[48] Senator Durbin pressed Alito to comment on John Roberts's testimony that *Roe v. Wade* was "settled law." Alito disagreed, saying that the issue could return to the Court, but explaining, "When a decision is challenged and reaffirmed, it increases its value. The more times it happens, the more respect it has."[49]

The committee split on party lines for the first time since Louis Brandeis in 1916, approving Alito's nomination 10–8. Chances for a successful filibuster seemed remote, but John Kerry pressed for one while at the World Economic Forum in Davos. The White House made light of this gambit, with Press Secretary Scott McClellan remarking, "I think even for a senator, it takes some pretty serious yodeling to call for a filibuster from a five-star ski resort in the Swiss Alps."[50] Cloture was easily invoked 72–25, although a majority of Democrats voted to sustain the filibuster, including party leaders Reid and Durbin, plus Biden, Clinton, Schumer, and Obama—who a decade later expressed regret for this vote. The next day, January 31, 2005, Alito was confirmed 58–42, with four Democrats in favor and one Republican against, Lin-coln Chafee (R.I.), who later switched parties.

Alito became a reliable conservative vote—a big shift from O'Connor—but one different than Justice Scalia or Thomas. Reflect-ing his prosecutorial past, he's the closest thing to a "law and order" conservative the Court has had in some time. Where Scalia was the criminal defendant's best friend on Fourth and Sixth Amendment cases—and Gorsuch is downright libertarian—Alito is more likely to defer to police. He's also less likely to support certain free speech claims, as in *United States v. Stevens* (2010) and *Snyder v. Phelps* (2011), where he dissented alone in cases on animal "crush" videos and funeral protests, respectively.

At the same time, he's been the Court's leader in protecting work-ers' First Amendment rights. Alito authored 5–4 opinions in a trio of cases that chipped away at, and in *Janus v. AFSCME* (2018) finally overturned, *Abood v. Detroit Board of Education* (1977), which allowed states to give unions the power to charge nonmembers "agency fees" for the "benefits" of their collective bargaining. A couple of other notable Alito opinions were *McDonald v. City of Chicago* (2010), extending to the states the individual right to keep and bear arms that the Court had found to be protected by the Second Amendment, and *Burwell v. Hobby Lobby Stores* (2014), holding that the federal Religious Freedom Restoration Act allowed closely held corporations not to pay for certain contraceptive coverage, contrary to an Obamacare regulation.

Because of Justice Alito's consistent jurisprudence, having a different conservative in that seat would've been unlikely to make a substantial impact on the Court's rulings, except possibly in elevating originalism more to the forefront. Had, however, Harriett Miers or someone else with a less-developed record of judicial or intellectual writings been confirmed in 2005–06, it's likely that a number of the Court's closer decisions may have gone the other way.

Back to the Lower Courts

Later in 2006, a new controversy arose over three circuit nominees who had not been specifically mentioned in the Gang of 14 deal but were still subject to its provisions. These nominations were returned to the White House ahead of the Senate's annual August recess. They were all renominated, but again no action was taken before the break for the midterm elections, after which Chairman Specter declined to process the nominees during the lame duck session.

The Gang of 14 deal expired in January 2007, but the Democrats now had a 51–49 Senate majority anyway. President Bush didn't resubmit some of his more controversial candidates, but the

Democrats still blocked several nominees without resorting to fili-buster, typically by not giving them a hearing. At the same time, there was less confirmation drama than there had been, and more com-promise candidates. Only two of ten circuit nominees received any no votes in 2007–08, compared to six of sixteen in 2005–07, and the last two years of Bush's term also saw many more district judges confirmed (fifty-eight) than in the previous two years (thirty-five). In September 2008, Senator Leahy referenced the Thurmond Rule of not confirming judicial nominees in the months leading up to a presidential election, but in the context of making exceptions to it. As it happened, judges were confirmed after July 1, ten of them by unanimous consent in September.

If a justice had retired during this time, it would have been easy for Democrats to block a replacement in committee, or by a party-line vote on the Senate floor. No vacancy arose, but Senator Schumer still declared in July 2007 that the Senate should only confirm another Bush justice in "extraordinary circumstances," because the high court was "dangerously out of balance."[51] This affirmation of the Biden Rule would come back to bite the Democrats.

CHAPTER 16

The Wise Latina and the Nuclear Senate

B arack Obama was one of twenty-two Democrats who voted against Chief Justice John Roberts, citing doubts over the nominee's "heart" in cases about racial discrimination or the right to privacy. The freshman senator from Illinois explained that 95 percent of cases can be decided based on precedent or standard rules of constitutional or statutory construction "so that both a Scalia and a Ginsburg will arrive at the same place most of the time," but the remaining cases "can only be determined on the basis of one's deepest values, one's core concerns, one's broader perspectives on how the world works, and the depth and breadth of one's empathy...in those difficult cases, the critical ingredient is supplied by what is in the judge's heart."[1]

He would elaborate on this "empathy" standard as a presidential candidate, saying that "we need somebody who's got the heart—the empathy—to recognize what it's like to be a young teenage mom. The empathy to understand what it's like to be poor or African-American or gay or disabled or old—and that's the criteria by which I'll be selecting my judges."[2] An exit poll released the day after the 2008 election showed that 53 percent of voters preferred judges "who will apply the law the same to each person regardless of an individual's background, cultural or economic circumstance"—which was how losing candidate John McCain answered the same question—while only 43 percent preferred Obama's formulation.[3] That result suggests that judges were less important in an election held in the teeth of the Great Recession.

But Obama would be true to his word. As president he would value judicial nominees' "lived experience," even over ideology. Even more than Bill Clinton, he would seek out racial and gender—and now sexual-orientation—diversity above all else, including academic qualifications and other objective measures of merit.[4] Only 25 percent of his circuit and 30 percent of district court nominees were white males, as compared to 52 and 52 for Clinton, and 64 and 67 for George W. Bush. They were all liberal-progressive in some sense, but more than finding the antidote to Republican presidents' conservative-originalist vanguard, Obama focused on what Clinton would've called a bench that "looks like America."

That concept would extend to his Supreme Court nominees, the first two of which would come in his first two years, as they had for Clinton. Obama's team was already preparing for any vacancies during their transition. John Paul Stevens was pushing 90, while David Souter, a spry 69, had expressed a desire to return to New Hampshire. Given Justice O'Connor's retirement three years earlier, NPR's Nina Totenberg reported before the election that "observers of the Supreme Court agree about one thing: The next nominee is likely to be a woman."[5]

Sonia Sotomayor

In mid-April 2009, Justice Souter notified the White House that he would be departing at the term's end. He made it official with a

May 1 letter to the president, who made an unscheduled appearance at that day's press briefing to announce the news. Given the relative youth of the recent GOP appointments, there was strong incentive to pick someone younger, with Obama "looking for a justice who will be an intellectual force on the court for many years to come."[6]

About a week into the process, the White House had a nine-person list, with the leading candidates being Second Circuit Judge Sonia Sotomayor, Seventh Circuit Judge Diane Wood, and Solicitor General Elena Kagan. Amid a flurry of speculation, the White House tried to keep interest groups quiet as it went about its deliberations, but the ultimate contenders didn't make progressive hearts race. Part of that is President Obama's penchant for avoiding "drama." "Would I like to be on the Supreme Court?" Stanford law professor and self-described "snarky" liberal Pamela Karlan asked before answering her own question. "You bet I would. But not enough to have trimmed my sails for half a lifetime."[7]

But part of it is the Democratic establishment's recognition that the role of the courts, for their purposes, is different than it was in the 1960s and '70s. Candidate Obama himself had said that, even as several Warren Court justices were his heroes, "that doesn't necessarily mean that I think their judicial philosophy is appropriate for today.... In fact, I would be troubled if you had that same kind of activism in circumstances today."[8] In his view, social change was supposed to be driven by the political process, because judicial tools are inapt for addressing modern society's problems. "The Warren court heroically took on entrenched systems that were utterly inconsistent with constitutional equality and fairness," explained Duke law professor Walter Dellinger, who had been acting solicitor general under President Clinton. "But that is history.... Judicial power is now often used to strike down or limit progressive measures adopted by Congress or the states."[9]

On May 26, 2009, the president announced that he was going
with Sotomayor, who had been favored from the start. In making the
announcement, he emphasized that she had "worked at almost every
level of our judicial system, providing her with a depth of experience
and a breadth of perspective that will be invaluable as a Supreme
Court justice."[10] The nominee was the embodiment of the American
dream, having grown up in a Bronx public housing project as the
daughter of poor Puerto Rican parents before becoming high school
valedictorian and graduating Princeton *summa cum laude*. She
admitted that affirmative action helped her get in and that she was
initially unprepared, but worked hard and took full advantage of the
opportunities presented to her.

After a few years as a hard-working assistant district attorney,
Sotomayor went into private practice. She was also tapped by Gov-
ernor Mario Cuomo to serve on the New York State Mortgage
Agency, and by Mayor Ed Koch on the New York City Campaign
Finance Board. Under an agreement between New York Senators
Daniel Patrick Moynihan (D) and Alfonse D'Amato (R), President
George H. W. Bush nominated her to the Southern District of New
York. She became the youngest judge on the court (thirty-eight) and
the first Hispanic federal judge in New York state. In that role, she
ended the 1994 Major League Baseball strike on the eve of the 1995
season by stopping the MLB from implementing a new collective-
bargaining agreement and using replacement players.[11] In 1991,
President Clinton tapped her for the Second Circuit, a nomination
that languished for over a year, as everyone recognized that she was
being positioned for further elevation. She was ultimately confirmed
67–29 in an experience that left her embittered and blaming ethnic
stereotyping for the ideological resistance she faced.

Although the naysayers weren't necessarily wrong in their assess-
ment, they could gather her liberal inclinations more from her

extracurricular activities than her Second Circuit rulings. Judge Sotomayor tended to write narrow, technical opinions, using workman-
like prose. Although some cases had anti-property rights aspects,
there was no overarching theoretical construct. Civil litigation expert
Walter Olson, then at the Manhattan Institute and now my colleague
at Cato, had some uneasiness about Sotomayor's views, but said "she
will not be as liberal as many of the Republicans are saying—but no
one could be that liberal, even if they tried."[12] Still, her unremarkable
judicial record showed that she was a representational pick; if she'd
been Sonia Smith from the Upper West Side, it's unlikely she would've
been considered.[13]

A 2001 speech she gave at Berkeley generated criticism. Playing
off a Justice O'Connor line in discussing gender and judging, Sotomayor said: "I would hope that a wise Latina woman with the rich-
ness of her experiences would more often than not reach a better
conclusion than a white male who hasn't lived that life."[14] She had
made similar remarks in other speeches, including one she submitted
as part of a judiciary committee questionnaire for her Second Circuit
nomination, but they had attracted little attention. It was a different
story now, with attacks coming quick and strong. It became a recur-
ring theme of her confirmation hearing, where she explained that
she merely "meant to inspire" young people, but that her play on
O'Connor's words "fell flat. It was bad."[15]

Although the usual suspects came out for and against the nomination, conservatives calling her a race-focused judicial activist, liberals praising her as thoughtful and trailblazing, there were some
surprises. "While I would have liked to see a more conservative libertarian type on the high court," said Larry Klayman, the founder of
the conservative watchdog groups Freedom Watch and Judicial
Watch, the selection "was a very prudent and wise decision from a
far left liberal like Obama."[16] President George H. W. Bush criticized

Newt Gingrich and Rush Limbaugh for accusing her of being racist, calling it "not fair" and "not right," praising her "distinguished record on the bench," and saying that she was entitled to a fair hearing.[17]

Judge Sotomayor would get her hearing in mid-July. In addition to the "wise Latina" speech, she was of course asked about abortion. Occasionally interrupted by pro-life protestors, Sotomayor said that *Roe v. Wade* was "settled law" but that she would have to look at the specifics of respective states' laws in applying it. Under questioning by Orrin Hatch (R-Utah) and Jon Kyl (R-Ariz.), Sotomayor distanced herself from President Obama's "empathy" standard. She returned to her theme that judges should just "apply the law" and that "if you look at my history on the bench, you will know that I do not believe that any ethnic, gender or race group has an advantage in sound judging."[18]

Sotomayor followed the standard formula of speaking slowly and deliberately, avoiding personal opinions, declining to take positions on controversial issues, agreeing with senators from both parties, and repeatedly affirming that as a justice she would just follow the law wherever it led. The judiciary committee approved her 13-6, with only one Republican in favor, Lindsey Graham (S.C.). The following week, the Senate confirmed her 68-31, with all Democrats and nine Republicans in favor. It's possible that a few more Republicans might have voted yes, but the NRA had announced that it was "scoring" the vote, counting it towards its influential legislative scorecard.

Justice Sotomayor quickly became a reliable liberal vote. Indeed, the only competition she has for being the most liberal justice is the one she agrees with most, Ruth Bader Ginsburg.[19] The two are often on the losing side of 7-2 splits, as in *NFIB v. Sebelius* (2012), where all the others agreed that Obamacare's Medicaid expansion uncon-stitutionally coerced the states. One 2015 analysis placed Sotomayor as having the most liberal voting history of all the then-sitting jus-tices, and slightly less liberal than Thurgood Marshall and John

Marshall Harlan II.[20] She's second only to Justice Clarence Thomas in the number of solo dissents and is typically least in the majority.[21]

Consequently, most of her notable opinions are dissents, as in *Schuette v. Coalition to Defend Affirmative Action* (2014), where the Court allowed Michigan to outlaw race and gender preferences in public education and employment. Sotomayor wrote a charged dissent arguing that voters had "changed the basic rules of the political process in that State in a manner that uniquely disadvantaged racial minorities."[22] Observers speculated that parts of the opinion were adapted from a planned dissent in *Fisher v. UT-Austin* (2013), when it looked like a 5–4 majority might outlaw the use of race in college admissions altogether. That case ended up being a 7–1 decision (Ginsburg in dissent, Kagan not participating) to remand to the lower courts for greater scrutiny of the administrators' motives, but Sotomayor obviously had a statement to make about the treatment of race in public policy. Responding to Chief Justice Roberts's earlier suggestion about how to stop racial discrimination, she wrote, "The way to stop discrimination on the basis of race is to speak openly and candidly on the subject of race, and to apply the Constitution with eyes open to the unfortunate effects of centuries of racial discrimination."[23]

One area where Justice Sotomayor's writings have been more influential is on criminal justice. Belying her prosecutorial background, she has staked out an expansive view of Fourth Amendment protection against warrantless and otherwise unreasonable searches and seizures. This is an area where she has come to unexpected agreement with the principled originalism of Justice Scalia, and now Justice Neil Gorsuch—albeit for different reasons.

Having now been on the Court for a decade, Justice Sotomayor has found her own voice, no longer technocratically following precedent as she did on the lower courts. And that voice speaks frequently, as she has come to ask by far the most questions at oral argument, stepping into the large rhetorical gap that Justice Scalia left.[24] As one reporter put it in a 2019 feature, "Her voice, in all its forms, has become the liberal conscience on a conservative court, one that speaks out in defense of minorities, immigrants, criminal defendants and death row inmates."[25] Barack Obama is no doubt pleased.

Elena Kagan

A year after Justice Souter left, it would be the turn of the third-longest-serving justice ever, John Paul Stevens, to depart. Stevens announced on April 9, 2010 that he would be retiring at the end of the term. The White House was ready, with a short list that largely tracked the previous year's, with the addition of Ninth Circuit Judge Sidney Thomas. President Obama first interviewed Thomas, then D.C. Circuit Judge Merrick Garland—who had been among the final nine before—then two others whom he had met with the previous year, Elena Kagan and Diane Wood. Garland was impressive and had a lot of institutional support, but Obama, recognizing that the Democrats might lose the Senate, wanted to save him for more difficult political terrain. On May 10, he announced that Kagan was his choice, praising her as a "consensus builder" and "one of the nation's foremost legal minds."[26]

Kagan was born and raised in Manhattan, the granddaughter of Russian-Jewish immigrants. She was the student body president at the elite Hunter College High School, where, somewhat akin to Sam Alito in college, she posed in her yearbook with a judge's robe and gavel. Also like Alito (and Sotomayor), Kagan graduated *summa cum laude* from Princeton. She clerked for D.C. Circuit Judge Abner Mika and Justice Thurgood Marshall, who called her "shorty." After a brief stint in private practice, Kagan joined the faculty of the University of Chicago Law School, where she met Obama, took time off to serve as a counsel on the Judiciary Committee for Justice Ginsburg's nomination, and made tenure "despite the reservations of some colleagues who thought she had not published enough."[27]

At that point, Mikva was President Clinton's counsel and hired Kagan. In June 1999, Clinton nominated Kagan to the D.C. Circuit but, as with John Roberts at the end of the Bush I presidency, the Senate took no action. Returning to academia, Kagan soon became a full-time professor at Harvard Law School and then its dean, in which capacity she both improved student life and diversified the faculty intellectually. "I love the Federalist Society," she would say to the organization's national student symposium in 2005, also demonstrating her people skills. "But you know, you are not my people."[28] Although she lost out on Harvard's presidency in 2007, she would gain an even bigger prize when President Obama tapped her to be the first female solicitor general in 2009. Although she'd never argued before the Supreme Court, she was confirmed relatively easily. Remarkably, her first argument would be the rehearing of *Citizens United v. FEC*. She would serve all of fifteen months in the job before ascending further.

Kagan's confirmation process proceeded *pro forma*, with all playing their assigned roles and the generally opposed Senate Republicans, who were down to forty-one members, ruling out the filibuster. "The filibuster should be relegated to extreme circumstances, and I don't think Elena Kagan represents that," admitted Minority Whip Jon Kyl.[29] Kagan faced a relatively subdued hearing, with questioning about how political she had been in her career and some frustrations at her evasiveness. Ironically, fifteen years earlier, Kagan as a professor had written a law review article criticizing judicial nominees for being too cagey.[30] But sitting in the hot seat herself, it became apparent why they were: there's no incentive to be more forthright and thus open yourself to attack, and every incentive just to demonstrate deep knowledge and an easygoing manner—which is precisely what Kagan did. One lighter moment came in response to a question by Senator Graham about where she had been on Christmas Day 2009, when a Nigerian man—the "underwear bomber"—attempted to take down a U.S.-bound plane with a plastic explosive. "You know," she dead-panned, "like all Jews, I was probably at a Chinese restaurant."[31] She got Graham's vote, as the committee otherwise approved her on party lines. Although the NRA announced that, as for Justice Sotomayor, it would be scoring the final vote, on August 5, 2010, the Senate confirmed her 63–37, with five Republicans in favor and one Demo-crat, Ben Nelson of Nebraska, against.

Justice Kagan's replacement of Justice Stevens was symbolic in many ways. She was the youngest justice (50), replacing someone nearly forty years her senior, and also the first justice in nearly forty years—since William Rehnquist and Lewis Powell were confirmed in 1972—with no judicial experience. This would be the first time there were three women on the bench, but also the first time there were no Protestants; the Court would now have six Catholics and three Jews. Remarkably, four of the nine justices were from New York City, each from a different borough: Scalia (Queens), Ginsburg (Brooklyn), Sotomayor (Bronx), and Kagan (Manhattan), plus Alito from New Jersey. And all the justices had gone to either Harvard or Yale Law Schools, though Ginsburg's degree was from Columbia. Most important for our purposes, although the Court's ideological balance didn't change, all the liberals were now appointed by Demo-crats and all the conservatives by Republicans. That seems like a banal truism and something that a decade later we're quite used to, but it was a first for the modern Court.

Kagan is an intellectual force who counters the big brains on the Court's right flank and, as a pragmatist, pulls Chief Justice Roberts towards the middle. On the former point, Justice Ginsburg, as senior justice in dissent, has assigned her many of the dissents in high-profile 5–4 cases that split on ideological lines. On the pragmatism point, Justice Kagan's joining the conservatives in finding that Obamacare's Medicaid expansion improperly coerced the states may have been part of a deal to get the chief justice's vote on the individual mandate question on which the constitutionality of the whole law turned. And during the fourteen months between Justice Scalia's death and Justice Gorsuch's confirmation, Kagan and Roberts, along with Justices Breyer and Kennedy, controlled the mushy middle to minimize 4–4 splits and other controversies at a time when the Court was already at the center of political debate. Part of Kagan's effectiveness as a justice is what has made her effective at every stage of her career: she asks the right questions, listens to people to build consensus, and communicates decisions well. Like Roberts, she writes few "optional" opinions and has never authored a solo dissent. And like her academic career, she doesn't publish much but what she does publish gets noticed.

Indeed, Kagan's seminal contribution to legal academia is her 2001 law review article "Presidential Administration," in which she spends more than 140 pages defending President Clinton's leveraging of regulatory agencies to pursue his agenda.[32] Just as Professor Kagan argued that executive control of a vigorous administrative state comports with the Constitution, Justice Kagan in 2019 wrote two opinions defending regulatory prerogatives. These two cases, *Gundy v. United States* and *Kisor v. Wilkie*—in both of which Justice Gorsuch led the dissenters—represent the continued battle over the separation of powers at the federal level. While not as sexy as the culture war, these issues tease out the differences between liberal and conservative interpretive theories and thus play a central role in confirmation battles.

Facing the Tea Party Senate

The fights over President Obama's lower court nominees, to which his judicial-selection team was able to turn after being pleasantly sidetracked by Supreme Court fights, would highlight different visions of federal power. The White House didn't initially focus on judges. The 2009 stimulus package, 2010 health care law, and two wars sucked up all the energy, and the administration didn't want to spend political capital on the judiciary—plus the initial process included too many interest groups. But Obama's first term did see 171 judges confirmed, in addition to Justices Sotomayor and Kagan. Some nominees faced political opposition that blocked them from a final vote, whether through filibuster, non-return of blue slips, or other tactics.

Caitlin Halligan, New York's solicitor general, was nominated to the D.C. Circuit in September 2010, but was filibustered for statements hostile to the Second Amendment and other touchstones. President Obama ultimately withdrew her nomination in March 2013. Ninth Circuit nominee, Andrew Hurwitz of Arizona, barely passed a cloture motion with sixty votes in June 2012, while other nominees, including those to the district courts, similarly faced delays and filibusters. In February 2012, Senator Chuck Grassley commented that more judges could have been confirmed had Obama not made recess appointments while the Senate was in session.[33] Unlike his predecessors, President Obama never recess-appointed any judges, but he did use the mechanism for executive officials, which the unanimous Supreme Court would say was improper in *NLRB v. Noel Canning* (2014).

After President Obama's reelection in 2012, when Democrats increased their Senate majority to 55–45, the administration became frustrated at the Republicans' slow-down efforts. The judicial battles reached a head in November 2013, over nominations to the remaining three D.C. Circuit vacancies. Republicans, having confirmed one judge to that court in May 2013, argued that a light docket plus the history of contentiousness—one vacancy was created by John Roberts's elevation eight years earlier—meant that the Democrats' insistence amounted to "court-packing." Majority Leader Harry Reid, citing Republicans' increased use of the filibuster—82 of the 168 cloture motions on nominations in our history had been filed under Obama, a number that would be trounced under President Trump— and the many waiting nominees, invoked the "nuclear option."[34] Since 1975, Senate Rules required a vote of three-fifths of senators to end a filibuster, while also allowing a "two-track" system whereby the Senate continued normal business and didn't require filibustering senators to physically hold the floor.[35] Now, without changing that rule but overriding the presiding officer's interpretation of the threshold, the Senate voted 52–48 to require only a bare majority to end debate on all nominations except for the Supreme Court. All Republicans and three Democrats voted against the change, which ended a practice that Reid himself had begun a decade earlier.

Nuking the Senate paved the way for the confirmation of the three stalled D.C. Circuit nominees, as well as four other circuit nominees who were confirmed with fewer than sixty votes. After the Republicans won back the Senate in 2014, giving them a 54–46 majority replete with Tea Party-aligned senators who saw judges as a key line of defense against an out-of-control federal government, the filibuster issue became moot and only two more circuit judges would be confirmed. President Obama ended up with twenty-five circuit judges his second term and a total of fifty-five, seven fewer than Bush and eleven fewer than Clinton. His total of 329 Article III judges beat George W. Bush's 326, however, even as they both lagged Clinton's 378.[36]

That battle over lower-court judges, with finger-pointing between partisans about hypocrisy and payback left over from the Clinton and Bush years, would pale compared to what came next. On February 13, 2016, with the Senate already in heightened tension and dysfunction and seventeen Republicans on the campaign trail, champing at the bit to succeed a president less popular among their party faithful than any in modern memory, the world turned upside down. Justice Scalia, an avid hunter, was found dead in his bed at a ranch in West Texas. The loss of the larger-than-life figure sent shockwaves through the legal and political establishments.

CHAPTER 17

The Garland Blockade, but Gorsuch

Before Scalia, the last two justices to die in office were William Rehnquist in 2005 and Robert Jackson in 1954, but those weren't presidential election years and the balance of the Court wasn't at stake. This was the first time a Democratic president would face a Republican Senate on a Supreme Court nomination since 1895. And if the nominee were confirmed, it would be the first time a majority of the Court would be made up of Democratic-appointed justices since 1970.

The last time a vacancy arose in a presidential election year was 1968, when Chief Justice Earl Warren attempted to retire. The time before that was 1956, when Sherman Minton informed President Eisenhower of his intention to retire two months before the election and Ike recess-appointed William Brennan (a Democrat). Before that, Oliver Wendell Holmes retired at age ninety in January 1932; President Hoover's nomination of Benjamin Cardozo was promptly acclaimed by the Republican Senate—the last time an election-year nominee was confirmed. The last time the Senate confirmed a nominee from a president of the opposing party to a high-court vacancy arising during a presidential election year was 1888. The opportunities just aren't common.

Senate Majority Leader Mitch McConnell, within an hour of Scalia's death hitting the national news, and without consulting his caucus, announced that the vacancy shouldn't be filled until after the election. It was a profoundly controversial move, but the argument was that the American people, having reelected President Obama in 2012 and then handed the Senate to the GOP in 2014, deserved to have a say in who got to appoint the next justice. With the election less than nine months away, the Court could survive with eight members. Democrats were understandably outraged, although they went overboard and harmed their credibility by suggesting that Republicans were questioning President Obama's legitimacy or denying his authority to nominate judges, or that the Constitution required a hearing.

It was also an extreme political risk; Republicans could lose the Senate in the election and therefore any bargaining power, let alone having a Democrat with a new mandate in the White House. Wouldn't it be better to work out a deal for some moderate than risk getting Goodwin Liu or Pam Karlan? But Judiciary Committee Chairman Chuck Grassley immediately reinforced McConnell's move and no Republican senators spoke against it. This was hugely important, because bottling up a nominee in committee would make it harder for Minority Leader Harry Reid to force a vote. Ten days later, February 23, all eleven Republican judiciary committee members signed a letter indicating an intent to withhold consent on *any* nominee and specifying that no hearings would occur until after the election. The next day, leading progressive scholars issued an open letter, organized by the leadership of the American Constitution Society, urging President Obama to nominate and the Senate to vote on that nomination.

At the same time, this wasn't a "scholars versus politicians" situation. The libertarian law professors at the Volokh Conspiracy blog gave variations of the argument that the Constitution imposes no duty on the Senate to do much of anything in this circumstance. Jonathan Adler, David Bernstein, Ilya Somin, and Eugene Volokh explained that here it was politics all the way down. Liberal Harvard law professor Noah Feldman wrote that "that the Constitution really doesn't answer the question of what the president or the Senate must do after the death of Justice Scalia. It sets the ground rules for a political battle."[1] Indeed, much like the Senate can decline to vote on bills passed by the House, or to ratify a treaty the president has signed, it can delay or ignore any nomination. Whether it should is, again, a political question.

Debate also raged over the "Biden Rule," referring to Joe Biden's June 25, 1992, speech where he warned the first President Bush not to follow the failed examples of Presidents Millard Fillmore (1852) and Lyndon Johnson (1968) in pressing election-year nominations. Now vice president, Biden issued a statement explaining that he believed that the president and Senate should "work together to overcome partisan differences," apparently disclaiming the part of his speech where he said that "Senate consideration of a nominee under these circumstances is not fair to the President, to the nominee, or to the Senate itself."[2] It later came out that Senator Chuck Schumer made similar remarks in 2007, which wasn't even an election year.

And in May 2005—in the *first year* of President Bush's second term—Harry Reid, facing criticism for obstructing judicial nominees, had said, "Nowhere in [the Constitution] does it say that the Senate has a duty to give Presidential nominees a vote. It says that appointments shall be made with the advice and consent of the Senate. That's very different than saying that every nominee receives a vote."[3]

Merrick Garland

Even in this extraordinary time, President Obama went about his normal selection process—which was risky, because the longer there wasn't a nominee, the stronger McConnell's position became. Speculation ran rampant about whether he would select an ideological or representational nominee that could help the Democrats politically in the election, or a compromise pick to put pressure on Republicans. Reid even suggested Nevada Governor Brian Sandoval, a very moderate Republican and former federal district judge.

By March 2016, Obama scheduled interviews with five candidates, before narrowing the list down to Merrick Garland, Sri Srinivasan (a pre-nuclear D.C. Circuit appointee), and Ninth Circuit Judge Paul Watford. Senator Orrin Hatch, who in 2010 had urged Obama to nominate Garland as a "consensus nominee," said at a Federalist Society lunch on March 11 that the GOP refusal to consider any Obama nominee was "the chickens coming home to roost" after the filibuster battles and the Biden Rule.[4] On March 16, Obama picked Garland. "To suggest that someone as qualified and respected as Merrick Garland does not even deserve a hearing, let alone an up-or-down vote," the president intoned, "that would be unprecedented."[5]

Originally from Chicago, Garland had graduated with honors from Harvard College and Law School, where editing William Brennan's famous article on state constitutions helped him land a clerkship with the justice. After working for President Carter's attorney general, Benjamin Civiletti, Garland spent time in private practice and teaching before becoming a federal prosecutor and, under President Clinton, principal deputy assistant attorney general in the Justice Department's criminal division. In that role, Garland worked on high-profile domestic terrorism cases, most notably the Oklahoma City bombing.

In 1995, President Clinton, at the urging of Judge Abner Mikva and Justice Brennan, nominated Garland to the retiring Mikva's seat on the D.C. Circuit. Judiciary committee Republicans gave him a hearing but not a vote, citing no need for an eleventh judge on that court. He was eventually renominated and confirmed after Clinton's reelection. By 2016, Garland was 63, the oldest nominee since Lewis Powell, and his nineteen years of judicial service would've been a record for a justice. Generally regarded as a brilliant moderate with a pro-prosecution bent—someone who defers to the government on everything, including law enforcement—Garland was about the best that conservatives, if not libertarians, could've hoped for from an Obama nominee.

But the Garland nomination didn't resolve the impasse, because it didn't affect the argument McConnell had been making from the very beginning: let the voters in the coming election choose who gets to fill the seat. As Hatch said, "I think well of Merrick Garland. I think he is a fine person. But his nomination does not in any way change current circumstances."[6]

As Garland began making his Senate rounds, the #NoHearing-NoVote position was hardening. By early April, a handful of Republican senators, notably Hatch and Jeff Flake (Ariz.), said that the nomination should be taken up during the lame duck session if presumptive Democratic nominee Hillary Clinton won the election—but thirty had announced that even after the election, regardless of its outcome, they wouldn't consider it.[7] Two Republicans, after previously supporting the idea of holding hearings, reversed their positions. Two others expressed support for hearings and a vote, with Susan Collins (Maine) also supporting Garland's nomination.

Despite those cracks, the GOP caucus held together. Although one normally wouldn't get rich betting on the steel in senators' spines, McConnell's crew survived the initial onslaught and the issue faded into the larger debate over the Court's direction. That August, McConnell heralded the party's uncompromising intransigence, declaring to a crowd in in his home state of Kentucky, "One of my proudest moments was when I looked at Barack Obama in the eye and I said, 'Mr. President, you will not fill the Supreme Court vacancy.'"[8]

The Court had rarely been more ideologically split, with three conservatives, four progressives who never defect on major cases, and a swing vote who represented the last bulwark against the evisceration of the First and Second Amendments, the separation of powers, and any other limits on federal power or the administrative state. The idea that in these circumstances a pivotal seat would be filled by one of the most polarizing presidents in American history who, especially in his second term, thought that when Congress didn't act, he got to enact his agenda regardless, was a compelling rallying cry. Moreover, President Obama's attempt at compromise by nominating an older moderate didn't move the needle. After all, a "moderate" isn't much different from a "liberal" on high-profile controversies—and the New York Times adjudged Garland to be to the left of Justices Breyer and Kagan, almost as far as Justices Ginsburg and Sotomayor.[9]

If the Republicans were going to stick with the position that there should be no pre-election confirmation, then not scheduling committee hearings was the honest procedural posture for implementing that strategy. After all, what's the point of holding a hearing without any intent to approve the nominee? Why engage in any process if the Senate as a whole won't take up any nominee? Garland is an honorable man with a sterling resumé. That alone doesn't merit his elevation—judicial philosophy matters—but it does earn him respectful treatment. Turning what was already a toxic situation into a charade wouldn't have served any purpose. It was politically cleaner to be straight at the outset and tell him, "it's not you, it's the fate of the nation."

The 2016 Election

On the campaign trail, meanwhile, the Supreme Court and judicial nominations became a campaign issue unlike at any other time in the nation's history. The very night after Justice Scalia's death, February 13, 2016, the Republicans held their ninth presidential debate. With Senator Ted Cruz (R-Tex.) having attacked Donald Trump on abortion and his past support for Democratic politicians, part of Trump's response to the debate's very first question was to name Judges Bill Pryor and Diane Sykes as the types of people he would put on the Supreme Court. These solid Bush II appointees were well known in legal circles and signaled to Republican elites that the unorthodox frontrunner was thinking about this crucial policy area.

It was an unusual move; presidential contenders don't typically float potential cabinet members, judges, or other officials, because doing so puts a target on their backs. But Trump needed to make assurances to Republicans, as well as clean up his earlier joking reference to his 78-year-old liberal sister, Third Circuit Judge Maryanne Trump Barry as a "phenomenal" potential justice. And for Cruz, who had clerked for Chief Justice Rehnquist and argued eight cases in the Supreme Court, and who would become Trump's biggest rival, judges were a major calling card. So Trump needled him, and Jeb Bush, about having supported John Roberts.

Trump was ready with names because his counsel, Donald F. McGahn II, former Federal Election Commission chairman and one of the few Washington insiders on the campaign, was giving him good advice. McGahn would tell a story at the Federalist Society lawyers convention in November 2017 about the time before the Iowa caucuses when the Federalist Society's director of external relations Jonathan Bunch asked about Trump's views on judges. McGahn explained that John Sununu was handling the issue, and that Sununu had prepared two lists, one of easily confirmable pragmatic moderates and another of conservatives with paper trails. Bunch asked what they would do with the two lists; McGahn said that the first would be thrown in the trash, while the second would be rammed through the Senate.[10] McGahn, a libertarian-minded amateur musician who would become Trump's White House counsel, could be a wicked jokester. Naming the man who had pushed David Souter on the first President Bush was an example of his keen wit—and showed that he understood the issue.

The gambit worked so well that Trump decided to make a list of potential nominees to further cement his standing with primary voters and defuse Cruz's attacks. To get on the list, a would-be justice had to have (1) an originalist-textualist judicial philosophy, (2) a record of applying that philosophy, and (3) examples of demonstrating the previous criteria in difficult or controversial situations.[11] The goal was to prevent the sorts of misfires that had plagued previous Republican administrations, to avoid not only justices who would move left, like Stevens and Souter, or squishy moderates like Kennedy, but also those like Roberts who prized restraint over applying the jurisprudential theories that had made Scalia and Thomas the gold standard.

McGahn asked Leonard Leo, the Federalist Society's executive vice president, to draw up some names, which he put on a card that Trump eventually took from a meeting they had. On March 21, Trump held a press conference in front of the Trump Hotel in Washington, then under construction, and in response to a question about the Scalia vacancy, announced that he'd be "making up a list" and "distributing that list in the very near future."[12] A week later, John Malcolm, the director of the Heritage Foundation's Edwin Meese

Center for Legal and Judicial Studies, came up with his list of eight people, making it public so anyone could use it, not just Trump.[13]

McGahn's team went to work, focusing on people who were already judges; who were scholarly, not just voting "the right way"; and who were from outside the Beltway. In the end, on May 18, 2016, after Trump won the Indiana primary and became the presumptive nominee, he released a list of eleven people: Sykes, Pryor, four other circuit judges, and five state supreme court justices. The list was solid, with nothing "Trumpy" about it: no Judge Judy or Rudy Giuliani.

But other people would still be under consideration—and many Republican-inclined voters were skeptical that the list was worth more than the pixels it was printed with. Accordingly, on September 23, three days before his first debate with Hillary Clinton, Trump put out another ten names, promising, "This [combined] list is definitive and I will choose only from it."[14] The supplemental list contained two more circuit judges, including Neil Gorsuch of the Tenth Circuit; two district judges, including Amul Thapar of Kentucky, whom Trump would elevate to the Sixth Circuit as his very first lower-court nominee; four more state supreme court justices; Senator Mike Lee (R-Utah), whose brother Thomas, a justice on Utah's supreme court, had been on the initial list; and Judge Margaret Ryan of the U.S. Court of Appeals for the Armed Forces. The combined list of twenty-one was high-powered and distinguished, and featured nobody from either coast except for Ryan, whose military service and unique court could hardly be painted as "swampy." Senator Lee, who had clerked for Justice Alito and was known as being a principled constitutionalist, was included at the last moment at the request of Cruz, who was preparing to endorse Trump after having declined to do so at the Republican convention.

On the Democratic side, however, the Scalia vacancy and fate of the Supreme Court faded from view. Hillary Clinton, who outlasted Senator Bernie Sanders in the primaries, barely mentioned Merrick

Garland on the stump, as she was in the awkward position of having to support President Obama's nominee while not necessarily committing to this compromise candidate should she become president. In the final presidential debate on October 19, she offered a litmus test for prospective justices: supporting *Roe v. Wade*, expanding LGBTQ rights, and reversing *Citizens United*.[15]

It looked like that would be good enough, that Clinton was cruising toward election on the basis of her "blue wall" of coastal and Midwestern states. Accordingly, on the eve of the election, some Republicans suggested that the Senate might not confirm any nominee to replace Scalia if Democrats retained control of the presidency.[16] That would've been unprecedented; the longest vacancy in our history was 841 days, starting in John Tyler's embattled presidency in 1844 after the Whigs had kicked him out of their party. Although there were a handful of vacancies that persisted longer than a year in the 1800s, the longest vacancy since the turn of the 20th-century came in the Nixon years, concluding in 1970 after 391 days. What these Republicans were saying is that, given that the Constitution allows the Senate maximal leeway and that Clinton had effectively pledged to nominate young, result-oriented progressives, they couldn't in good faith vote for them. There was little appetite even for confirming Garland during the lame duck. As Senator Lee put it, "[T]he last Democratic nominee to the Supreme Court...who voted independently" was Byron White.[17]

In any case, we didn't face the prospect of massive resistance to Clinton nominees, as Donald Trump's election victory shocked the world. Adam Liptak, the *New York Times* Supreme Court reporter, asked for my reaction early the next morning. "Senate Republicans' strategy of not even considering Garland, of letting the American people decide who gets to fill Scalia's seat, worked," I told him. "Not only that, but it didn't at all hurt vulnerable senators running for re-election."[18] Indeed, right where I was in Des Moines, ahead of a talk at Drake University—coincidentally at the same hotel as the Iowa GOP victory party—Chuck Grassley was reelected by nearly twenty-five points despite millions of dollars spent attacking him for the Garland blockade.

Neil Gorsuch

The Trump campaign itself was surprised to have won, leading to a chaotic transition—except on the Supreme Court vacancy. The president-elect knew that this one issue was the primary factor behind more than a quarter of his votes—read Salena Zito and Brad Todd's remarkable *The Great Revolt* if you doubt that Iowa farmers and Michigan waitresses weren't paying attention to the fight for Justice Scalia's seat—so he wanted to get it right.[19] He told his inner circle what he wanted: someone young enough to serve for decades; "extraordinarily well qualified," preferably with "name brand" degrees and a wealth of writings; "not weak," with the courage to make controversial rulings; and who would interpret the Constitution consistent with the Framers' intent.[20] Leonard Leo, who took an immediate leave from the Federalist Society to work on the transition, provided a list of six names, all of them among the expanded list of twenty-one Trump had promised to pick from in September: Gorsuch, Pryor, Sykes, Thapar, Eighth Circuit Judge Steve Colloton, and Third Circuit Judge Thomas Hardiman. After preliminary interviews with McGahn—including the "sex, drugs, and rock-and-roll" questions about embarrassing things in the candidates' pasts—there was a panel that added Vice President-elect Mike Pence, strategist Steve Bannon, incoming chief of staff Reince Priebus, and Pence's counsel Mark Paoletta, who had worked on the Clarence Thomas confirmation. The Pence panel focused on preventing the leftward slide that all too many GOP nominees experienced, as well as asking the candidates whom they would pick if it wasn't them: Gorsuch came up a lot. McGahn also spearheaded meetings with senators to smooth the way for the eventual nominee, the main upshot of which was that Pryor would face headwinds, including among certain Republicans, for his unapologetic social conservatism.[21]

After being coached by McGahn not to ask litmus-test-type questions—because the judiciary committee would ask—President-elect Trump interviewed four finalists: Hardiman, who came highly recommended by Judge Trump Barry, which was significant because she disagreed with him on many issues; Gorsuch, who had the most gold-plated resume; Pryor, who was supported by Attorney General-designate Jeff Sessions; and Thapar, who was being pushed by McConnell. Although Trump got along swimmingly with Hardiman, whose working-class background and Pennsylvania home made him a proxy for Trump voters, the president decided to go with the person whom the others picked if it wasn't to be them—Neil Gorsuch.[22] As the media tracked the finalists' movements to discern who the final choice might be, President Trump achieved a show-business reveal. On January 31, 2017, he announced the pick in an East Room ceremony, asking, "Are you surprised?" Gorsuch showed his light touch in his remarks by noting that he had clerked for Byron White, "the last Coloradan to serve on the Supreme Court and the only justice to lead the NFL in rushing."[23]

Garland's nomination, meanwhile, had expired on January 3, with the end of the 114th Congress, after languishing 293 days. Kathryn Ruemmler, who had been President Obama's White House counsel from 2011 to 2014, acknowledged at a post-election panel that if the roles had been reversed, she would've recommended that Senate Democrats take the same course that Republicans had.[24] In May 2019, McConnell would be asked what he would do if a vacancy arose in

2020, another presidential election year. He replied that he would fill it, later explaining that it's a different circumstance when the White House and Senate are politically aligned.

Neil Gorsuch was a Supreme Court nominee from central casting. Just 49 years old, with a silver coif that somehow projected wisdom and energy at the same time, he had spent his formative years in Colorado before moving to D.C. for high school, when his mother became administrator of the EPA under President Reagan. He was two years behind Brett Kavanaugh at Georgetown Preparatory School, and the two ended up clerking together for Justice Anthony Kennedy. After graduating with honors from Columbia and Harvard Law School, where he was classmates with Barack Obama, he won a Marshall Scholarship to attend Oxford, where he met his wife and would eventually be awarded a doctorate in legal philosophy. After clerking for D.C. Circuit Judge David Sentelle and Justices White and Kennedy (White had just retired), Gorsuch spent a decade in private practice before becoming principal deputy associate attorney general, helping oversee the Justice Department's civil litigation components. In 2006, George W. Bush nominated him to the Tenth Circuit, and he was confirmed by voice vote.

Gorsuch was like Scalia in the ways that made Scalia legendary, but unlike him on the measures that prevented the great Nino from having even more of an impact. There were no rough edges, no acerbic barbs. And yet the commitment to enforcing the text of a law was clear, the devotion to a Constitution whose structure protects liberty is complete. Gorsuch's best line as a circuit judge was from *U.S. v. Krueger* (2015), on a motion to suppress evidence seized in Oklahoma under a warrant issued by a magistrate judge in Kansas. "Ours is not supposed to be the government of the Hunger Games with power centralized in one district, but a government of diffused and divided power, the better to prevent its abuse."[25] The nominee was witty and erudite, a Westerner who loved skiing and fishing but was also comfortable in the halls of power.

After some time to digest Gorsuch's 212 lower-court opinions and 140,000 documents relating to his work in the Bush II administration, the judiciary committee scheduled hearings for the third week of March. The first day was largely spent by senators of both parties rehashing arguments about the handling of the Garland nomination. Cruz argued that the Gorsuch nomination had "super-legitimacy"—perhaps harkening to Arlen Specter's "super-duper precedent"—because the American people had gotten to weigh in on who should make it.[26] Gorsuch himself emphasized the role of the judge to faithfully apply the law, joking that a judge who likes all of his rulings is "probably a pretty bad judge."[27]

As questioning began on the second day, Democrats tried to make the nominee appear against "the little guy." Senator Dianne Feinstein (Calif.) literally asked, "How do we have confidence in you that you won't be just for the big corporations? That you will be for the little man?" Gorsuch replied with a list of cases where he had ruled for an individual against a corporation.[28] Senator Sheldon Whitehouse (R.I.) tried to get Gorsuch to commit to unmasking donors who had paid for advertising opposing Garland and supporting him, asking whether Gorsuch would join the Roberts majority in subverting our democracy.[29] The nominee demurred from such loaded questions, and generally stayed on his script of being personable yet not saying anything that could be used to derail his confirmation.

Democratic senators repeatedly criticized Gorsuch for a dissent from his colleagues' ruling in favor of a truck driver who, after waiting hours for relief, abandoned his trailer in freezing conditions. The case turned on an unforgiving bit of statutory language.[30] Senator Dick Durbin (D-Ill.) also attacked Gorsuch's opinion in the Hobby Lobby case that the Religious Freedom Restoration Act protected corporations, not just individuals—which the Supreme Court ultimately affirmed.[31] He and others probed the skepticism that Gorsuch had expressed in his opinions about judicial deference to administrative agencies, to make it look like he was against environmental and safety regulations. Gorsuch explained that it was Congress that should be making those sorts of decisions, and it was his job as a judge to enforce the law that Congress enacted.

Republicans focused on humanizing Gorsuch against accusations that he was a heartless tool of the far right. Cruz asked about the meaning of life as relayed in *The Hitchhiker's Guide to Galaxy* (forty-two), mutton-busting (look it up), and judicial basketball at "the highest court in the land." Graham asked how he would have reacted if during his interview, the president had asked him to vote against *Roe v. Wade*. Gorsuch replied, "I would have walked out the door."[32]

Toward the end of the hearings, the Supreme Court issued a ruling reversing a Tenth Circuit decision that had relied on an opinion Gorsuch had written regarding individual education plans for children with disabilities, which in turn was based on circuit precedent that bound him.[33] Senate Minority Leader Chuck Schumer said it demonstrated "a continued, troubling pattern of Judge Gorsuch deciding against everyday Americans, even children who require special assistance at school."[34] Schumer then announced his intent to filibuster the nomination.

Nothing particularly damaging had come out, and yet Gorsuch would have only a slim majority supporting him. The judiciary committee voted 11–9 on party lines to approve him, sending him to the Senate floor, where three days later the filibuster began. A cloture vote under the 60-vote threshold fell four votes short, with Democrats Michael Bennet (Colo.), Joe Donnelly (Ind.), Heidi Heitkamp (N.D.), and Joe Manchin (W.Va.) joining all fifty-two Republicans. Mitch McConnell then used the same procedure Harry Reid had four years earlier to end filibusters of lower-court nominees, invoking the "thermonuclear" option to require a bare majority for cloture on Supreme Court picks. John McCain (Ariz.) had been reluctant to take this step, but said that the Democrats' intransigence gave him no choice. Susan Collins (Maine) unsuccessfully tried to broker a deal to approve Gorsuch but preserve the filibuster. The next day, April 7, 2017, the Senate moved to a final vote, confirming Gorsuch 54–45, with one Republican absent and three Democrats who had previously voted for cloture supporting him—all from states Trump had won handily—but not fellow Coloradan Bennet.

The Court was effectively returned to the status quo before Scalia's death. Gorsuch, the youngest justice since Clarence Thomas, the lone Protestant (but raised Catholic), and the first one to serve alongside a justice for whom he clerked, was expected to vote like Scalia on the hot-button issues that broke 5–4, and also on cases that joined the left and right against the middle, like constitutional criminal procedure. "Wouldn't it be a lot easier if we just followed the plain text of the statute?" he asked at his first argument, in an otherwise forgettable case.[35] In that first abbreviated term, Gorsuch agreed with Thomas on all seventeen cases they heard together; they continue to be closely aligned, but not unanimously.

While early reports, based on unsubstantiated rumors, spoke of tensions between Gorsuch and several of his new colleagues, he quickly settled in, establishing himself as an evocative writer and libertarian darling. In his first full term, he was assigned to write for the majority in more 5–4 rulings than any junior justice since Anthony Kennedy in 1988–89. And he was behind only the chief justice and Justice Kennedy in being on the winning side of cases.

Those who hoped for (or feared) a smooth-writing originalist got what they expected. "Originalism has regained its place at the table [and] textualism has triumphed," he explained to more than 2,000 celebrants at the Federalist Society's annual dinner in November 2017, "and neither one is going anywhere on my watch."[36] Moreover, Gorsuch has continued his campaign against the awesome power of the administrative state, both in terms of judicial over-deference and congressional over-delegation of legislative power. In the 2018-19 term, in which Gorsuch was in the majority of more 5–4 cases than anyone else, two such cases where Gorsuch was in dissent illustrate this commitment to the separation of powers. In *Gundy v. United States*, Gorsuch led the opposition to a ruling that okayed the congressional delegation of power to write sex-offender registry rules, criticizing a statute that "gave the attorney general free rein to write the rules for virtually the entire existing sex offender population in this country."[37] In *Kisor v. Wilkie*, he decried the refusal to erase the deference courts give to regulatory reinterpretations, saying that the majority's rewrite "has maimed and enfeebled—in truth, zombified" what was known as *Auer* deference, keeping it "on life support" but depriving lower courts of clarity and litigants of the judicial independence that the Constitution guarantees.[38]

In this pen-and-phone-and-tweet era, it's refreshing to see a jurist recognize the lack of accountability in a system driven by bureaucrats rather than legislators. And this is a nonpartisan complaint; agencies are run by administrations of both parties and can promulgate rules that achieve both conservative and progressive results. It's unclear why Democratic senators want President Trump's cabinet secretaries to have more power, but that's what they were implying in their attacks on Gorsuch for wanting to cut back agency discretion. Gorsuch's work in this area is not what you'd get from a "judicial restraint" conservative, and signals the sway he'll have in coming years over the debate on the proper scope and distribution of federal power.

CHAPTER 18

Kavanaugh and Beyond

J ustice Gorsuch only got to serve one full term with his former boss. On June 27, 2018, Justice Kennedy announced his retirement. Although progressives hailed Kennedy when he ruled their way, his decision to depart provoked paroxysmal spasms of alarm. MSNBC's Chris Matthews argued that Senate Democrats should keep the seat open through the midterms, in hopes that they take back the Senate, where the GOP majority had slipped to 51–49.[1] How they were supposed to do this after pushing the Republicans to eliminate the filibuster to seat Gorsuch was unclear, although the judiciary committee did have only a one-vote margin now, 11–10.

Selection Process

President Trump confirmed that he would again pick someone from his list. That list now had twenty-five people on it, having been updated in November 2017, adding two newly confirmed federal judges, Amy Coney Barrett of the Seventh Circuit and Kevin Newsom of the Eleventh Circuit; two young state supreme court justices, Britt Grant of Georgia (now on the Eleventh Circuit) and Patrick

Wyrick of Oklahoma (now a district judge); and Brett Kavanaugh, who had been on the D.C. Circuit for twelve years. Washington insiders raised their eyebrows at the latter, who had been a contender for some time but was the only one on the list from the Acela corridor.

In due course, a short list of appealing personalities emerged, ranging in background about as much as federal judges could. There was Amul Thapar, the son of Indian immigrants who was born in Toledo and made a name for himself in Kentucky; Barrett, a brilliant law professor and mother of seven from Indiana; Raymond Kethledge, an introverted Michigander who preferred the solitude of his wilderness cabin to the stifling Washington swamp; Thomas Hardiman, a Pittsburgher who was the first in his family to graduate college and put himself through law school by driving a taxi; and of course Kavanaugh, the boyish D.C. insider with strong opinions on the separation of powers, the only Ivy Leaguer in the bunch. The "swing senators" were also consulted: Republicans Susan Collins (Maine) and Lisa Murkowski (Alaska), plus Democrats Joe Donnelly (Ind.), Heidi Heitkamp (N.D.), and Joe Manchin (W.Va.).

The judges' former clerks and other surrogates advocated their champions; the deluge of case summaries and legal memoranda became overwhelming and sometimes annoying. Then came the op-eds praising this or that judge's originalism and his or her capacity to help in the midterm elections, or to see the law exactly like Justice Scalia, or to be Justice Gorsuch 2.0. The process finished with a July 9 prime-time special that appropriately ran right after the latest episode of *The Bachelor*. The anticipation and Law Twitter gossip all day leading up to it must be how normal people feel about that other reality-TV show. I half-expected the final pair to be up there on stage in the East Room, with the president turning to the runner-up and saying, "sorry, pack your robes and go."

Poor Hardiman was the runner-up for the second consecutive time. Kavanaugh had been the frontrunner all along. He was known to be the favorite of Don McGahn, now the White House counsel, and was by far the most connected to the legal elite who, even in Trump's Washington, hold tremendous sway over these sorts of things. He also passed Trump's test of being well-qualified, an originalist, and "not weak." Still, it was a little odd to see this inside-the-Beltway double-Yale swamp creature—having grown up in tony Bethesda, Maryland, just across the D.C. line—who had worked so closely with Independent Counsel Ken Starr and then President George W. Bush, be on stage. Despite the plot twists, the unconventional president went with the conventional choice.

The fact that Kavanaugh wasn't a consensus first choice shows the deep bench Republicans have. It was also telling that the worry was never that Kavanaugh would be a Souter (stealth candidate who moved left) or Kennedy (inscrutable moderate), but a Roberts (more committed to minimalism than originalism). The nominee had displayed a strong record of enforcing constitutional text, but his political caginess worried the conservative cognoscenti, who felt heartburn over Roberts's Obamacare betrayal. "There's a difference between a home run and a grand slam," wrote David French in *National Review*, of the baseball-fan jurist.[2]

Kavanaugh was like Justice Kennedy in his dedication to the Constitution's *structural* protections for liberty—as opposed to the Bill of Rights or other explicit guarantees—a theme he returned to again and again during the process. He also believes, as he put it at the nomination ceremony, that a judge "must be independent and must interpret the law, not make the law. A judge must interpret statutes as written. And a judge must interpret the Constitution as written, informed by history and tradition and precedent."[3] That all seems straightforward, but Kavanaugh has a long track record of enforcing the separation of powers. His steadfast defense of civil rights, including the freedom of speech, religion, and armed self-defense, were notable. His 300+ opinions were scholarly and influential, often cited by the Supreme Court itself.

Kavanaugh's willingness to push back on the excesses of the regulatory state made him a man for the moment. Yet he approaches this task from a different angle than Gorsuch. Whereas Gorsuch wants to pare back the scope of judicial deference, Kavanaugh has focused on reducing the occasions where deference is applied in the first place. For example, under the famous *Chevron* doctrine, judges defer to agencies when the operational statute is ambiguous, but Kavanaugh would rather that judges work not to find (or manufacture) that ambiguity.

He's likely better on civil liberties and criminal justice than many libertarians think, just differentiating domestic law enforcement from national security.[4] And on most of the top issues causing progressive rage—corporate power, campaign finance, workers' rights, health care—he's no worse for progressives than Kennedy was.[5] The main concern that those on the right have about Kavanaugh is that he might be too much like Chief Justice Roberts, playing the long game rather than simply calling balls and strikes. That's what may have happened in *Seven-Sky v. Holder* (2011), the D.C. Circuit Obamacare case where, instead of ruling on the individual mandate's constitutionality, Kavanaugh would have dismissed the suit for lack of jurisdiction under a technical tax statute. Still, unlike Roberts, Kavanaugh has long been involved with the Federalist Society, which signals a commitment to ideas rather than mere party loyalty, and was endorsed by plenty of conservatives.

The ABA rated him "well qualified"—although after Kavanaugh was accused of sexual impropriety, the committee reopened the evaluation "regarding temperament," closing it after he was confirmed. This was a replay of his drawn-out D.C. Circuit nomination, when the ABA initially rated him "well qualified" but three years later downgraded him to "qualified."

Senate Republicans expressed immediate support, while leading Democrats, particularly those running for president, announced their opposition.[6] Given the slim GOP majority, there was little margin for error. Demand Justice, a left-wing group led by Brian Fallon, Hillary Clinton's former spokesman, announced plans to spend $1 million against the nomination even before there was a nominee, while on the right the Judicial Crisis Network ramped up its own rapid-response and digital-media operation. Much as the opposition to Gorsuch was driven by resentment from the inaction on Garland, the Kavanaugh opposition was based on his replacing the Court's longtime swing vote. On the night the nomination was announced, protestors outside the Court, not wanting to repeat the ridiculous spectacle of "Stop [fill in the blank]" signs they had for Gorsuch, this time were ready with preprinted placards featuring the finalists. Still, the occasional "Stop Hardiman" or "Stop Kethledge" sign appeared in crowd broadcasts, while the Women's March issued a statement opposing "Trump's nomination of XX."[7]

The legal establishment seemed to be in Kavanaugh's favor, about as much as it had been for Gorsuch, recognizing that he was a normal pick for a Republican president. Yale law professor Akhil Amar wrote "A Liberal's Case for Brett Kavanaugh."[8] Amar would testify in support of the nomination, as would liberal appellate lawyer Lisa Blatt, who has argued more Supreme Court cases than any other woman. Former acting solicitor general Neal Katyal tweeted, "Given Judge Kavanaugh's credentials, hardworking nature, and much more, it would be such a different confirmation process if for a different seat (like Justice Thomas's) or if he were nominated by a different President (like, any of them who weren't subjects of criminal investigations and multiple suits)."⁹ Indeed, the pendency of the Robert Mueller investigation was the pretext many senators cited as reason for delaying the nomination indefinitely.

The Spartacus Hearing

Initially, no Democratic senators save the centrist Joe Manchin would meet with Kavanaugh, citing the need to review the copious documents from his work in the Bush White House, on the 2000 Florida election recount, and as counsel in the Starr investigation. As the hearings drew closer, several Democrats finally did meet with him, in part to press him on those documents. By the time the hearings started, nearly half a million pages of documents had been released to the committee—nearly triple the previous high (for Gorsuch).¹⁰ The Trump administration blocked another one hundred thousand pages, citing executive privilege. Kavanaugh had been staff secretary, such that essentially all documents circulating through the White House would've crossed his computer, so Chairman Chuck Grassley tried to work with the Democrats to narrow their request.¹¹ Although he negotiated a deal with Ranking Member Dianne Feinstein, it fell apart once staff got involved, so Republicans simply requested a manageable amount of documents.¹² Had the Democrats requested a large but still reasonable set of documents, they could've delayed the nomination for months. But a focus on "document obstruction," without good-faith negotiations, didn't damage the nomination.¹³

The first day of the hearings, September 4, 2018, was supposed to be the typical set-piece of opening statements, before questioning began on day two. But the carnival atmosphere outside the room— including a line of silent protesters dressed as handmaidens from *A Handmaid's Tale*—spilled inside, waving signs and screaming, largely about the alleged threat to abortion rights that Kavanaugh posed.

The Capitol Police reported that seventeen protestors were arrested in the first hour of the hearing. Ultimately, seventy people were arrested that day and more than 200 over the course of the four-day hearing, with most being charged with disorderly conduct and paying a small fine.[14] This was a coordinated action, organized by Planned Parenthood, the Women's March, Code Pink, and other radical organizations.[15]

Democratic senators also got into the act, with a sort of rolling filibuster that interrupted Chairman Grassley's opening statement. One after another they objected to the process for document review, especially 42,000 pages released by Bush lawyers the day before.[16] Senators Cory Booker of New Jersey and Kamala Harris of California were particularly vocal, effectively using the hearing to launch their presidential campaigns. The delays lasted over an hour, with protestor interruptions throughout the day. Senator Dick Durbin (D-Ill.) called it "the noise of democracy," while Senator John Cornyn (R-Tex.) called it "mob rule," adding that it was "hard to take the [the process objections] seriously when every single one of our colleagues in the Senate Judiciary Committee on the Democratic side have announced their opposition to this nominee even before today's hearing."[17]

The second day began with Senator Leahy's probing Kavanaugh's knowledge of Republican committee staffers' accessing sensitive Democratic memos during the 2001–03 impasse over the Miguel Estrada nomination, when Leahy was chairman (see chapter 15). Despite Democratic assertions to the contrary, there was no "scandal" here, because the memos had been saved on a shared server and there was no hacking or other unethical behavior—and in any case Kavanaugh was removed from what judiciary committee staffers were doing.[18] Senators also asked about Kavanaugh's positions on legal controversies. The nominee testified that *Roe* was "settled as a precedent" and that *Casey* was "precedent on precedent," but beyond that he could offer "no hints, no forecasts, no previews"—quoting Justice Ginsburg—on any types of cases.[19]

There were several contentious exchanges out of left field. Senator Harris asked whether Kavanaugh had ever discussed the Mueller investigation with anyone at the law firm founded by Donald Trump's personal lawyer Marc Kasowitz. Kavanaugh was unsure how to answer because he didn't know everyone who worked at the firm, so he tried to get Harris to clarify what she had in mind. "I think you're thinking of someone and you don't want to tell us," she replied ominously. It turned out that Kavanaugh hadn't talked to anyone at the firm about Mueller. Harris's line of attack, presaging her presidential run, was a nothingburger.

The third day began with an announcement by Senator Booker that he was going to break Senate rules by releasing "committee confidential" emails that purported to show Kavanaugh's support for racial profiling. Booker had hinted at these emails before, but now said that he would risk expulsion from the Senate to make them public, "the closest I'll probably ever have in my life to an 'I am Spartacus' moment."[20] Never mind that he used an inapt analogy—the 1960 Kirk Douglas movie featured a group of slaves all claiming to be Spartacus to avoid the latter's crucifixion—the documents at issue had already been cleared for release *pursuant to Booker's own request the previous day.* After fruitless questions about President Trump's tweets, the committee concluded its questioning with an hourlong closed session that would cover confidential topics, including any issues uncovered by the FBI background investigation. No ethical concerns were raised; Ranking Member Feinstein didn't even attend.[21]

The hearing was as contentious as any save those for Bork and Thomas, but Kavanaugh seemed cruising for confirmation, with a final vote expected to match Gorsuch's. "This week's hearing lacked the sordidness of the Thomas hearing but made up for it in vitriol," concluded the *Washington Times*.[22] Grassley set the committee vote for September 20. In the meantime, Kavanaugh had to answer a record number of written "questions for the record," a process started with the Stevens nomination in 1975 that's meant to clarify points raised during the hearing or related issues that didn't get covered. He received 1,287, more than those received by all previous nominees *combined*. All but four of the questions came from Democrats, almost all of whom had already announced they would be voting no. The previous record was 324, for Gorsuch; Thomas had gotten 18, Bork 15, and Scalia 3.[23]

"This Is a Circus"

The nominee and the White House thought that was the final obstacle, but a funny thing happened on the way to One First Street. After a pro forma committee meeting a week before the scheduled vote, Feinstein pulled Grassley aside and told him about a letter she had gotten from a constituent in late July regarding an incident involving Kavanaugh from decades earlier. A woman had made certain allegations but requested confidentiality, so all Feinstein did was refer the matter to the FBI, which placed the letter in Kavanaugh's file per standard procedure, thus allowing the White House to see it for the first time. Sensitive issues like these would normally be handled in a standard process, but Feinstein had sat on this information for two months, only releasing it in this limited way after the hearing failed to derail the nomination.

The following day, September 14, the *New Yorker* published a story about the allegations, without naming the accuser: a woman claimed that, during a 1982 high school party, Kavanaugh had held

her down and tried to force himself on her.[24] Two days after that, the
Washington Post published a more detailed story, identifying the
accuser as Christine Blasey Ford, a psychology professor at Palo Alto
University.[25] Ford, who had attended an all-girls school in the same
D.C. suburb as Kavanaugh, had hired Debra Katz, a media-savvy
sexual harassment lawyer, and decided to go public once the story
began leaking in order to tell her own version of it.

On September 17, Kavanaugh issued a categorical denial, saying
that he has "never done anything like what the accuser describes."[26]
Several Republican senators, notably Flake and Graham, stated a
desire to hear from Ford; President Trump said that "a little delay"
would be okay.[27] Katz offered to have Ford appear before the committee, at which point Grassley, who had wanted to avoid a repeat of
the Thomas debacle, postponed the vote and set a hearing for September 24, the earliest he could under the rules. His staff had a hard
time communicating with Ford—Katz didn't relay an offer to have
staffers interview her in California—but arranged to have her testify
on September 27. Around the same time, Ford's high school friend
Leland Keyser, whom Ford had named in the *Post* account as being
at the get-together where the alleged incident took place, denied ever
meeting Kavanaugh or being at a party where he was present.[28]

A few days before the new hearing, another woman, Yale classmate Deborah Ramirez, alleged that Kavanaugh exposed himself
to her at a dorm party in 1983–84.[29] Although reporters contacted
dozens of classmates, the only "witness" they could find was an
anonymous claim to have heard about the incident third-hand.
The *New York Times* reported that Ramirez herself wasn't certain
that Kavanaugh was the one involved.[30] The nominee again issued
a total denial.

At this point, breathless rumor came from all sides, as the media
reported on the social lives of suburban teenagers and Ivy League

underclassmen. Michael Avenatti, who had made a name for himself representing Stormy Daniels in various lawsuits against Donald Trump—and who would later be convicted for tax evasion, fraud, and extortion—tweeted out insinuations and then an affidavit from Julie Swetnick accusing high-school Kavanaugh of having plied girls with drugs and alcohol to facilitate gang-rapes.[31] A woman from Oceanside, California, sent Feinstein an anonymous letter claiming Kavanaugh had raped her, later admitting she was just trying to get attention.[32] A man in Rhode Island sent Senator Sheldon Whitehouse (D-R.I.) a letter claiming that Kavanaugh and a friend had raped an acquaintance on a boat in Newport thirty years earlier, also later recanting.[33] What had been shaping up as a repeat of the Clarence Thomas process became a media-driven farce, as the attempt to make Kavanaugh into a serial sex-abuser backfired, casting even Ford's original claims into a miasma of incredulity.

After that phony war, which polarized the pro- and anti-Kavanaugh sides, nobody could be sure that Ford would show up to testify. Grassley and his staff had agreed to various accommodations—only one TV camera, frequent breaks, Kavanaugh not in the room, a security detail—but declined to have Kavanaugh testify first (as Thomas had done, in a sort of pointless "prebuttal") or to limit questioning to senators. The Republicans on the judiciary committee, all men, recognizing the sensitivities involved and the need to get facts rather than score political points, hired a well-respected Arizona prosecutor who is one of the leading interviewers of sex-crime victims, Rachel Mitchell, to handle their questioning.

Grassley opened the hearing by apologizing to both Ford and Kavanaugh and said that it was the timing of the allegations that had derailed the process, that if Feinstein had shared Ford's letter in July, it could've been investigated through proper channels in advance of any hearings. He explained that the FBI could ask questions and take

statements but didn't make conclusions, which was a job for the committee, and that lawyers for the other accusers were not cooperative
and had made no attempt to substantiate any claims. Feinstein admitted that she had sat on the letter; it came out that she did so because,
unlike her staff, she didn't find the claims relevant.[34]

Ford began her testimony by detailing the claims that were by
now well known: in the summer of 1982, at a small evening gathering
at a house in Bethesda, she was pushed into a bedroom, where Kavanaugh pinned her down, pawed at her clothes, and covered her
mouth so she couldn't scream, before his friend Mark Judge jumped
on the bed—Judge later sent the committee a sworn letter saying he
had no memory of this—causing Kavanaugh to fall off and allowing
Ford to escape. Ford said she told nobody about the incident at the
time; she had only mentioned a sexual assault to her husband and
described it in marital counseling. She said the assault had been
"seared into my memory and haunted me episodically" and that initially she wanted to keep the information confidential, before deciding it was her civic duty to testify.[35]

Although Mitchell's questioning brought out some inconsisten-
cies, Ford's sympathetic and credible account put Kavanaugh behind
the eight-ball. The nominee would have to give the performance of
his life to survive.

Kavanaugh's testimony was by no means perfect—he lost his cool
a couple of times, though that in itself was understandable given the
accusations against him—but it showed a personal side that often
gets lost in the political strategery of these high-stakes hearings. Taking McGahn's advice to be himself and fight, the nominee first laid
out the evidence—denying the allegations "immediately, categori-
cally, and unequivocally"—and then went on the offensive. "This
confirmation process has become a national disgrace," he said. "You
have replaced 'advice and consent' with 'search and destroy.'"[36] He

reminded the senators that many of them had made extreme statements about him even before the Ford allegations. Booker had called him "complicit in evil." Schumer vowed to fight him with everything he had. Then he listed all the last-minute smears: "Crazy stuff. Gangs, illegitimate children, fights on boats in Rhode Island. All nonsense. Reported breathlessly and often uncritically by the media. This has destroyed my family and my good name. A good name built up through decades of very hard work and public service at the highest levels of the American government." While he would later be criticized for bringing up "revenge on behalf of the Clintons," and "outside left-wing opposition groups," it's not because what he said wasn't true, just that you're not supposed to bring up motives or make allusions to background politics.

Kavanaugh then made a broader point that relates to the larger theme of this book: "This is a circus. The consequences will extend long past my nomination. The consequences will be with us for decades. This grotesque and coordinated character assassination will dissuade confident and good people of all political persuasions from serving our country." What do we gain from confirmation hearings if almost everybody's mind is made up going in, we learn nothing new, and the reputations of all involved take a hit? He feared for the future, but would not be intimidated: "You may defeat me in the final vote, but you will never get me to quit." Kavanaugh went on to detail the six FBI investigations he had passed, the intensely scrutinized positions he held, and the fact that no untoward allegations had been made against him before. He also pointed to his calendars—marvelously spoofed by Matt Damon on "Saturday Night Live"—as further evidence that he wouldn't have been at the party central to Ford's claim.

The Democrats questioned Kavanaugh about his drinking and sexual activity—particularly several goofy, cryptic notations in his high school yearbook. The nominee explained that he drank plenty of beer in high school, when the drinking age was 18, but had only respectful relationships with girls. Several senators asked whether he wanted an FBI inquiry, to which he replied that he wasn't going to tell them how to do their jobs but that committee staff could ask questions as well as the FBI, and similarly under penalty of felony. The Republicans were quiet, letting Rachel Mitchell firm up factual details, but then it was Lindsey Graham's turn. After a few questions to show Feinstein's secrecy and bad faith, the South Carolina senator launched into a tirade of rising indignation. Turning to his Democratic colleagues, whom he reminded of his votes for Justices Sotomayor and Kagan, he accused them of perpetrating the "most unethical sham since I've been in politics." "If you wanted an FBI investigation, you could've come to us. What you want to do is destroy this guy's life, hold this seat open, and hope you win in 2020," he continued. "Boy, y'all want power. God, I hope you never get it."[37]

The next day, the judiciary committee approved Kavanaugh 11–10, on party lines. Senator Jeff Flake made his vote contingent on the FBI conducting a new investigation, to be completed within a week.[38] The non-committee senators who were in play—Republicans Susan Collins and Lisa Murkowski, and Democrat Joe Manchin—supported that plan, which President Trump directed the FBI to execute. The further week's delay frustrated Kavanaugh's supporters but proved to be good for his nomination, as doubts began creeping in about the missing details from Ford's account and Swetnick's allegations kept shifting and ultimately lost any remaining credibility. Swetnick and her lawyer Avenatti would in late October be referred to the Justice Department for making false statements to the judiciary committee, a federal offense. Ramirez's story also never really came together. Senator Graham, accosted by a protestor who demanded that Kavanaugh take a polygraph to resolve the situation, responded, "Why don't we dunk him in water and see if he floats?"[39]

The investigation concluded on October 4, with the final report, a compilation of witness interviews, held in a secure Senate room with no possibility of photocopying or other distribution to avoid any more Spartacus moments. The room was open twenty-four hours for senators to come in and review the files. The next day, the Senate held its cloture vote, which was less dramatic than it could've been. By filibustering Gorsuch, Democrats had destroyed their leverage over this latest, more consequential vacancy. Moderate Republican senators would've been unlikely to go for a "nuclear option" to seat Kavanaugh, but now they didn't face that dilemma. Accordingly, the vote to move to a final vote was 51–49, along party lines except Murkowski voted no and Manchin—running for reelection in a deep-Trump state—yes.

The final vote would take place the next day, October 6, and it was by no means assured; Justice Alito had gotten 73 votes for cloture but only 58 for confirmation. It would come down to Collins, as Manchin would use her for electoral cover either way. The Maine moderate was besieged at home and in the office, and her female staff harassed by so-called women's rights groups. Progressive activists raised over a million dollars that they promised to spend against her in 2020 if Collins voted for Kavanaugh, which fight she's still waging as this book goes to press.

As Collins went to the Senate floor to announce her vote, behind her sat two other Republican women, Cindy Hyde-Smith of Mississippi and Shelley Moore Capito of West Virginia. She began her remarks by lamenting the devolution of the process into a "gutter-level political campaign."[40] "Our Supreme Court confirmation process has been in steady decline for more than 30 years," she said. "One can only hope that the Kavanaugh nomination is where the process has finally hit rock bottom." After reviewing Kavanaugh's qualifications and respect for precedent, she explained that this wasn't a criminal trial, so Ford's allegations need not be proven beyond a reasonable doubt. But they fail even a more lenient "more likely than not" standard, concluding that she would vote to confirm. Murkowski remained opposed, but she would ultimately "pair" with Senator Steve Daines, who was home in Montana for his daughter's wedding during the final vote. According to the old Senate tradition, neither would vote, so the final tally was 50–48, the narrowest margin since Stanley Matthews's 24–23 in 1881 and slightly narrower than that as a percentage. Justice Brett Kavanaugh was sworn in later that day, as hundreds of protestors milled about on the plaza outside the Supreme Court.

The Court's ideological dynamic that we'd all gotten used to, with four liberals, four conservatives, and a "swing," was now done. After that bruising confirmation fight, Kavanaugh took his seat on the Court in the second week of the 2018–19 term. Replacing the predictably unpredictable Justice Kennedy, he seemed poised to move the Court to the right. But looks can be deceiving. In a few high-stakes cases and, especially, petition rejections and other votes on the "shadow docket" (not fully briefed and argued cases), in his first term Kavanaugh was pragmatic rather than ideological. Notably, he was the deciding vote to allow an antitrust lawsuit to proceed against Apple, in a case where the dissent was led by his fellow Trump appointee Gorsuch. I'm still not sure who's right, but it showed two lively minds at work.

And Kavanaugh tried to keep a low and agreeable profile, easily becoming the justice most often in the majority (88 percent of the time). He also showed how different he was from Gorsuch, and not just on antitrust. Kavanaugh actually aligned as much with Justices Stephen Breyer and Elena Kagan as with Gorsuch (70 percent).

That's the lowest level of agreement between any two justices appointed by the same president in their first terms together going back at least to JFK.[41]

In Kavanaugh's second term, the newest justice was still in the majority in all but four cases—second only to Roberts, with whom he agreed more than any other pairing of justices—but he was much more in line with Gorsuch, and without the chief justice's strategic deviations. My fervent hope is that in those politically sensitive cases where Roberts may be inclined to tweak a law in order to save it, Kavanaugh will be more like Justices Scalia and Thomas and let external concerns fall by the wayside.

Of course, the debate we lived in 2018 wasn't really about Kavanaugh. While the people on Trump's judicial list differed in various ways, they were all in the conservative-originalist-textualist mainstream. The opposition to Kavanaugh was part of the continued refusal to accept the 2016 election, a frustration that Hillary Clinton wasn't making the pick.

The Judicial-Confirmation Machine

President Trump, meanwhile, who wouldn't have won had it not been for the Scalia vacancy, has now ensured that a major part of his legacy is in the judiciary. Having appointed nearly a third of all circuit judges—a record thirty in his first two years, about the same as Bush and Obama *combined* at that point in their presidencies, and fifty in three years (where Obama had fifty-five in eight years)—he has also had back-to-back Supreme Court picks. And Justices Ginsburg (87), Breyer (82), and Thomas (72) aren't getting any younger.

That's a big deal, because a president has few constitutional powers more important than picking judges. Legislative victories can be short-lived, regulations can be rescinded, and policy guidance isn't worth the paper it's written on. But judicial appointments are for life; those black-robed arbiters continue shaping our world long after the president who appointed them has left the White House. And all this goes just as much or more for the lower courts, which decide fifty thousand cases annually, dwarfing the Supreme Court's output. An important ruling on nonprofit-donor disclosures was made in April 2016 by a district judge appointed by Lyndon Johnson.[42]

Every four years, a president appoints 20 percent or more of the federal judiciary. To put it another way, when President Obama took office, only one of the thirteen federal appellate courts had majorities of Democratic appointees—the west-coast Ninth Circuit—but when he left nine did. When Trump was inaugurated in January 2017, there were 108 vacancies in the lower courts, which rose to about 150 before a Senate rule change enabled speedier confirmations. The remaining vacancies—all in district courts—are mostly in states where both Democratic senators refused to negotiate any sort of deal, preferring to leave their states shorthanded rather than allow Trump to get any say in their judges.[43]

These judicial slots were real wildcards. If a constitutional lawyer who had been president of the *Harvard Law Review* (Obama) deprioritized judicial nominations in his first few years, how much would a celebrity real-estate developer care? Would Trump see these as patronage posts for his casino lawyers and others he encountered in the entertainment world? Would he just focus on immigration and trade and let the judiciary erode away?

To his credit, the president let the White House Counsel's office run the show. Senators will occasionally insist on cronies, but the ratio of solid, "movement" nominees to establishmentarian hacks is exceedingly high. The result has been Trump's biggest success, with judges of the same kind and caliber as those conservative-constitutionalist Ted Cruz would have picked—and probably better than Jeb Bush or

Mitt Romney. This administration has surpassed even George W. Bush in picking committed and youthful originalists, particularly in the circuit courts, and getting them through the Senate. There is little concern of anyone moving left or being a "squish." McGahn likes to say that, rather than "outsourcing" judicial selection to the Federalist Society, he had "insourced" the operation, meaning that his team, which was far leaner than in previous administrations, were all "Fed Soc" members who understood the need for solid judges with a record of accomplishment.

That's why it's no surprise that so many of Trump's nominees are intellectual superstars, and why the Democrats have tried to smear them in various ways. Senator Feinstein said about Seventh Circuit Judge Amy Coney Barrett, the odds-on favorite to be elevated if Justice Ginsburg's seat becomes vacant, that "the dogma lives loudly within you"—which sounds like a rejected Star Wars line.[44] Fifth Circuit Judge Don Willett was assailed for humorous tweets, particularly one about a constitutional right to marry bacon. D.C. Circuit Judge Neomi Rao and Second Circuit Judge Steven Menashi were attacked for their (standard conservative-libertarian) collegiate writings, as was Ryan Bounds, a Ninth Circuit nominee who ultimately withdrew when two Republican senators, Tim Scott (S.C.) and Marco Rubio (Fla.), unreasonably declined to support him. California senators Feinstein and Harris tried especially hard to block Patrick Bumatay, who became the first openly gay Ninth Circuit judge and first circuit judge of Filipino descent. Unlike some of their colleagues in deep-blue states, including Schumer, they also haven't played ball on district judges, despite judicial emergencies in California's federal courts. The ABA too has been a source of renewed controversy, with nine nominees rated "not qualified," including three circuit nominees whose ratings seem based almost entirely on ideological disagreements.

Returning to numbers, on Inauguration Day, Republican-appointed majorities remained only in the Fifth, Sixth, Seventh, and Eighth Circuits, basically the middle of the country. While those majorities have grown and gotten younger, and more originalist, more interesting is how Trump and McConnell have been able to reverse the tide in the other nine circuits. For only the second time, the Senate confirmed double-digit circuit judges three years in a row.

The Third Circuit, based in Philadelphia, was the first one to flip from Democratic-appointed majorities to Republican-appointed ones. Then in quick succession came the New York-based Second and the Atlanta-based Eleventh. A far more significant shift has occurred on the Ninth Circuit, which has moved from nineteen Democrat-appointed judges, nine Republican-appointed, and one vacancy, to sixteen Democrat and thirteen Republican. The resulting ratio of D:R appointees is lower than in five other circuits, which ideological rebalancing is already being felt in the makeup of three-judge case panels and, unique to this court, the "limited" *en banc* panels of eleven. And the Ninth Circuit skews old, so if Trump is reelected, it could end up with a GOP-appointed majority for the first time since before the Carter-era judiciary expansion.

Realizing the danger in all this to a jurisprudential non-theory of social-justice-seeking, Democratic senators have used every parliamentary trick in their power to slow this Trump train. They no longer have the biggest brake, the filibuster—McConnell frequently thanks Harry Reid for having gotten rid of it for lower-court judges—so they've forced more cloture votes than in all previous presidencies combined. Nearly 80 percent of Trump's judicial nominees have faced cloture votes, including many who are confirmed with upwards of ninety votes. In comparison, about three percent of Obama's nominees faced cloture votes and fewer than two percent in the previous five presidencies. Until the Senate majority voted to cut back on floor time, Democrats also demanded the full thirty hours of floor time per nominee the rules allowed, even on judges who ultimately got approved by voice vote. Democrats are also refusing to return "blue slips," the home-state senators' prerogative to have significant say in whether to let a nominee be considered. Grassley thus made them non-dispositive for circuit nominees, assuming that the White House engaged in good-faith consultation—a policy Graham has continued as chairman.

As it happens, Trump's 200 Article III judicial appointees have received more than 4,400 no votes, while all 329 of Obama's judges got 2,039.[45] Trump's judges have received nearly half of all no votes in U.S. history, an average of about 22 per judge (and about 36 per circuit judge)—as compared to just over 6 per judge under Obama, 2 under George W. Bush, 1.3 under Clinton, and the rest fewer than one. In 2019 alone, when the Senate confirmed 102 judges, 12 percent of the total and second-highest ever for one year, those judges received 88 percent more no votes than all 2,680 judges confirmed in the 20th century. The number confirmed in 2019 is eclipsed only by the 135 in 1979, when Congress had just created 150 new judgeships and President Carter's Democrats had a 59–41 Senate majority. Judiciary Chairman Ted Kennedy even considered seven circuit nominees in one hearing and the Senate confirmed more than twenty judges on a single day at least twice, confirming more than 97 percent of judges on voice vote and taking *no* cloture votes. It was a different world.

One final statistic: The average Democrat has voted against nearly half of all Trump judicial nominees, while the average Republican voted against fewer than ten percent of Obama nominees and—get this—since the turn of the 20th century, senators of one party voted against fewer than two percent of nominees of the other. It's a shame that quality nominees are confirmed on party-line votes; only sixteen of fifty-three circuit judges confirmed under Trump have gotten more than sixty votes. But we've gotten here because we're at the culmination of a long trend whereby different legal theories map onto ideologically sorted parties. Federal judges are a big deal, so it's understandable that senators try to advance or block as many as possible.

That's why I'd never tell senators to vote for a nominee they think will do damage to the Constitution and the rule of law. Senator Graham really impressed me in the Kavanaugh fight, but he and Senator Collins are wrong to simply defer to presidents from both parties so long as their judicial nominees are qualified as a matter of intellect and experience. For senators and citizens alike, it's absolutely appropriate to question judicial philosophy. Judicial nominations are now properly an election issue, so it's heartening that voters are paying attention.

Part III—Future

Diagnoses and Reforms

CHAPTER 19

What Have We Learned?

T
he last few years have shown that the Supreme Court is now part of the same toxic cloud that has enveloped all of the nation's public discourse. Although the Court is still respected more than most institutions, it's increasingly viewed through a political lens. I discuss the Court's "legitimacy" in chapter 22—that's what most concerns people about the politics of judicial nominations—but what lessons can we draw from the sweep of confirmation battles?

Politics Has Always Been Part of the Process

Politics has always been part of the process of selecting judicial nominees, and even more part of the process of confirming them. From the beginning of the republic, presidents have picked justices for reasons that include balancing regional interests, supporting policy priorities, and providing representation to key constituencies. Whether looking to candidates' partisan labels or "real" politics, they've tried to find people in line with their own political thinking, and that of their party and supporters. Even in the earliest days, it was rare for someone to be on the Supreme Court "short list" of presidents from different parties. Look at the judicial battles of Adams and Jefferson, with the Midnight Judges Act—the original court-packing—as well as Jefferson's failed attempts to appoint justices to counter the great Federalist John Marshall. In the years that followed, when U.S. politics was defined by rivalries *within* the Democratic-Republican Party and its successors, ambitious lawyers knew that their careers depended on navigating the intra-party split. There has never been a golden age when "merit" as an objective measure of brain power and legal acumen was the sole consideration for judicial selection.

When those nominees got to the Senate, they faced another gauntlet, particularly when the president's party didn't have a majority. Historically, the Senate has confirmed fewer than 60 percent of Supreme Court nominees under divided government, as compared to just under 90 percent when the president's party controlled the Senate.[1] Timing matters too: over 80 percent of nominees in the first three years of a presidential term have been confirmed, but barely more than half in the fourth (election) year.

Nearly half the presidents have had at least one unsuccessful nomination, starting with George Washington and running all the way through George W. Bush and Barack Obama. James Madison had a nominee rejected, while John Quincy Adams had one "postponed indefinitely"—gotta love that euphemism. Andrew Jackson was able to appoint Roger Taney only after a change in Senate composition, while poor John Tyler, a political orphan after the Whigs kicked him out of their party, had only one successful nomination in nine attempts. Most 19th-century presidents had trouble filling seats before we had a run from 1894 until 1968 where only one nominee was rejected, John Parker under Herbert Hoover in 1930. Since LBJ, all presidents who have gotten more than one nomination had one fail, except George H. W. Bush and Bill Clinton. Donald Trump has thus far avoided that fate, but has had two of the most contentious nominations in our history.

In all, of 163 nominations formally sent to the Senate (counting each submission, even if the same person), only 126 were confirmed, which represents a success rate of 77 percent. Of those 126, one died before taking office and seven declined to serve, the last one in 1882—an occurrence unlikely ever to happen again. Of the rest, twelve were rejected, twelve were withdrawn, ten expired without the Senate's taking any action, and six were postponed or tabled. In other words, for various reasons, fewer than three-quarters of high court nominees have ended up serving.

Based on relative rates of unsuccessful nominations, the argument could be made that the nomination and confirmation process was more political during the nation's first century than since. Both the presidency and the Court were relatively weak and the process was more of an insider's game, with many picks based on personal loyalty and political philosophy rather than approach to the law. Of the fifty-seven justices confirmed between 1789 and 1898, seventeen lacked significant judicial experience.[2] As the judiciary took on a greater role, however, nominations attracted more public attention, and also more transparency. Interest groups began to matter—unions and the NAACP contributed to Parker's 1930 rejection—as public relations became just as important as Senate relations. Politics came back into the process, but in a different way. The battle became one over ideology and public perception rather than satisfying intra-party or regional factions.

Confirmation Fights Are Now Driven by Judicial Philosophy

As we've seen over the long sweep of American history, confirmation controversies are hardly unprecedented. To a certain extent, the politicization of Supreme Court appointments has tracked political divisions nationally. But the reasons for such controversies in the last few decades are largely unprecedented. While inter- and intra-party politics have always played a role, couching opposition in terms of judicial philosophy is a relatively new phenomenon that represents a departure from the past.

Pre-modern controversies tended to revolve around either the president's relationship with the Senate or deviations from shared understandings of the factors that go into nominations for particular seats—especially geography and patronage. That dynamic is markedly different from the ideological considerations we see now for at least two reasons. First, modern fights transcend any particular nominee or even president, evolving and growing and filtering into the lower courts. Second, ideological litmus tests cause more of a problem than the geographic, patronage, religious, and other past criteria because there's no longer widespread acceptance that a president gets to have his choice as long he meets those other, more neutral criteria. With the two major parties adopting essentially incompatible judicial philosophies, it's impossible for a president to find an "uncontroversial" nominee.

The conservative legal movement, meanwhile, has learned its lesson; "no more Souters" means there has to be a proven record, not simply center-right views and affiliations, showing not telling a commitment to originalism and textualism. That's one reason why, for example, former solicitor general Paul Clement, possibly the best Supreme Court lawyer in the country, wasn't added to Trump's list of potential high court picks. Once you consider someone who doesn't have a long judicial record, or at least academic writings to the same originalist-textualist effect, it opens the door to the sort of unmoored presidential discretion that has led to so many misfires.

The entire reason candidate Trump released his list was to convince Republicans, as well as cultural conservatives who may otherwise have stayed home or voted Democrat, that he could be trusted to appoint the right kind of judges. This was a real innovation, and we could see lists become standard practice, even if candidates from the two parties might use different criteria for shaping those lists, with more concern for demographic representation among the Democrats, who have a broader swath of lawyers—if not necessarily federal judges—to choose from.

The current emphasis on judicial philosophy may well be an updating of the "real politics" approach favored by presidents in the early 1900s—except now applied to intellectual commitments instead of trying to find (or avoid) progressive Republicans or conservative Democrats. But the problem is that there aren't really too many progressive originalists or conservative living-constitutionalists, at least not in any way where the ideological appellation doesn't swallow the philosophical one. Even Merrick Garland, who's about as much of a moderate as President Obama could find, didn't budge the Republican Senate.

Modern Confirmations Are Different Because the Political Culture Is Different

The inflection point for our legal culture, as for our social and political culture, was 1968, which ended that seventy-year near-perfect run of nominations. Until that point, most justices were confirmed by voice vote, without having to take a roll call. Since then, there hasn't been a single voice vote, not even for the five justices confirmed unanimously or the four whose no votes were in the single digits. And despite those "easy" confirmations, we've seen an upswing in no votes. Five of the closest eight confirmation margins have come in the last thirty years. Not surprisingly, the increased opposition and scrutiny has also signaled an increase in the time it takes to confirm a justice; six of the eight longest confirmations—and all but one that took longer than eighty days—have come since 1986. Every confirmation since the mid-1970s except O'Connor and Ginsburg has taken more than two months.

There are many factors going into the contentiousness of the last half-century: the Warren Court's activism and then *Roe v. Wade*, spawning a conservative reaction; the growth of presidential power to the point where the Senate felt the need to reassert itself; the culture of scandal and loss of institutional trust since Watergate; a desire for transparency when technology allows not just a 24-hour media cycle but a constant *and instant* delivery of information and opinion; and, fundamentally, more divided government.[3] As the Senate has grown less deferential, and presidential picks have become more ideological, seeking to achieve a certain legal agenda or empower a certain kind of jurisprudence rather than merely appointing a good party man, the clashes have grown.

And as these philosophical battle lines have hardened, so have the widespread media campaigns orchestrated by supporters and opponents of any given nominee. There's a straight line from the national TV ads against Bork to the tens of millions of dollars spent supporting and opposing Kavanaugh, including sophisticated targeting of digital media to voters in states whose senators are the deciding votes. "It's a war," explains Leonard Leo, who now chairs the public affairs firm CRC Advisors, "and you have to have troops, tanks, air, and ground support."[4]

To put a finer point on it, all but one failed nomination since Fortas have come when the opposite party controlled the Senate. The one exception is Harriet Miers, who withdrew because she was the first nominee since Harrold Carswell in 1969 to be seen as not up to the task. The last nominee rejected by a Senate whose majority was the same party as the president was Parker, by two votes in 1930. For that matter, this turbulent modern period has seen few outright rejections—Nixon's two and Bork are the only ones, in fifty-two years—with pre-nomination vetting and Senate consultation obviating most problematic picks.

At the same time, the inability to object to qualifications has led to manufactured outrage and scandal-mongering. This was more evident before considerations of judicial philosophy became standard practice, when Bork was an outlier. "Many people sneer at the notion of litmus tests for purposes of judicial selection or confirmation— even as they unknowingly conduct such tests themselves," Harvard law professor Randall Kennedy wrote nearly twenty years ago. The real problem, as he saw it, was that not being able to discuss ideology led to a search for scandal. "A transparent process in which ideological objections to judicial candidates are candidly voiced," he concluded, "is a much-needed antidote to the murky 'politics of personal destruction.'"[5] Sounding the same refrain was one Chuck Schumer: "The taboo [on invoking ideology] has led senators who oppose a nominee for ideological reasons to justify their opposition by finding non-ideological factors, like small financial improprieties from long ago. This 'gotcha' politics has warped the confirmation process and harmed the Senate's reputation."[6]

Well, that taboo no longer exists—which is a good, honest thing, because vetting a nominee's judicial philosophy is important—and yet we still got the Kavanaugh hearings.

Hearings Have Become Kabuki Theater

Public confirmation hearings have only been around for a century, starting with Brandeis's nomination in 1916. But Brandeis didn't testify at his own hearing; the first hearing where the nominee took unrestricted questions in an open hearing was Felix Frankfurter in 1938. It simply wasn't regular practice until the 1950s. At that point, the hearings became an opportunity for Southern Democrats to rail against *Brown v. Board of Education*. Few senators other than the segregationists even asked the nominees questions. Otherwise, hearings became perfunctory discussions of personal biography, as with Charles Whittaker in 1957 or the man who succeeded him in 1962, Byron White, whose hearing opens this book. John Paul Stevens, the first nominee after *Roe v. Wade*, wasn't even asked about that case—which was already controversial, have no doubt. The focus in that post-Fortas, post-Watergate time was on ethics, and Stevens was confirmed nineteen days after nomination.

Things changed in the 1980s, not coincidentally when the hearings began to be televised. Now all senators ask questions, especially about key controversies and fundamental issues, but nominees largely refuse to answer, creating what Elena Kagan twenty-five years ago called a "vapid and hollow charade."[7] But even with this conventional narrative, there has been a subtle shift; from Robert Bork in 1987 through Stephen Breyer in 1994, nominees went into some detail about doctrine.[8] "This is not to say that nominees during those years made commitments about how they would rule on contested legal issues. But they did discuss their judicial philosophies, their past writings and their beliefs about the role of judges."[9] Justice Thomas discussed natural law and the role that the Declaration of Independence plays in constitutional interpretation. Justice Ginsburg talked about gender equality and the relationship between liberty and privacy.

Beginning with John Roberts in 2005, however, the nominees still covered the holdings of cases and what lawyers call "black letter law"—what you need to know to get a good grade in law school—but there has been little revelation of personal opinions. The nominees speak in platitudes: Roberts and his judicial umpire, Sotomayor saying that fidelity to the law was her only guidepost, Kagan accepting that "we're all originalists now." President Trump's nominees, starting with Gorsuch and filtering down to lower-court nominees, have even been hesitant to take a view on whether iconic cases like *Brown* were correctly decided, lest their inability to similarly approve of another longstanding precedent (notably *Roe*) cast doubt on its validity.

These days, senators try to get nominees to admit that certain controversial cases are "settled law," whether *Roe* when coming from a Democrat or *Heller* from a Republican. Of course, when you're dealing with the Supreme Court, law is settled until it isn't, so nominees have come to say that every ruling is "due all the respect of a precedent of the Supreme Court," or some such. Which may or may not be a lot of respect, depending on the future justice's view of the merits and of the weight of *stare decisis*—the idea that some erroneous precedent should be allowed to stand to preserve stability in the law and protect reliance interests. And that's before we even get to the "gotcha" questions, or last-minute accusations of sexual impropriety.

Every Nomination Can Have a Significant Impact

The actual hearings, and the confirmation process more broadly, have very little to do with being a judge or justice. Once that spectacle is over, the new justice takes his or her seat among new colleagues—a lifetime "team of nine," as Justice Kavanaugh called it at his confirmation hearing—to begin reading briefs and considering technical legal issues. It must be a surreal experience, having run an American Ninja Warrior course to win a life of quiet contemplation and oracular pronouncements. Or, as President Trump's first White House Counsel Don McGahn put it, "[I]t's a Hollywood audition to join a monastery."[10]

Regardless, once you're in, you're in. As Justice White told Justice Thomas when the latter first joined the Court, "It doesn't matter how you got here. All that matters now is what you do here."[11] After all the nomination hoopla, the Supreme Court is still a court, albeit with a new composition that affects both internal dynamics and external results. White was also fond of saying that every justice creates a new Court, so each change shakes up the previous balance—regardless how close in "expected" philosophy a new justice might be to his or her predecessor.

That's why every single vacancy is important. Not all historically significant cases would've turned out differently if a single justice were replaced—*Marbury v. Madison* and other Marshall Court cases were typically unanimous, *Dred Scott* was 7–2, *Plessy* was 8–1, *Korematsu* was 6–3, *Wickard v. Filburn* was unanimous, as was *Brown*, while *Roe* was 7–2—but some would have. And not simply by changing the party of the president making the appointment. The *Slaughterhouse Cases*, which eviscerated the Fourteenth Amendment's protections against state action, were a 5–4 ruling with Lincoln appointees split 2–3, Grant appointees split 2–1, and a Buchanan appointee breaking the tie. *Lochner* was another 5–4, with Republican appointees split 3–3 and Democratic appointees split 2–1. The early New Deal cases typically split 6–3 or 5–4 against expansions of federal power, aligning the Four Horsemen (three Republican appointees and McReynolds) against the Three Musketeers (two Republican appointees and Brandeis), with two other Republican appointees in the middle, culminating in 1937's "switch in time that saved nine."

And all that's before we get to the modern era, when we got used to first Justices Stewart and Powell, then O'Connor and Kennedy, as the swing votes on issues ranging from affirmative action and redistricting to religion in the public square and gay rights. So many cases would've been decided differently had the conservative Bork been confirmed instead of the moderate Kennedy, and differently still had the libertarian Douglas Ginsburg occupied that seat. For that matter, had Edith Jones been nominated in 1990 instead of David Souter,

Kennedy wouldn't have been the median vote from 2005 to 2018—John Roberts would've been. And if Michael Luttig had been picked instead of Roberts in 2005—whether as chief justice or with Scalia elevated and Alito in Scalia's place—it would've been a *very* different Court these last fifteen years.

Moreover, Court majorities are fragile and subject to affinities and clashes. Chief Justice Marshall drew people toward him who normally wouldn't agree with him. Justice McReynolds pushed everyone away. Justice Brennan was gregarious and a skilled tactician, often outmaneuvering Chief Justice Burger. Justice O'Connor may have shaded left in response to Justice Scalia's provocations, or to balance the arrival of the more conservative Justice Thomas.

In part because they've been burned so many times, Republicans focus on the Court as an election issue much more than Democrats. *Bush v. Gore, Citizens United,* and *Shelby County,* the three biggest progressive losses of the last twenty years, have riled activists and elites, and ratcheted up confirmation battles, but haven't translated into campaigns regarding judges as such. "Republicans seem conditioned to feel that when they're not paying attention, the courts will cause them all kinds of trouble," Obama White House counsel Bob Bauer explains. "Democrats have come to have a similar concern, but for a long time, with visions of Warren, Brennan, Stevens and the like, they were more optimistic—maybe to a fault."[12]

Democrats may now be catching up, even though during the Garland experience they didn't make much of the vacancy or the Republicans' blockade. The result of the 2016 presidential election is that, for the first time in the modern era, and perhaps more clearly than ever, different judicial methodologies and approaches to legal interpretations line up with partisan preferences. For the foreseeable future, every Supreme Court vacancy is an opportunity to either prolong one party's control of a particular seat or "flip" it.

Another reason why filling each vacancy is such a big deal is that justices now serve longer. In the late 1700s, when life expectancy was under 40—skewed by infant mortality, of course—the average age of a Supreme Court nominee was about 50. In the late 1900s/early 2000s, when life expectancy in the United States is just under 80—more than that for those who are already in late middle age—the average age of a Supreme Court nominee is still not much above 50. And that includes the outlier Merrick Garland, who at 63 wouldn't have been picked had it not been for the unusual situation in which President Obama tried to offer a compromise. Since 1972, only one of 16 justices was over 55 at confirmation, Ruth Bader Ginsburg.

To put it another way, before 1970, the average tenure of a Supreme Court justice was less than fifteen years. Since then, it's been more than twenty-five. The life expectancy of justices once confirmed has grown from about eight years at the beginning of the Republic to twenty-five–thirty today. Justices appointed at or before age fifty, like John Roberts, Elena Kagan, and Neil Gorsuch, are likely to serve thirty-five years, or about nine presidential terms, projecting the legal-policy impact of Presidents Bush, Obama, and Trump, respectively, as far into the future as Antonin Scalia and Anthony Kennedy did for President Reagan. Clarence Thomas, who was forty-three when he joined the Court and has already served nearly thirty years, could serve another decade!

The Hardest Confirmations Come When There's a Potential for a Big Shift

In addition to divided government, at a time when the Court's ideological profile is more clearly defined, the most contentious nominations are those that threaten a shift in the Court's jurisprudence. Replacing the centrist Powell with the conservative Bork provoked a firestorm, but putting another moderate in that seat was easy.

Replacing liberal lion Thurgood Marshall with counterculture conservative Clarence Thomas was a fight, but appointing Antonin Scalia to William Rehnquist's seat when Rehnquist was elevated was a cakewalk. Would Kavanaugh have faced such strong opposition had he been nominated for Thomas's seat? Probably not.

There are only two modern moves in a more liberal direction. The first was Ruth Bader Ginsburg's replacement of Byron White, but that smooth confirmation came at a time when the Democrats had a significant Senate majority (57–43), newly elected Bill Clinton was enjoying his honeymoon—remember when presidents had those?—and White himself had been appointed by a Democratic president. The second was Merrick Garland's nomination to replace Scalia.

Think of it this way: regardless of which party controls the Senate, would there be a bigger political battle if President Trump gets to replace Ginsburg or Thomas? Would the fight to replace Breyer be fiercer under Trump or a Democratic president?

Of course, presidents aren't always successful in moving the Court in their preferred direction. Thomas Jefferson tried valiantly to dislodge the powerful Federalist judicial impulse, only to see his nominees fall under John Marshall's sway. Abraham Lincoln named Treasury Secretary Salmon P. Chase as chief justice, partly to get him out of his hair, but more importantly to uphold the legislation by which the federal government had financed the Civil War, and which Chase had helped draft. Instead, Chief Justice Chase wrote the opinion finding the Legal Tender Act unconstitutional. Ulysses Grant wanted to mold the Court for the post-Civil War world, but it took him eight nominations to seat four justices of varying quality and political direction. Teddy Roosevelt should've been pleased with the great progressive Oliver Wendell Holmes, but after a vote in the major antitrust case of the time, TR inveighed that "I could carve out of a banana a judge with more backbone than that."[13]

Woodrow Wilson named another storied progressive, Louis Brandeis, but also the most retrograde justice of that or possibly any time, James McReynolds, who didn't seem to share any of Wilson's views other than with regard to antitrust (and bigotry). Calvin Coolidge's sole nominee, Harlan F. Stone, would end up betraying his benefactor's laissez-faire proclivities by joining with Justices Holmes and Brandeis in taking the Court in a judicially restrained, and therefore progressive, direction. Harry Truman called putting Tom Clark on the Supreme Court his "biggest mistake" after Justice Clark ruled against his 1952 seizure of steel mills.[14] Dwight Eisenhower was disappointed with both Earl Warren and William Brennan, although the latter was more of a political calculation ahead of the 1956 election, intended to help with the Catholic (and crossover Democrat) vote. Nixon's appointment of Harry Blackmun similarly mitigated the reversal of the Warren Court that he had hoped to achieve, particularly given that Warren Burger wasn't a particularly strong leader and Lewis Powell became more of a moderate.

Ronald Reagan too advanced his own legal-policy agenda only with Scalia—elevating Rehnquist didn't add any votes—as O'Connor and Kennedy occupied the Court's middle rather than pushing originalism, strict construction, law-and-order conservatism, or any other articulation of what Republicans wanted. George H.W. Bush of course had Souter in addition to Thomas. His son, looking for reliable conservatives, checked that box with Roberts and Alito but didn't realize that a focus on judicial restraint could also lead to unpleasant results.

While a justice might feel "loyal to the president who appointed him," then-Justice Rehnquist told a law school audience in 1984, "institutional pressures...weaken and diffuse the outside loyalties of any new appointee."[15] At the same time, he explained, "one may look at a legal question differently as a judge than one did as a member of the executive branch"—and Rehnquist would know, having been a high Justice Department official. Moreover, a nominee picked for his views on the issues of the day—government expansion under FDR, executive power over national security under George W. Bush—might act contrary to type when the issue constellation changes. The judicial restraint of Felix Frankfurter, a New Deal progressive who co-founded the ACLU, made him a conservative in the postwar era, while John Roberts's similar restraint leads him to defer both to a wartime president and a peacetime Congress.

The Court Rules on So Many Controversies That Political Battles Are Unavoidable

Under the Framers' Constitution, by which the country lived for its first 150 years, the Supreme Court hardly ever had to curtail a federal law. If you read the Congressional Record of the 18th and 19th centuries, Congress debated whether particular legislation was constitutional much more than whether something was a good idea. Debates focused on whether something was genuinely for the general welfare or whether it only served a parochial or regional interest. "Do we have the power to do this?" was the central issue. In 1887, Grover Cleveland vetoed an appropriation of $10,000 for seeds to Texas farmers who were suffering from a terrible drought because he could find no warrant for such appropriation in the Constitution.[16] Twenty years later, the Supreme Court declared, "the proposition that there are legislative powers affecting the nation as a whole although not expressed in the specific grant of powers is in direct conflict with the doctrine that this is a government of enumerated powers."[17]

We also had a stable system of rights that went beyond those listed in the Bill of Rights. These rights were retained by the people under the Ninth Amendment—and similarly the Tenth Amendment was redundant of the whole structure of powers, which was based on the idea that we have a government of delegated and enumerated, and therefore limited, powers.

Judges play bigger roles today; as the Court has allowed the federal government to grow, so has its own power to police the programs its own jurisprudence enabled. For example, the idea that the General Welfare Clause justifies any legislation that gains a majority in Congress—as opposed to *limiting* federal reach to national issues— emerged in the Progressive Era. In 1935, FDR wrote to the chairman of the House Ways and Means Committee, "I hope your committee will not permit doubts as to constitutionality, however reasonable, to block the suggested legislation."[18] Decades later, Rexford Tugwell, a New Deal architect, wrote that "to the extent that these [policies] developed they were tortured interpretations of a document intended to prevent them."[19] In the 1930s and '40s, we thus had the perverse expansion of the Commerce Clause with cases like *NLRB v. Jones & Laughlin* and *Wickard v. Filburn*, which gained renewed prominence in the constitutional debate over Obamacare. After the "switch in time that saved nine," when the Court began approving grandiose legislation it had previously rejected, no federal legislation would be set aside as going beyond congressional power until 1995.

We also had the flip side of the expansion of powers: the warping of rights. In 1938, the infamous Footnote Four in the *Carolene Products* case bifurcated our rights such that certain rights are more equal than others in a kind of *Animal Farm* approach to the Constitution. So it's the New Deal Court that politicized the Constitution, and thus also the confirmation process, by laying the foundation for judicial mischief of every stripe—but particularly letting laws sail through that should be invalidated. The Warren Court picked up that baton by rewriting laws in areas that are best left to the political branches, micro-managing cultural disputes in a way that made the justices into philosopher kings, elevating and sharpening society's ideological tensions.

In that light, modern confirmation battles—whether you look at Bork, Thomas, the filibustering of George W. Bush's lower-court nominees, the scrutiny of Sotomayor's "wise Latina" comment, or the party-line votes on Gorsuch and Kavanaugh—are all part of, and a logical response to, political incentives given judges' novel expansive role. When judges act as super-legislators, the media and the public want to scrutinize their ideology for that very reason.

As Roger Pilon wrote presciently nearly 20 years ago, "Because constitutional principles limiting federal power to enumerated ends have been ignored, the scope of federal power and the subjects open to federal concern are determined now by politics alone. Because the rights that would limit the exercise of that power are grounded increasingly not in the Constitution's first principles but in the subjective understandings of judges about evolving social values, they too increasingly reflect the politics of the day."[20]

The ever-expanding size and scope of the federal government has increased the number and complexity of issues brought under Washington's control, while the collection of those new federal powers into the administrative state has transferred ultimate decision-making authority to the courts. The imbalance between the executive branch and Congress—especially the latter's abdication of its leading constitutional role by delegating what would otherwise be legislative responsibilities—has made the Supreme Court into the decider both of controversial social issues and complex policy disputes. Senator Ben Sasse (R-Neb.) wrote about this dynamic in a *Wall Street Journal* op-ed adapted from his opening remarks at the Kavanaugh hearings:

> For the past century, more legislative authority has been delegated to the executive branch every year. Both parties

do it. The legislature is weak, and most people here in Congress want their jobs more than they want to do legislative work. So they punt most of the work to the next branch.

The consequence of this transfer of power is that people yearn for a place where politics can actually be done. When we don't do a lot of big political debating here in Congress, we transfer it to the Supreme Court. And that's why the court is increasingly a substitute political battleground. We badly need to restore the proper duties and the balance of power to our constitutional system.[21]

In other words, Congress doesn't complete its work so it can pass the political buck to a faceless bureaucracy, and to a judiciary that ultimately has to evaluate if what these alphabet agencies come up with is within spitting distance of what the law allows. What's supposed to be the most democratically accountable branch has been punting its duties and avoiding hard choices since long before the current polarization.

Gridlock is a feature of a legislative process that's meant to be hard by design, but compounded of late by citizens of all political views being fed up with a situation where nothing changes regardless of which party is elected. Washington has become a perpetual-motion machine—and the courts are the only actors able to throw in an occasional monkey wrench. "Punting difficult issues to the Court is not a new thing," says C. Boyden Gray, White House counsel under President Bush I, noting that Alexis de Tocqueville had recognized the dynamic in the 1830s. "What's made it so fraught is the way the administrative state has been used the last two decades."[22] That's why people are concerned about the views of judicial nominees—and why there are more protests outside the Supreme Court than outside Congress.

CHAPTER 20

Term Limits

T erm limits for justices has been an evergreen reform proposal that flares up whenever there hasn't been a vacancy in several years, or when justices stay in office past a certain age. William O. Douglas, who served on the Court longer than anyone else, didn't want to leave despite having suffered a debilitating stroke, causing his colleagues to hold over any cases in which he was the deciding vote. Thurgood Marshall, near-blind and in poor health, tried to outlast Republican presidents before finally retiring in George H. W. Bush's third year. William Rehnquist's decision to stay on despite illness led Sandra Day O'Connor to have an awkward lame duck period, with consecutive vacancies for George W. Bush to fill. There's now morbid interest in the health of eighty-seven-year-old Ruth Bader Ginsburg, who was criticized for not retiring when Democrats controlled both the White House and Senate.

After Robert Bork's failed nomination, scholars and pundits began whispering about the possibility of term limits as a way to defuse tensions over the Supreme Court, whose importance was exacerbated by the lifetime power that each justice held. But the Court was in a period of rapid turnover, with six new justices in eight years (1986–1994), so it seemed like term limits were beside the point. Then, as time passed after Stephen Breyer joined the bench in 1994 and no further vacancies were in the offing, the drumbeat for term limits grew.

The scholarship culminated in a proposal that Northwestern law professors Steven Calabresi—one of the founders of the Federalist Society—and James Lindgren published in 2006.[1] They argued for staggered 18-year terms, such that a vacancy would occur every two years, in non-election years, giving each presidential term two appointments. They also analyzed various possibilities of enacting such a reform by statute and found them wanting—Article III says federal judges "shall hold their Offices during good Behaviour"—thus requiring a constitutional amendment to achieve this goal.

Of course, the idea for limited judicial tenures is hardly a new one; it was debated at the Founding. Back then, the idea of lifetime appointments seemed the best way to establish an independent judiciary, insulating judges from the political forces that might endanger constitutional rights and liberties. But has the pendulum swung too far the other way, with a high court either unresponsive to or too reflective of contemporary political fights? Even if the justices behave the same way they always have on the bench, if the public perception is that they're out-of-touch ideologues, that isn't good for the Supreme Court as an institution or our body politic more broadly. And given the difficulty in ratifying a constitutional amendment—three quarters of state legislatures have to approve, if term limits were instituted, they would represent significant bipartisan consensus.

Even if the Court's jurisprudence wouldn't change, and even if justices' average age didn't decline too much—because people in their 60s would again be considered—a more regular rotation, without unexpected vacancies or superannuated tenures, might help with public confidence, which is no small matter. At the same time, given the guaranteed two appointments every four years, the Court would play a more prominent and regular role in presidential elections, thus shifting at least some of the political battle from the confirmation process to the campaigns, where they're a healthier fit. Both of these changes would be good.

From Founding Times till Today

Thomas Jefferson denounced life tenure as contrary to an ordered republic, proposing terms of four or six years for federal judges—even though he had earlier supported life terms.[2] On the other side stood Jefferson's frequent rival, Alexander Hamilton, who argued in *Federalist* 78 that judicial life tenure was "the best expedient which can be devised in any government to secure a steady, upright, and impartial administration of the laws." The debate was thus over how and to what degree the country's judiciary should be beholden to popular opinion, reflecting conflicting visions for the young republic.

These early debates died down as the Supreme Court and inferior federal courts settled into predictable routines. From 1801 to 1835, the Court, led by Chief Justice Marshall, navigated some rough waters, but its stability legitimized it. While the Court faced serious crises after Marshall—most notably following *Dred Scott* (1857), which contributed to the Civil War—there were no serious proposals to end life tenure until the modern era.

After a decade without a Supreme Court vacancy, scholars in the mid-2000s began to ponder term limits more seriously. In April 2005, law professors from across the country gathered at Duke University to discuss possibilities for reform, which would eventually be compiled into an edited volume.[3] A common thread was that the greatest danger posed by lifetime tenure was not physical or even mental decrepitude, but that it practically deifies the Court and thus makes it too important in politics and culture. The centerpiece of the symposium was the developing Calabresi-Lindgren proposal for fixed, staggered, non-renewable 18-year terms, achieved through constitutional amendment, with a new seat to open every two years.

The reasons for the change are clear. First, the average length of tenure has increased as a result of rising life expectancies, increased prestige of the job, and a reduction in the difficulties associated with service. Justices' ages at confirmation are remarkably clustered between fifty-two and fifty-seven throughout history, so "the expansion of life tenure is caused not by Presidents' appointing younger Justices, but by the Justices' living longer and retiring later."[4] Second, life tenure enables justices to time their retirements for political purposes. Third, the longer justices serve, the less accountable they become to democratic sentiments and the more detached they are from the cultural zeitgeist that inevitably informs the public's response to the Court's rulings. Finally, "the irregular occurrence of vacancies on the Supreme Court means that when one does arise, the stakes are enormous," and the brutal and often drawn-out political combat that results affects the Court "directly, since it is deprived of one of its nine members, and indirectly, since rancorous confirmation battles lower the prestige of the Court."[5]

The structure and clarity of these arguments made the Calabresi-Lindgren piece the gold standard of the modern debate—though the scholars rejected a statutory version of their proposal as both unconstitutional and undesirable, given the partisan tug-of-war it could elicit from one Congress to the next. The statutory route is simply subject to too strong a constitutional challenge. What's more, as a practical matter, it could very well accelerate the politicization of the Court that it's meant to address. No longer would politics simply intrude on confirmation battles and the occasional lighting-rod ruling. Instead, it could foster a brave new world in which the federal law of Supreme Court term limits is constantly repealed, reenacted, and readjusted with each rebalancing of the Senate's majority.

A Democratic Senate could block nominations through four years of a Republican presidency, and then with two vacancies, repeal the fixed term and give four or more of the justices lifetime posts, ensuring a left-leaning majority for generations. Republicans could do the same; neither party is immune to the perverse incentives that would be at work. In this light, a constitutional amendment is the only depoliticizing avenue.

Setting aside the question of *how* to accomplish term limits, Calabresi and Lindgren are persuasive in their *why*. First, 18-year terms would obviously reduce the post-1970 average tenure of more than twenty-five years. Second, if presidents continue to appoint justices in their mid-50s, ages at retirement would drop, thus reducing the risk of mental or physical decrepitude. Third, the proposal would solve what Calabresi and Lindgren call the "problem of hot spots": the irregular vacancies that are often clustered. Since Justice O'Connor was confirmed in 1981, each of the last six presidents has been limited to two appointment opportunities in consecutive years. If vacancies were set to occur once every two years, every president would be able to pick two justices each term, except for death or retirement, which would "reduce the stakes of the nomination process and eliminate the uncertainty that now exists regarding when vacancies will occur," making the Court "more democratically accountable and legitimate by providing for regular updating of the Court's membership."[6] In other words, there would be a more direct connection between the will of the people, as expressed through their presidential ballot, and the direction of the Court.

Still, having a closer—or at least more tangible—connection between presidential elections and Supreme Court nominations won't necessarily lower tensions. Imagine a scenario in which a GOP-controlled Senate blocks a Democratic president's 2025 and 2027 nominations. A Republican president is then elected in 2028 and the Senate confirms four of her nominees: in 2029 and 2031 to serve the regular 18-year terms, and the two empty seats with forteen and sixteen years left on their terms, respectively. Again, this could happen in every cycle of divided government, and would exacerbate, not lessen, the politicization of the confirmation process. But perhaps there's something to having that regularity, with a midterm or presidential election the following year to provide instant popular feedback on each party's tactics.

There are also transition problems. Since term limits almost certainly wouldn't apply to sitting justices, for decades we would have term-limited justices serving alongside life-tenured ones. Moreover, it would take decades to get each seat's 18-year term aligned with all the others. Whenever the first vacancy occurs after a new president takes office, the new "transitional" justice would be put into the 18-year slot that either starts that year or the following year. For the next vacancies, if a transitional justice is already occupying that term, then the 18-year clock would begin two years later (or four, or six, etc.). But during this phase-in, future vacancies wouldn't arise in an orderly manner, so some transitional justice could serve five or ten years before another one arrives; at a certain point, someone could end up "limited" to twenty, twenty-five, or even thirty-five years. There could be fixes put in to prevent all this, but at some point, the complications become more trouble than they're worth. The problem of having a vacancy before a term is up looks easy in comparison: the president just nominates someone to fill the rest of the term who is ineligible for reappointment.

Could the Court weather accusations of illegitimacy and special-interest capture in these novel circumstances? And, as some commentators have indicated, eighteen years is still a long time—more than the pre-1970 average tenure!—so even with a biennial vacancy, the stakes will remain high, especially for those confirmation fights in which the Court's ideological balance is at stake.

Where Are We Now?

Naturally, some scholars have voiced continuing support for life tenure, both before and after the publication of that seminal Calabresi-Lindgren proposal. Once such earlier voice was Ward Farnsworth, now dean of UT-Austin Law School, who has maintained that life tenures serve a valuable role in slowing the lawmaking process. Put simply, "the Court is supposed to be undemocratic, at least in part."[7] Of course the Court should be at least partly undemocratic. How else would we protect the rights of minority or otherwise unpopular actors from the threats of majoritarianism? But is life tenure necessary to insulate justices from outside pressure, to maintain independence?

Northwestern law professor Martin Redish thinks so, insisting that "Article III's provision of life tenure is quite obviously intended to insulate federal judges from undue external political pressures on their decision making, which would undermine and possibly preclude effective performance of the federal judiciary's function in our system."[8] Even if that point were valid for lower-court judges, however, the Supreme Court is a prestigious place. Ascending to the high court is a dream shared by many ambitious lawyers, enough to keep qualified appointees rolling into 18-year terms. Veneration of judicial service is real, and is associated with the office itself, not with the accoutrements or post-service opportunities it offers.

Similar to Farnsworth's defense of life tenure was Justice Kennedy's assertion, at his confirmation hearing, that "life tenure is in part a constitutional mandate to the federal judiciary to proceed with caution, to avoid reaching issues not necessary to the resolution of the suit at hand, and to defer to the political process."[9] This argument is not without merit. Term-limited justices, eager to cement their legacies, might jump at any opportunity to rule on an important case, to cast the swing vote on a decision that'll make the history books. Of course, lifers have hardly been immune to this urge, though it makes sense that the itch to cast a historic vote might be marginally harder to resist when a justice knows just how much time he or she has left.

Post-publication critiques of Calabresi-Lindgren proposal are, for the most part, challenges to the need for such a drastic overhaul, rather than a Kennedy-style defense of lifetime appointments. While the proposal has garnered a largely warm reception within academic and media circles, a notable criticism, that of professors David R. Stras and Ryan W. Scott (the former now an Eighth Circuit judge), is that the repeated reference to a post-1970 increase in the average length of service is a false premise. Scott and Stras argue that the Court's history is replete with long tenures, and that the only difference is that there haven't been any very short tenures in the modern era to drag down the average. But, as Stras and Scott emphasize, "tenures actually were *higher* before 1940, so the trend looks more like a random walk than a steady climb."[10] Moreover, cutting off the trendline at 1970 rather than 1975 assigns to the "modern" era the abnormally long tenures of Hugo Black (thirty-four years) and William O. Douglas (thirty-six years).

While long tenures have been a regular feature of Court history, that fact doesn't necessarily vindicate a system charged with being unduly politicized. Such whataboutism doesn't do any argument any good, especially when the political and cultural consequences of long tenures are greater now than they were before.

Term-limit debates have continued into the 2010s. In 2012, former *New York Times* Supreme Court correspondent Linda Greenhouse wrote that when she first heard about judicial term limits, "I thought it was a bad, if not crazy idea that threatened the Framers' plan to guarantee judicial independence. But more recently, against my instincts, I have found myself drawn to the notion."[11] And Greenhouse is in good (and crowded) company. Proponents of term limits for Supreme Court justices now include a myriad senators, governors, lawyers, academics, and commentators who run the ideological gamut—plus offhand comments by Justices Breyer and Kagan, and a young John Roberts in a 1983 White House memo.[12]

So where are we now? Do term limits have a real chance? There's certainly an itch for reforming the Court; in 2015, 66 percent of Americans supported the idea of limiting justices' tenure, while in 2018, that number went up to 78 percent—without much differentiation by party affiliation.[13] And after the Garland blockade and Kavanaugh debacle, the public may well be just one or two controversies away from bringing the proposal into serious political contention.

The Trump era has been particularly kind to the idea of Supreme Court term limits, not least because the administration and GOP-controlled Senate have been so successful in filling the courts with young originalist judges, which has peeved those on the left who might otherwise applaud the lifetime appointment of the next Ruth Bader Ginsburg. These calls for reform accelerated around Justice Kennedy's retirement, and reached a fever pitch once it became clear that his successor would be confirmed after a blistering confirmation fight. Just after Kennedy announced he was to leave the bench, a *Vox* writer, endorsing term limits, warned that if Democrats regain the White House and Senate, "they might be tempted to expand the number of justices to 15, as payback for the 'stolen' Merrick Garland seat."[14] That's a decent point, but it seems strange that Republicans are being asked to bear the weight of the Court's recent politicization—that it's up to them to avoid the Democrats' wrath.

That view of where things stand permeates recent calls for term limits, though cooler minds have emerged. Professor Lindgren, writing in the *L.A. Times* after Kavanaugh's nomination but before the confirmation firestorm, argued that "[l]ong tenures on the court…provoke a fear, reasonable or not, that an ill-considered appointment could damage the nation for a long time."[15] In contrast, a *Reason* piece written during the Kavanaugh controversy cautioned against expecting too much from term limits: "Would the stakes really be that much lower if Kavanaugh were in the running for an 18-year term on the court?"[16] What's more, if these 18-year terms had been around the last few decades, the Court's makeup would hardly be different; there would now be three Bush II appointees, four Obama appointees, and two Trump appointees. In the last fifty years, there have been thirty years of Republican presidents and twenty years of Democratic ones; yet if anything, liberal voices have been overrepresented on the Court.

But even if term limits won't change the Court's decision making, they might be worth trying anyway because at least there would be less randomness about when vacancies arise. As Berkeley law professor Orin Kerr (then at the University of Southern California) put it, "If the Supreme Court is going to have an ideological direction— which, for better or worse, history suggests it will—it is better to have that direction hinge on a more democratically accountable basis than the health of one or two octogenarians."[17]

The best argument for term limits is that maybe, just maybe, they'll help restore public confidence in the confirmation process.

CHAPTER 21

More Radical Reforms

While term limits aren't a new idea, the last few years have seen an explosion of more creative reform proposals to respond to unpopular decisions and other controversies. On the extremes are calls for electing justices—or at least retention elections, as Ted Cruz proposed after the 2015 rulings on Obamacare and same-sex marriage[1]—and even abolishing the Supreme Court altogether, as Harvard law professor Mark Tushnet suggested after Justice Kavanaugh's confirmation.[2] This phenomenon has accelerated in the wake of the 2016 election, with progressives' dual frustration at (1) Donald Trump's unexpected victory that (2) vindicated the Republicans' risky strategy of not acting on the Merrick Garland nomination.

Politicians and academics alike have proposed a host of changes to both the Supreme Court's structure and the process for confirming justices. These proposals aim to remedy issues that go beyond the usual complaint that justices stay on the bench too long, serving as a sort of dead hand of long-departed presidential administrations. They address both Garland's "stolen" seat and, more broadly, the politicization of the judiciary, in an attempt to end the tit-for-tat escalations documented in Part II.

From the politicians' perspective, Democrats have finally decided to make judicial nominations an election issue. After ceding the ground to Republicans for decades—in 2016, Hillary Clinton barely addressed the Supreme Court vacancy, and Garland's name wasn't mentioned at the Democratic National Convention—in 2020 they went all in. Even more than calling for "non-ideological" judges who will nonetheless rule in the "right" way on certain litmus-test issues, the Democrats chose a bolder approach going into the latest presidential election. They aimed to fundamentally restructure the Court, adding justices, changing the way they're picked, and even altering how rulings are made and on what subjects.[3]

Why are progressives so up in arms, not just learning the lessons of past elections by activating their base voters but calling for radical change? It's a combination of frustration about the past and despair for the future. In other words, for the same reasons that the judiciary has been a base-activating issue for conservatives, who have long felt themselves to be one vote shy on the things that really matter: abortion, affirmative action, Obamacare, same-sex marriage. Even if the left has won its fair share of judicial victories in recent years, it has felt increasingly on defense, one step away from the precipice.

The 2016 election was supposed to mark a move away from that posture. In May of that year, Mark Tushnet—the same Harvard professor who would later talk of abolishing the Court—called for abandoning "defensive crouch liberal constitutionalism," while cautioning that "all bets are off if Donald Trump becomes President."[4] The Garland blockade, as vindicated by Trump's inside-straight win, felt like a sucker punch. *Janus v. AFSCME*, where Gorsuch in his first term provided the deciding vote that freed workers from being forced to pay "agency fees" to public-sector unions, thus jeopardizing a key Democratic funding source, was the last straw. The Kavanaugh imbroglio added insult to injury.

Before Trump, progressives complained vociferously about *Citizens United*, *Shelby County*, and partisan gerrymandering, as examples of structural advantages that corporate interests, conservatives, and Republicans—all the same thing in this telling—enjoyed. Once Trump took the oath of office, all that was dialed up to twelve, even as Clinton handily outspent the Trump campaign and the chamber of Congress that Democrats have been unable to take back is the non-gerrymanderable Senate.

"Because the Court has undermined the institutions of democracy, court packing is the only way to restore the integrity of the political system," the progressive activist group Pack the Courts said in March 2019. "To be taken seriously, presidential candidates must explain how they will restore democracy over the objections of a hostile and partisan Court."[5]

Democrats thus added the court-packing initiative to their cornucopia of "systemic" reforms, which have included the elimination of the Electoral College and lowering the voting age to sixteen, as well as a smorgasbord of power-grabs and speech restrictions in H.R. 1, the first bill the Democrats proposed after taking over the House in the 2018 elections.[6] Those polarizing initiatives would make the nation safe for left-wing populism, as a direct response to what Trump has engineered on the right. How any of them is supposed to "depoliticize" the Court or any other institution is anyone's guess. "The Founders had a pretty good system" that prevented federal excess, said former attorney general Ed Meese, and that's why "these reform ideas primarily come from the left."[7]

Adding More Justices

It's no surprise that court-packing emerged as the first litmus test of the 2020 Democrats. "I think the Kavanaugh nomination has put a fire under progressives," said Caroline Fredrickson, then-president of the American Constitution Society (lefty counterpart to the Federalist Society), adding that it's "not written in stone that the court has nine seats."[8]

Indeed, the Constitution doesn't specify the number of justices, but each expansion was historically accompanied by political mischief, as we learned in the first few chapters of this book. The Judiciary Act of 1789 set out six, but then the 1801 Midnight Judges Act would've reduced the Court to five members at its next vacancy, to thwart the incoming president, Thomas Jefferson. In 1802, Congress restored the Court to six seats, a move Justice Samuel Chase opposed, which led to his impeachment (but not removal; see chapter one). As the country grew, Congress created new circuits, with new justices appointed to each one. That all seems innocuous, but there were also convenient political reasons for adding them, ones that didn't always inure to the nation's benefit.[9]

A seventh seat was added in 1807, in part because Jefferson wanted to temper Chief Justice John Marshall's Federalist proclivities, an unsuccessful maneuver given Marshall's skill at swaying new colleagues. The eighth and ninth seats added in 1837 allowed a Jacksonian reshaping with the new justices supporting Roger Taney's authorship of *Dred Scott*. Then a tenth seat was added in 1863, in part to allow Abraham Lincoln more leeway.

That tenth seat was never filled and, to prevent Andrew Johnson from naming anyone—and at the request of Chief Justice Salmon Chase, who presided over Johnson's impeachment trial—Congress in 1866 cut the Court to seven members, such that the next three departing justices wouldn't be replaced. In 1869, however, after two seats had been lost to that attrition, the Circuit Judges Act fixed the bench at nine seats, a number that has survived 150 years, allowing the Court to get the stability and prestige it never had previously.

The most famous example of attempted court-packing is, of course, FDR's Judicial Procedures Reform Bill of 1937 (see chapter 5). The president was fresh off a massive reelection—the famous "as goes Maine, so goes Vermont" year, when Roosevelt won 523–8 in the Electoral College—and unhappy about a series of rulings against his New Deal programs. He proposed adding a new justice for every sitting justice older than seventy and a half, up to a maximum bench of fifteen. The plan met heavy, bipartisan opposition from Congress and faced public opposition by the justices *and FDR's own vice president*. The plan led to huge Democratic losses in the 1938 election, with Republicans gaining eighty-one seats in the House and seven in the Senate.

No real calls for court-packing have come between FDR's time and now, though of course there were calls to "Impeach Earl Warren" in the Jim Crow South. As with most such proposals in our history, the partisan appeal is both evident and heavy-handed. But if Democrats think they'd be reuniting the country, then they deserve the political losses that such ends-justify-the-means radicalism would inevitably cause. And if they think that packing the Court would restore "norms," then they really didn't understand the nature of governance. Just as two wrongs don't make a right, you don't restore norms by transforming institutions, particularly when doing so would mean eliminating the legislative filibuster—there's still a 60-vote threshold for most legislation—which would open an even bigger can of worms.

Yet there's nothing inherently ideological about a larger Supreme Court. Presidents of both parties nominate however many justices there are, just as presidents of both parties nominate lower-court judges in both the reddest and bluest states. In addition to issues of judicial administration—maybe the Court could hear more cases and more efficiently process cert petitions with more personnel—there would logically be less significance to each of, say, nineteen seats than nine (and presumably fewer 10–9 decisions than 5–4 ones now), so there would be less of a battle royale over each vacancy. For that matter, you could set an even number of justices, as some countries do, which would require at least a two-vote margin to take any action and ensure that there's no one swing vote. You could also go back to the earlier practice of having as many Supreme Court seats as there are geographical circuits, which might mean a return, at least marginally, of the norm of regional representation on the high bench.

The problem comes in getting to the new number, whatever it is. If we were designing a Constitution from scratch, or passing the first judiciary act, we could be writing on a blank slate and could implement whatever structure we thought best. But we're not, so how do you get to an expansion of any kind that won't result in a similar expansion the next time the opposing party is in power? Even if there were a deal whereby each party gets to add a justice every two years, the GOP would turn it down because a 5–4 ratio is better than 7–6, 9–8, and so on.

Presumably you would need a transition period, such that the reform only takes effect far enough into the future that we don't know who will be in the White House. Would twelve years (three presidential elections) be enough? Twenty? Politicos tend to be risk-averse, so I'm not sure this is viable—and in any case, a future Congress could eliminate or change the planned expansion. Even if one of these "delayed packing" plans went through, wouldn't the same sort of natural attrition that ultimately benefited FDR also benefit today's Democrats? Except they'd have to suffer the "damage" from the current Court in the intervening years. So we're back to the simple (and nakedly partisan) escalations.

The current number of nine justices is not some golden ideal. It was set not through debate and deliberation, incorporating the best that 19th-century social science had to offer, but simply because there were nine circuits at the time.[10] Still, Senator Marco Rubio (R-Fla.) and Rep. Mark Green (R-Tenn.), joined by various colleagues, have proposed constitutional amendments capping the Court's size at nine.[11] As one might expect, these proposals react to the nakedly partisan court-packing scheme rather than making arguments for the Court's optimal size in the abstract—and they have no chance of getting two-thirds of each house of Congress to approve them and three-quarters of state legislatures to ratify them.

Restructuring the Court

Recognizing that term limits faced a constitutional stumbling block and that expanding the Court wouldn't depoliticize it, scholars have begun thinking outside the box. Dan Epps of Washington University in St. Louis (who clerked for Justice Kennedy) and Ganesh Sitaraman of Vanderbilt (who had been Elizabeth Warren's counsel) in 2019 published a provocative *Yale Law Journal* article that floated two major reforms. Titled "How to Save the Supreme Court," the authors proposed a "Supreme Court lottery" whereby lower-court judges rotate through sittings on the high court or, in the alternative, an expanded but politically "balanced" bench.[12] These ideas have been much-discussed—Epps and Sitaraman went about as "viral" as a law review article can get—and attracted the attention of several presidential candidates, but also faced significant pushback, most substantively by Duke law professor Stephen Sachs (who clerked for Chief Justice Roberts).[13]

1. Supreme Court Lottery

Under this proposal, every circuit judge would also be appointed as an associate justice. Each would then be eligible to be randomly called to Washington to hear Supreme Court cases in two-week rotations as panels of nine, with no more than five members appointed by presidents of the same party. Further, a 6–3 majority would be required to invalidate any act of Congress—although overruling prior decisions, even so-called super-duper precedents, would continue to rest on counting to five. While empaneled, the supreme lottery winners would conduct the Court's regular business on the "shadow docket": granting and denying petitions for review (in cases some future panel would decide), ruling on motions to stay lower-court judgments or executions pending appeal, and everything that the justices do in addition to hearing cases.

It's hard to foresee all the effects this system would have on Court decision-making. For one thing, it would likely create a shift in the deference due pre- versus post-lottery decisions. Epps and Sitaraman believe the irregularity of panel service would yield greater deference for prior panel decisions, but it's equally likely that panels would *not* apply much precedential weight at all to a case decided just the previous year by a randomly assigned panel, which would effectively require several rulings going in one direction for a legal issue to be as "settled" as precedents generated under the current regime. Of course, that may be a feature, not a bug. Currently, "bad" decisions are enshrined because the justices that originally decided a case will then reiterate the decision time and time again, until it becomes "longstanding" precedent.[14] With quickly rotating panels, poorly reasoned decisions will not stand the test of time. Still, there may be more "bad" decisions because not all circuit judges are equal and, quite apart from judicial philosophy, most would not be considered for elevation by presidents of either party.

But is the chance for "better" decisions, such as it would be, worth the trade-off in lost finality and stability in the law? Citing statistics showing that circuit judges give less weight to the opinions of justices who have left the bench and that short time horizons hurt cooperation, Sachs suggests that the short-term appointments would create a "judicial goat rodeo" of wildly fluctuating law.[15] Defending a similar suggestion in 2012, Josh Hawley, who clerked for Chief Justice Roberts and is now a Republican senator from Missouri, argued that justices who would one day return to the circuit court may be more circumspect about altering constitutional rules,[16] but Sachs points out that this "ephemeral tenure might also encourage justices to get their licks in while they can."[17]

Whatever its effect on stability and ideology, the judicial lottery would undoubtedly remedy one complaint that people have about the Supreme Court: that it skews toward the coasts. There are 179 federal circuit judgeships, allocated proportionately by population across circuits. And yet, all the justices except Gorsuch hail from eastern states and circuits, particularly the Boston-Washington "Acela corridor." Justice Scalia—one of the then-five justices born and raised in metro New York City—noted in his *Obergefell* dissent that there was nobody from the West, because Justice Kennedy's California "does not count."[18] So it might be nice to have more regional variation, even if there would still be too many Harvard and Yale alums.

Then there are some atmospheric issues. A Supreme Court lottery limited to circuit judges would exclude very capable potential justices from other legal walks of life. No state jurists (like Cardozo or O'Connor), nor executive-branch officials (Taft, Murphy, Jackson, Rehnquist, Kagan), nor senators, professors, or anyone else.

And finally, if one of the goals of this whole endeavor is to depoliticize judicial confirmations, raising the stakes on lower-court nominees hardly helps with that project. Most of President Trump's circuit judges have been confirmed with fewer than sixty votes, many after wild accusations involving collegiate writings, tweets, and other assorted smears; making them all into justices-in-waiting (even more than some already are) will not improve that situation.

2. A "Balanced Court"

Epps and Sitaraman also suggest a completely different idea, a 15-member Court composed of five Democratic- and five Republican-affiliated justices, plus five others who would have to be selected *unanimously* by the partisan justices. These "neutrals" would be picked two years in advance to serve for a single year. If there were no agreement on this slate, then the Court would lack a quorum and couldn't hear cases that year. The professors argue that this political makeup would increase public confidence in the Court's legitimacy because any decision in ideologically salient cases would have to gain the support of three centrists.

But how would one even determine whether a judge is an R or a D? Why not switch parties to maximize chances of selection? Would it be constitutional to exclude members of third parties or independents? A Republican dying during a Democratic presidency could lead to a Souter or a Stevens—or at the very least someone who wouldn't be picked by a president of his own nominal party. The Epps-Sitaraman idea that the Senate leader opposed to the president could provide a list of choices is unworkable as a plain violation of the Appointments Clause, which gives the president the sole power to "nominate...Judges of the supreme Court." So we're talking another constitutional amendment.

Moreover, while some high-profile cases are split ideologically, many are not. For example, any criminal defendant would prefer that his case be decided by a Gorsuch or a Sotomayor rather than an Alito or a Breyer (or a Garland, for that matter). This plan values public acceptance through perceived moderation over correct legal conclusions, resting on an assumption that there are generally equally wrong or extreme partisan answers and the best legal option is a centrist compromise between the two. But that in itself privileges a political method of judicial decision making, splitting the baby and treading as lightly as possible rather than wrestling with what the correct answer might be.

The balanced Court idea has entered the political discourse. Mayor Pete Buttigieg even included a rough sketch on his presidential campaign website. But *New York Times* columnist Jamelle Bouie, in one of the rare times I've agreed with him, argued that "no reform short of ending the power of judicial review will disentangle [the Court] from ordinary, partisan politics."[19] At the same time, unlike court-packing, the "balanced Court" wouldn't be associated with a progressive agenda and would effectively remove the Supreme Court as an issue in presidential election campaigns.

But the biggest problem with this proposal is that, in the name of depoliticizing the Court it would affix scarlet partisan letters to two-thirds of the justices, making it appear as a mini-legislature all the more. This structure also advantages those who call for judicial restraint, whether on the left (for fear of a conservative majority) or the right (who would rather defer to the political branches). It's completely foreseeable that at least some years the "partisan" justices wouldn't be able to agree on a slate of five—or even one "neutral" after allowing two effective partisans on each side—which would both empower the circuit and state courts whence the cases come and result in cases dragging on until a quorum is reached.

Underlying both the "judicial lottery" and "balanced court" proposals is a problem with the proponents' premise, that the Court needs saving in the first place. The Court isn't in crisis, but liberals—and especially legal elites, who have relied on it to solve social ills they can't remedy at the ballot box—are *very* unhappy with its nascent conservative majority. For Epps and Sitaraman, the Court's legitimacy means the sociological acceptance of the Court's role, but, as the polling data I discuss in chapter 22 shows, the Court is more popular than other government institutions.

3. Other Proposals

Beyond the Epps-Sitaraman proposals that have gained some traction—or at least attention—among the chattering classes, a few other interesting structural reforms are floating around, some a sort of evergreen that, like term limits, crops up every time there's dissatisfaction with the Court.

A decade ago, Vanderbilt law professors Tracey George (now vice provost) and Chris Guthrie (now dean) suggested court-packing-plus: expanding the Court to fifteen, but then having it hear cases in three-justice panels, like the circuit courts (and the high courts of certain countries, plus Delaware and Mississippi).[20] It's an interesting idea that addresses a technical concern about the current Supreme Court: that it hears too few cases, half the number it was hearing thirty years ago and less than a third of what it decided fifty years ago, despite a large increase in lower-court rulings. Setting aside the same transition problems that make regular court-packing a political non-starter— George and Guthrie suggest adding a new justice in every two-year period when there's not otherwise a vacancy—the proposal makes intuitive sense.

But there are two main drawbacks: (1) there's nothing to stop the current Court from taking up more cases, so simply expanding capacity won't guarantee that this capacity is used any more than it is now, and (2) there will be petitions for plenary *en banc* review in every case, so the jump in administrative workload will swallow some of the excess capacity—introducing an extra level of appellate review—and we'll see more political debate over the Supreme Court's deciding to grant this or that case. Epps and Sitaraman worry that every politically charged case would go *en banc* and that the Court would take up even more controversial cases.[21] Indeed, there are many on both the left and the right who think the Court ought to decide *fewer* cases—I don't share this perspective, at least not while federal power is so broad and skewed toward the administrative state—so this fix may not even be part of the same conversation.

What is part of the conversation over the judiciary's politicization is the idea that judicial celebrity has contributed to the Supreme Court's being "broken." Suzanna Sherry, yet another Vanderbilt law professor—the water in Nashville must be reform-flavored—describes the issue thus: "Justices seeking to enhance their own reputations ignore the potential effect on the institutional legitimacy and reputation of the Court. They overinvest in their individual reputations at the expense of the reputation of the judiciary as a whole."[22] Sherry suggests a law requiring opinions to be published anonymously and without concurrences or dissents, or even vote counts—what are known as *per curiam* ("by the court") rulings. Indeed, recent studies show that people adjust their level of agreement with a judicial opinion based on the author rather than the decision itself, and *per curiam* opinions garnered the greatest level of support of all.[23]

But it's odd to argue, when surveys show that most Americans can't name even one justice, that cults of personality lead to institutional decay. The causation arrow goes the other way: there are few justices and they decide important issues, so of course the leading voices on either side, plus the swing votes, will get attention. Trying to minimize the attention given to the "Notorious RBG" is all well and good, but Justice Ginsburg accrued that notoriety because of the votes she casts and her longevity, not because of a colorful personality. The wars over the Scalia vacancy and the replacement of Justice Kennedy would've been just as fierce if the succeeding justices no longer signed opinions. And that's before we even get to the loss of the value of having separate opinions to the development of the law, as well as signaling when there's real consensus and when there's not.[24] *Per curiam* opinions may have worked in John Marshall's day, but that's not the legal world we live in now.

One final structural reform bears mentioning. If the problem, as many scholars and pundits suggest, is that the Supreme Court (and the judiciary as a whole) makes too many important, political decisions, then why not take some of those issues off the docket? Lawyers call this idea "jurisdiction-stripping." Just as conservatives in the past, angered by the Warren Court and various other controversies over the decades, have called on Congress to limit the scope of judicial purvey, progressives are now saying the same thing in the light of the new conservative majority.

The problems with this approach are both procedural and substantive. On procedure, even though Congress has immense power over the Court's appellate jurisdiction, the Supreme Court has held in the past that it will always have jurisdiction to determine whether it has the power to hear a case, typically finding that Congress has failed to properly strip that jurisdiction.[25] And it's doubtful that Congress can strip jurisdiction on constitutional claims, which abortion and racial preferences certainly are.[26]

On substance, be careful what you wish for. What a successful jurisdictional strip would accomplish is effectively an evisceration of the Constitution, such that states would have full power to intrude on people's freedoms, while the federal government would be even less constrained than it is now. A court without judicial review is no court at all—which only appeals to people who not only think that the Supreme Court is illegitimate, but that the Constitution is "undemocratic" and should be undone.

Changes to Confirmation Hearings

Setting aside Supreme Court structure, what about the confirmation process itself? Should we have rules for how many days after a nomination there must be a hearing and then a vote? Maybe we should consider restoring the filibuster for nominees—although Gorsuch was the first and only Supreme Court nominee subjected to partisan filibuster. (Recall that Justice Fortas lacked even a bare majority of announced support for his elevation to chief justice, while Justices Thomas and Alito were confirmed with fewer than sixty votes.) Of course, if we had the political alignment for these kinds of changes, we wouldn't have the "toxified" atmosphere we're in, so it's a chicken-and-egg problem.

Henry Saad, a former Michigan court of appeals judge whose nomination to the Sixth Circuit was filibustered under George W. Bush, recently proposed a number of reforms to the nomination and confirmation process, most of which are only relevant to the lower courts.[27] For example, he suggests that each of the three branches should have a committee for evaluating judicial candidates, as should each state, and federal judges themselves should conduct interviews and issue ratings (in lieu of the discredited ABA). I'm not sure how realistic these pre-nomination proposals are, both in light of political realities—some states already have commissions, particularly for district judgeships, but that system breaks down when the relevant senators are opposed to the White House—and the constitutional powers of presidential appointment and senatorial advice and consent. And how many judges would really want to evaluate their future colleagues, even if their eventual reports are supposed to say confidential?

With respect to reforms that would apply equally to Supreme Court nominees, Saad would make it a violation of judicial ethics for nominees to give their opinions about a case, while making hearings untelevised, with questions submitted in writing, restricted to professional qualifications, and asked by the chief counsel for each party's judiciary committee members. Some committees allow this in other contexts, and while it didn't seem to work very well for Republicans in the supplemental Kavanaugh hearing, that was largely a function of the five-minute increments the counsel questioning was forced into. Any personal information or ethical concerns could be handled in the confidential session that the judiciary committee already has to discuss the FBI background investigation and other sensitive matters.

These sorts of post-nomination proposals are healthy, because they target the spectacle that confirmations have become, with senators either not equipped to handle the required lines of questioning or grandstanding to produce a gotcha moment, or at least B-roll for campaign videos. "It's like testifying in a restaurant," quips former White House counsel Don McGahn, with photographers clicking away in front and protestors haranguing in the back.[28] And it's not like we learn anything about nominees, who are now coached to avoid saying anything newsworthy.

I've come to the conclusion that we should get rid of hearings altogether, that they've served their purpose for a century but now inflict greater cost on the Court, Senate, and rule of law than any informational or educational benefit gained. Given the voluminous and instantly searchable records nominees have these days—going back to collegiate writings and other digitized archives—is there any need to subject them, and the country, to a public inquisition? At the very least, the Senate could hold nomination hearings entirely in closed session.

■   ■   ■

Outside-the-box thinking should be commended and proposals to reimagine the Court or improve the confirmation process shouldn't be discounted lightly, even if—particularly if—cosmetic or easy changes would enhance public confidence in the Supreme Court's integrity. I'm willing to consider anything that would help show that there's a difference between interpreting the law and making it, between judging and legislating.

But I'm not sure any of these formalistic changes would do anything given that it's not a breakdown in the rules that caused the poisonous atmosphere surrounding nominations, but the other way around. Senators have—correctly—come to see judges as just as or more important than legislation, so they started applying the same bareknuckle political plays to them.

In the end, all of this "reform" discussion boils down to re-arranging the deck chairs on the Titanic. And this Titanic is not the appointment process, but the ship of state. The fundamental problem we face, and that the Supreme Court faces, is the politicization not of the *process* but of the *product*. The only way judicial confirmations will be detoxified, and the only way we reverse the trend whereby people increasingly see judges as "Trump judges" and "Obama judges," is for the Supreme Court to restore our constitutional order by returning improperly amassed federal power to the states; securing all of our rights, enumerated and unenumerated alike; and forcing Congress to legislate on the remaining truly national issues rather than delegating that legislative power to executive-branch agencies.

All the rest is window dressing. As Adam Liptak, the *New York Times* Supreme Court reporter, said at a Princeton conference on the politics of judicial nominations in March 2020, "people aren't sure what exactly we're trying to reform. The focus should not be on tinkering with the inputs, but on achieving the only output that matters in this context: legitimacy."[29]

CHAPTER 22

A Question of Legitimacy

Since the nominations of Justices Neil Gorsuch and Brett Kavanaugh, progressives have feared a radical right-turn on the court. Such a dramatic shift has yet to materialize, yet there still has been plenty of handwringing about judicial partisanship and ominous warnings, sometimes more like threats, about the Court's "legitimacy" being in jeopardy. If Gorsuch is an illegitimate justice because he "stole" Merrick Garland's seat, Kavanaugh's illegitimacy—even before the sexual-assault allegations—stems from the continual investigations of President Trump, and thus that he was selected to grant the president some newfangled immunity.

The background insinuation is clear: if the justices rule in ways that disagree with progressive orthodoxy, there will be hell to pay. It's a nice Court you have there, wouldn't want anything to happen to it. More precisely, to quote a recent brief from five senators in a Second Amendment case, with Senator Sheldon Whitehouse (D-R.I.) as counsel of record, "The Supreme Court is not well. And the people know it. Perhaps the Court can heal itself before the public demands it be restructured in order to reduce the influence of politics."[1] The morning of last term's big abortion case, *June Medical Services v.*

Russo, Senate Minority Leader Chuck Schumer said before a cheering crowd on the courthouse steps, "I want to tell you, Gorsuch. I want to tell you, Kavanaugh. You have released the whirlwind, and you will pay the price." The New York Democrat added, "You won't know what hit you if you go forward with these awful decisions."[2] Chief Justice Roberts issued a rare press statement later that day, saying, "Justices know that criticism comes with the territory, but threatening statements of this sort from the highest levels of government are not only inappropriate, they are dangerous."[3] It recalled the November 2018 contretemps Roberts had with President Trump over "Obama judges," except there the president was complaining about decisions that went against him—something presidents have done since the dawn of the republic—not making threats about pending cases.

We've come to expect this sort of "working the refs," a cynical tactic that will continue so long as it appears to be an effective guilt trip against "institutionalist" judges like Roberts himself. Now the Court's median vote, the chief justice has continued his never-ending quest to preserve the Court's reputation. In the 2018–19 term, his first in the "swing seat" after Justice Anthony Kennedy's retirement, he cast the key votes (and wrote the controlling opinions) in decisions to (1) remove federal courts from policing partisan gerrymandering[4]—seen as a "conservative" ruling even though both parties do it; and (2) reject a question regarding citizenship for the 2020 Census, but allowing the Commerce Department to try again in future with a better rationale.[5] In doing so, Roberts has responded to a host of political and ideological pressures that coalesce under the umbrella category of the Court's "legitimacy."[6]

These moves came after Roberts faced a more-than-whisper campaign that allowing partisan gerrymandering and, especially, the census question would damage the Court's legitimacy. Joshua Geltzer, executive director of Georgetown's Institute for Constitutional Advocacy and Protection, warned in a *New York Times* op-ed that the Court had to "get the census case right" (rule against the administration) "[f]or the sake of its own legitimacy."[7] UC-Irvine law professor Richard Hasen, who had urged Roberts to "show in these cases that he is above politics," later despaired that the census case had echoes of *Bush v. Gore*, the ur-legitimacy-buster where the justices "let politics get in the way of a fair decision."[8]

We saw a similar dynamic in the most recently concluded term, when Roberts generally joined the conservatives but "defected" in the high-profile abortion, immigration, and employment discrimination cases. And again when he assembled 7–2 majorities to (1) reject President Trump's claim of absolute immunity from state grand jury subpoenas; but (2) rein in congressional power to investigate the president. To be fair, more populist conservatives also assail "judicial supremacy," particularly when it involves district courts' nationwide injunctions. But their prescription is either for the Supreme Court to cut down on lower-court mischief—well yes, that's how the system works—or for Congress to strip jurisdiction over certain types of claims. Or for the administration to become more aggressive in pushing back on judicial rulings by seeking more stays and leap-frogging over the circuit courts to go straight to the top—which it has been doing, even drawing a rebuke from Justice Sonia Sotomayor, who also chastised her colleagues for being too quick to grant the government favors as it battles lower-court resistance to its policy agenda.[9] It's largely an aspirational position, unless you also argue that judicial review is itself improper or that the executive branch should ignore court rulings—which nobody seriously does (yet!), but which would indeed signal a debate over legitimacy, as well as a potential constitutional crisis.

My point isn't to present the definitive theory of judicial or institutional legitimacy, but to show how this question plays out now and is both a contributor to and symptom of the politicization of the judicial confirmation process. Modern legitimacy concerns can be traced to three key moments: *Bush v. Gore* (2000), the battle over Obamacare (2010–12), and the early Trump era (2016–18)—the combination of Mitch McConnell's blocking of Merrick Garland and Donald Trump's winning the presidency while losing the popular vote, thus getting to replace not just Scalia but the swing-vote Kennedy (with a reputationally damaged Kavanaugh at that).

In the wake of *Bush v. Gore*, prominent progressive lawyers rent their garments over the end of the rule of law. In January 2001, over six hundred law professors signed an ad in the *New York Times* decrying the decision.[10] Neal Katyal, one of Al Gore's lawyers and later acting solicitor general under President Obama, described George W. Bush's victory as the Supreme Court's "immolation": "By elevating politics over principle, the court revealed itself to be no better than any other institution or actor that touched this election." Katyal also compared the case to *Dred Scott* as a time when the Court hurt itself by playing politics.[11]

Harvard law professor Alan Dershowitz, who wrote a book about the case, argued that the majority's decision to "substitute their political judgment for that of the people threatens to undermine the moral authority of the high court for generations." "Unless steps are taken to mitigate the damage inflicted on the Court by these five justices, the balance struck by our Constitution between popular democracy and judicial oligarchy will remain askew," Dershowitz wrote, presaging today's populists.[12]

Yale law professor Bruce Ackerman built on Justice John Paul Stevens's dissenting lament that *Bush v. Gore* had shaken "the Nation's confidence in the judge as an impartial guardian of the rule of law."[13] Ackerman suggested that Bush himself was an illegitimate president. "If such a president is allowed to fill the Court, he will be acting as an agent of the narrow right-wing majority that secured his victory in the first place," so Congress should prevent Bush from appointing new justices like it did during Reconstruction by preventing Andrew Johnson from doing the same by cutting seats.[14] In other words, in a refrain that should sound familiar from the 2020 election campaign, restructuring the Court—or preventing a Republican president from adding justices—was the only way to preserve legitimacy.

The pushback to these attacks was encapsulated in a concise law review article by Berkeley law professor John Yoo that was appropriately entitled "In Defense of the Court's Legitimacy."[15] Yoo argued that *Bush v. Gore* would not have a sustained impact on the Court's legitimacy when viewed through the lenses of public opinion, history, and impartiality. First, it turns out that people's confidence in the Court remained relatively stable, at least in the short term. Next, Yoo compared the moment to other times when the Court's legitimacy was in doubt: the early Republic, the *Dred Scott* era, initial resistance to the New Deal, and the Warren Court's fight against segregation and expansion of civil liberties. "Close inspection of these periods show that they bear little resemblance to *Bush v Gore*. The defining characteristic of several of these periods was the persistent, central role of the Court in the political disputes of the day." Finally, "only by acting in a manner that suggests that its decisions are the product of law rather than politics can the Court maintain its legitimacy."

More important than his specific analysis of *Bush v. Gore* is Yoo's exposition of factors that arise when critics argue the Court's illegitimacy.

1. *Public opinion.* Because the Court's authority derives wholly from people following its decisions, public opinion matters. The critic might use data to show that the public has less confidence in the Court, argue that the Court shouldn't overturn democratically enacted laws, or suggest that justices appointed by a president who

didn't win the popular vote are illegitimate. These sorts of claims can be summed up as: "The Court didn't rule my way but the political winds are blowing in my favor, so democracy, not the Court, should win out."

2. *Historical precedent.* In what previous circumstances has the Court's legitimacy been in doubt? Except that when critics rely on historical precedent, they often compare current cases to past ones they feel were wrongly decided or to overturned cases that are so different from the one at hand that the comparison becomes hyperbolic at best— comparing the Trump administration's travel ban to *Korematsu*, *Bush v. Gore* to *Dred Scott*, etc.

3. *Impartiality.* Those who say the Court fails this consideration accuse justices of partisanship, lawless ideology, or bias toward a particular kind of party (for example, big business). These accusations become more common when the Court issues opinions on divisive issues, or, increasingly, if the justices subscribe to a coherent legal philosophy like originalism—reading the Constitution for the original public meaning its text had when ratified.

Arguments on these three grounds are found in every criticism of the Court's legitimacy, and they've been increasingly used in the last twenty years, not just after rulings, but ahead of them, to influence swing votes. Most notable in that regard, at least until Donald Trump came down his escalator in 2015, was the Obamacare litigation. The first lawsuit was filed the same day President Obama signed the Affordable Care Act into law in March 2010. Initially the challengers' legal claims were treated as frivolous sour grapes after losing a political fight. But when rulings started going against the government, illegitimacy claims began. After Judge Roger

Vinson invalidated the individual mandate in January 2011, Yale's Akhil Amar compared Vinson to Roger Taney, author of *Dred Scott*, in an op-ed that for some reason no longer appears on the *L.A. Times* website.[16]

Fast forward to the end of March 2012, when Supreme Court oral arguments did not go well for the government. *The New Republic's* Jonathan Cohn argued that the "legitimacy of the Supreme Court" is at stake, singling out Justice Samuel Alito as opposing welfare programs on policy grounds while also appealing to "tens of millions of Americans" because "nobody has said they want to stop government from providing universal access to health care."[17]

Cohn was neither the last nor most prominent critic calling into question a potential ruling against the ACA. President Obama himself said it would be "conservative judicial activism,"[18] an attack Senate Judiciary Committee Chairman Pat Leahy later repeated. Leahy further admonished John Roberts from the Senate floor: "I trust that he will be Chief Justice for all of us and that he has a strong institutional sense of the proper role of the judicial branch. It is the Supreme Court of the United States, not the Supreme Court of the Democratic Party or the Republican Party, not the Supreme Court of liberals or conservatives."[19]

Of course, Roberts did switch his vote to preserve Obamacare in *NFIB v. Sebelius*, on a bizarre taxing-power theory that most people recognize was a "twistification," his best attempt to uphold the law while not expanding Congress's regulatory authority. *Slate's* David Franklin wrote that a decision to strike down the law "would have been received by the general public as yet more proof that the court is merely an extension of the nation's polarized politics."[20] He also compared the chief to another Justice (Owen) Roberts, who made the "switch in time" in 1937 that started approving New Deal programs.

As I wrote in chapter 15, the sad thing about the episode is that the chief justice didn't have to do what he did to "save the Court." Most importantly, Roberts only damaged his own reputation by making the move after those warnings from pundits and politicians. As Jan Crawford described in breaking the story, "Roberts pays attention to media coverage. As chief justice, he is keenly aware of his leadership role on the court, and he also is sensitive to how the court is perceived by the public. There were countless news articles warning of damage to the court—and to Roberts' reputation—if the court were to strike down the mandate."[21]

Now, I don't think that impolitic pressure had much to do with his ultimate vote, but much of the American public probably does. Indeed, if Justice Kennedy had agreed with the liberals that there are no structural limits on federal power, there would have been disappointment, but it would have been understandable given the conventional left-right rubric. But to lose in an extra-legal way was a sucker punch, belying the idea that there's a difference between law and politics and that the judiciary is a counter-majoritarian check on the political branches.

The whole reason we care about the Court's independence is so it can make tough decisions while letting the political chips fall where they may. Had the Court struck down Obamacare, it would have been the sort of thing for which it needs all that accrued legitimacy. Instead, we got some strategic judicial lawmaking. In refraining from making the sort of balls-and-strikes call he invoked at his confirmation hearing, Roberts actually decreased respect for the Court, thereby showing why judges shouldn't play politics.

In other words, when justices occasionally switch their votes to maintain some sort of perceived external legitimacy, they undermine the internal legitimacy of the judicial process—the very idea that the

Supreme Court is a court of law, not just another political body. As Justice Kagan put it in remarks at Princeton on the eve of Justice Kavanaugh's confirmation, "[p]art of the court's legitimacy depends on people not seeing the court in the way that people see the rest of the governing structures of this country."[22] And what undermines that public view more than justices' changing their votes to a position that they don't believe to be legally correct, in the search for public acceptance. Whether Owen Roberts's "switch in time" or John Roberts's Obamacare maneuver, they may have curried political legitimacy—though that, too, is in dispute—but they unmistakably hurt the Court's legal legitimacy.[23]

Nor have the pressures against which Chief Justice Roberts has been reacting, in his self-appointed mission to protect the Court's legitimacy, come entirely from the outside. Justice Sotomayor, speaking alongside Justice Kagan, expressed a fear that her colleagues' commitment to their judicial philosophies might come with an unwanted partisan overtone. "When the political parties adopted that language as their own, they superimposed that on the court," she explained, referencing the Republican Party's rhetorical commitment to originalism, which "institutionally, has hurt the court a lot and may continue to do so."[24] Apart from failing to take originalist claims seriously on their own terms—namely the idea that a fidelity to original public meaning is a necessary component of judicial legitimacy—Sotomayor's view demonstrates that it's not only court-watchers who view jurisprudential disputes as a proxy partisan battle.

Given that arguments against the Court's legitimacy have focused on specific justices, 5–4 decisions—particularly those where Bush and Trump appointees have voted together—have been eyed with more suspicion. For some progressives, this is doubly true when cases are perceived as favoring "powerful interests" aligned with the GOP.[25]

Justice Ruth Bader Ginsburg herself has stated that "I don't think that 5–4 decisions have the same clout as a unanimous decision." Legal progressives may be misperceiving the public legitimacy of those split opinions. A 2009 study found that public support for controversial decisions was not dependent on the size of the majority in a particular case.[26] A 2015 study by Harvard law professor Cass Sunstein likewise concluded that the legitimizing value of consensus on the Court has long been overestimated.[27]

On the other hand, Justice Ginsburg was correct if we understand "clout" to mean staying power as a precedent. A 2001 study found that a 5–4 decision was 54 percent more likely to be overturned than other splits.[28]

And so we've arrived at the Trump era, where nothing the administration does is seen as legitimate by a large segment of the population, but especially in the Supreme Court context because of the Garland saga. It's not surprising that in fall 2018, *The Nation* published an article asserting "How the US Supreme Court Lost Its Legitimacy" that's hardly different from one called "The Supreme Court's Legitimacy Crisis" in the *New York Times*.[29] The latter argued for the double illegitimacy of Justices Gorsuch and Kavanaugh because they were nominated by a president who didn't win the popular vote and confirmed by senators who collectively won fewer votes in their last election than senators who voted against their confirmation. Berkeley Law Dean Erwin Chemerinsky upped the ante with a remarkable assertion that, assuming Kavanaugh "or someone like him" was confirmed (he was writing a few days before the final vote), "each of the five conservative justices...came on to the Court in a manner that lacks legitimacy."[30]

After the Kavanaugh confirmation, Senator Dianne Feinstein, the judiciary committee's ranking member, went on to tweet that Justice

Kavanaugh's confirmation "undermines the legitimacy of the Supreme Court." Former attorney general Eric Holder likewise tweeted: "The legitimacy of the Supreme Court can justifiably be questioned."[31]

Indignation at the thought of a minority-appointed Supreme Court has, at the extremes, found expression in paranoia over the influence of conservative legal groups, especially the Federalist Society, even to the point of full-fledged conspiracy-theorizing. For example, the author of that *Nation* essay wrote that the Federalists have "understood that cultural and demographic trends are poised to strip the power of its wealthy, predominantly white male sponsors" and striven to engineer an undemocratically appointed court.[32] The goal of all this, he claims, has been to protect the "untraceable 'dark money' and gerrymandering" used by Republicans to thwart the popular will. Senator Whitehouse similarly lambasted the "Third Federalist Society," beyond the law school debating society and "high-brow think tank," the one that is "the nerve center for a complicated apparatus that does not care much about conservative principles like judicial restraint, or originalism, or textualism. This Federalist Society is the vehicle for powerful interests, which seek not to simply 'reorder' the judiciary, but to acquire control of the judiciary to benefit their interests."[33]

Hanging over the debate on Supreme Court legitimacy is the possibility that some actors—lower courts, agencies, states—may begin to practice "open defiance" of controversial decisions with which they disagree. The judiciary is the "least dangerous branch," as Alexander Hamilton dubbed it, because it relies on the institutions it governs to accept its constitutional authority as an arbiter of legal disputes. Chief Justice Taney discovered the limits of that moral authority during a clash with President Lincoln over the suspension of the writ of habeas corpus during the Civil War. Unable to enforce a writ the executive would not recognize, Taney despaired, "I have exercised all the power which the Constitution and laws confer on me, but that power has been resisted by a force too strong for me to overcome."[34]

Outside such exceptional circumstances, however, the Court's decisions have been recognized and obeyed, if sometimes grudgingly. While lower courts sometimes apply Supreme Court precedent so narrowly as to render certain decisions effectively toothless—the way *District of Columbia v. Heller*, the landmark Second Amendment case, has been interpreted in some circuits is a good example—these decisions remain open to clarification and correction.

Observing a "crisis of legitimacy" created by the Kavanaugh confirmation, however, *Slate*'s legal correspondent gleefully speculated that a future Democratic administration might give in to street protestors demanding that it ignore decisions by a majority-GOP-appointed Court, citing even southern resistance to *Brown v. Board of Education* as an uncomfortable precedent. "What can the Supreme Court do? Send its tiny police force to storm the White House?"[35]

Some progressive critics have gone so far to call for the impeachment of conservative justices as a remedy to their underlying illegitimacy. A core inconsistency would seem to be inherent in these proposals: the illegitimacy of a gerrymandered house and non-proportional Senate, which is said to have brought this situation to pass, would make the constitutional impeachment process itself illegitimate.

No Supreme Court justice has ever been removed from office, and only one, Samuel Chase in 1805 (as detailed in chapter 1), has ever been impeached. Although Chase's impeachment, animated by the belief that the Court was packed with partisan Federalists but revolving around his judicial misconduct, might make an interesting contemporary comparison, it led to acquittal. Only William O.

Douglas, who was investigated twice, has faced a House impeach-ment since Chase. The first Douglas affair, revolving around his brief stay of execution for Julius and Ethel Rosenburg, lasted less than a month. A second effort, led by then House Minority Leader Gerald Ford and mentioned in chapter twelve, focused on Douglas's personal life and ties to a corrupt foundation, and ended with no public vote. In none of these instances was the impeachment attempt premised on an invalid appointment or anything of the sort.

There was at least one justice who did serve despite legitimate concerns over his appointment. Franklin Roosevelt nominated Sen-ator Hugo Black despite the fact that Black had voted for pension increases for justices, which violates the constitutional prohibition on appointments of members of Congress to federal offices whose "emoluments" were increased during their time in that elected office.[36] Few worried then, and few worry now, that any serious cloud hangs over either Black's opinions or votes, because "the real source of constitutional settlement in our system is not always judicial deci-sion, but sometimes sheer practice."[37]

In contrast to oft-expressed concerns over legitimacy, polling tells conflicting stories as to the Court's standing among the public. Gal-lup has the Court's approval rating declining somewhat from a high of 62 percent at the beginning of the 21st century, but the numbers don't map onto conventional narratives of recent judicial politics. According to the poll, the Court's approval reached its nadir in 2016 at 42 percent (with disapproval of 52 percent), but that has since reversed to 54–42.[38] These numbers suggest that the cautious eight-member Court after Justice Scalia's passing marked a peak of public distrust, with Americans' concerns being assuaged by President Trump's subsequent nominations. Over a longer term since 1973, the number of Americans with a high degree of confidence in the Court has declined only slightly, from the low 40s to the high 30s, while the number with little to no confidence has remained steady in the high teens and the number with "some" confidence has modestly increased to about 40 percent.[39]

So what are we to make of all this? Is it simply that where you stand on the question of judicial legitimacy now also parallels where you sit politically? In two words, pretty much. Political scientists even have an expression for this dynamic: "Legitimacy is for losers," because those who like an outcome generally don't question the Court's decision making.[40] A more recent *FiveThirtyEight* analysis shows that views of the Court "are fairly malleable, and tend to shift around big events or decisions," typically in opposite directions by ideological or partisan affinity in response to the latest politically salient case or confirmation battle.[41] According to the Pew Research Center, the share of Democrats who saw the Court in a positive light plunged from 63 to 49 percent from January to July 2019. Republicans, meanwhile, who as recently as July 2015—after rulings that upheld Obamacare and required states to license same-sex marriages—only gave the Court a 33 percent approval rate, went up to 82 percent in January 2019, before dropping slightly to 75 percent in July of that year.[42]

That 26-point partisan gap is significant, but it's not unprecedented, either historically or in recent decades. It's easy to see why people are attacking the Court's legitimacy when we apply Yoo's considerations: when big issues are on the docket and we have the culmination of trends whereby divergent judicial theories map onto ideologically distinct parties.

And that goes as well for the related debate over the preservation of old precedents. Where you stand on how sacrosanct precedent is depends on which precedent you have in mind. For all the gnashing of teeth over *Citizens United* or *Janus*—or similar pearl-clutching about overturning precedent in lesser cases that serve as a proxy war over *Roe v. Wade*—is there any doubt that a progressive majority would act the same way toward conservative shibboleths?

Anyway, that's all overblown. As the *New York Times* described in its 2019 term wrap-up, "When [the Supreme Court] overruled precedents, it was in technical cases that attracted little attention."[43] Moreover, Case Western law professor Jonathan Adler has shown that the Roberts Court overturns precedents at a significantly lower rate than its predecessors.[44]

Michael Greve, a professor at the Antonin Scalia Law School at George Mason University, wrote recently that the Court's perceived legitimacy has been the victim of certain long term trends, which he identifies as (1) the decline of "latent" legitimacy, Americans' inherited presumption that the Court is a legitimate arbiter rather than politicians in robes, and (2) "constitutional rot," the decline of extra-textual norms like refraining from personal attacks on judges by politicians of both parties.[45] To these two trends, Greve adds an important historical contingency, the likely longevity of a conservative majority in a deeply polarized country. This last factor is a source of frustration, but also an opportunity for the Court to rescue itself by putting the political ball back in Congress's court: forcing Congress to hash out policy disagreements and then write laws with more specificity, as well as returning power to the states instead of mandating one-size-fits-all solutions on a large and pluralistic country. This would be playing the "long game," but in a very different way than what Chief Justice Roberts is credited and blamed for doing, tacking this way and that and avoiding sweeping movements, in a way that will, by some magical mechanism, keep the Court out of political debates.

One factor, according to Greve, adding to the impression that the Court is increasingly under a magnifying glass is the cultural process of "disintermediation" by which ordinary citizens, acting as part of activist pressure groups, seek to project their views onto the Court. Beginning in the 1970s with the advent of mass mailing, new information technology has made it increasingly easy for Americans to circumvent the political branches, traditional media, and all other established institutions through which they had previously related to the judiciary. Today a protest outside the Supreme Court building may be organized on social media and large amounts crowdfunded to support a focused pressure campaign.

That effect has had a profound impact on confirmation fights, with pre-made t-shirts and signs to signal opposition to whichever nominee a president makes. Twitter storms and digital broadcasting reinforce each in a vicious cycle of gotcha politics. Judicial deliberations are also now subject to instant and exhaustive coverage, with court-watchers parsing oral arguments for the slightest hints of voting intentions. The obvious conclusion is that the openness of modern nomination processes detracts from the legitimacy of the judicial branch as a whole and the Supreme Court in particular. The public-relations set pieces and rapid-response tactics make justices seem like just another piece of political flotsam, while the disingenuous hearings serve less of an informational function and more of an entertainment one, the apotheosis of our grand political sport. It's great reality TV—the current occupant of the White House understands this better than anyone else—but it's terrible for institutional preservation.

In the end, the only measure of the Court's legitimacy that matters—not the "playing the refs" nonsense we see each spring—is the extent to which it gets the law right and applies it correctly. The reason for these legitimacy disputes isn't that the Court is partisan or that the confirmation process is broken, but that (1) the Court and judicial nominations can't be divorced from the larger political scene, and (2) sometimes justices seem to make decisions not based on their legal principles but for strategic purposes. The public can see through that; it's when justices think about "legitimacy" and try to avoid political controversy that they act most illegitimately.

Conclusion

A s one Court watcher wrote a quarter-century ago, "Today's confirmation battles are no longer government affairs between the President and the Senate; they are public affairs open to a broad range of players. Thus, overt lobbying, public opinion polls, advertising campaigns, focus groups, and public appeals have all become a routine part of the process."[1] Those trends have only accelerated in the intervening twenty-five years, such that Supreme Court nominations are perhaps the highest-profile set-pieces in the American political system. Not even set-pieces, but months-long slogs. Once the inside game of picking the nominee ends—that traditional dance between president and Senate—the outside game begins, culminating in the literally made-for-TV hearing and then a vote that, as we learned with Justice Kavanaugh, can be just as dramatic.

It's not good, but we've gotten here because Congress and the presidency have gradually taken more power for themselves, and the Supreme Court has allowed them to get away with it, aggrandizing itself in the process. As the Court has let both the legislative and executive branches swell beyond their constitutionally authorized powers, so have the laws and regulations that it now interprets. Competing theories battle for control of both the U.S. Code and Federal Register, as well as determine—often at the whim of one "swing vote"—what rights will be recognized. As we've gone down that warped jurisprudential track, the judiciary now affects the direction of public policy more than ever. So of course judicial confirmations are going to be fraught, particularly as competing interpretive theories essentially map onto political parties that are more ideologically coherent than ever.

That's also why the judicial nomination and confirmation processes are more cognizant of partisan considerations. This wasn't as much of a problem when partisanship mainly meant rewarding your cronies. But it's a modern phenomenon for our parties to be so ideologically polarized, and therefore for judges nominated by presidents from different parties to have notably different views on constitutional interpretation.

There are two big buckets of cases where that dynamic has contributed to the ratcheting up of tensions that has both crumbled Senate norms and filtered down into lower-court nominations: (1) cultural issues, ranging from abortion and LGBTQ issues to the Second Amendment and death penalty, and (2) what I'll call "size of government" issues, which encompass everything from environmental regulations to Obamacare, guidance documents to enforcement practices. And then there's an overlay of "structural" cases: *Bush v. Gore*, *Citizens United*, *Shelby County*, and partisan gerrymandering—whose legal issues in the abstract shouldn't have partisan valence, but in the real world of American politics obviously do.

As the response of the conservative legal movement to various judicial provocations has shifted, the debate over the Court's posture has crystallized. From calls for restraint in the face of the Warren Court's making up social policy out of whole cloth—which ultimately led to too much deference to the political branches, and thus a long-term loss for constitutional governance—the focus now is on engaging with the law. That approach often calls for invalidating the laws being reviewed rather than exercising "passive virtues." Indeed, "activism" has become a vacuous term that conveys nothing more than disagreement with the judge or opinion being criticized. The battle has been joined over the legal theory rather than judicial process.

That is, so long as we accept that judicial review is constitutional and appropriate in the first place—how a judiciary is supposed to ensure that the government secures and protects our liberties without it is beyond me—then we should be concerned only that a court "gets it right," regardless of whether that correct interpretation leads to the challenged law being upheld or overturned. To paraphrase Neil Gorsuch at his confirmation hearings, the "little guy" should win when he's in the right, and the big corporation should win when it's in the right. The dividing line, then, is not between judicial activism and judicial restraint, but between legitimate and vigorous judicial engagement and illegitimate judicial imperialism or abdication.

It's a generational battle: Do you get into the fight over federalism and the separation of powers or do you sit back and let the political branches handle that sort of thing, preferring not to mess up your judicial robes? And that gets us back to the debate over the administrative state, regarding deference doctrines, congressional delegation of legislative powers, and even more arcane areas of regulatory law. Which is why judicial selection is so consequential. "If you get the administrative stuff right, everything else will fall into place," explains former White House counsel Don McGahn, the architect of President Trump's judicial-nominations strategy.[2]

In any event, the balanced Court that we were accustomed to, with one or two human jump-balls between separate ideological blocs, is over. The Court is moving right, if only incrementally.

While Chief Justice Roberts now has even more incentive to indulge his minimalist fantasies and lead the Court from the squishy commanding heights, he is a surer vote for conservatives—maybe not libertarians—than Justice Kennedy was. What that means in the long term only time will tell, though of course Roberts will only remain in the middle of the Court if a Democratic president gets to replace Justices Ginsburg and Breyer. If it's President Trump making one or both of those nominations, the resulting war will make the Bork, Thomas, and Kavanaugh processes look like those old-school same-day confirmations.

But the judicial debates we've seen the last few decades were never really about the nominees themselves—just like the proposals for court-packing and the like aren't about "good government." They're about the direction of the Court. The left in particular needs its social and regulatory agendas, as promulgated by the executive branch, to get through the judiciary, because they would never pass as legislation at the national level. That's why progressive forces pull out all the stops against originalist nominees who would enforce limits on federal power. Indeed, all of the big nominee blowups in modern times—since the bipartisan opposition to Abe Fortas in 1968—have come with Republican appointments. The one quasi-exception didn't involve any attacks on the nominee, but the rare case of an election-year vacancy arising under divided government; Merrick Garland would've been confirmed had Antonin Scalia died a year earlier.

Not that any of this is a good thing. "I really, really don't like where we are right now," sighs former solicitor general Don Verrilli, who had worked on nominations under Presidents Clinton and Obama and laments the evermore toxic atmosphere. "Something needs to be done to change the situation."[3] If nominations were depoliticized, whether through term limits or any other reforms, or some unpredictable shock that recalibrated norms, that would likewise depoliticize the exercise of judicial power, both in perception and reality.

But term limits would take a constitutional amendment (see chapter 20) and everything else is either completely unworkable or doesn't actually solve the identified problem (see chapter 21). We can't just wave a magic wand and go back to some halcyon age where the issues we faced as a country, the development of the law, and the political dynamic, were all different. "If they could truly, truly go back, I hear from most senators that they would prefer a return to the pre-nuclear-option days," observes Ron Klain, former chief of staff to Vice Presidents Gore and Biden, "but in many ways, it's easier for them now, because there's very little constituency for voting for the other party's nominees."[4]

The only lasting solution to what ails our body juridic is to return to the Founders' Constitution by rebalancing and devolving power, so Washington isn't making so many big decisions for the whole country. Depoliticizing the judiciary and toning down our confirmation process is a laudable goal, but that'll happen only when judges go back to judging rather than bending over backwards to ratify the constitutional abuses of the other branches.

The judiciary needs to once again hold politicians'—and bureaucrats'—feet to the constitutional fire by rejecting overly broad legislation of dubious constitutional warrant, thus curbing executive-agency overreach and putting the ball back in Congress's court. And by returning power back to the states, and the people, while ensuring that majorities on the local level don't invade individual constitutional rights. After all, the separation of powers and federalism exist not as some dry exercise in Madisonian political theory but as a means to that singular end of protecting our freedom.

These structural protections are the Framers' best stab at answering the eternal question of how you empower government to secure liberty while also building internal controls for self-policing. Or, as Madison famously put it in *Federalist 51*, his disquisition on man's non-angelic nature, "In framing a government which is to be administered by men over men, the great difficulty lies in this: you must first enable the government to control the governed; and in the next place oblige it to control itself."

Ultimately, judicial power is not a means to an end, but an enforcement mechanism for the strictures of a founding document intended just as much to curtail the excesses of democracy as to empower its exercise. In a country ruled by law, and not men, the proper response to an unpopular legal decision is to change the law or amend the Constitution. Any other method leads to a sort of judicial abdication and the loss of those very rights and liberties that can only be vindicated through the judicial process. Or to government by black-robed philosopher kings—and as Justice Scalia liked to say, why would we choose nine lawyers for that job?

The reason we have these heated court battles is that the federal government is simply making too many decisions at a national level for such a large, diverse, and pluralistic country. There's no more reason that there needs to be a one-size-fits-all health care system, for example, than that zoning laws must be uniform in every city. Let federal legislators make the hard calls about truly national issues like defense or (actually) interstate (actual) commerce, but let states and localities make most of the decisions that affect our daily lives. Let Texas be Texas and California be California. That's the only way we're going to defuse tensions in Washington, whether in the halls of Congress or in the marble palace of the highest court in the land.

Acknowledgments

This book would not have been possible without the encouragement, advice, assistance, hard work, and support of many people.

For several years, over a series of emails, phone calls, and cocktails, I had noodled ideas for a book about the Supreme Court and our constitutional order with Keith Urbahn. Unlike many of my friends, Keith to his credit never went to law school but instead founded a literary agency, Javelin, that has been quite successful in selling books to a range of publishers. He helped shape my thoughts into an attractive proposal, and worked tirelessly as my agent to sell it. His colleagues Matt Lattimer and Dylan Colligan also handled some of that legwork.

Then when it came time to actually write the thing—first you sell, then you write!—I wouldn't have gotten very far, at least not in the time I had, without the help of four young lawyers whose tenure in the Cato Institute's annual legal associates program coincided with this project. Michael Collins, Dennis Garcia, James Knight, and Sam Spiegelman produced historical outlines and research memos, calculated confirmation rates, organized historical data, tracked down details, suggested edits, formatted footnotes, and did whatever else I asked whenever I fired off missives from the depths of my manuscript. I'm not sure this is what they signed up for when they agreed to come work for us, but I hope that this book work was a nice break from the legal briefs, op-eds, and policy analyses they were otherwise working on.

Speaking of institutional support, I can't imagine a better circumstance in which to write a book than at a think tank that encourages its scholars to write books. I finalized my book proposal soon after becoming the director of the Robert A. Levy Center for Constitutional Studies, so it was already a period of adjustment and new responsibilities, but Cato supported me in my ambitious goals. Executive Vice President David Boaz read an early version of the manuscript—about a third longer than what you have here—and pushed me to further clarify the differences between conservatives and libertarians, a tension reflected in the debates over judicial restraint versus engagement and protections for unenumerated rights. Jason Kuznicki, the editor of Cato Books, also read that long manuscript, and gave comments far more detailed than I could've ever hoped far, particularly since I wasn't publishing this under his imprint.

Then there's Roger Pilon. Roger founded Cato's constitutional center and served as its director for thirty years. He read a later version of my manuscript, taking time away from his own book-writing to give useful and characteristically precise comments. But even more importantly in the grand scheme of things, he saved me from toiling away in Big Law, taking a chance on this opinionated young associate and launching me in a more fruitful direction.

Randy Barnett also read the near-final version of the book, giving several useful corrections. I had only asked him for a blurb, but he insisted on making sure I knew what I was talking about.

I'm indebted to several other people who reviewed certain chapters based on their own experience: Steven Duffield, who now runs his own public policy consulting firm after being a longtime Senate Judiciary Committee staffer, provided deep knowledge of the Clinton and Bush confirmation battles; C. Boyden Gray, who was President George H.W. Bush's White House counsel, made sure I got the Souter and Thomas nominations right; Mark Paoletta, now general counsel to the Office of Management and Budget, was a key player in the Thomas confirmation and helped me sort through the important moments there; Peter Wallison, who had been White House counsel in 1986–87, gave me pointers on both President Reagan's selection process and the effect of the Supreme Court's role in expanding the administrative state on judicial politics.

Also invaluable were discussions with several other judicial-selection advisers, counsel, and strategists, including Bob Bauer, Jonathan Bunch, Ron Klain, Leonard Leo, Don McGahn, and Don Verrilli. They were generous with their time in helping this outside observer understand the way things really worked in the halls of power, as well as talking through the "where do we go from here?" issues.

Quite fortuitously, and completely coincidentally, less than a month before my manuscript was due, my alma mater Princeton University held a conference on "The Politics of Judicial Nominations in an Age of Mistrust." Co-sponsored by Princeton's Center for the Study of Democratic Politics and its James Madison Program in American Ideals and Institutions, this event gave me good food for thought, filled in important gaps, and provided an opportunity to test out part of my narrative on leading scholars, practitioners, and journalists. My great thanks to Professors Brandice Canes-Wrone and Robby George for organizing this timely confab and inviting me to participate.

The team at Regnery Publishing has been a pleasure to work with. Tom Spence was enthusiastic about this project from the beginning.

Although in one sense I lament that he became Regnery's president before my editing process even began, it's also not a bad thing for your publisher's head honcho to have a soft spot for your book. Moreover, the guy who then became my first-line editor, Paul Choix, did a fantastic job. After I turned in way too many words—it turns out that an author can indeed be *too* comprehensive—Paul guided me through a process that wasn't so much separating the wheat from the chaff as ensuring that only the parts necessary to tell my story and make my arguments remained. The "director's cut" had some more amusing vignettes and curious trivia, but it wasn't as strong a book.

Since before I even had a first draft of a book proposal, let alone a contract or a manuscript, friends and professional acquaintances would ask, "when are you gonna write your Supreme Court book?" There are too many such people to list here, but once I was actually in the trenches, I especially appreciated the regular check-ins from Adam Kwasman and Eddie Loya. And the judge I clerked for, E. Grady Jolly, was a constant voice in my head, ensuring that I brought integrity, rigor, and clarity to the project.

Finally, everything I do I owe to my family. My wife Kristin, who's a better lawyer than I am, assumed more childcare duties so I could hole up in my study to work on my *magnum opus*, and was tolerant of my moods when I periodically emerged. I don't recommend writing a book while raising two preschoolers unless you're married to her. My mother-in-law and father-in-law, Diane and Roger Feeley, who moved from Kansas and built their home on our property, provide us type-A big-city lawyers some common sense and practical skills (and more childcare). Multi-generational living, once the norm, is now a growing trend, and I can see why; I don't know how busy couples raise kids without this kind of setup.

My dad Leonid, who with my late mother Galina took me away from Soviet Russia nearly 40 years ago, has never stopped believing in me. This book is as much his dream as mine.

Bibliography

Abraham, Henry J. *Justices, Presidents, and Senators*, 5th ed. Lanham, Maryland: Rowman & Littlefield, 2008.

Biskupic, Joan. *American Original: The Life and Constitution of Supreme Court Justice Antonin Scalia*. New York: Farrar, Straus and Giroux, 2009.

———. *Breaking In: The Rise of Sonia Sotomayor and the Politics of Justice*. New York: Farrar, Straus and Giroux, 2014.

———. *The Chief: The Life and Turbulent Times of Chief Justice John Roberts*. New York: Basic Books, 2019.

Carter, Stephen L. *The Confirmation Mess: Cleaning Up the Federal Appointments Process*. New York: Basic Books, 1994.

Collins, Paul M. Jr., and Lori A. Ringhand. *Supreme Court Confirmation Hearings and Constitutional Change*. Cambridge, United Kingdom: Cambridge University Press, 2013.

Cramton, Roger C., and Paul D. Carrington, eds. *Reforming the Court: Term Limits for Supreme Court Justices*. Durham, North Carolina: Carolina Academic Press, 2006.

Davis, Richard. *Electing Justice: Fixing the Supreme Court Nomination Process*. New York: Oxford University Press, 2005.

Eisgruber, Christopher L. *The Next Justice: Repairing the Supreme Court Appointments Process*. Princeton: Princeton University Press, 2007.

Epstein, Lee, and Jeffrey A. Segal. *Advice and Consent: The Politics of Judicial Appointments*. New York: Oxford University Press, 2007.

Graetz, Michael J., and Linda Greenhouse. *The Burger Court and the Rise of the Judicial Right.* New York: Simon & Schuster, 2016.

Greenburg, Jan Crawford. *Supreme Conflict: The Inside Story of the Struggle for Control of the United States Supreme Court.* New York: Penguin Press, 2007.

Greenhouse, Linda. *Becoming Justice Blackmun: Harry Blackmun's Supreme Court Journey.* New York: Henry Holt and Company, 2005.

Hemingway, Mollie, and Carrie Severino. *Justice on Trial: The Kavanaugh Confirmation and the Future of the Supreme Court.* Washington, D.C.: Regnery, 2019.

Knowles, Helen J. *The Tie Goes to Freedom: Justice Anthony M. Kennedy on Liberty.* Lanham, Maryland: Rowman & Littlefield Publishers, Inc., 2009.

Merida, Kevin, and Michael Fletcher. *Supreme Discomfort: The Divided Soul of Clarence Thomas.* New York: Doubleday, 2007.

Nemacheck, Christine L. *Strategic Selection: Presidential Nomination of Supreme Court Justices from Herbert Hoover through George W. Bush.* Charlottesville: University of Virginia Press, 2008.

O'Brien, David M. *Storm Center: The Supreme Court in American Politics,* 9th ed. New York: W.W. Norton & Company, 2011.

Peretti, Terri Jennings. *In Defense of a Political Court.* Princeton: Princeton University Press, 1999.

Rosen, Jeffrey. *Louis D. Brandeis: American Prophet.* New Haven, Connecticut: Yale University Press, 2016.

———. *William Howard Taft.* New York: Times Books, 2018.

Silverstein, Mark. *Judicious Choices: The Politics of Supreme Court Confirmations,* 2nd ed. New York: W.W. Norton & Company, 2007.

Simon, Paul. A*dvice & Consent: Clarence Thomas, Robert Bork and the Intriguing History of the Supreme Court's Nomination Battles.* Washington, D.C.: National Press Books, 1992.

Thomas, Clarence. *My Grandfather's Son.* New York: Harper, 2007.

Thomas, Evan. *First: Sandra Day O'Connor.* New York: Random House, 2019.

Wallison, Peter J. *Ronald Reagan: The Power of Conviction and the Success of His Presidency.* New York: Basic Books, 2004.

Woodward, Bob, and Scott Armstrong. *The Brethren: Inside the Supreme Court.* New York: Simon & Schuster, 1979.

Yalof, David Alistair. *Pursuit of Justices: Presidential Politics and the Selection of Supreme Court Nominees.* Chicago: University of Chicago Press, 2001.

Notes

This book turned out to be a larger undertaking than I imagined. Piecing together historical and journalistic accounts, as well as academic research, proved to be an effective way to understand the current state of Supreme Court politics and judicial nominations, how we got there, and where we're going (or should be going).

I didn't spend time in archives or reviewing primary historical documents, so you won't find anything here that wasn't already discovered, but I hope that I put it all together in a way that updates the narrative. I also didn't spend too much time interviewing the players from various modern confirmation battles, although conversations with former White House counsels and others who had a hand in selecting and vetting judges and justices, as well as with a few judges who went through the process, proved invaluable.

In addition to the chapter notes that appear below, a list of key books—histories, biographies, and political-science analyses—appears in the bibliography. Those that were particularly helpful in telling the story of *Supreme Disorder* were Henry Abraham's magisterial *Justices, Presidents, and Senators*, Senator Paul Simon's unique perspective in *Advice & Consent*, Jan Crawford's readable inside scoop *Supreme Conflict*, and Mollie Hemingway and Carrie Severino's ripped-from-the-headlines *Justice on Trial*. My legal associates and I called Abraham's tome "the bible" and I was saddened that its remarkable author passed away a month before I turned in my manuscript, before I could convey my gratitude. For more detailed historical information about all Supreme Court nominations and justices, as well as statistics on modern judicial confirmation processes, visit SupremeDisorder.com.

Chapter 1: The Early Court

1. Henry J. Abraham, *Justices, Presidents, and Senators*, 5th ed. (Lanham, Maryland: Rowman & Littlefield, 2008), 20.
2. Paul Simon, *Advice & Consent: Thomas, Robert Bork and the Intriguing History of the Supreme Court's Nomination Battles* (Washington: National Press Books, 1992), 157.
3. "Supreme Court Nominations (1789-Present)," United States Senate, https://www.senate.gov/legislative/nominations/SupremeCourtNominations1789present.htm.
4. Abraham, *Justices, Presidents, and Senators*, 57.
5. Fred L. Israel, "John Blair," in Leon Friedman and Fred L. Israel, eds., *The Justices of the United States Supreme Court, 1789–1969: Their Lives and Major Opinions*, (New York: Chelsea House Publishers and Bowker & Co., 1969) 1:111.
6. *South Carolina State-Gazette* (Charleston), July 17, 1795, as shown in *The Documentary History of the Supreme Court of the United States, 1789–1800* (New York: Columbia University Press, 1985), 1:767.
7. Simon, *Advice & Consent*, 167–68.
8. John Maltese, *The Selling of Supreme Court Nominees* (Baltimore: Johns Hopkins University Press, 1998), 30–31.
9. Samuel Eliot Morison, Henry Steele Commager, and William E. Leuchtenberg, *The Growth of the American Republic*, 6th ed. (New York: Oxford University Press, 1969), 1:346.
10. Simon, *Advice & Consent*, 172.
11. William H. Rehnquist, *Grand Inquests: The Historic Impeachments of Justice Samuel Chase and President Andrew Johnson* (New York: William Morrow & Co., 1992), 52.
12. Henry J. Abraham, *The Judicial Process: An Introductory Analysis of the Courts of the United States, England, and France*, 7th ed. (New York: Oxford University Press, 1998), 340.
13. R. Kent Newmeyer, "A Note on the Whig Politics of Justice Joseph Story," 48 *Mississippi Valley Historical Review* 480 (Dec. 1961): 482.
14. R. Kent Newmeyer, *Supreme Court Justice Joseph Story: Statesman of the Old Republic* (Chapel Hill: University of North Carolina Press, 1985).
15. Henry Clay to John Crittenden, January 27, 1829, Warren, *The Supreme Court*, 1:704.

Chapter 2: Prelude to Civil War

1. John Marshall to Senator Benjamin W. Leigh, undated, in Samuel Taylor, *Memoir of Roger B. Taney* (1872; repr., Boston: Da Capo Press, 1970), 240.
2. Simon, *Advice & Consent*, 175.
3. Quoted in Joseph Harris, *The Advice and Consent of the Senate: A Study of the Confirmation of Appointments by the United States Senate* (Berkeley: University of California Press, 1953), 63.
4. *New York Courier*, January 23, 1836, quoted in Warren, *The Supreme Court*, 2:11.
5. Quoted in Bernard Schwartz, *Basic History of the U.S. Supreme Court* (Princeton: Van Nostrand Co., 1968), 29.
6. Simon, *Advice & Consent*, 176. They had six daughters.
7. See Mark A. Graber, "The Jacksonian Makings of the Taney Court," *University of Maryland Legal Studies Research Paper November 2005-63* (Nov. 2005), https://papers.ssrn.com/sol3/papers.cfm?abstract_id=842184.
8. Abraham, *Justices, Senators, and Presidents*, 83.

9. *Bank of the United States, Report of the Majority*, 22nd Congress, 1st Sess., appendix to *Register of Debates in Congress* 8, March 14, 1832, 3:76.

10. Abraham, *Justices, Presidents, and Senators*, 88.

11. *See* Keith E. Whittington, "The Road Not Taken: *Dred Scott*, Judicial Authority and Political Questions," *Journal of Politics* 2 (May 2001): 365–91; Stuart Streichler, *Justice Curtis in the Civil War Era: At the Crossroads of American Constitutionalism* (Charlottesville: University of Virginia Press, 2005).

12. James Buchanan, "Inaugural Address," March 4, 1857, *Presidential Speeches: James Buchanan Presidency*, Miller Center of Public Affairs at the University of Virginia, transcript, https://millercenter.org/the-presidency/presidential-speeches/march-4-1857-inaugural-address.

13. Simon, *Advice & Consent*, 192.

Chapter 3: The Civil War and After

1. Roy P. Basler, ed., *Collected Works of Abraham Lincoln* (New Brunswick, New Jersey: Rutgers University Press, 1953), 3:9.

2. Brian Doherty, *Radicals for Capitalism: A Freewheeling History of the Modern American Libertarian Movement* (New York: PublicAffairs, 2007), 28.

3. *Hepburn v. Griswold*, 75 U.S. 603 (1870) (invalidating the Legal Tender Act of 1862); *Legal Tender Cases*, 79 U.S. 457 (1871) (overruling *Hepburn*).

4. Abraham, *Justices, Presidents, and Senators*, 98.

5. Ibid., 99.

6. Loren P. Beth, "President Hayes Appoints a Justice," *Yearbook 1989* (Washington: Supreme Court Historical Society, 1989), 73.

7. Linda Przybyszewski, *The Republic According to John Marshall Harlan* (Chapel Hill: University of North Carolina Press, 1999).

8. Tinsley E. Yarbrough, *Judicial Enigma: The First Justice Harlan* (Oxford: Oxford University Press, 1995), viii.

9. Abraham, *Justices, Presidents, and Senators*, 109.

10. Page 1 on March 15 and 13, 1881, respectively, quoted in Abraham, *Justices, Presidents, and Senators*, 109.

11. Abraham, *Justices, Presidents, and Senators*, 111.

12. For a detailed account of Lamar's fascinating confirmation process, *see* Daniel J. Meador, "Lamar to the Supreme Court: Last Step to National Reunion," in *Yearbook 1986* (Washington: Supreme Court Historical Society, 1986), 27-47.

13. Abraham, *Justices, Presidents, and Senators*, 114, quoting *Supreme Court Historical Society Quarterly* (Spring 1983), 2.

14. Abraham, *Justices, Presidents, and Senators*, 117.

15. Allan Nevins, *Grover Cleveland: A Study in Courage* (New York: Dodd, Mead & Co., 1932), 415.

16. *See* David E. Bernstein, *Rehabilitating Lochner: Defending Individual Rights against Progressive Reform* (Chicago: University of Chicago Press, 2011).

17. "Annual Message to Congress," 60th Cong., 2nd sess., Congressional Record 43, December 8, 1908, 1:21.

18. Woodrow Wilson, *Constitutional Government in the United States* (New York: Columbia Univ. Press), 54–62.

19. Abraham, *Justices, Presidents, and Senators*, 125.

20. *Lochner v. New York*, 198 U.S. 45, 75 (1905) (Holmes, J., dissenting).

21. *Buck v. Bell*, 274 U.S. 200, 207 (1927).

22. Holmes to Laski, March 4, 1920, reported in *Holmes-Laski Letters: The Correspondence of Mr. Justice Holmes and Harold J. Laski, 1916–1935*, ed. Mark DeWolfe Howe (Cambridge: Harvard University Press, 1953), 1:249.

23. The *Letters of Theodore Roosevelt*, vol. 5, *The Big Stick*, eds. Elting E. Morison, John M. Blum, and John J. Buckley (Cambridge: Harvard University Press, 1952), 396.

24. "Books: The Great Dissenter," *Time*, May 8, 1944, http://content.time.com/time/magazine/article/0,9171,933394,00.html.

25. Alpheus Thomas Mason, *William Howard Taft: Chief Justice* (New York: Simon & Schuster, 1965), 15.

26. *See, e.g., Houston East & West Texas Ry. Co. v. United States*, 234 U.S. 342 (1914) (also known as the *Shreveport Rate Case*, upholding the Interstate Commerce Commission's decision to void discriminatory railroad rates imposed by the Texas Railroad Commission).

27. Howard Ball, *Hugo L. Black: Cold Steel Warrior* (New York: Oxford University Press, 1996), 89.

28. C. Dickerman Williams, "The 1924 Term: Recollections of Chief Justice Taft's Law Clerk," *Yearbook 1989* (Washington: Supreme Court Historical Society, 1989), 49.

29. Robert Battle, comp., "Ancestry of Christopher Reeve," http://www.wargs.com/other/reeve.html.

30. *See, e.g., Coppage v. Kansas*, 236 U.S. 1 (1915) (holding that it was unconstitutional for states to exercise their police powers to try to "equalize" bargaining power in employment negotiations).

31. Mason, *William Howard Taft*, 213; Pringle, *Life and Times of William Howard Taft*, 971.

32. Richard A. Epstein, John Yoo, and Troy Senik, "Recess Appointments," February 4, 2013, in *Law Talk with Epstein and Yoo*, podcast, https://ricochet.com/podcast/law-talk/recess-appointments.

33. "Video: Richard Epstein Defends the 'Classical Liberal' Constitution," *Constitution Daily*, National Constitution Center, September 11, 2014, https://constitutioncenter.org/blog/video-richard-epstein-defends-the-classical-liberal-constitution.

Chapter 4: The Court Resists the Progressives

1. Terry Bimes and Stephen Skowronek, "Woodrow Wilson's Critique of Popular Leadership: Reassessing the Modern-Traditional Divide in Presidential History," *Polity* 29, no. 1 (Autumn 1996): 29.

2. Josephus Daniels, *The Wilson Era*, vol. 1, *Years of Peace: 1910-1916* (Chapel Hill: University of North Carolina Press, 1968), 302.

3. Liva Baker, *The Justice from Beacon Hill: The Life and Times of Oliver Wendell Holmes* (New York: HarperCollins, 1991), 465.

4. Philippa Strum, *Louis D. Brandeis: Justice for the People* (Cambridge: Harvard University Press, 1984), 371.

5. Drew Pearson and Robert S. Allen, *The Nine Old Men* (Garden City, New York: Doubleday, Doran, 1936), 131.

6. Samuel D. Warren and Louis D. Brandeis, "The Right to Privacy," 4 Harv. L. Rev. 193 (1890).

7. Jeffrey Rosen, "Judge Garland's Nomination, Day 126," *New York Times*, July 20, 2016, A23 (Rosen is, among other things, author of *Louis Brandeis: American Prophet*); Harris, *The Advice and Consent of the Senate*, 102–03.

8. Lewis J. Paper, *Brandeis* (Englewood Cliffs, New Jersey: Prentice-Hall, 1983), 213.

9. Diana Klebanow and Franklin L. Jonas, *People's Lawyers: Crusaders for Justice in American History* (Armonk, New York: M.E. Sharpe, Inc., 2003), 82.

10. A. L. Todd, *Justice on Trial: The Case of Louis D. Brandeis* (New York: McGraw-Hill, 1964), 73.

11. William O. Douglas, "Louis Brandeis: Dangerous Because Incorruptible," review of *Justice on Trial*, by A.L. Todd, *New York Times*, July 5, 1964.

12. Abraham, *Justices, Presidents, and Senators*, 143.

13. Woodrow Wilson, *Selected Addresses and Public Papers of Woodrow Wilson* (New York: Boni and Liveright, Inc., 1918), 119.

14. Simon, *Advice & Consent*, 240.

15. Alpheus Thomas Mason, "William Howard Taft," in Friedman and Israel, eds., *The Justices of the United States Supreme Court*, 3:2113.

16. C. Herman Pritchett, *The Roosevelt Court: A Study in Judicial Politics and Values, 1937–1947* (New York: Macmillan, 1948),18.

17. Donald F. Anderson, "Building National Consensus: The Career of William Howard Taft," 68 U. Cin. L. Rev. 323, 349–50 (2000).

18. Abraham, *Justices, Presidents, and Senators*, 149.

19. *See* Daniel J. Danelski, *A Supreme Court Justice Is Appointed* (New York: Random House, 1964).

20. Mason, *William Howard Taft: Chief Justice*, 15.

21. Theodore M. Vestal, "Harlan Fiske Stone: New Deal Prudence," Oklahoma State University (accessed from Archive Today, https://archive.is/20121214230233/http://fp.okstate.edu/vestal/polsci4983/Articles/Chief_Justice_Stone.htm).

22. *See* Daniel J. Danelski, "Ideology as a Ground for the Rejection of Robert Bork," 84 Nw. L. Rev. 900 (1990).

23. U.S. Congress, Senate, Committee on the Judiciary, *Reorganization of the Federal Judiciary*, 75th Cong., 1st Sess., 1937, S. Rep. 711, 1.

24. "The participation of the Negro in politics is a source of evil and danger to both races and is not desired by the wise men in either race or by the Republican Party of North Carolina." U.S. Congress, Senate, Committee on the Judiciary, *Hearings before the Subcommittee of the Committee on the Judiciary, on the Confirmation of John J. Parker to Be an Associate Justice of the Supreme Court of the United States*, 71st Cong., 2nd Sess., 1930, 74.

25. Abraham, *Justices, Presidents, and Senators*, 33.

26. Ibid., 159.

27. Laura Kalman, "The Constitution, the Supreme Court, and the New Deal," 110 Am. Hist. Rev. 1052, 1055 (2005).

28. Abraham, *Justices, Presidents, and Senators*, 159.

29. Alpheus Thomas Mason, *Harlan Fiske Stone: Pillar of the Law* (New York: Viking, 1956), 336.

30. *Steward Machine Co. v. Davis*, 301 U.S. 548 (1937) (unemployment insurance); *Helvering v. Davis*, 301 U.S. 619 (1937) (Social Security); *Palko v. Connecticut*, 302 U.S. 319 (1937) (selective incorporation).

Chapter 5: Roosevelt's Court

1. Franklin D. Roosevelt, "Court-Packing" (speech, Washington, D.C., March 9, 1937), *Presidential Speeches: Franklin D. Roosevelt Presidency*, Miller Center of Public Affairs at the University of Virginia, https://millercenter.org/the-presidency/presidential-speeches/march-9-1937-fireside-chat-9-court-packing.
2. Ronald Steel, *Walter Lippman and the American Century* (Boston: Little, Brown, 1980), 320.
3. "Found Dead Alone; Heart Attack Is Fatal to Majority Leader Who Ignored Symptoms," *New York Times*, July 15, 1937, 13.
4. Joseph Alsop and Turner Catledge, *The 168 Days* (Garden City, New York: Doubleday, Doran, 1938), 296.
5. Hugo L. Black Jr., *My Father: A Remembrance* (New York: Random House, 1975), 16-17.
6. Abraham, *Justices, Presidents, and Senators*, 168.
7. John P. Frank, *Mr. Justice Black: The Man and His Opinions* (New York: Alfred A. Knopf, 1949), 105.
8. *Ex parte Levitt*, 302 U.S. 633 (1937). *See also* Andrew Hamm, "A Look Back at Justice Hugo Black's First Day on the Bench," SCOTUSblog, October 9, 2018, https://www.scotusblog.com/2018/10/a-look-back-at-justice-hugo-blacks-first-day-on-the-bench.
9. *See* William Baude, "The Unconstitutionality of Justice Black," 98 Tex. L. Rev. 327 (2019).
10. Liva Baker, *Felix Frankfurter* (New York: Coward-McCann, 1969), 201-06.
11. Abraham, *Justices, Presidents, and Senators*, 173.
12. *See, e.g., Rochin v. California*, 342 U.S. 165 (1952) (applying that test to the Fourth Amendment).
13. Abraham, *Justices, Presidents, and Senators*, 177.
14. John P. Frank, "William O. Douglas," in Friedman and Israel, eds., *The Justices of the United States Supreme Court*, 4:2454.
15. 381 U.S. 479, 484 (1965).
16. John Dean, "When Supreme Court Justices Refuse to Retire: Why We Need More Media Coverage, and a Constitutional Amendment," *Find Law's Legal Commentary*, July 20, 2001, https://supreme.findlaw.com/legal-commentary/when-supreme-court-justices-refuse-to-retire.html; J. Woodford Howard Jr., *Mr. Justice Murphy: A Political Biography* (Princeton: Princeton University Press, 1968), 215–16.
17. 323 U.S. 214, 202 (cleaned up).
18. Jeffrey S. Lehman, "Student Profile: The Honorable Frank William Murphy, Class of 1914," *History and Traditions*, University of Michigan Law School, http://www.law.umich.edu/HISTORYANDTRADITIONS/STUDENTS/Pages/ProfilePage.aspx?SID=9470&Year=1914.
19. As quoted in Mason, *Harlan Fiske Stone*, 184.
20. Mason, *Harlan Fiske Stone*, 191.
21. Abraham, *Justices, Presidents, and Senators*, 183.
22. Ibid., 184.
23. Dennis J. Hutchison, "The Black-Jackson Feud," 1988 Sup. Ct. Rev. 203 (1988).

Chapter 6: The Post-War Settlement

1. Abraham, *Justices, Presidents, and Senators*, 188.
2. James F. Simon, *Independent Journey: The Life of William O. Douglas*, (New York: Harper & Row, 1980), 274.
3. Robert E. Riggs, "When Every Vote Counts: 5–4 Decisions in the United States Supreme Court, 1900-90," 21 Hofstra L. Rev. 667 (1993); "Stat Pack Archive," SCOTUSblog, https://www.scotusblog.com/reference/stat-pack.
4. Kim Isaac Eisler, *The Last Liberal: Justice William J. Brennan, Jr. and the Decisions that Transformed America* (1993, repr., Washington: Beard Books, 2005), 76.
5. William Franklin Radcliff, Sherman Minton: Indiana's Supreme Court Justice (Indianapolis: Guild Press of Indiana, 1996), 137.
6. Dwight D. Eisenhower, *Mandate for Change, 1953–1956: The White House Years* (Garden City, New York: Doubleday, 1963), 226-30.
7. Joseph L. Rauh Jr., "The Chief," New Republic, August 9, 1982, 31.
8. Eisenhower, *Mandate for Change*, 228.
9. Dwight D. Eisenhower to Milton Stover Eisenhower, October 9, 1953, from The Presidential Papers of Dwight David Eisenhower, https://web.archive.org/web/20120118180711/http://www.eisenhowermemorial.org/presidential-papers/first-term/documents/460.cfm (accessed from the Internet Archive Wayback Machine), originally in The Papers of Dwight David Eisenhower, vol. 14, *The Presidency: The Middle Way* (Baltimore, The Johns Hopkins University Press, 1996), part III, chap. 6.
10. G. Edward White, *Earl Warren: A Public Life* (New York: Oxford University Press, 1982), 127, 129.
11. Eisenhower, *Mandate for Change*, 228.
12. G. Edward White, *Earl Warren*, 152.
13. Michael R. Belknap, *The Supreme Court under Earl Warren, 1953–1969* (Columbia: University of South Carolina Press, 2005),13–14.
14. *See* Dennis J. Hutchinson, "Hail to the Chief: Earl Warren and the Supreme Court," 81 Michigan Law Review 922 (1983).
15. Anthony Lewis, "Earl Warren," in Friedman and Israel, eds., The Justices of the United States Supreme Court, 4:2721.
16. Abraham, *Justices, Presidents, and Senators*, 206.
17. James Taranto and Leonard Leo, eds., *Presidential Leadership: Rating the Best and the Worst in the White House* (New York: Free Press, 2004).
18. 443 U.S. 193, 201 (1979).
19. Brian Walsh "In the opinion of many, Justice Brennan was the most influential member in the US Supreme Court's history," Irish Times, August 20, 1997, https://www.irishtimes.com/news/in-the-opinion-of-many-justice-brennan-was-the-most-influential-member-in-the-us-supreme-court-s-history-1.98377; Rory K. Little, "Reading Justice Brennan: Is There a 'Right' to Dissent?" 50 Hasting L.J. 683, 683 n. 2 (1999).
20. Patricia Brennan, "Seven Justices, On Camera," Washington Post, October 6, 1996, https://www.washingtonpost.com/wp-srv/national/longterm/supcourt/brennan/brennan1.htm.
21. David N. Atkinson, *Leaving the Bench: Supreme Court Justices at the End* (Lawrence: University Press of Kansas, 1999), 128.

22. Richard Lawrence Miller, *Whittaker: Struggles of a Supreme Court* Justice (Westport, Connecticut: Greenwood Press, 2002), 202.

23. As quoted in Abraham, *Justices, Presidents, and Senators,* 211.

24. Congressional Record, 86th Cong., 1st sess., May 5, 1959, 7472; Anthony Lewis, "Stewart Hearing Opens in a Clash," *New York Times,* April 10, 1959, 1.

25. "Two Senators Blast Naming Of Stewart," *Cincinnati Post & Times-Star,* April 30, 1959, 4. Senator Eastland made a similar statement during the floor debate. Congressional Record, 86th Cong., 1st Sess., May 5, 1959, 7465 (1959).

26. Lyndon Johnson, then a senator from Texas, and majority leader, voted yes. For more on the Stewart confirmation battle, see Joel Jacobsen, "Remembered Justice: The Background, Early Career and Judicial Appointments of Justice Potter Stewart," 35 Akron L. Rev. 227 (2002).

27. *Jacobellis v. Ohio,* 378 U.S. 184, 197 (Stewart, J., concurring).

28. Stephen J. Wermiel, "The Nomination of Justice Brennan: Eisenhower's Mistake? A Look at the Historical Record," 11 Const. Comment. 515, 534-37 (1995).

29. Chester J. Pach Jr. and Elmo Richardson, *The Presidency of Dwight D. Eisenhower,* rev. ed. (Lawrence: University Press of Kansas, 1991), 141.

30. Wermiel, "The Nomination of Justice Brennan," 536 (noting that the memorandum is in the Arthur Krock Papers at Seeley G. Mudd Manuscript Library at Princeton University).

Chapter 7: The New Frontier

1. David Bernstein, "Flashback: Senate Democrats in 1960 Pass Resolution Against Election-Year Supreme Court Recess Appointments," The Volokh Conspiracy (blog), *Washington Post,* February 13, 2016, https://www.washingtonpost.com/news/volokh-conspiracy/wp/2016/02/13/flashback-senate-democrats-in-1960-pass-resolution-against-election-year-supreme-court-recess-appointments.

2. Abraham, *Justices, Presidents, and Senators,* 217.

3. Ibid., 217–18.

4. "Detroit Signs 'Whizzer' White," *St. Petersburg Times,* August 20, 1940, 10, https://news.google.com/newspapers?id=GU8wAAAAIBAJ&sjid=XEoDAAAAIBAJ&pg=2116%2C4008675; Bob French, "Whizzer White Still a Student," *Toledo Blade,* August 27, 1941, 22, https://news.google.com/newspapers?id=MfEjAAAAIBAJ&sjid=7f4DAAAAIBAJ&pg=2132%2C3776085.

5. For more on Byron White's fascinating life and career, *see* Dennis J. Hutchinson, "The Man Who Once Was Whizzer White," 103 Yale L.J. 43 (1993), which eventually became a book: *The Man Who Once Was Whizzer White: A Portrait of Justice Byron R. White* (New York: Free Press, 1998) https://www.amazon.com/Man-Who-Once-Whizzer-White/dp/0684827948.

6. Abraham, *Justices, Presidents, and Senators,* 221.

7. 381 U.S. 479, 488 (1965) (Goldberg, J., concurring).

8. David L. Stebenne, *Arthur J. Goldberg, New Deal Liberal* (New York: Oxford University Press, 1996), 348-51.

9. Stebenne, *Arthur J. Goldberg,* 373.

10. Lyndon B. Johnson, *The Vantage Point: Perspectives of the Presidency, 1963–1969* (New York: Holt, Rinehart and Winston, 1971), 544–45.

11. Bruce Allen Murphy, *Abe Fortas: The Rise and Ruin of a Supreme Court Justice* (New York: William Morrow & Co., 1988), chaps. 8, 10, 24.

12. Walter Dellinger, "SCOTUS End of Term: Will Ruth Bader Ginsburg Retire?" June 25, 2014, *Slate*, https://slate.com/news-and-politics/2014/06/scotus-end-of-term-will-ruth-bader-ginsburg-retire.html; David Alistair Yalof, *Pursuit of Justices: Presidential Politics and the Selection of Supreme Court Nominees* (Chicago: University of Chicago Press, 1999).

13. Congressional Record, one-hundredth Cong., 1st Sess., December 18, 1987, 36,163 Lyndon Johnson, then a senator from Texas, and majority leader, voted yes. (transcript of *Thurgood Marshall, The Man* (CBS one-hour special)).

14. Linda Sheryl Greene, "A Tale of Two Jusitces: Brandeis, Marshall, and Federal Court Judicial Diversity," 2017 Wis. L. Rev. 401, 409 (2017).

15. Congressional Record, 90th Cong., 1st Sess., August 30, 1967, 24,589.

16. Charlie Savage, "Kagan's Link to Marshall Cuts 2 Ways," *New York Times*, May 13, 2010, A16.

17. Abraham, *Justices, Presidents, and Senators*, 231, citing Paul J. Wahlbeck, James F. Spriggs II, and Lee Sigelman, "Ghostwriters on the Court? A Stylistic Analysis of the U.S. Supreme Court Opinion Drafts" (paper presented at the annual meeting of the Midwest Political Science Association, Chicago, April 15–17, 1998).

18. William J. Daniels, "Justice Thurgood Marshall: The Race for Equal Justice," in Charles M. Lamb and Stephen C. Halpern, eds., *The Burger Court: Political and Judicial Profiles* (Urbana: University of Illinois Press, 1991), 235.

19. Jim Newton, *Justice for All: Earl Warren and the Nation He Made* (New York: Riverhead Books, 2006), 491.

20. Abraham, *Justices, Presidents, and Senators*, 227.

21. Congressional Record, 90th Cong., 2nd Sess., June 21, 1968, 18,171; Laura Kalman, *Abe Fortas: A Biography* (New Haven: Yale University Press, 1990), 331.

22. Kalman, *Abe Fortas*, 331 (quoting a petition by 17 senators stating that "the next Chief Justice of the Supreme Court should be designated by the next President of the United States").

23. Newton, *Justice for All*, 493.

24. Kalman, *Abe Fortas*, 337.

25. Simon, *Advice & Consent*, 283.

26. Patrick J. Buchanan, "Nixon, LBJ, and the First Shot in the Judges' War," *The American Conservative*, April 7, 2017, https://www.theamericanconservative.com/buchanan/nixon-lbj-and-the-first-shots-in-the-judges-war/

27. Fred Graham, "Fortas Approved by Senate Panel," *New York Times*, September 18, 1968.

28. William Lambert, "Fortas of the Supreme Court: A Question of Ethics," *Life*, May 5, 1969.

29. *See* Gerard Magliocca, "The Legacy of Chief Justice Fortas," 18 Green Bag 2d 361 (2015).

30. The other such retirements were Oliver Ellsworth (1800), Alfred Moore (1804), Samuel Nelson (1872), William Strong (1880), Charles Evans Hughes (1916), and Oliver Wendell Holmes (1932).

Chapter 8: The Burger Court and the Conservative Revolt

1. Richard Nixon, campaign speech, November 2, 1968, quoted in 27 *Congressional Quarterly Weekly Report*, May 23, 1969, 798.

2. John Cloud, "William Rehnquist: 1924–2005, *Time*, September 4, 2005, http://content. time.com/time/nation/article/0,8599,1101296,00.html.

3. *Louisville Courier-Journal*, May 23, 1969, A1, as quoted in Abraham, *Justices, Presidents, and Senators*, 237.

4. Simon, *Advice & Consent*, 289.

5. *Alexander v. Holmes County Board of Education*, 396 U.S. 19 (1969). Burger had a hand in editing a draft orchestrated by the liberal justices. Bob Woodward and Scott Armstrong, *The Brethren: Inside the Supreme Court* (New York: Simon & Schuster, 1979), 51–55.

6. *Swann v. Charlotte-Mecklenburg Board of Education*, 402 U.S. 1 (1971).

7. *Lamb's Chapel v. Ctr. Moriches Union Free Sch. Dist.*, 508 U.S. 384, 398 (1993).

8. Kim Isaac Eisler, *A Justice for All: William J. Brennan, Jr., and the Decisions That Transformed America*, (New York: Simon & Schuster, 1993), 252.

9. *See* Edward A. Tamm and Paul Reardon, "Warren Burger and the Administration of Justice," 1981 BYU L. Rev. 447 (1981).

10. Alfonso A. Narvaez, "Clement Haynsworth Dies at 77; Lost Struggle for High Court Seat, *New York Times*, November 23, 1989, D21.

11. Simon, *Advice & Consent*, 290.

12. Lewis Powell Jr., foreword to John P. Frank, *Clement Haynsworth, the Senate, and the Supreme Court* (Charlottesville: University of Virginia Press, 1991). Powell also resented the linkage of Haynsworth with the next nominee, G. Harrold Carswell, calling it "a mindless misjoinder of names."

13. Northern Florida being part of the South, and the Fifth Circuit still including that state, plus Alabama and Georgia, the three of which became the new Eleventh Circuit in 1982.

14. Richard Harris, *Decision* (New York: E.P. Dutton & Company, 1971), 15–16.

15. *Irwinton Bulletin* (Georgia), August 13, 1948, quoted in U.S. Congress, Senate, *Hearings before the Committee on the Judiciary on the Nomination of George Harrold Carswell, of Florida, to be an Associate Justice of the Supreme Court*, 91st Cong., 2nd Sess., January 27, 1970, 22.

16. Henry Lee Moon, "The Carswell Defeat: Again Racism Repulsed," *The Crisis* 144, 147 (April 1970). *The Crisis* was the official NAACP magazine.

17. Harris, *The Advice and Consent of the Senate*, 28.

18. Abraham, *Justice, Presidents, and Senators*, 12.

19. Harris, *The Advice and Consent of the Senate*, 16.

20. A. Mitchell McConnell Jr., "Haynsworth and Carswell: A New Senate Standard of Excellence," 59 Ky. L.J. 43 (1970).

21. Congressional Record, 91st Cong., 2nd Sess., March 18, 1970, 7881.

22. Ibid., 7487.

23. Richard Nixon, presidential television address, April 9, 1970, in *Public Papers of the Presidents of the United States, Richard Nixon, 1970* (Washington: U.S. Government Printing Office, 1999), 345.

24. Fred P. Graham, "Burger and Blackmun: Opinions Similar," *New York Times*, April 15, 1970, 34.

25. Fred P. Graham, "Blackmun May Prove a Surprise for Nixon," *New York Times*, April 19, 1970, 10.

26. Linda Greenhouse, *Becoming Justice Blackmun: Harry Blackmun's Supreme Court Journey* (New York: Times Books, 2006), 186.

27. Woodward and Armstrong, *The Brethren*, 506.

28. Greenhouse, *Becoming Justice Blackmun*, 186.

29. *Roe v. Wade*, 410 U.S. 113 (1973), together with its companion case, *Doe v. Bolton*, 410 U.S. 179 (1973).

30. *Roe*, 410 U.S. at 163.

31. *Doe*, 410 U.S. at 208 (Burger, C.J., concurring).

32. John Hart Ely, "The Wages of Crying Wolf: A Comment on *Roe v. Wade*," 82 Yale L.J. 920, 947 (1973) (footnotes omitted).

33. Laurence H. Tribe, "The Supreme Court, 1972 Term – Foreword: Toward a Model of Roles in the Due Process of Life and Law," 87 Harv. L. Rev. 1, 7 (1973).

34. Jeffrey Rosen, "The Dissenter, Justice John Paul Stevens," *New York Times Magazine*, September 23, 2007, 50.

35. Ruth Bader Ginsburg, "Some Thoughts on Autonomy and Equality in Relation to *Roe v. Wade*", 63 N.C. L. Rev. 375, 385-86 (1985) ("The political process was moving in the early 1970s, not swiftly enough for advocates of quick, complete change, but majoritarian institutions were listening and acting. Heavy-handed judicial intervention was difficult to justify and appears to have provoked, not resolved, conflict.") (footnotes omitted).

36. Jonathan Bullington, "Justice Ginsburg: *Roe v. Wade* Not Woman-centered," *Chicago Tribune*, May 11, 2013, https://www.chicagotribune.com/news/breaking/chi-justice-ginsburg-roe-v-wade-not-womancentered-20130511-story.html.

37. *Callins v. Collins*, 510 U.S. 1141, 1145 (1994) (Blackmun, J., dissenting from denial of cert.).

38. *Planned Parenthood v. Casey*, 505 U.S. 833, 943 (Blackmun, J., concurring in part, concurring in judgment in part, and dissenting in part).

39. Linda Greenhouse, "Friends for Decades but Years on Court Left Them Strangers," *New York Times Magazine*, March 5, 2004, 16.

40. Dean, *The Rehnquist Choice*, xii-xiv.

41. Ibid., 51.

42. Abraham, *Justices, Presidents, and Senators*, 15.

43. "Fuck the ABA!" he had exclaimed, as reported by James Goodman, "The Politics of Picking Federal Judges," *Juris Doctor* (June 1977), 26.

44. Dean, *The Rehnquist Choice*, 163.

45. Fred P. Graham, "Senate Confirms Powell by 89 to 1 for Supreme Court," *New York Times*, December 7, 1971, 1.

46. Ibid.

47. *United States v. U.S. Dist. Court for Eastern Dist. of Mich.*, 407 U.S. 297 (1972).

48. Abraham, *Justices, Presidents, and Senators*, 251, quoting tape of conversation by Richard M. Nixon with John Ehrlichman and Egil (Bud) Krogh, July 24, 1971. *See also* Jeffrey Rosen, "Renchburg's the One!," *New York Times*, November 4, 2001, 7/15.

49. As quoted in *Time*, November 1, 1971, 10.

50. George Lardner Jr., "Nixon on Appointing Rehnquist," *Washington Post*, October 30, 2000, A25.

51. 283 Civil Liberties 8 (January 1972). *Civil Liberties* was the ACLU's in-house publication, and this position was circulated in a letter to all senators in November 1971.]

52. 443 U.S. 193, 227 (1979) (Rehnquist, J., dissenting).

53. Ibid., 219. During congressional debates over the Civil Rights Act of 1964, the bill's proponents made clear that racial quotas and set-asides weren't part of the plan.

54. Thomas, "Reagan's Mr. Right," June 30, 1986.

Chapter 9: The Swinging Seventies

1. Remarks by Rep. Gerald R. Ford, Republican leader, prepared for delivery on the Floor of the U.S. House of Representatives (speech, Washington, D.C., April 15, 1970), 8–21, https://www.fordlibrarymuseum.gov/library/speeches/700415.pdf.

2. David M. O'Brien, "Filling Justice William O. Douglas's Seat: President Gerald R. Ford's Appointment of John Paul Stevens," *Yearbook 1989* (Washington: Supreme Court Historical Society, 1989), 20–40. This actually wasn't the first time that Douglas faced impeachment. In 1953, after he stayed the execution of Ethel and Julius Rosenberg, who had been convicted of spying for the Soviets, congressional opponents initiated proceedings that didn't get very far. "House Move to Impeach Douglas Bogs Down; Sponsor Is Told He Fails to Prove His Case," *New York Times*, July 1, 1953, 18.

3. O'Brien, "Appointment of John Paul Stevens," 30.

4. Abraham, *Justices, Presidents, and Senators*, 54, table 7 (statistics through 2007, so not including Obama or Trump).

5. Gerald R. Ford, *A Time to Heal: The Autobiography of Gerald R. Ford* (New York: Harper & Row, 1979), 335.

6. U.S. Senate, 94th Cong., 2nd Sess., Committee on the Judiciary, Subcommittee on Separate of Powers, "Advice and Consent on Supreme Court Nominations," November 21, 1975, 2, https://ufdc.ufl.edu/AA00022582/00001/3.

7. *New York Times*, November 17, 1975, 18, as quoted in Abraham, *Justices, Presidents, and Senators*, 258.

8. Abraham, *Justices, Presidents, and Senators*, 258.

9. *See* Linda Greenhouse, "Justice John Paul Stevens as Abortion-Rights Strategist," 43 U.C. Davis L. Rev. 749, 752 n. 9 (2010).

10. Ford, *A Time to Heal*, 335.

11. *See, e.g.,* Gerald R. Ford letter to William M. Treanor, "RE: Justice John Paul Stevens, 30 Years on the Supreme Court," published in *USA Today*, September 21, 2005, https://usatoday30.usatoday.com/news/opinion/forum/2010-04-14-fordletter_N.htm.

12. *See* Ilya Shapiro and Nathan Harvey, "Break Up the Ninth Circuit," 26 Geo. Mason L. Rev. 1, 3 (2019), http://georgemasonlawreview.org/wp-content/uploads/2019/08/26-4_ShapiroHarvey_Web.pdf.

13. U.S. Library of Congress, Congressional Research Service, Dennis Steven Rutkus and Kevin M. Scott, *Nomination and Confirmation of Lower Federal Court Judges in Presidential Election Years*, RL34615 (2008), https://fas.org/sgp/crs/misc/RL34615.pdf.

14. Russell Wheeler, "Judicial Confirmations: What Thurmond Rule?" *Issues in Governance Studies* 45 (March 2012), https://www.brookings.edu/wp-content/uploads/2016/06/03_judicial_wheeler.pdf.

15. *New York Times*, February 13, 1979, A16 (emphasis added), as quoted in Abraham, *Justices, Senators, and Presidents*, 264.

16. "Executive Order 12059, United States Circuit Court Nominating Commission," May 11, 1978, *Federal Register* 43 (May 16, 1978): 20,949.

17. White House press conference, Dec. 7, 1978, as quoted in Abraham, *Justices, Presidents, and Senators*, 264.

18. Author's search of the Federal Judicial Database, https://www.fjc.gov/history/judges/search/advanced-search.

19. Elliott Slotnick, "A Historical Perspective on Federal Judicial Selection," 86 *Judicature* 1, 13 (2002). These figures are always inexact because of ambiguities in self-identification.

20. David M. O'Brien, *Storm Center: The Supreme Court in American Politics*, 6th ed. (New York: W.W. Norton & Co., 2003), 69.

21. *New York Times*, July 8, 1981, A12, as quoted in Abraham, *Justices, Presidents, and Senators*, 265.

22. William French Smith, "Memorandum on Judicial Selection Procedures," April 1981, reprinted in 64 *Judicature* 9, 428 (1981).

23. Abraham, *Justices, Presidents, and Senators*, 265.

24. *Washington Post*, July 8, 1981, 11, as quoted in ibid.

25. *Time*, July 20, 1981, 11, as quoted in Abraham, *Justice, Presidents, and Senators*, 266.

26. Abraham, *Justices, Presidents, and Senators*, 266, 361 n.185 (relaying what O'Connor herself told Abraham).

27. Nina Totenberg, "O'Connor, Rehnquist and a Supreme Marriage Proposal," *NPR*, October 31, 2018, https://www.npr.org/2018/10/31/662293127/a-supreme-marriage-proposal.

28. Linda Greenhouse, "Bar Group Backs Judge O'Connor on Eve of Confirmation Hearings," *New York Times*, Sept. 9, 1981, A24.

29. *Washington Post*, July 8, 1981, A7, as quoted in Abraham, *Justices, Presidents, and Senators*, 266.

30. Ed Magnusson, "The Brethren's First Sister," *Time*, February 22, 2002, http://content.time.com/time/magazine/article/0,9171,212563,00.html.

31. Jan Crawford Greenburg, *Supreme Conflict: The Inside Story of the Struggle for Control of the United States Supreme Court* (New York: Penguin Press, 2007), 222.

32. Magnusson, "Brethren's First Sister, February 22, 2002.

33. "Transcript of GOP Debate at Reagan Library," *CNN*, June 30, 2008, http://edition.cnn.com/2008/POLITICS/01/30/GOPdebate.transcript.

34. Greenburg, *Supreme Conflict*, 222.

35. U.S. Congress, Senate, *Hearings Before the Committee on the Judiciary on the Nomination of Judge Sandra Day O'Connor of Arizona to Serve as an Associate Justice of the Supreme Court of the United States*, 97th Cong., 1st Sess., September 9–11, 1981, 68.

36. Linda Greenhouse, "Panel Approves Judge O'Connor," *New York Times*, September 16, 1981, A16.

37. Greenburg, *Supreme Conflict*, 68; Herman Schwartz, "O'Connor as a Centrist? Not When Minorities Are Involved," *Los Angeles Times*, April 12, 1998, https://www.latimes.com/archives/la-xpm-1998-apr-12-op-38686-story.html.

38. Robert J. Jackson Jr. and Thiruvendran Vignarajah, "Nine Justices, Ten Years: A Statistical Retrospective," 118 Harv. L. Rev. 510, 521 (2004).

39. Abraham, *Justices, Presidents, and Senators*, 273.

40. *Grutter v. Bollinger*, 549 U.S. 306, 343 (2003).

Chapter 10: The Calm before the Storm

1. Al Kamen, "Rehnquist Confirmed in 65–33 Senate Vote," *Washington Post*, September 18, 1986, https://www.washingtonpost.com/archive/politics/1986/09/18/rehnquist-confirmed-in-65-33-senate-vote/a1d9c510-e342-4452-a18c-52aa34689b96.

2. Edward M. Kennedy, "He's Too Extreme on Race, Women's Rights, Speech . . ." *Los Angeles Times*, July 30, 1986, https://www.latimes.com/archives/la-xpm-1986-07-30-me-18627-story.html.

3. Stuart Taylor Jr., "Senate Opens Rehnquist Hearing, and the Lines of Battle are Drawn," *New York Times*, July 30, 1986, A1.

4. Ibid.

5. Ronald J. Ostrow and Robert L. Jackson, "Opponents Quiz Rehnquist on Race Covenant," *Los Angeles Times*, August 1, 1986, https://www.latimes.com/archives/la-xpm-1986-08-01-mn-18978-story.html.

6. Adam Liptak, "The Memo That Rehnquist Wrote and Had to Disown," *New York Times*, September 11, 2005, https://www.nytimes.com/2005/09/11/weekinreview/the-memo-that-rehnquist-wrote-and-had-to-disown.html.

7. *United States v. Lopez*, 514 U.S. 549, 552 (1995).

8. John Yoo, "He Advocated Limitations of Public Power," *Philadelphia Inquirer*, April 27, 2005.

9. *New Republic*, June 10, 1985, 16, as quoted in Abraham, *Justices, Presidents, and Senators*, 277. See also Jeffrey Segal and Harold Spaeth, "If a Supreme Court Vacancy Occurs, Will the Senate Confirm a Reagan Nominee?" 69 *Judicature* 4 (1986), 186–90.

10. *Time*, June 30, 1986, 32, as quoted in Abraham, *Justices, Presidents, and Senators*, 278.

11. *New York Times*, June 18, 1986, 32, as quoted in *ibid*.

12. Peter J. Wallison, *Ronald Reagan: The Power of Conviction and the Success of His Presidency* (Boulder, Colorado: Westview Press, 2004), 151.

13. Richard A. Posner, "The Court of Celebrity," *New Republic*, May 5, 2011, https://newrepublic.com/article/87880/supreme-court-burger-blackmum-media-celebrity.

14. *New.York Times*, June 18, 1986, 32, as quoted in Abraham, *Justices, Presidents, and Senators*, 278.

15. Al Kamen, "Rehnquist Confirmed."

16. "Scalia on Women," *Legal Times*, February 17, 1992.

17. Antonin Scalia, Madison Lecture (lecture, Chapman University Fowler School of Law, August 29, 2005).

18. Edwin Meese III, Speech before the American Bar Association, July 9, 1985, https://www.justice.gov/sites/default/files/ag/legacy/2011/08/23/07-09-1985.pdf. See also Stuart Taylor Jr., "Meese, in Bar Group Speech, Criticizes High Court," *New York Times*, July 10, 1985, A13.

19. Margalit Fox, "Bernard Siegan, 81, Legal Scholar and Reagan Nominee, Dies," *New York Times*, April 1, 2006, B8.

20. Linda Greenhouse, "Reagan Nominee for Judgeship Urged to Withdraw," *New York Times*, March 26, 1988, 1/6.

Chapter 11: The Original Sin of Robert Bork

1. Stuart Taylor Jr., "Powell Leaves High Court; Took Key Role on Abortion and on Affirmative Action," *New York Times*, June 27, 1987, 1/1.

2. Jonathan Fuerbringer, "Byrd Says Bork Nomination Would Face Senate Trouble," *New York Times*, June 30, 1987, B20.

3. George F. Will, "Biden v. Bork," *Washington Post*, July 2, 1987, https://www. washingtonpost.com/archive/opinions/1987/07/02/biden-v-bork/be124295-d2a5-4353-ad3a-a05c20eee0c32.

4. "Bork: Nixon Offered Next High Court Vacancy in '73," *Yahoo News*, February 25, 2013, https://news.yahoo.com/bork-nixon-offered-next-high-court-vacancy-73-215747517.html

5. Simon, *Advice & Consent*, 68.

6. *New York Times*, July 2, 1987, as quoted in Abraham, *Justices, Presidents, and Senators*, 282.

7. James Reston, "Kennedy and Bork," *New York Times*, July 5, 1987, https://www.nytimes.com/1987/07/05/opinion/washington-kennedy-and-bork.html.

8. Robert H. Bork, *The Tempting of America: The Political Seduction of the Law* (New York: The Free Press, 1990), 130.

9. Roger Pilon, "Rethinking Judicial Restraint," *Wall Street Journal*, February 1, 1991.

10. Carol Rose, "Judicial Selection and the Mask of Nonpartisanship," 84 Nw. L. Rev. 929 (1989).

11. Robert Drinan, "Senate to Anti-Bork Vote Would Fit U.S. Tradition," *National Catholic Reporter*, July 31, 1987, as quoted in Simon, *Advice & Consent*, 51.

12. Rick Lyman, "NAACP to Fight Bork 'Til Hell Freezes Over," *Philadelphia Inquirer*, July 6, 1987, A1.

13. Stuart Taylor Jr., "A.B.A. Panel Gives Bork a Top Rating but Vote Is Split," *New York Times*, September 10, 1987, A1.

14. Simon, *Advice & Consent*, 52.

15. U.S. Congress, Senate, *Hearings Before the Committee on the Judiciary on the Nomination of Robert H. Bork to Be Associate Justice of the Supreme Court of the United States* (hereafter "Bork Hearings"), 100th Cong., 1st Sess., September 15-19, 21-23, 25, 28-30, 1987 (Washington: Government Printing Office, 1989), part 1, 10.

16. Ibid., 33–34.

17. Ibid., 67.

18. Ethan Bronner, *Battle for Justice: How the Bork Nomination Shook America* (New York: W.W. Norton & Co., 1989), 227.

19. Bork Hearings, 34.

20. *Oil, Chem. & Atomic Workers Int'l Union v. Am. Cyanamid Co.*, 741 F.2d 444 (D.C. Cir. 1984).

21. Bork Hearings, part 2, 2556–57.

22. Bork Hearings, part 1, 150.

23. Ibid., 117.

24. *See, e.g.*, Randy Barnett, "The Ninth Amendment: It Means What It Says," 85 Texas L. Rev. 1 (2006).

25. Simon, Advice & Consent, 57.

26. Robert H. Bork, "Neutral Principles and Some First Amendment Problems," 47 Ind. L.J. 1 (1971).

27. Bork Hearings, part 1, 35.

28. Ibid., 37.
29. Jeffrey A. Segal, "Amicus Curiae Briefs by the Solicitor General during the Warren and Burger Courts: A Research Note," 41 *Western Political Quarterly* 135 (1988); Karen O'Connor, "The Amicus Curiae Role of the U.S. Solicitor General in Supreme Court Litigation," 66 *Judicature* 256 (1983).
30. Bork Hearings, part 1, 384.
31. Bork Hearings, part 2, 2101.
32. Ibid., 1368.
33. Ibid., 2158.
34. Bork Hearings, part 3, 2807.
35. Bork Hearings, part 2, 4249.
36. Aric Press, "Trying to Leave a Conservative Legacy," *Newsweek*, July 13, 1987.
37. Walter F. Murphy and Joseph Tanenhaus, "Publicity, Public Opinion, and the Court," 84 Nw. U. L. Rev. 985 (1990).
38. "Bork Gives Reasons for Continuing Fight," *New York Times*, October 10, 1987, 1/13.
39. Congressional Record, 100th Cong., 1st Sess., Oct. 15, 1987, 14572.

Chapter 12: Insult after Injury

1. *Public Papers of the Presidents of the United States, Ronald Reagan, 1987* (Washington: Government Printing Office, 1989), 1175. The *Washington Post* had quoted Reagan as saying he would "a nominee that they would object to just as much as Judge Bork," November 12, 1987, 38.
2. Greenburg, *Supreme Conflict*, 56.
3. "Reagan Studying a Short List of Candidates for High Court," *New York Times*, October 25, 1987, 1/28.
4. Joel Brinkley, "President Selects Appellate Judge to Become Justice," *New York Times*, October 30, 1987, A1.
5. Simon, *Advice & Consent*, 67.
6. Abraham, *Justices, Presidents, and Senators*, 284.
7. Linda Greenhouse, "Senate, 97 to 0, Confirms Kennedy to High Court," *New York Times*, February 4, 1988, A18.
8. Nadine Cohodas, "Kennedy Finds an Easy Act to Follow," 45 *Congressional Quarterly Weekly Report* 2989 (1987).
9. U.S. Congress, Senate, *Hearings Before the Committee on the Judiciary on the Nomination of Anthony M. Kennedy to Be an Associate Justice of the Supreme Court*, 100th Cong., 1st Sess., December 14-16, 1987 (Washington: Government Printing Office, 1989), 164.
10. "The Questions Begin: 'Who is Anthony Kennedy?'" *New York Times*, December 15, 1987, B16.
11. Al Kamen, "Kennedy Moves Court to the Right; Justice More Conservative Than Expected," *Washington Post*, April 11, 1989.
12. Linda Greenhouse, "The Year the Court Turned to the Right," *New York Times*, July 7, 1989, A1.
13. Helen J. Knowles, *The Tie Goes to Freedom: Justice Anthony M. Kennedy on Liberty* (Lanham, Maryland: Rowman & Littlefield Publishers, Inc., 2009), 163.
14. *Grutter v. Bollinger*, 539 U.S. 306, 389 (Kennedy, J., dissenting).

15. Randy Barnett, "Kennedy's Libertarian Revolution," *National Review*, July 10, 2003, https://www.nationalreview.com/2003/07/kennedys-libertarian-revolution-randy-barnett.

16. *Obergefell v. Hodges*, 135 S. Ct. 2584, 2593 (2015).

17. Eugene Volokh, "How the Justices Voted in Free Speech Cases, 1994–2002," https://www2.law.ucla.edu/volokh/howvoted.htm.

18. *Bond v. United States*, 564 U.S. 211, 222.

19. *NFIB v. Sebelius*, 567 U.S. 519, 707 (Scalia, Kennedy, Thomas, and Alito, JJ., dissenting).

20. Andrew M. Duehren, "At Law School, Justice Kennedy Reflects on Cases, Time as Student," *Harvard Crimson*, October 23, 2015, https://www.thecrimson.com/article/2015/10/23/justice-kennedy-harvard-law.

21. "Law-and-Order Issues Top Supreme Court Docket," *CNN*, September 30, 2007, https://www.cnn.com/2007/US/law/09/30/scotus.preview/index.html.

22. *See* Ilya Shapiro, "Justice Kennedy Has Harmed the Rule of Law," *Washington Post*, June 28, 2018, https://www.washingtonpost.com/opinions/i-agree-with-a-lot-of-justice-kennedys-decisions-but-he-has-harmed-the-rule-of-law/2018/06/27/646f8a0c-59fd-11e7-a9f6-7c3296387341_story.html.

23. Greenhouse, "Senate, 97 to 0, Confirms Kennedy to High Court."

Chapter 13: The Souter Disappointment and the Thomas Travesty

1. Ann Devroy, "In the End, Souter Fit Politically," *Washington Post*, July 25, 1990, A6.

2. Alpheus Thomas Mason & Donald Grier Stephenson Jr., *American Constitutional Law: Introductory Essays and Selected Cases*, 12th ed. (Upper Saddle River, New Jersey: Prentice Hall, 1999), 14.

3. Maureen Dowd, "Souter, New Hampshire Judge, Named by Bush for High Court; No 'Litmus Test,' President Says," *New York Times*, July 24, 1990, A1.

4. Al Kamen, "For Liberals, Easy Does It with Roberts," *Washington Post*, September 19, 2005, https://www.washingtonpost.com/wp-dyn/content/article/2005/09/18/AR2005091801188.html.

5. *Casey*, 505 U.S. at 867.

6. Leonard Gilroy, "Justice Souter: First Kelo Victim?" *Reason*, June 27, 2005, https://reason.org/commentary/justice-souter-first-kelo-vict.

7. Greenburg, *Supreme Conflict*, 246.

8. Joan Biskupic, "Thomas Recalls His Reluctant Journey," *Washington Post*, August 2, 1999, A17.

9. Margo Jefferson, "The Thomas-Hill Question, Answered Anew," review of Jane Mayer and Jill Abramson, *Strange Justice: The Selling of Clarence Thomas* (New York: Houghton Mifflin Harcourt, 1994), *New York Times*, November 11, 1994, C29.

10. Clarence Thomas, "Civil Rights as Principle Versus Civil Rights as an Interest," in *Assessing the Reagan Years*, ed. David Boaz (Washington: Cato Institute, 1988), 397.

11. Michael J. Gerhardt, "Divided Justice: A Commentary on the Nomination and Confirmation of Justice Thomas," 60 Geo. Wash. L. Rev. 969, 977 (1992).

12. John Fund, "The Borking Begins," *Wall Street Journal*, January 8, 2001, https://www.wsj.com/articles/SB122417070632840737.

13. U.S. Congress, Senate, *Hearings Before the Committee on the Judiciary on the Nomination of Clarence Thomas to Be an Associate Justice of the Supreme Court of the United States*

(hereafter "Thomas Hearings"), 100th Cong., 1st Sess., September 10–13, 16–20, October 11–13, 1991, part 1, 2.

14. Thomas Hearings, part 1, 220–226 (exchange about *Roe* with Senator Leahy); *see also* David E. Rosenbaum, "No Comment Is Common at Hearings for Nominees," *New York Times*, July 12, 2005, A16.

15. David Boaz, "Joe Biden and Limited Government," Cato at Liberty (blog), Cato Institute, August 24, 2008, https://www.cato.org/blog/joe-biden-limited-government.

16. Thomas Hearings, part 1, 24.

17. Ibid., at 40.

18. Ibid., 143.

19. Ibid., 236.

20. Ibid., 471–74.

21. Ibid., part 2, 49563.

22. Abraham, *Justices, Presidents, and Senators*, 298.

23. Simon, *Advice & Consent*, 99.

24. Thomas, *My Grandfather's Son*, 249.

25. Nina Totenberg, "A Timeline of Clarence Thomas-Anita Hill Controversy as Kavanaugh to Face Accuser," *NPR*, September 23, 2018, https://www.npr.org/2018/09/23/650138049/a-timeline-of-clarence-thomas-anita-hill-controversy-as-kavanaugh-to-face-accuse.

26. Jan Crawford Greenburg, "Clarence Thomas: A Silent Justice Speaks Out," *ABC News*, October 1, 2007, https://abcnews.go.com/TheLaw/story?id=3665221&page=1.

27. Thomas, *My Grandfather's Son*, 250.

28. Thomas Hearings, part 4, 38 (opening statement of Anita Hill).

29. Ibid., 212–14.

30. Ibid., 206.

31. Ibid., 158.

32. Ibid., 157.

33. Ibid., 257.

34. Ibid., 341.

35. Ibid., 355.

36. Ibid., 344.

37. "The Thomas Nomination; On the Hearing Schedule: Eight Further Witnesses," *New York Times*, October 13, 1991, 1/34.

38. Thomas Hearings, part 4, 236.

39. Ibid., at 521; Kevin Merida and Michael A. Fletcher, Supreme Discomfort: The Divided Soul of Clarence Thomas (New York: Broadway Books, 2007), 194.

40. Ruth Marcus, "One Angry Man," *Washington Post*, October 3, 2007, https://www.washingtonpost.com/wp-dyn/content/article/2007/10/02/AR2007100201822.html.

41. Simon *Advice & Consent*, 122 (citing a *USA Today* poll that showed 47 percent believing Thomas, 24 percent Hill, and 55 percent supporting confirmation, as well as a Gallup poll that showed 54 percent for Thomas versus 27 percent for Hill).

42. "The Thomas Nomination," *Washington Post*, October 15, 1991, https://www.washingtonpost.com/archive/opinions/1991/10/15/the-thomas-nomination/37fd8396-fd2d-4dc4-9bc7-85ff90687abd.

43. Sheryl Gay Stolberg and Carl Hulse, "Joe Biden Expresses Regret to Anita Hill, but She Says 'I'm Sorry' Is Not Enough," *New York Times*, April 25, 2019, A1.

44. Richard L. Berke, "The Thomas Nomination; Senators Who Switched Tell of Political Torment," *New York Times*, October 16, 1991, A19.

45. Marcus, "One Angry Man."

46. "New Justice Calls for Healing, Not Anger, After Senate Ordeal," *Associated Press*, October 15, 1991.

47. Merida and Fletcher, *Supreme Discomfort*, 250.

48. *Hudson v. McMillian*, 503 U.S. 1, 28 (1992) (Thomas, J., dissenting).

49. *Lawrence v. Texas*, 539 U.S. 558, 605 (2005) (Thomas, J., dissenting).

50. *See* Scott Douglas Gerber, *First Principles: The Jurisprudence of Clarence Thomas* (New York: New York University Press, 1999).

51. *Gonzales v. Raich*, 545 U.S. 1, 58, 69 (2005) (Thomas, J., dissenting) (citing Federalist No. 45).

52. "Final Stat Pack for October Term 2018," *SCOTUSblog*, July 30, 2019, https://www.scotusblog.com/wp-content/uploads/2019/07/StatPack_OT18-7_30_19.pdf, 15 (showing that Justice Thomas has averaged more than two solo dissents annually, while the next-closest justice, Sotomayor, has averaged fewer than one).

53. Abraham, *Justices, Presidents, and Senators*, 295.

Chapter 14: Ginsburg's Pincer Movement and Breyer's Safe Pick

1. Joseph Biden, "Supreme Court Confirmation Process," *C-SPAN* video, June 25, 1992, https://www.c-span.org/video/?c4581759/sen-joe-biden-supreme-court-confirmation-process

2. Ibid.; *see also* Mike DeBonis, "Joe Biden in 1992: No Nominations to the Supreme Court in an Election Year," *Washington Post*, February 22, 2016, https://www.washingtonpost.com/politics/joe-biden-in-1992-no-nominations-to-the-supreme-court-in-an-election-year/2016/02/22/ea8cde5a-d9b1-11e5-925f-1d10062cc82d_story.html.

3. Kenneth T. Walsh, "He's Not Barrister Bill," *U.S. News & World Report*, July 26, 1993, 32; Bork Hearings, part 4, 4320 (statement of Governor Bill Clinton).

4. Ronald Stidham, Robert A. Carp, and Donald R. Songer, "The Voting Behavior of President Clinton's Judicial Appointees," in Elliot R. Slotnick, ed., *Judicial Politics: Readings from Judicature*, 2d ed. (Chicago: American Judicature Society, 1999), 86.

5. "Bush v. Clinton," 78 *ABA Journal* 51 (1992).

6. Ruth Marcus and Joan Biskupic, "Justice White to Retire after 31 Years," *Washington Post*, March 20, 1993, A1.

7. Byron York, "Advice and Consent? How Clinton Chose Ginsburg," National Review, July 5, 2005, accessed from the Internet Archive Wayback Machine), https://web.archive.org/web/20060624200217/http://article.nationalreview.com/?q=NzdlNTFmNjNmOTBlZDJiNTZhYTM3YmEwNzEzOWYyZmU%3D.

8. Abraham, *Justices, Presidents, and Senators*, 304, 368 n. 142.

9. *See, e.g.*, David Von Drehle, "Redefining Fair with a Simple Careful Assault," *Washington Post*, July 19, 1993, accessed from the Internet Archive Wayback Machine), https://web. archive.org/web/20100902061856/http://www.washingtonpost.com/wp-dyn/content/ article/2007/08/23/AR2007082300903_pf.html.

10. Barbara A. Perry and Henry J. Abraham, "A 'Representative' Supreme Court?: The Thomas, Ginsburg, and Breyer Appointments," 81 *Judicature* 4 (February 1998), 162.

11. Antonin Scalia, "Ruth Bader Ginsburg," *Time*. April 16, 2015 (profile for the Time 100), https://time.com/3823889/ruth-bader-ginsburg-2015-time-100.

12. Ruth Bader Ginsburg, James Madison Lecture on Constitutional Law, New York University Law School, May 9, 1993, reprinted as "Speaking in a Judicial Voice," 67 NYU L. Rev. 1185 (1992) (law reviews are often late to publish, so this 1992 volume would've come out in late 1993); *see also* Olivia B. Waxman, "Ruth Bader Ginsburg Wishes This Case Had Legalized Abortion Instead of *Roe v. Wade*," *Time*, August 2, 2018, https://time. com/5354490/ruth-bader-ginsburg-roe-v-wade.

13. Ruth Marcus, "Judge Ruth Ginsburg Named to High Court," *Washington Post*, June 15, 1993, https://www.washingtonpost.com/archive/politics/1993/06/15/judge-ruth-ginsburg-named-to-high-court/e09bd5db-8f1c-4404-86ba-9d2e754932fb.

14. Waxman, "Ruth Bader Ginsburg Wishes This Case Had Legalized Abortion Instead of *Roe v. Wade.*"

15. Adam Liptak, "Avoid, Sidestep, Retreat: Justices' Advice on Confirmation Tactics," *New York Times*, March 19, 2017, A16, https://www.nytimes.com/2017/03/19/us/politics/supreme-court-justices-confirmation-tactics.html.

16. *See* Linda Greenhouse, "In Dissent, Ginsburg Finds Her Voice at Supreme Court," *New York Times*, May 31, 2007, https://www.nytimes.com/2007/05/31/world/americas/31iht-court.4.5946972.html.

17. *See, e.g.*, Ilya Shapiro, "Liberal Supreme Court Justices Vote in Lockstep, Not the Conservative Justices," *USA Today*, September 10, 2019, https://www.usatoday.com/story/opinion/2019/09/10/liberal-supreme-court-justices-vote-in-lockstep-not-the-conservative-justices-column/2028450001.

18. Adam Liptak, "Ruth Bader Ginsburg, No Fan of Donald Trump, Critiques Latest Term," *New York Times*, July 10, 2016, A1. A few days later, she apologized for her remarks, calling them "ill advised." Michael D. Shear, "Ruth Bader Ginsburg Expresses Regret for Criticizing Donald Trump," *New York Times*, July 14, 2016, A1.

19. *See, e.g.*, Amy Davidson Sorkin, "Ruth Bader Ginsburg's Retirement Dissent," *New Yorker*, September 24, 2014, https://www.newyorker.com/news/amy-davidson/ruth-bader-ginsburgs-retirement-dissent.

20. Abraham, *Justices, Presidents, and Senators*, 309–10.

21. Neil A. Lewis, "As Political Terrain Shifts, Breyer Lands on His Feet," *New York Times*, May 15, 1994, A1, A30.

22. Neil A. Lewis, "Friends and Foes Testify About Breyer," *New York Times*, July 16, 1994, 1/10.

23. Abraham, *Justices, Presidents, and Senators*, 312.

24. Cass R. Sunstein, "Justice Breyer's Democratic Pragmatism," 115 Yale L.J., 1719, 1722 (2006) (citing Lori A. Ringhand, "Judicial Activism and the Rehnquist Court" (September 7, 2005) (unpublished manuscript), later published as "Judicial Activism: An Empirical Examination

of Voting Behavior on the Rehnquist Natural Court," 24 Constitutional Commentary 43 (Spring 2007)); Thomas J. Miles and Cass R. Sunstein, "Do Judges Make Regulatory Policy? An Empirical Investigation of *Chevron*," 73 U. Chi. L. Rev. 823, 826 (2006).

25. Antonin Scalia and Stephen Breyer, "Constitutional Relevant of Foreign Court Decisions," *C-SPAN* video, January 13, 2005, https://www.c-span.org/video/?185122-1/constitutional-relevance-foreign-court-decisions.

26. *See* U.S Library of Congress, Congressional Research Service, Dennis Steven Rutkus, *Judicial Nominations by President Clinton During the 103rd-106th Congresses*, Order Code 98-510 GOV (2008), https://fas.org/sgp/crs/misc/98-510.pdf.

27. *See, e.g.,* Office of Senator Patrick Leahy, "Statement of Senator Patrick Leahy on Republican Filibuster of the District Court Nomination of Jack McConnell," Press Release, May 3, 2011, https://www.leahy.senate.gov/press/statement-of-senator-patrick-leahy-on-republican-filibuster-of-the-district-court-nomination-of-jack-mcconnell. ("I hope we are not returning to the situation we had during the Clinton administration when my friends on the Republican side of the aisle pocket filibustered 61 of his nominees.").

28. Carl Tobias, "Judicial Selection at the Clinton Administration's End," 19 Law & Ineq. 159, 180–81 (2001).

Chapter 15: Filibusters and Umpires

1. Bruce Ackerman, "The Court Packs Itself," *The American Prospect*, February, 12, 2001, accessed from the Internet Archive Wayback Machine, https://web.archive.org/web/20041224170504/http://www.prospect.org/web/page.ww?section=root&name=ViewPrint&articleId=5663.

2. Office of the Press Secretary, The White House, "Remarks by the President during Federal Judicial Appointees Announcement," Press Release, May 9, 2001, archived at https://georgewbush-whitehouse.archives.gov/news/releases/2001/05/20010509-3.html.

3. Neil A. Lewis, "Bush to Nominate 11 to Judgeships Today," *New York Times*, May 9, 2001, A24.

4. Ibid.

5. *Trafficking Victims Protection Act of 2000*, HR 3244, *Conference Report*, 106th Cong., 2nd Sess., Congressional Record 146, part 15, 22,052.

6. Carl Hulse and David Stout, "Embattled Estrada Withdraws as Nominee for Federal Bench," *New York Times*, September 4, 2003, https://www.nytimes.com/2003/09/04/politics/embattled-estrada-withdraws-as-nominee-for-federal-bench.html.

7. William Safire, "Nuclear Options," *New York Times*, March 20, 2005, 6/26.

8. David S. Law, "Appointing Federal Judges: The President, the Senate, and the Prisoner's Dilemma," University of San Diego Public Law & Legal Theory Research Paper Series (2004) (quoting Sen. Mark Pryor (D-Ark.), as quoted in Helen Dewar, "Confirmed Frustration With Judicial Nomination Process," *Washington Post*, Mar.10, 2003, A19).

9. Democratic Policy Committee, "Judicial Nominations Update: Bush Judicial Nominees Confirmed at a Rate Better Than or Equal to Recent Presidents, Report, October 7, 2004, accessed from the Internet Archive Wayback Machine, https://web.archive.org/web/20100727153537/http://democrats.senate.gov/dpc/dpc-new.cfm?doc_name=fs-108-2-282.

10. "Senators Compromise on Filibusters," *CNN*, May 24, 2005, https://www.cnn.com/2005/POLITICS/05/24/filibuster.fight/index.html.

11. Sandra Day O'Connor, Letter to George W. Bush, tendering her resignation from the Supreme Court, July 1, 2005, https://www.supremecourt.gov/publicinfo/press/oconnor070105.pdf.

12. Sheryl Gay Stolberg and Elisabeth Bumiller, "Senate Confirms Roberts as 17th Chief Justice, *New York Times*, September 30, 2005, https://www.nytimes.com/2005/09/30/politics/politicsspecial1/senate-confirms-roberts-as-17th-chief-justice.html.

13. *See, e.g.*, John R. Lott Jr. and Sonya D. Jones, "Unserious Suggestions," *National Review*, July 19, 2005, https://www.nationalreview.com/2005/07/unserious-suggestions-john-r-lott-jr-sonya-d-jones.

14. "First Lady Wants New Female Justice," *Washington Post*, July 13, 2005, https://www.washingtonpost.com/wp-dyn/content/article/2005/07/12/AR2005071200456.html.

15. *See* Greenburg, *Supreme Conflict*, 190-93.

16. Gail Russell Chaddock, "A Judicial Think Tank—Or a Plot," *Christian Science Monitor*, August 4, 2005, https://www.csmonitor.com/2005/0804/p01s01-uspo.html.

17. Sheryl Gay Stolberg and David D. Kirkpatrick, "Court Nominee Advised Group on Gay Rights," *New York Times*, August 5, 2005, A1.

18. "Some Civil Rights Group Members Support Roberts," *CNN*, August 27, 2005, https://www.cnn.com/2005/POLITICS/08/25/roberts.supporters.

19. Roberts Hearings, 56; "Roberts: 'My Job Is to Call Balls and Strikes and Not to Pitch or Bat,'" *CNN*, September 12, 2005, https://www.cnn.com/2005/POLITICS/09/12/roberts.statement/.

20. John M. Broder and Carolyn Marshall, "White House Memos Offer Opinions on Supreme Court," *New York Times*, July 30, 2005, A11.

21. Roberts Hearings, 143. *See also* Kenneth Jost, "Privacy, Precedents Dominate Roberts Session," *NPR*, September 13, 2005, https://www.npr.org/templates/story/story.php?storyId=4845368.

22. Richard W. Stevenson, "President Names Roberts as Choice for Chief Justices," *New York Times*, September 6, 2005, A1.

23. Akin, Gump, Strauss, Hauer & Feld, LLP, "End of Term Statistics and Analysis – October Term 2005," *SCOTUSblog*, June 29, 2006, https://www.scotusblog.com/archives/EndofTermAnalysis.pdf.

24. "Stat Pack for October Term 2013," *SCOTUSblog*, July 3, 2014, http://sblog.s3.amazonaws.com/wp-content/uploads/2014/07/SCOTUSblog_Stat_Pack_for_OT13.pdf.

25. "Final Stat Pack for October Term 2018," 15.

26. Ibid., 18.

27. "Chief Justice Says His Goal Is More Consensus on the Court," *New York Times*, May 22, 2006 (reprint of Associated Press article), https://www.nytimes.com/2006/05/22/washington/22justice.html.

28. *Parents Involved*, 551 U.S. at 748.

29. *NFIB v. Sebelius*, 567 U.S. 519, 706 (2012) (Scalia, Kennedy, Thomas, and Alito, JJ., dissenting).

30. For more of this line of analysis, *see* Ilya Shapiro, "Against Judicial Restraint," *National Affairs* (Fall 2016), and Ilya Shapiro, "Like Eastwood Talking to a Chair: The Good, the Bad, and the Ugly of the Obamacare Ruling," 1 Tex. Rev. L. & Pol. 17 (2013).

31. Frank Newport, Jeffrey M. Jones and Lydia Saad, "Gallup Editors: Americans' Views on the Healthcare Law, *Gallup*, June 22, 2012, https://news.gallup.com/poll/155300/gallup-editors-americans-views-healthcare-law.aspx.

32. "Senate Presses for Quick Miers Confirmation," *NBC News*, October 3, 2005, http://www.nbcnews.com/id/9566882/ns/us_news-the_changing_court/t/senate-presses-quick-miers-confirmation.

33. "Bush Picks White House Counsel for Supreme Court," *CNN*, October 4, 2005, https://www.cnn.com/2005/POLITICS/10/03/scotus.miers/index.html.

34. *See, e.g.*, George Will, "Can This Nomination Be Justified?" *Washington Post*, October 5, 2005, https://www.washingtonpost.com/wp-dyn/content/article/2005/10/04/AR2005100400954.html.

35. David Frum, "Madame Justice," *National Review*, October 3, 2005, accessed from the Internet Archive Wayback Machine, https://web.archive.org/web/20081004003034/http://frum.nationalreview.com/post/?q=ZjM1NDExNTgwNmFkYjc5ODJkNWFjNTdmYzgoMDIyMGQ=.

36. Peggy Noonan, "The Miers Misstep," *Wall Street Journal*, October 6, 2005, https://www.wsj.com/articles/SB122487886536967577.

37. Robert H. Bork, "Slouching Towards Miers," *Wall Street Journal*, October 19, 2005, https://www.wsj.com/articles/SB112968557638772718.

38. Shailagh Murray and Charles Babington, "Miers Makes Rounds on Hill," *Washington Post*, October 7, 2005, https://www.washingtonpost.com/wp-dyn/content/article/2005/10/06/AR2005100601713.html.

39. Charles Krauthammer, "Miers: The Only Exit Strategy," *Washington Post*, October 21, 2005, https://www.washingtonpost.com/wp-dyn/content/article/2005/10/20/AR2005102001635.html.

40. David D. Kirkpatrick, "Court Nominee Is Asked to Redo Reply to Questions," *New York Times*, October 20, 2005, A1.

41. Greenburg, *Supreme Conflict*, 282-84.

42. "Text of Bush, Alito Remarks at Nomination Announcement," *USA Today*, October 31, 2005 (reprint of Associated Press report), https://usatoday30.usatoday.com/news/washington/2005-10-31-text-bush-alito_x.htm.

43. Bill Mears, "Alito's Record, Character on Display at Hearings," *CNN*, January 9, 2006, https://www.cnn.com/2006/POLITICS/01/09/alito.hearing.preview/index.html.

44. "ACLU Opposes Nomination of Judge Alito," American Civil Liberties Union, accessed from the Internet Archive Wayback Machine, https://web.archive.org/web/20060112124104/http://www.aclu.org/scotus/alito/.

45. Senator Barack Obama "Obama Statement on President Bush's Nomination of Judge Samuel Alito to the Supreme Court," Press Release, October 31, 2005, accessed from the Internet Archive Wayback Machine, https://web.archive.org/web/20051102043214/http://obama.senate.gov/press/051031-obama_statement_on_president_bushs_nomination_of_judge_samuel_alito_to_the_supreme_court/index.html.

46. Senator John Kerry, "Statement by John Kerry on the Nomination of Judge Samuel Alito to the Supreme Court," Press Release, October 31, 2005 (accessed February 26, 2020, from the Internet Archive Wayback Machine), https://web.archive.org/web/20051128052246/http://kerry.senate.gov/v3/cfm/record.cfm?id=248050.

47. U.S. Congress, Senate, *Confirmation Hearing on the Nomination of Samuel A. Alito, Jr. to Be an Associate Justice of the Supreme Court of the United States* (hereafter "Alito Hearings"), 109th Cong., 2nd Sess., January 9-13, 2006, https://www.govinfo.gov/content/pkg/GPO-CHRG-ALITO/pdf/GPO-CHRG-ALITO.pdf, at 441.

48. Liz Marlantes, "Alito Grilling Gets Too Intense for Some," *ABC News*, January 12, 2006, https://abcnews.go.com/WNT/SupremeCourt/story?id=1495804.

49. Alito Hearings, 455.

50. Maura Reynolds, "Filibuster Option on Alito Divides Senate Democrats," *SFGate*, January 28, 2006 (reprint of *L.A. Times* report), https://www.sfgate.com/politics/article/Filibuster-option-on-Alito-divides-Senate-2542729.php.

51. "Opening Statement of Chairman Patrick Leahy" to the *Hearing on Nominations* of the Senate Committee on the Judiciary, September 23, 2008, accessed from the Internet Archive Wayback Machine, https://web.archive.org/web.

52. 20100615053539/http:/judiciary.senate.gov/hearings/testimony.cfm?id=3585&wit_id=2629; Carrie Budoff Brown, "Schumer to Fight New Bush High Court Picks," *Politico*, July 27, 2007, https://www.politico.com/story/2007/07/schumer-to-fight-new-bush-high-court-picks-005146.

Chapter 16: The Wise Latina and the Nuclear Senate

1. Senator Barack Obama, "Remarks of Senator Barack Obama on the Confirmation of Judge John Roberts," Press Release, September 22, 2005, accessed from the Internet Archive Wayback Machine), https://web.archive.org/web/20081030231631/http://obama.senate.gov/press/050922-remarks_of_sena.

2. Eric Zuckerman, "Obama: We Need a Justice with 'Empathy,'" *The Hill*, May 1, 2009, https://thehill.com/blogs/blog-briefing-room/news/36170-obama-we-need-a-justice-with-empathy.

3. Kellyanne Conway, "Key Findings from a National Survey of 800 Actual Voters," *Federalist Society*, November 5, 2008, https://fedsoc.org/commentary/publications/key-findings-from-a-national-survey-of-800-actual-voters.

4. *See, e.g.,* Charlie Savage, "Ratings Shrink President's List for Judgeships," *New York Times*, November 22, 2011, A1.

5. Nina Totenberg, "Law School Past Shapes Obama's View on Justices," *NPR*, October 30, 2008, https://www.npr.org/templates/story/story.php?storyId=96337196.

6. Bill Mears, "Sources: High Court Selection Process Down to Finalists," *CNN*. May 13, 2009. https://www.cnn.com/2009/POLITICS/05/13/scotus.obama.index.html.

7. Peter Baker, "Favorites of Left Don't Make Obama's Court List," *New York Times*, May 25, 2009, https://www.nytimes.com/2009/05/26/us/politics/26court.html.

8. David G. Savage, "Supreme Chance to Alter the Court," *Los Angeles Times*, November 17, 20008, https://www.latimes.com/archives/la-xpm-2008-nov-17-na-courtobama17-story.html.

9. Peter Baker and Adam Nagourney, "Sotomayor Pick a Product of Lessons from Past Battles," *New York Times*, May 27, 2009, https://www.nytimes.com/2009/05/28/us/politics/28select.html.

10. Peter Baker and Jeff Zeleny, "Obama Hails Judge as 'Inspiring,'" *New York Times*, May 26, 2009, https://www.nytimes.com/2009/05/27/us/politics/27court.html.

11. *Silverman v. Major League Baseball Player Relations Comm., Inc.*, 880 F. Supp. 246 (S.D.N.Y. 1995).

12. John Schwartz, "Sotomayor's Appellate Opinions Are Unpredictable, Lawyers and Scholars Say," *New York Times*, May 27, 2009, https://www.nytimes.com/2009/05/28/us/politics/28circuit.html.

13. See Ilya Shapiro, "Commentary: Sotomayor Pick Not Based on Merit," *CNN*, May 27, 2009, https://www.cnn.com/2009/POLITICS/05/27/shapiro.scotus.identity/index.html.

14. "Supreme Court Nominee Sonia Sotomayor's Speech at Berkeley Law in 2001," October 26, 2001, originally published in Berkeley La Raza L.J. (2002), posted to the website of the University of California, Berkeley School of Law on May 26, 2009, https://www.law.berkeley.edu/article/supreme-court-nominee-sonia-sotomayors-speech-at-berkeley-law-in-2001.

15. U.S. Congress, Senate, *Confirmation Hearing on the Nomination of Hon. Sonia Sotomayor, to Be an Associate Justice of the Supreme Court of the United States* (hereafter "Sotomayor Hearings"), 111th Cong., 1st Sess., July 13-16, 2009, 73.

16. Mark Murray, "Legal Conservative Praises Sotomayor," *MSNBC*, May 26, 2009 (accessed February 26, 2020 from the Internet Archive Wayback Machine), https://web.archive.org/web/20090531093129/http://firstread.msnbc.msn.com/archive/2009/05/26/1943875.aspx.

17. Andy Barr, "Elder Bush Defends Sotomayor," *Politico*, June 12, 2009, https://www.politico.com/story/2009/06/elder-bush-defends-sotomayor-023686.

18. Sotomayor Hearings, 126.

19. "Final Stat Pack for October Term 2018," 26 (judicial agreement rates); "Sonia Sotomayor," Ballotpedia, accessed February 26, 2020, https://ballotpedia.org/Sonia_Sotomayor; "Martin-Quinn Scores, Measures," accessed February 26, 2020, https://mqscores.lsa.umich.edu/measures.php (Martin-Quinn scores).

20. Alex Greer, "Ranking the Most Liberal Modern Supreme Court Justices," *Yahoo News*, July 6, 2015, https://www.yahoo.com/news/ranking-most-liberal-modern-supreme-court-justices-214720805.html.

21. "Final Stat Pack for October Term 2018," 15 (solo dissents), 18 (frequency in the majority).

22. *Schuette v. Coalition to Defend Affirmative Action*, 572 U.S. 291, 329 (2014) (Sotomayor, J., dissenting).

23. Ibid., 381.

24. "Final Stat Pack for October Term 2018," 32 (oral argument statistics for October Term 2018).

25. Richard Wolf, "'The People's Justice': After Decade on Supreme Court, Sonia Sotomayor Is Most Outspoken on Bench and Off," *USA Today*, August 8, 2019, https://www.usatoday.com/story/news/politics/2019/08/08/justice-sonia-sotomayor-supreme-court-liberal-hispanic-decade-bench/1882245001.

26. "Kagan Likely to Be Pressed on Writings, Experience," *NPR*, May 10, 2010, https://www.npr.org/templates/story/story.php?storyId=126657976.

27. Sheryl Gay Stolberg, Katharine Q. Seelye and Lisa W. Foderaro, "A Climb Marked by Confidence and Canniness," *New York Times*, May 10, 2010, https://www.nytimes.com/2010/05/10/us/politics/10kagan.html.

28. Jim Lindgren, "Elena Kagan: 'I LOVE the Federalist Society! I LOVE the Federalist Society!'" The Volokh Conspiracy (blog), May 10, 2010, http://volokh.com/2010/05/10/elena-kagan-i-love-the-federalist-society-i-love-the-federalist-society.

29. Kendra Marr, "Kyl: GOP Won't Filibuster Kagan," *Politico*, May 16, 2010, https://www.politico.com/story/2010/05/kyl-gop-wont-filibuster-kagan-037308.

30. Elena Kagan, "Confirmation Messes, Old and New," review of Stephen L. Carter, *The Confirmation Mess: Cleaning Up the Federal Appointments Process* (New York: Basic Books, 1994), 62 U. Chi. L. Rev. 919 (1995).

31. U.S. Congress, Senate, *The Nomination of Elena Kagan to Be an Associate Justice of the Supreme Court of the United States*, 111th Cong., 2nd Sess., June 28-30, July 1, 2010, 144.

32. Elena Kagan, "Presidential Administration," 114 Harv. L. Rev. 2245 (2001).

33. Larry Margasak, "Senate Confirms Cuban-born Judge to 11th Circuit," *Athens Banner-Herald* (Georgia), February 15, 2012, https://www.onlineathens.com/local-news/2012-02-15/senate-confirms-cuban-born-judge-11th-circuit.

34. U.S. Library of Congress, Congressional Research Service, Richard S. Beth, Elizabeth Rybicki and Michael Greene, *Cloture Attempts on Nominations: Data and Historical Development Through November 30, 2013*, RL32878 (2018).

35. From 1917 to 1975, the rule was two thirds, while before 1917 there were no restrictions on debate.

36. This tracking counts only Fourth Circuit Judge Roger Gregory's recess appointment under Clinton without double-counting his renomination and confirmation under Bush. Bush did have one recess appointee who was never confirmed: Fifth Circuit Judge Charles W. Pickering, who served most of the 2004 calendar year.

Chapter 17: The Garland Blockade, but Gorsuch

1. Noah Feldman, "Obama and Republicans Are Both Wrong about Constitution," *Bloomberg*, February 17, 2016, https://www.bloomberg.com/opinion/articles/2016-02-17/obama-and-senate-are-both-wrong-about-the-constitution.

2. Julie Hirschfeld Davis, "Joe Biden Argued for Delaying Supreme Court Picks in 1992," February 22, 2016, *New York Times*, https://www.nytimes.com/2016/02/23/us/politics/joe-biden-argued-for-delaying-supreme-court-picks-in-1992.html.

3. Mitch McConnell and Chuck Grassley, "Democrats Shouldn't Rob Voters of Chance to Replace Scalia," *Washington Post*, February 18, 2016, https://www.washingtonpost.com/opinions/mcconnell-and-grassley-democrats-shouldnt-rob-voters-of-chance-to-replace-scalia/2016/02/18/e5ae9bdc-d68a-11e5-be55-2cc3c1e4b76b_story.html, quoting from and linking to Harry Reid, "No Duty to Give Nominees a Vote," *C-SPAN* video, May 19, 2005, https://www.c-span.org/video/?c4581302/user-clip-reid-duty-give-nominees-vote.

4. John Gizzi, "Orrin Hatch Says GOP SCOTUS Refusal Just 'The Chickens Coming Home to Roost,'" *Newsmax*, March 13, 2016, https://www.newsmax.com/Newsfront/john-gizzi-orrin-hatch-obama-will-nominate/2016/03/13/id/718871.

5. Michael D. Shear, Julie Hirschfeld Davis and Gardiner Harris, "Obama Chooses Merrick Garland for Supreme Court," *New York Times*, Mar. 17, 2016, A1.

6. "Republican Senator Weighs in on Supreme Court Nomination," *NPR*, March 17, 2016 (transcript to radio interview), https://www.npr.org/2016/03/17/470776592/republican-senator-weighs-in-on-supreme-court-nomination.

7. "Where Republican Senators Stand on the Supreme Court Nomination," *New York Times*, April 21, 2016, https://www.nytimes.com/interactive/2016/03/21/us/politics/where-republican-senators-stand-on-the-supreme-court-nomination.html.

8. Alex Roarty, "Tea Party-Aligned Kentucky Gov May End 95-Year Democratic Reign," *Roll Call*, August 6, 2016, https://www.rollcall.com/2016/08/06/tea-party-aligned-kentucky-gov-may-end-95-year-democratic-reign/.

9. Sarah Almukhtar, "Why Obama Nominated Merrick Garland for the Supreme Court," *New York Times*, March 16, 2016, https://www.nytimes.com/interactive/2016/03/16/us/politics/garland-supreme-court-nomination.html.

10. Donald F. McGahn II, 17th Annual Barbara K. Olson Memorial Lecture, Federalist Society National Lawyers Convention, Washington D.C., November 17, 2017, https://fedsoc.org/conferences/2017-national-lawyers-convention?#agenda-item-barbara-k-olson-memorial-lecture.

11. Mollie Hemingway and Carrie Severino, *Justice on Trial: The Kavanaugh Confirmation* (Washington: Regnery, 2019), 50.

12. Donald Trump, Press Conference, *C-SPAN* video, March 21, 2016, https://www.c-span.org/video/?407049-1/donald-trump-news-conference-washington-dc.

13. John G. Malcolm, "The Next Supreme Court Justice," *Daily Signal*, March 30, 2016, https://www.dailysignal.com/2016/03/30/the-next-supreme-court-justice/?.

14. Adam Liptak, "Trump's Supreme Court List: Ivy League? Out. The Heartland? In." *New York Times*, November 14, 2016, A21.

15. Hemingway and Severino, *Justice on Trial*, 58.

16. Christopher Ingraham, "Republican Talk of Holding a Supreme Court Seat Vacant for Four Years Is Without Precedent," *Washington Post*, November 1, 2016, https://www.washingtonpost.com/news/wonk/wp/2016/11/01.republican-talk-of-holding-a-supreme-court-seat-vacant-for-four-years-is-without-precedent.

17. James Hohmann, "Mike Lee Explains Why the GOP Will Block Garland Even if Clinton Wins," *Washington Post*, October 13, 2016, https://www.washingtonpost.com/news/powerpost/wp/2016/10/13/mike-lee-explains-why-the-gop-will-block-garland-even-if-clinton-wins.

18. Adam Liptak, "What the Trump Presidency Means for the Supreme Court," *New York Times*, November 9, 2016, 7.

19. Philip Bump, "A Quarter of Republicans Voted for Trump to Get Supreme Court Picks—And It Paid Off," *Washington Post*, June 26, 2018, https://www.washingtonpost.com/news/politics/wp/2018/06/26/a-quarter-of-republicans-voted-for-trump-to-get-supreme-court-picks-and-it-paid-off.

20. Philip Rucker and Seung Min Kim, "'We Have to Pick a Great One': Inside Trump's Plan for a New Supreme Court Justice," *Washington Post*, June 30, 2018, https://www.washingtonpost.com/politics/we-have-to-pick-a-great-one-inside-trumps-plan-for-a-new-supreme-court-justice/2018/06/30/610dcd4e-7bb0-11e8-80be-6d32e182a3bc_story.html.

21. Hemingway and Severino, *Justice on Trial*, 60.

22. Shane Goldmacher, Eliana Johnson and Josh Gerstein, "How Trump Got to Yes on Gorsuch," *Politico*, January 31, 2017, https://www.politico.com/story/2017/01/trump-supreme-court-gorsuch-234474.

23. David Jackson, "Why Trump Chose Neil Gorsuch as His Supreme Court Nominee," *USA Today*, January 31, 2017, https://www.usatoday.com/story/news/politics/2017/01/31/donald-trump-neil-gorsuch-antonin-scalia/97306468/.

24. Ed Whelan, "Top Obama Lawyer: I Would Have Recommended Republican Strategy on Scalia Vacancy," *National Review*, November 18, 2016, https://www.nationalreview.com/bench-memos/ruemmler-garland-strategy.

25. *U.S. v. Krueger*, 809 F.3d 1109, 1125 (10th Cir. 2015) (Gorsuch, J., concurring in the judgment).

26. Matt Flegenheimer, "Gorsuch Tries to Put Himself above Politics in Confirmation Hearing," *New York Times*, March 20, 2017, A20.

27. U.S. Congress, Senate, *Confirmation Hearing on the Nomination of Hon. Neil Gorsuch to Be an Associate Justice of the Supreme Court of the United States* (hereafter "Gorsuch Hearings"), 115th Cong., 1st Sess., March 20–23, 2017, 67.

28. Gorsuch Hearings, 85–86.

29. Ibid., 132–39.

30. *TransAm Trucking, Inc. v. Administrative Review Board*, 833 F.3d 1206 (2016).

31. *Hobby Lobby Stores, Inc. v. Sebelius*, 723 F.3d 1114 (10th Cir. 2013) (Gorsuch, J., concurring), aff'd sub nom. *Burwell v. Hobby Lobby Stores, Inc.*, 573 U.S. 682 (2014).

32. Gorsuch Hearings, 107.

33. *Endrew F. v. Douglas Cnty. Sch. Dist. RE-1*, 798 F.3d 1329 (10th Cir. 2015), vacated, *Endrew F. v. Douglas Cnty. Sch. Dist. RE-1*, 137 S. Ct. 988 (2017).

34. Adam Liptak and Matt Flegenheimer, "Democrats Fail to Move Gorsuch Off Script and beyond Generalities," *New York Times*, March 22, 2017, A17.

35. *Anthony W. Perry v. Merit Systems Protection Board*, No. 16-399, Tr. of Oral Arg., April 17, 2017, 47 https://www.supremecourt.gov/oral_arguments/argument_transcripts/2016/16-399_3f14.pdf.

36. Rachel Del Guidice, "Gorsuch Touts Originalism, Textualism in Address to Conservative Legal Society," The Daily Signal, November 17, 2017, https://www.dailysignal.com/2017/11/17/gorsuch-touts-originalism-textualism-in-address-to-conservative-legal-society.

37. *Gundy v. United States*, 139 S. Ct. 2116, 2132 (2019) (Gorsuch, J., dissenting).

38. *Kisor v. Wilkie*, 139 S. Ct. 2400, 2425 (2019) (Gorsuch, J., dissenting).

Chapter 18: Kavanaugh and Beyond

1. David Choi, "'It's Time for Democrats to Play Hardball': TV Host Chris Matthews Urges Democrats to Resist Mitch McConnell after Justice Kennedy Announces Retirement," *Business Insider*, June 27, 2018, https://www.businessinsider.com/chris-matthews-hardball-democrats-resist-mitch-mcconnell-anthony-kennedy-2018-6.

2. David French, "Brett Kavanaugh Is an Excellent Judge, but Is He the Best Choice?" *National Review*, July 5, 2018, https://www.nationalreview.com/2018/07/brett-kavanaugh-supreme-court-potential-pick.

3. "Remarks by President Trump Announcing Judge Brett M. Kavanaugh as the Nominee for Associate Justice of the Supreme Court of the United States," Press Release, July 9, 2018,

https://www.whitehouse.gov/briefings-statements/remarks-president-trump-announcing-judge-brett-m-kavanaugh-nominee-associate-justice-supreme-court-united-states.

4. I wrote an op-ed on that subject at the time, leading "libertarianish" Senator Rand Paul (R-Ky.) to endorse him less than 24 hours later. Ilya Shapiro, "Here's the Libertarian Case for Brett Kavanaugh's Supreme Court Nomination," *The Federalist*, July 29, 2018, https://thefederalist.com/2018/07/29/heres-libertarian-case-brett-kavanaughs-supreme-court-nomination; Elana Schor, "Rand Paul Backs Kavanaugh for Supreme Court," *Politico*, July 30, 2018, https://www.politico.com/story/2018/07/30/rand-paul-supposed-kavanaugh-748254.

5. *See* Ilya Shapiro, "Don't Worry (Too Much) about Kavanaugh Changing the Supreme Court," *The Hill*, July 17, 2018, https://thehill.com/opinion/judiciary/397248-dont-worry-too-much-about-kavanaugh-changing-the-supreme-court.

6. Nicole Darrah, "Kavanaugh Nomination to Supreme Court Cheered by Conservatives," Fox News, July 9, 2018, https://www.foxnews.com/politics/kavanaugh-nomination-to-supreme-court-cheered-by-conservatives.

7. Davis Richardson, "Liberal Activist Prepared to Protest All of Trump's SCOTUS Picks," *Observer*, July 10, 2018, https://observer.com/2018/07/liberal-activist-groups-protest-trump-scotus-pick/; William Cummings, "Women's March Slammed for Goof in Statement on Kavanaugh Supreme Court Nomination," *USA Today*, July 10, 2018, https://www.usatoday.com/story/news/politics/onpolitics/2018/07/10/womens-march-gaffe-kavanaugh-statement-derided-and-mocked/773650002.

8. Akhil Reed Amar, "A Liberal's Case for Brett Kavanaugh," *New York Times*, July 9, 2018, https://www.nytimes.com/2018/07/09/opinion/brett-kavanaugh-supreme-court-trump.html.

9. Neal Katyal, Twitter, July 10, 2018, 12:46 a.m., "Given J.Kavanaugh's credentials,hardworking nature&much more, it would be such a difft confirmation process if for a difft seat (like Justice Thomas') or if he were nominated by a difft President (like, any of them who weren't subjects of criminal investigations + multiple suits)," https://twitter.com/neal_katyal/status/1016544059517800449 (cleaned up).

10. Fred Barbash and Seung Min Kim, "Hours before Kavanaugh Nomination Hearings, Bush Lawyer Releases 42,000 Pages of Documents to Judiciary Committee," *Washington Post*, September 3, 2018, https://www.washingtonpost.com/news/morning-mix/wp/2018/09/03/hours-before-kavanaugh-nomination-hearings-bush-lawyer-releases-42000-pages-of-documents-to-judiciary-committee.

11. Yuval Levin, "The Kavanaugh Paper Flow," *National Review*, July 11, 2018, https://www.nationalreview.com/corner/the-kavanaugh-paper-flow.

12. Senator Chuck Grassley, "Kavanaugh Review Will Be Thorough and Fair, but No Taxpayer-Funded Fishing Expedition," Press Release, July 18, 2018, https://www.grassley.senate.gov/news/news-releases/grassley-kavanaugh-review-will-be-thorough-and-fair-no-taxpayer-funded-fishing.

13. *See* Hemingway and Severino, *Justice on Trial*, 95–98.

14. Sheryl Gay Stolberg and Adam Liptak, "Kavanaugh Portrayed as a Hopeless Partisan as Hearings on Supreme Court Nominee Open," *New York Times*, September 4, 2018, A1.

15. Hemingway and Severino, *Justice on Trial*, 10.

16. Dylan Stableford, "Kavanaugh Hearing Starts with a Bang as Protestors, Dems Interrupt Opening Statements," Yahoo! News, September 4, 2018, https://www.yahoo.com/news/

kavanaugh-hearing-starts-bang-protesters-dems-interrupt-opening-statements-150945260.html.

17. Jeffrey Cimmino, "Cornyn: Kavanaugh Hearing Is First I've Seen Run 'Basically According to Mob Rule,'" *Washington Free Beacon*, September 4, 2018, https://freebeacon.com/politics/cornyn-kavanaugh-hearing-first-run-basically-according-mob-rule.

18. Ed Whelan, "Refuting Anti-Kavanaugh Smears—Manny Miranda Controversy," *National Review*, September 10, 2018, https://www.nationalreview.com/bench-memos/refuting-anti-kavanaugh-smears-manny-miranda-controversy.

19. PBS Newshour, "Judge Brett Kavanaugh Supreme Court Confirmation Hearings—Day 2," YouTube video, September 5, 2018, https://www.youtube.com/watch?time_continue=1&v=x9fHsoqAkLU&feature=emb_logo.

20. Kathleen Parker, "Cory Booker's 'Spartacus' Moment," *Washington Post*, September 7, 2018. https://www.washingtonpost.com/opinions/cory-bookers-spartacus-moment/2018/09/07/8c97eaee-b2f6-11e8-aed9-001309990777_story.html.

21. Hemingway and Severino, *Justice on Trial*, 114.

22. David Sherfinski, Alex Swoyer, and Stephen Dinan, "Accusations Fly against Kavanaugh in Craziest Supreme Court Confirmation Hearings in Decades," *Washington Times*, September 6, 2018. https://www.washingtontimes.com/news/2018/sep/6/brett-kavanaugh-confirmation-hearings-feature-wild.

23. U.S. Congress, Senate, Committee on the Judiciary, "Committee Democrats Continue Delay Tactics with Volume of Written Questions for Kavanaugh," Press Release, September 12, 2018, https://www.judiciary.senate.gov/press/rep/releases/scotus_committee-democrats-continue-delay-tactics-with-volume-of-written-questions-for-kavanaugh.

24. Ronan Farrow and Jane Mayer, "A Sexual-Misconduct Allegation against the Supreme Court Nominee Brett Kavanaugh Stirs Tension among Democrats in Congress," *New Yorker*, September 14, 2018, https://www.newyorker.com/news/news-desk/a-sexual-misconduct-allegation-against-the-supreme-court-nominee-brett-kavanaugh-stirs-tension-among-democrats-in-congress.

25. Emma Brown, "California Professor, Writer of Confidential Brett Kavanaugh Letter, Speaks Out about Her Allegation of Sexual Assault," *Washington Post*, September 16, 2018, https://www.washingtonpost.com/investigations/california-professor-writer-of-confidential-brett-kavanaugh-letter-speaks-out-about-her-allegation-of-sexual-assault/2018/09/16/46982194-b846-11e8-94eb-3bd52dfe917b_story.html.

26. "Kavanaugh Again Denies Sexual Assault Allegations," *Axios*, September 17, 2018, https://www.axios.com/brett-kavanaugh-responds-sexual-assault-allegations-9061dc4d-39b3-4bbb-9a18-0fb164294600.html.

27. Christina Wilkie, "Trump on Kavanaugh: 'If It Takes a Little Delay,' That's OK," *CNBC*, September 17, 2018, https://www.cnbc.com/2018/09/17/trump-on-kavanaugh-if-it-takes-a-little-delay-thats-ok-.html.

28. Hemingway and Severino, *Justice on Trial*, 154–55.

29. Ronan Farrow and Jane Mayer, "Senate Democrats Investigate a New Allegation of Sexual Misconduct, from Brett Kavanaugh's College Years," *New Yorker*, September 23, 2018, https://www.newyorker.com/news/news-desk/senate-democrats-investigate-a-new-allegation-of-sexual-misconduct-from-the-supreme-court-nominee-brett-kavanaughs-college-years-deborah-ramirez.

30. Sheryl Gay Stolberg and Nicholas Fandos, "Christene Blasey Ford Reaches Deal to Testify at Kavanaugh Hearing," *New York Times*, September 23, 2018, https://www.nytimes.com/2018/09/23/us/politics/brett-kavanaugh-christine-blasey-ford-testify.html.

31. Emily Stewart, "Michael Avenatti's Client Says She Witnessed Kavanaugh Sexually Assault Girls in High School," *Vox*, September 26, 2018, https://www.vox.com/policy-and-politics/2018/9/26/17905908/julie-swetnick-michael-avenatti-twitter-brett-kavanaugh.

32. Christal Hayes, "'I was Angry and I Sent It': Another Kavanaugh Accuser Referred to FBI after Recanting," *USA Today*, November 3, 2018, https://www.usatoday.com/story/news/politics/2018/11/02/brett-kavanaugh-accuser-referred-fbi-doj-investigation/1863210002.

33. Jessica A. Botelho, "RI Man Apologizes for Claiming Kavanaugh Sexually Assaulted Woman on Boat in Newport," *NBC 10 News* (Rhode Island), September 26, 2018, https://turnto10.com/news/local/kavanaugh-accused-of-sexually-assaulting-woman-on-boat-in-ri-in-1985.

34. *See, e.g.*, Laura McGann, "Dianne Feinstein Silenced Kavanaugh's Accuser to Protect the Status Quo," Sept. 14, 2018, https://www.vox.com/2018/9/14/17861350/dianne-feinstein-supreme-court-brett-kavanaugh-letter-sexual-assault-high-school.

35. Anthony Zurcher, "Christine Blasey Ford and Brett Kavanaugh: What We Learned," BBC, September 27, 2018, https://www.bbc.com/news/world-us-canada-45660297.

36. "Brett Kavanaugh's Opening Statement: Full Transcript," *New York Times*, September 26, 2018, https://www.nytimes.com/2018/09/26/us/politics/read-brett-kavanaughs-complete-opening-statement.html.

37. CNN, "Lindsey Graham Erupts: Kavanaugh Hearing an Unethical Sham," YouTube video, September 27, 2018, https://www.youtube.com/watch?v=RTBxPPx62s4.

38. *See* Hemingway and Severino, *Justice on Trial*, 237-45.

39. Megan Keller, "Graham Spars with Protester Over Kavanaugh: 'Why Don't We Dunk Him in Water and See If He Floats,'" *The Hill*, October 4, 2018, accessed from: https://thehill.com/homenews/senate/409907-graham-why-dont-we-dunk-kavanaugh-in-water-see-if-he-floats.

40. Stavros Agorakis, "Read the Full Transcript of Sen. Collins's Speech Announcing She'll Vote to Confirm Brett Kavanaugh," *Vox*, October 5, 2018, https://www.vox.com/2018/10/5/17943276/susan-collins-speech-transcript-full-text-kavanaugh-vote.

41. Adam Feldman, "So Happy Together: 2018 Term, Justices, Votes," *Empirical SCOTUS*, May 22, 2019, https://empiricalscotus.com/2019/05/22/so-happy-together; "Final Stat Pack for October 2018," 23.

42. *Americans for Prosperity Found. v. Harris*, 2015 U.S. Dist. LEXIS 188240 (C.D. Cal. 2015). Judge Manuel Real, who became the last LBJ nominee on the federal bench, was appointed in 1966, took senior status in November 2018, and died in June 2019.

43. *See* Madison Alder, "Blue States Create Hurdle for Trump's 2020 Judicial Appointments," *Bloomberg Law*, February 11, 2020, https://news.bloomberglaw.com/us-law-week/blue-states-create-hurdle-for-trumps-2020-judicial-appointments.

44. Alexandra Desanctis, "Dianne Feinstein Attacks Judicial Nominee's Catholic Faith," *National Review*, September 6, 2017, https://www.nationalreview.com/corner/dianne-feinstein-amy-coney-barrett-senator-attacks-catholic-judicial-nominee.

45. "Biographical Directory of Article III Federal Judges: Export," Federal Judicial Center, last accessed July 15, 2020, https://www.fjc.gov/history/judges/biographical-directory-article-iii-federal-judges-export.

Chapter 19: What Have We Learned?

1. Lee Epstein and Jeffrey A. Segal, *Advice and Consent: The Politics of Judicial Appointments*, (New York: Oxford University Press, 2005), 107. The authors were writing before the Supreme Court nominations of Presidents George W. Bush (all under united government), Obama (Sotomayor and Kagan under united, Garland under divided), and Trump (united), but the statistic holds.

2. *See* Timothy S. Heubner, "The Supreme Court Confirmation Process Is Actually Less Political Than It Once Was," *Washington Post*, December 12, 2018, https://www.washingtonpost.com/outlook/2018/12/12/supreme-court-confirmation-process-is-actually-less-political-than-it-once-was.

3. *See* David Greenberg, "The New Politics of Supreme Court Appointments," *Daedelus* (Summer 2005), 5.

4. Phone interview with author, March 19, 2020.

5. Randall Kennedy, "The Case for Borking," *The American Prospect*, July 2–16, 2001, 26.

6. Charles E. Schumer, "Judging by Ideology," *New York Times*, June 26, 2001, A19.

7. Elena Kagan, "Confirmation Messes, Old and New," review of Stephen L. Carter, *The Confirmation Mess: Cleaning Up the Federal Appointments Process* (New York: Basic Books, 1994), 62 U. Chi. L. Rev. 919, 941 (1995).

8. *See* Paul M. Collins, Jr., and Lori A. Ringhand, Chapter 4: "An Issue-by-Issue Look at the Hearings," *Supreme Court Confirmation Hearings and Constitutional Change* (New York: Cambridge University Press, 2013), 100-39.

9. Carolyn Shapiro, "Putting Supreme Court Confirmation Hearings in Context," SCOTUSblog, August 28, 2018, https://www.scotusblog.com/2018/08/putting-supreme-court-confirmation-hearings-in-context.

10. Donald F. McGahn, remarks at conference on "The Politics of Judicial Nominations in an Age of Mistrust," Princeton University, March 6, 2020.

11. Thomas, *My Grandfather's Son*, 286.

12. Interview with author, March 2, 2020.

13. George F. Will, "Liberals Put the Squeeze to Justice Roberts," *Washington Post*, May 25, 2012, https://www.washingtonpost.com/opinions/liberals-put-the-squeeze-to-justice-roberts/2012/05/25/gJQANa4hqU_story.html.

14. Merle Miller, *Plain Speaking* (New York: Berkeley Medallion Edition, 1973), 242–43.

15. Todd S. Purdum, "Presidents, Picking Justices, Can Have Backfires," *New York Times*, July 5, 2005, A1.

16. 18 Cong. Rec. 1,875 (1887).

17. *Kansas v. Colorado*, 206 U.S. 46, 89 (1907).

18. Letter from Franklin D. Roosevelt to Rep. Samuel B. Hill (July 6, 1935) in 4 *The Public Papers and Addresses of Franklin D. Roosevelt* 91-92 (Samuel I. Rosenman ed., 1938).

19. Rexford G. Tugwell, "A Center Report: Rewriting the Constitution," *Center Magazine*, (March 1968), 20.

20. Roger Pilon, "How Constitutional Corruption Has Led to Ideological Litmus Tests for Judicial Nominees," Cato Institute Policy Analysis No. 446, August 6, 2002, 11.

21. Ben Sasse, "Blame Congress for Politicizing the Court," *Wall Street Journal*, September 5, 2018, https://www.wsj.com/articles/blame-congress-for-politicizing-the-court-1536189015.

22. Interview with author, February 13, 2020.

Chapter 20: Term Limits

1. Steven G. Calabresi and James Lindgren, "Term Limits for the Supreme Court: Life Tenure Reconsidered," 29 Harv. J. L. & Pub. Pol'y 769 (Summer 2006).

2. Letter from Thomas Jefferson to William T. Barry (July 2, 1822), in 7 *The Writings of Thomas Jefferson* 255, 256 (H.A. Washington ed., 1854); Letter from Thomas Jefferson to William Branch Giles (April 20, 1807), in *Thomas Jefferson: A Biography in his Own Words* (Joseph L. Gardener *et al.* eds., 1974). *See also* Charles Cooper, "Federalist Society Symposium: Term Limits for Judges?" 13 J.L. & Pol. 669, 674 (1997) (discussing Jefferson's criticism of life tenure and his proposal for term limits); Michael J. Mazza, "A New Look at an Old Debate: Life Tenure and the Article III Judge," 39 Gonzaga L. Rev. 131, 136 (2003–04) (describing Jefferson's early writings).

3. *Reforming the Court: Term Limits for Supreme Court Justices* (Durham, NC: Carolina Academic Press, 2006, Roger C. Cramton and Paul D. Carrington, eds.).

4. Calabresi and Lindgren, "Term Limits for the Supreme Court," 29 Harv. J. L. & Pub. Pol'y, 784.

5. Ibid., 813.

6. Ibid., 832–33.

7. Ward Farnsworth, "The Regulation of Turnover on the Supreme Court," 2005 Ill. L. Rev. 407, 414, 424.

8. Martin H. Redish, "Judicial Discipline, Judicial Independence, and the Constitution: A Textual and Structural Analysis," 72 S. Cal. L. Rev. 673, 685 (1999).

9. Nadine Cohodas, "Kennedy Finds Bork an Easy Act to Follow," 45 Cong. Q. Wkly. Rep. 2989, 2989 (1987).

10. David R. Stras and Ryan W. Scott, "Retaining Life Tenure: The Case for a 'Golden Parachute," 83 Wash. U. L. Quarterly 1397, 1427 (2005).

11. Linda Greenhouse, "The 18-Year Bench," *Slate*, June 7, 2012, https://slate.com/news-and-politics/2012/06/linda-greenhouse-calls-for-supreme-court-term-limits.html.

12. *See* "Who's Talking Terms," SCOTUSTermLimits.org, https://scotustermlimits.org/whos-talking-terms.

13. Lawrence Hurley, "Americans Favor Supreme Court Term Limits: Reuters/Ipsos," Reuters, July 20, 2015, pollhttps://www.reuters.com/article/us-usa-court-poll-idUSKCN0PU09820150720; Lydia Wheeler, "Majority of Americans Support Term Limits for Supreme Court Justices, New Poll Finds," *The Hill*, November 1, 2018, https://thehill.com/regulation/court-battles/414264-majority-of-americans-support-term-limits-for-supreme-court-justices.

14. Lee Drutman, "It's Time for Term Limits for Supreme Court Justices," *Vox*, June 27, 2019, https://www.vox.com/polyarchy/2018/6/27/17511030/supreme-court-term-limits-retirement.

15. James Lindgren and Ross M. Stolzenberg, "Term Limits Could Fix the Dysfunction around Supreme Court Confirmations," *Los Angeles Times*, July 18, 2018, https://www.

latimes.com/opinion/op-ed/la-oe-lindgren-stolzenberg-scotus-term-limits-20180718-story.html.

16. Eric Boehm, "Term Limits for Supreme Court Justices Won't Save Us," *Reason*, October 3, 2018, https://reason.com/2018/10/03/term-limits-supreme-court-kavanaugh.

17. Ibid.

Chapter 21: More Radical Reforms

1. Ted Cruz, "Constitutional Remedies to a Lawless Supreme Court," *National Review*, June 26, 2015, https://www.nationalreview.com/2015/06/ted-cruz-supreme-court-constitutional-amendment.

2. Sean Illing, "The Case for Abolishing the Supreme Court," *Vox*, October 12, 2018, https://www.vox.com/2018/10/12/17950896/supreme-court-brett-kavanaugh-constitution.

3. This analysis builds on my previous work in, "Democrats Are Courting Disaster," *Washington Examiner*, April 5, 2019, https://www.washingtonexaminer.com/opinion/democrats-are-courting-disaster.

4. Mark Tushnet, "Abandoning Defensive Crouch Liberal Constitutionalism," Balkinization, May 6, 2016, https://balkin.blogspot.com/2016/05/abandoning-defensive-crouch-liberal.html.

5. Lukas Mikelionis, "Channeling FDR, Eric Holder Says Dems Should Consider Packing Supreme Court to Counter GOP 'Power Grab,'" Fox News, March 8, 2019, https://fxn.ws/3900yC1.

6. *See* Ilya Shapiro and Nathan Harvey, "What Left-Wing Populism Looks Like," *National Review*, March 7, 2019, https://www.nationalreview.com/2019/03/democrats-for-the-people-act-unconstitutional-left-wing-populism.

7. Telephone interview with author, March 2, 2020.

8. Jordain Carney and Rachel Frazin, "Court-Packing Becomes New Litmus Test on Left," *The Hill*, March 19, 2019, https://thehill.com/homenews/senate/434630-court-packing-becomes-new-litmus-test-on-left.

9. *See* Dan McLaughlin (@baseballcrank), Twitter, March 18, 2019, https://twitter.com/baseballcrank/status/1107659649652801536.

10. F. Andrew Hessick and Samuel P. Jordan, "Setting the Size of the Supreme Court," 41 Ariz. St. L.J. 645, 668-69, n. 106 (2009) (citing Cong. Globe, 41st Cong., 1st Sess. 29, 62 (1869)). The authors note, however, that all previous additions to the Court came when the same party controlled the presidency and Congress, and all reductions occurred when different parties controlled each branch. Ibid., 667–68.

11. Press Release, "Rubio, Colleagues Introduce Constitutional Amendment to Keep SCOTUS at Nine Justices," March 25, 2019, https://www.rubio.senate.gov/public/index.cfm/2019/3/rubio-colleagues-introduce-constitutional-amendment-to-keep-scotus-at-nine-justices; Press Release, "Rep. Green Introduces Constitutional Amendment Limiting SCOTUS Seats to Nine," March 21, 2019, https://markgreen.house.gov/2019/3/rep-green-introduces-constitutional-amendment-limiting-scotus-seats-to-nine.

12. Daniel Epps and Ganesh Sitaraman, "How to Save the Supreme Court," 129 Yale L.J. 148 (2019).

13. Stephen Sachs, "Supreme Court as Superweapon: A Response to Epps & Sitaraman," 129 Yale L.J. Forum 93 (Nov. 4, 2019). *See also*, Amanda Frost, "Academic Highlight: Sachs

Responds to 'How to Save the Supreme Court,'" SCOTUSBlog, February 4, 2020, https://www.scotusblog.com/2020/02/academic-highlight-sachs-responds-to-how-to-save-the-supreme-court.

14. *See* John G. Grove, "Reforming the Court," 42 *National Affairs* 58, No. 61 (Winter 2020) (calling this phenomenon "vox SCOTUS, vox Dei," a variation on Justice Jackson's famous saying, "We are not final because we're infallible, but we are infallible only because we are final.").

15. Sachs, "Supreme Court as Superweapon," 98 (citing Stuart Minor Benjamin and Georg Vanberg, "Judicial Retirements and the Staying Power of U.S. Supreme Court Decisions," 13 J. Empirical Legal Stud. 5 (2016); Matthew Embrey, et al., "Cooperation in the Finitely Repeated Prisoner's Dilemma," 133 Q.J. Econ. 509, 511 (2018)).

16. *See* Joshua D. Hawley, *The Most Dangerous Branch*, 13 *National Affairs* 29 (Fall 2012) (suggesting a lottery system where circuit judges take multi-year temporary assignments to the Supreme Court).

17. Sachs, "Supreme Court as Superweapon," 98.

18. *Obergefell v. Hodges*, 135 S. Ct. 2584, 2629 (Scalia, J., dissenting).

19. Jamelle Bouie, "Why Pete Buttigieg Is Wrong about the Supreme Court," *New York Times*, June 6, 2019, https://www.nytimes.com/2019/06/06/opinion/buttigieg-warren-supreme-court.html.

20. Tracey George & Chris Guthrie, "Remaking the United States Supreme Court in the Courts' of Appeals Image," 58 Duke L.J. 1439 (2009).

21. Epps and Sitaraman, "How to Save the Supreme Court," 175.

22. Suzanna Sherry, "Our Kardashian Court (and How to Fix It)," Vand. L. Research Paper No. 19–30 (January 9, 2020), at 9, https://papers.ssrn.com/sol3/papers.cfm?abstract_id=3425998.

23. Scott Boddery, "The One Change John Roberts Can Make to Depoliticize the Supreme Court," *Politico,* Mar. 18, 2020, https://www.politico.com/news/magazine/2020/03/18/john-roberts-political-supreme-court-opinions-135769.

24. *See, e.g.,* Ruth Bader Ginsburg, "The Role of Dissenting Opinions," 95 Minn. L. Rev. 1 (2010).

25. *See, e.g., INS v. St. Cyr*, 533 US 289 (2001) (holding that immigration statutes didn't strip federal courts of power to hear petitions from deportable aliens).

26. *See, e.g., Boumediene v. Bush*, 553 U.S. 723 (2008) (holding Congress can't stop federal courts from entertaining habeas corpus petitions from enemy combatants held in Guantanamo).

27. Henry Saad, remarks at conference on "The Politics of Judicial Nominations in an Age of Mistrust," Princeton University, March 6, 2020.

28. Interview with author, March 9, 2020.

29. Adam Liptak, remarks at conference on "The Politics of Judicial Nominations in an Age of Mistrust," Princeton University, March 6, 2020. *See also* Roger Pilon, "Judicial Confirmations and the Rule of Law," 2016-17 Cato Sup. Ct. Rev. ix (2017).

Chapter 22: A Question of Legitimacy

1. Brief of Senators Sheldon Whitehouse, Mazie Hirono, Richard Blumenthal, Richard Durbin, and Kirsten Gillibrand in Support of Respondents, *New York State Rifle & Pistol Ass'n, Inc., et al. v. City of New York, et al.*, citation pending (2020) (No. 18–280), 18.

Notes

Maired McArdle, "Schumer Claims Conservative Supreme Court Justices Will Pay Price
      If They Rule against Abortion Advocates," *National Review*, March 4, 2020, https://www.
      nationalreview.com/news/schumer-claims-conservative-supreme-court-justices-will-
      pay-the-price-if-they-rule-against-abortion-advocates.

Josh Gerstein, "Roberts Slams Schumer for 'Dangerous' Rhetoric against Justices," *Politico*,
      March 4, 2020, https://www.politico.com/news/2020/03/04/roberts-schumer-scotus-121490

Rucho v. Common Cause, 139 S. Ct. 2484 (2019).

Department of Commerce v. New York, 139 S. Ct. 2551 (2019).

This analysis builds on my previous work in, "How the Supreme Court Undermines Its
      Own Legitimacy," *Washington Examiner*, July 18, 2019, https://www.washingtonexaminer.
      com/opinion/how-the-supreme-court-undermines-its-own-legitimacy.

Joshua A. Geltzer, "Will the Legitimacy of the Supreme Court Survive the Census Case?"
      New York Times, May 31, 2019, https://www.nytimes.com/2019/05/31/opinion/census-
      citizenship-question-supreme-court-travel-ban.html.

Richard L. Hasen, "Roberts' Rules," *Slate*, March. 25, 2019, https://slate.com/news-and-
      politics/2019/03/john-roberts-supreme-court-gerrymandering-cases.html;   Richard   L.
      Hasen, "The Census Case Is Shaping Up to Be the Biggest Travesty Since *Bush v. Gore*," *Slate*,
      June 25, 2019, https://slate.com/news-and-politics/2019/06/census-case-john-roberts-bush-
      v-gore-tragedy.html.

Wolf v. Cook Cty., 2020 U.S. LEXIS 825 (2020), https://www.supremecourt.gov/
      opinions/19pdf/19a905_7m48.pdf.

10.   Jesse Merriam, "Stephen Presser's Love Letter to the Law, in Five Parts," review of Stephen
      B. Presser, *Law Professors: Three Centuries of Shaping American Law* (St. Paul: West
      Publishing, 2017), 33 Const. Comment. 71, 74 (2018).

11.   Neal Kumar Katyal, "Politics over Principle," *Washington Post*, December 14, 2000, https://
      www.washingtonpost.com/archive/opinions/2000/12/14/politics-over-
      principle/0621e3d5-77c9-4731-acdb-faa1f19fa5dd.

12.   Alan M. Dershowitz, "Supreme Injustice: How the High Court Hijacked Election 2000,"
      New York Times, July 15, 2001, https://www.nytimes.com/2001/07/15/books/chapters/
      quotsupreme-injustice-how-the-high-court-hijacked-election.html.

13.   *Bush v. Gore*, 531 U.S. 98, 129 (Stevens, J., dissenting).

14.   Bruce Ackerman, "The Court Packs Itself," *American Prospect*, December 4, 2001, https://
      prospect.org/features/court-packs.

15.   John C. Yoo, "In Defense of the Court's Legitimacy," 68 U. Chi. L. Rev. 775 (2001). I quote
      liberally from this article in the discussion that follows.

16.   See my discussion of his argument, "Responding to Akhil Amar on Obamacare," Cato at
      Liberty (blog), Cato Institute, February 7, 2011, https://www.cato.org/blog/responding-
      akhil-amar-obamacare.

17.   Jonathan Cohn, "Obamacare Is on Trial. So Is the Supreme Court," *The New Republic*,
      March 29, 2012, https://newrepublic.com/article/102204/supreme-court-roberts-kennedy-
      health-mandate-legitimacy.

18.   Jeff Mason, "Obama Takes a Shot at Supreme Court Over Healthcare," Reuters, April 2,
      2012, https://www.reuters.com/article/us-obama-healthcare-idUSBRE8310WP20120402.

19. "Sen. Patrick Leahy Tries to Intimidate Supreme Court Chief Justice Roberts into Upholding Obamacare," *The Right Scoop*, May 24, 2012, https://therightscoop.com/sen-patrick-leahy-tries-to-intimidate-supreme-court-chief-justice-roberts-into-upholding-obamacare.

20. David L. Franklin, "Why Did Roberts Do It?" *Slate*, June 28, 2012, https://slate.com/news-and-politics/2012/06/john-roberts-broke-with-conservatives-to-preserve-the-supreme-courts-legitimacy.html.

21. Jan Crawford, "Roberts Switched Views to Uphold Health Care Law," *CBS News*, July 2, 2012, https://www.cbsnews.com/news/roberts-switched-views-to-uphold-health-care-law/2.

22. Sophie Tatum, "Justice Kagan Worries about the 'Legitimacy' of a Politically Divided Supreme Court," CNN.com, October 5, 2018, https://www.cnn.com/2018/10/05/politics/supreme-court-elena-kagan-legitimacy/index.html.

23. *See* Tara Leigh Grove, "The Supreme Court's Legitimacy Dilemma," review of Richard B. Fallon, Jr., *Law and Legitimacy in the Supreme* Court (Cambridge, Massachusetts: Harvard University Press, 2018), 132 Harv. L. Rev. 2240, 2259 ("Even in our open and fluid constitutional practice, it is difficult to justify such a change as legally legitimate.").

24. Josh Gerstein, "Kagan Fears Supreme Court Losing Swing Justice," *Politico*, October 5, 2018, https://www.politico.com/story/2018/10/05/elena-kagan-supreme-court-kennedy-877288.

25. Adam Liptak, "On Supreme Court, Does 9-0 Add up to More than 5-4?" *New York Times*, August 11, 2014, A13.

26. Michael F. Salamone, Supreme Court Unity and Public Opinion: An Experimental Study (2009, last revised 2011), *American Political Science Association 2009 Toronto Meeting Paper*, 21, https://ssrn.com/abstract=1450847 ("Thus, it appears that whether or not a decision has a dissent, be it narrowly divided or not, has no real impact on whether or not one agrees with the decision or on how she feels about the court as an institution or the immediate issue on which it has ruled.").

27. Cass R. Sunstein, "Unanimity and Disagreement on the Supreme Court," 100 Cornell L. Rev. 769, 806 (2015) ("The results showed that the level of internal consensus had little effect on people's views.").

28. James F. Spriggs, II and Thomas G. Hansford, "Explaining the Overruling of U.S. Supreme Court Precedent," *The Journal of Politics*, vol. 63, no. 4 (November 2001): 1103-05, www.jstor.org/stable/2691808.

29. Lawrence Weschler, "How The US Supreme Court Lost Its Legitimacy," *The Nation*, September 17, 2018, https://www.thenation.com/article/how-the-us-supreme-court-lost-its-legitimacy; Michael Tomasky, "The Supreme Court's Legitimacy Crisis," *New York Times*, October 5, 2018, https://www.nytimes.com/2018/10/05/opinion/supreme-courts-legitimacy-crisis.html.

30. Erwin Chemerinsky, "A Very Tarnished Court," *American Prospect*, October 1, 2018, https://prospect.org/justice/tarnished-court.

31. "Who's Attacking Political Norms Now?" *Wall Street Journal*, October 14, 2018, https://www.wsj.com/articles/whos-attacking-political-norms-now-1539552494.

32. Weschler, "How The US Supreme Court Lost Its Legitimacy."

33. Senator Sheldon Whitehouse, "The Third Federalist Society" (U.S. Senate, Washington, D.C., March 27, 2019), https://www.whitehouse.senate.gov/news/speeches/the-third-federalist-society; also available on *C-SPAN*, video at 8:21:55, https://www.c-span.org/video/?459152-1/senate-session&start=30115.

34. *Ex parte Merryman*, 17 F. Cas. 144, 153 (No. 9,487) (C.C. Md. 1861).

35. Mark Joseph Stern, "How Liberals Could Declare War on Brett Kavanaugh's Supreme Court," *Slate*, October 4, 2018, https://slate.com/news-and-politics/2018/10/brett-kavanaugh-confirmation-constitutional-crisis.html.

36. "No Senator or Representative shall, during the Time for which he was elected, be appointed to any civil Office under the Authority of the United States...the Emoluments whereof shall have been encreased during such time." U.S. Const. art. 1, sec. 6, cl. 2—a.k.a. the (other) Emoluments Clause or the Ineligibility Clause.

37. William Baude, "The Unconstitutionality of Justice Black," 91 Tex. L. Rev. 327, 356 (2019).

38. Gallup, tracking poll of Supreme Court approval, https://news.gallup.com/poll/4732/supreme-court.aspx (last visited July 15, 2020).

39. Amelia Thomson-DeVeaux and Oliver Roeder, "Is the Supreme Court Facing a Legitimacy Crisis?" FiveThirtyEight, October 1, 2018, https://fivethirtyeight.com/features/is-the-supreme-court-facing-a-legitimacy-crisis.

40. *See, e.g.*, James L. Gibson et al., "Losing but Accepting: Legitimacy, Positivity Theory, and the Symbols of Judicial Authority," 48 Law & Society Rev. 837, No. 839 (2014) ("Legitimacy is for losers, since winners ordinarily accept decisions with which they agree.").

41. Amelia Thomson-DeVeaux, "Can the Supreme Court Stay Above the Partisan Fray?" FiveThirtyEight, August 12, 2019, https://fivethirtyeight.com/features/can-the-supreme-court-stay-above-the-partisan-fray.

42. Clare Brockway and Bradley Jones, "Partisan Gap Widens in Views of Supreme Court," Pew Research Center, August 7, 2019, https://www.pewresearch.org/fact-tank/2019/08/07/partisan-gap-widens-in-views-of-the-supreme-court.

43. Adam Liptak and Alicia Parlapiano, "A Supreme Court Term Marked by Shifting Alliances and Surprise Votes," *New York Times*, June 29, 2019, A26.

44. Jonathan H. Adler, "Is This Still the Stare Decisis Court?" The Volokh Conspiracy (blog), *Reason*, July 24, 2019, https://reason.com/2019/06/24/is-this-still-the-stare-decisis-court.

45. Michael S. Greve, "Is the Roberts Court Legitimate?" 42 *National Affairs* 43 (Winter 2020), https://www.nationalaffairs.com/publications/detail/is-the-roberts-court-legitimate.

Conclusion

1. John A. Maltese, *The Selling of the Supreme Court Nominees* (Baltimore: Johns Hopkins University Press, 1995), 143.

2. Interview with author, March 9, 2020.

3. Phone interview with author, March 19, 2020.

4. Phone interview with author, March 18, 2020.

Index

A

abolitionists, 27–29

abortion, 7, 311, 313, 330

Abraham, Henry, 33, 89, 175

Adams, John, 15, 17–19, 266

Adams, John Quincy, 16, 20–21, 266

administrative agencies, executive branch, 7, 237

administrative state, the, 47, 219281, 305, 331, 337
judges against, 230

Advice and Consent Clause, 12, 115, 225, 252, 308

affirmative action, 79, 106, 109, 125, 143, 164–65, 212
in judicial nominations, 119, 163

Alito, Samuel, 203–7, 218, 231, 275, 278, 317

American Bar Association, 75, 99, 107–8, 115, 141, 196, 202, 259

American Civil Liberties Union, 66, 110, 141, 204

antitrust law, 42, 149, 256, 277

Article III, 284, 289

B

Barnett, Randy, 145, 155

Biden, Joe, 138, 143, 148, 152, 166–68, 172
Biden rule, the, 177, 208, 225–26

Black, Hugo, 62, 64–66, 71, 74, 87, 290, 323

Blackmun, Harry, 79, 96, 103–4, 106–7, 125, 278

blue slips, 4, 187, 190, 220, 261

Bork, Robert, 2, 115, 128, 130, 133–34, 158–59, 161
consequences of confirmation hearing, 270–72, 276, 281
hearing, 135, 137–49, 151, 153, 166
the verb, 165

Brandeis, Louis, 47–52, 56–57, 61–62, 67, 92, 202, 278
Bork comparison with, 142,

146, 271

Brennan, William, 78–82, 89, 99, 122, 125, 160–62, 275

Breyer, Stephen, 118, 179, 182–86, 284

Brown v. Board of Education, 77, 97, 143, 272, 322

Buchanan, James, 29–30

Buck v. Bell, 41

Burger, Warren, 96–99, 101, 103–6, 111, 116, 126–27, 278
on abortion, 105

Burwell v. Hobby Lobby Stores, 207

Bush v. Gore, 185, 189, 275, 313–16, 330

business, 37, 54, 185, 316

Butler, Pierce, 49, 53–54, 68

Byrnes, James, 69–72

C

campaign finance, 6, 117, 199, 244

Cardozo, Benjamin, 43, 55–56, 58–59, 61, 223, 301

Carswell, G. Harrold, 100–102, 270

Carter, Jimmy, 6, 43, 117–19, 147

Catron, John, 25–26, 29, 31, 33

Chase, Salmon, 32–33, 277, 296

Chase, Samuel, 15–17, 296, 322–23

checks and balances, 41, 47

circuit courts, 259, 301, 313, 322
See also district courts; lower courts

circuit-riding, 11, 14, 17–18

Citizen United v. FEC, 199, 232, 275, 295, 330

civil rights, 36, 63–64, 68, 77, 79, 101, 128, 243
and Clarence Thomas, 163–65
and Robert Bork, 141, 144, 147–48
and Thurgood Marshall, 88–89, 95

civil war, 25, 28–29, 31, 277, 285, 321

Clarke, John, 52–53

classical liberalism, 40, 44–45

Clay, Henry, 21, 25

Cleveland, Grover, 4, 37–39, 279

Clifford, Nathan, 29–30

Clinton, Bill, 118–19, 178–80, 183–88, 210, 219, 227

Clinton, Hillary, 133, 178, 198, 206, 231–32, 257, 294–95

cloture votes, 187, 191–92, 221, 237–38, 255, 260–61

See also "nuclear option", the

Commerce Clause, 56, 109, 117, 129, 280

See also interstate commerce

conservatives, 39, 42, 54, 268, 294–95, 313

constitutional interpretation, 5, 89, 122, 149, 272, 330

See also statutory interpretation

Coolidge, Calvin, 54–56, 278

court-packing, 57, 64, 221, 266, 295–99, 304, 332

criminal procedure, 77, 81, 117, 133, 238

cronyism, 35, 74, 91, 95, 115, 179

Curtis, Benjamin Robbins, 27–28

D

D.C. v. Heller, 132, 273, 322

Danforth, John, 142, 165

O'Connor, Sandra Day, 121–26, 139, 159, 162, 196–97, 213, 275

Democratic-Republicans, 16, 19–21, 266

Department of Education, 168–69, 171

Dershowitz, Alan, 86, 314

Douglas, William, 50, 67–69, 73–74, 80, 113–14, 144, 283, 322–23

Dred Scott v. Sandford, 25, 28–29, 31, 285, 314

E

Eisenhower, Dwight, 4, 75–83, 122, 129, 278

"empathy" standard, 209, 214

Equal Employment Opportunity Commission (EEOC), 164–65, 168–71

equal protection, 143, 155, 181, 185

Establishment Clause, the, 98, 108

Estrada, Miguel, 191–93, 247

expansion of federal power, 7, 96, 274, 279–80

See also federal power

F

FBI, 75, 152, 168, 249, 251, 253–54

federal power, 61, 200, 281, 305, 309, 332

See also expansion of federal power

Federalist Society, the, 195–96, 239, 244, 259, 321

filibuster, the, 4–5, 191–93, 205–6, 217, 220–21, 237–38, 260, 307

flag-burning, 65, 117

Ford, Christine Blasey, 250–54

Ford, Gerald, 113–17, 142

Fortas, Abe, 4, 87, 89–92, 95, 99, 113–14

Four Horsemen, the, 44, 49, 56–57, 61, 274

Fourteenth Amendment, the, 32, 53–54, 104, 143–44, 181, 274

Fourth Amendment, the, 77, 108, 133, 215

Frankfurter, Felix, 66–67, 70, 74–76, 92, 138, 271

free speech, 65, 143, 145, 156, 206

G

Garfield, James, 36–37

Garland, Merrick, 216, 226–28, 232–33, 236, 245, 269, 277, 293–94, 332

geography, considerations of, 17, 34–35, 39–40, 63, 96, 268

Gideon v. Wainwright, 77, 87

Ginsburg, Douglas, 4, 151–52

Ginsburg, Ruth Bader, 105, 179–83, 185, 272, 283, 320

Goldberg, Arthur, 84–86

Gonzales v. Raich, 117, 157, 174

Gorsuch, Neil, 4–5, 206, 219, 233–39, 244, 256–57, 294, 331

Graham, Lindsey, 214, 218, 237, 250, 254, 261–62

Grant, Ulysses, 4, 33–34, 277

Grassley, Charles, 143, 220, 224, 246–47, 249–51, 261

Griswold v. Connecticut, 65, 68, 77, 85–86, 144, 153

H

habeas corpus, 32, 321

Hamilton, Alexander, 12, 15, 285, 321

Harding, Warren, 4, 49, 52–55

Harlan, John Marshall, 35–36, 78–79, 106

Hatch, Orrin, 146, 166 169, 226–27

Hayes, Rutherford B., 35–36

Haynsworth, Clement, 99–102

Hill, Anita, 168–72

Holmes, Oliver Wendell, Jr., 40–42, 56, 58, 140, 277

Hoover, Herbert, 56–59

Hughes, Charles Evans, 43, 51, 56–58, 61–63, 70

I

ideological balance, 6, 218, 289

impeachments, judicial, 16–17, 92, 114, 322–23

incorporation of the Bill of Rights, 59, 65

individual liberty, 32, 40, 71, 142

interstate commerce, 21, 44, 116, 129, 174

J

Jackson, Andrew, 3, 21, 23–27, 296

Jackson, Robert, 66, 69–71, 74, 78, 111

Janus v. AFSCME, 207, 294, 324

Jay, John, 3, 14–15, 17

Jefferson, Thomas, 16, 18–20, 266, 277, 285, 296

Jim Crow, 35, 77, 88

Johnson, Andrew, 33–34, 117, 296

Johnson, Lyndon, 86–89, 225

judicial activism, 68, 88, 120, 213, 317, 331

Judicial Procedures Reform Bill, 61, 297

K

Kagan, Elena, 132, 182, 185, 216–19, 272, 319

Kavanaugh, Brett, 2, 5, 193, 205, 242–57, 273, 292–95

Kennedy, Anthony, 124, 152–59, 199, 243

Kennedy, John F., 83–86,

Kennedy, Ted, 128, 139, 142, 144, 161, 167, 184

Kerry, John, 205–6

L

Lawrence v. Texas, 155–56, 173

Leahy, Pat, 123–24, 158, 167, 190–91, 208, 317

legal realism, 41, 55

Leo, Leonard, 230, 233, 270,

libertarianism, 53, 135, 152, 166

Lincoln, Abraham, 30–34, 63, 321

"living Constitution", 41, 88, 143

Lochner era, 32, 54, 56

Lochner v. New York, 39, 41

Loving v. Virginia, 77, 156

loyalty, 19, 23, 26, 34, 38, 63, 73, 267

M

Madison, James, 11–12, 19–20, 41, 139–40, 149, 174, 333–34

Marbury v. Madison, 19, 274

Marshall, John, 17–21, 24–27, 70, 266, 274, 296

Marshall, Thurgood, 87–89, 125, 163, 173

Masterpiece Cakeshop v. Colorado Civil Rights Commission, 182

Matthews, Stanley, 36–37

McCarthy, Joe, 79, 87

McConnell, Mitch, 4, 102, 224, 226–28, 234, 237, 260

McGahn, Don, 229–31, 233–34, 243, 259, 273, 331

McReynolds, James, 48–49, 52–54, 69, 278

Meese, Ed, 121–22, 130, 134, 151, 295

merit, in nominations, 37, 56, 73, 114, 120, 131, 138, 210, 266

Midnight Judges Act, 19, 266, 296

Miers, Harriet, 201–4, 207, 270

minimalism, 157, 199, 243

Miranda v. Arizona, 77, 129

N

NAACP, 57, 100, 108, 161, 165, 167, 267

National Abortion Rights Action League, 180, 204

natural law, 41, 164, 167, 272

natural rights, 53, 155

New Deal, the, 48–49, 55–57, 61, 63–64, 66–70, 72, 75, 149

New York Times v. United States, 98

NFIB v. Sebelius, 157, 182, 185, 200, 214, 317

Ninth Circuit, the, 118, 258, 260

Nixon, Richard, 76, 89, 95–100, 102–3, 106–10, 112–14, 125

"nuclear option", the, 4–5, 192–93, 221, 238, 255, 333

O

Obergefell v. Hodges, 132, 155–56, 301

obstruction, 4, 187

originalism, 122, 131, 149, 207, 238, 268, 316, 319

P

partisanship, 7, 17, 115, 311, 316, 330

party affiliation, 48, 96, 291

penumbras, 68, 85–86, 144

People for the American Way, 140, 205

Planned Parenthood v. Casey, 106, 125, 154, 162, 197

Plessy v. Ferguson, 36, 111, 128, 274

political calculations, 14, 97, 120, 278

pornography, 81, 90, 146, 170

Powell, Lewis, 96, 100, 107–12, 125, 137, 141, 152

pragmatism, 122, 178, 219

precedent, 68, 122, 145–46, 209, 243, 273, 322, 324
of Roe, 162, 197, 205, 247, 273

presidential election years, 38, 118, 175, 223–24, 235

privacy, 49, 65, 77, 85–86, 104–5, 144–45, 155, 180

private property, 32, 166

progressives, 39–40, 232, 244, 293–96, 306, 311, 319

progressivism, 48, 78

property rights, 21, 164, 213

R

Reagan, Ronald, 120–24, 127, 129–31, 134, 137–41, 151–53, 159, 278

"real politics", 41, 43–45, 48, 52, 83, 96, 112, 269

Reconstruction, 33–37, 315

Rehnquist, William, 105, 109–13, 121, 124–31, 133–34, 141, 196, 278–79

Reid, Harry, 193, 221, 224–26, 237, 260

Roberts, Owen, 57–58, 62, 317, 319

Roe v. Wade, 79, 85, 104–5, 124–25, 154, 162, 197, 232, 270

Roosevelt, Franklin Delano (FDR), 47–48, 57–58, 61–64, 66–67, 69–70, 72, 323

Roosevelt, Teddy, 39–43, 45

Rutledge, John, 3, 12, 14–15

S

Schumer, Chuck, 190, 198, 203, 206, 208, 225, 237, 253, 259, 271, 312

separation of powers, 26, 41, 219, 228, 239, 242, 244, 331, 333

Stewart, Potter, 80–81, 83, 85, 108, 120–21, 126,

Stone, Harlan, 51, 63, 70, 168

Story, Joseph, 20, 24, 68

substantive due process, 65, 85, 125

Sutherland, George, 53–54

"swing vote", 124, 173, 199, 330

"swing" justices, 57, 157

T

Textualism, 131, 238, 268, 321

Three Musketeers, the, 56–57, 62, 274

Thurmond, Strom, 70, 85, 88–90, 118–19, 148, 166, 184

Tribe, Laurence, 105, 178, 190

Truman, Harry, 73–75, 78, 278

Tyler, John, 3, 27, 232, 266

U

United States v. Lopez, 116, 129

United States v. Morrison, 117, 129

V

Van Devanter, Willis, 44, 49, 53, 63

Vinson, Fred, 74, 76, 85, 317

W

Wall Street, 56, 68

Warren, Earl, 75–76, 91–92, 95–96, 202–3, 223, 278, 297

Washington, George, 3, 8, 13, 23, 63, 135, 266

White, Byron, 1, 3, 84, 86, 105, 178, 232, 234, 272, 277

Wilson, Woodrow, 37, 40–41, 47–51, 278